STUDIES IN IMPERIALISM

General editor: Andrew S. Thompson

Founding editor: John M. MacKenzie

When the 'Studies in Imperialism' series was founded by Professor John M. MacKenzie more than thirty years ago, emphasis was laid upon the conviction that 'imperialism as a cultural phenomenon had as significant an effect on the dominant as on the subordinate societies'. With well over a hundred titles now published, this remains the prime concern of the series. Cross-disciplinary work has indeed appeared covering the full spectrum of cultural phenomena, as well as examining aspects of gender and sex, frontiers and law, science and the environment, language and literature, migration and patriotic societies, and much else. Moreover, the series has always wished to present comparative work on European and American imperialism, and particularly welcomes the submission of books in these areas. The fascination with imperialism, in all its aspects, shows no sign of abating, and this series will continue to lead the way in encouraging the widest possible range of studies in the field. 'Studies in Imperialism' is fully organic in its development, always seeking to be at the cutting edge, responding to the latest interests of scholars and the needs of this ever-expanding area of scholarship.

Learning femininity in colonial India, 1820–1932

MANCHESTER
1824

Manchester University Press

Learning femininity in colonial India, 1820–1932

Tim Allender

MANCHESTER UNIVERSITY PRESS

Published by MANCHESTER UNIVERSITY PRESS
ALTRINCHAM STREET, MANCHESTER M1 7JA
www.manchesteruniversitypress.co.uk

British Library Cataloguing-in-Publication Data
A catalogue record for this book is available from the British Library

ISBN 978 0 7190 8579 6 hardback
ISBN 978 1 5261 3431 8 paperback

First published by Manchester University Press in hardback 2016
This edition first published 2018

Typeset by Out of House Publishing

Frontispiece An accomplishments geography lesson learning about the 'mother country'.

This book is dedicated to the memory of
Doris Embling
A lifelong mentor and much loved friend

CONTENTS

ILLUSTRATIONS

PREFACE AND ACKNOWLEDGEMENTS

In some ways this book's history began over fifteen years ago while I was still a postgraduate student at Sydney University. Then my task was to try to find new ways to understand the impact of empire on India, particularly in new theoretical terms, drawing on what became important feedback offered to me by Professor Chris Bayly and others at a key conference in Kew in Melbourne. Their work, which engaged with this issue, was published not long after the conference. This was still at a time when talking about the European at all in India was an unfashionable enterprise – also signalling, as I imagined, to my more able and experienced peers, that here was a new scholar who lacked the imagination to escape the elitist white men's postcolonial approaches of the past. The naivety evident in my scholarship naturally pointed to the need for broader thinking as my research deepened. My ongoing academic insecurities were only slowly lifted – though still not fully – by the kind encouragement of Kathy Prior, Carey Watt and Indrani Chatterjee. They were fellow students whom I was fortunate enough to meet, between teaching commitments in Australia, during my trips to the India Office, which in those days was temporarily located at Blackfriars in London.

There were senior academics, as well, who were patient enough I think to see my struggles as a scholar in terms of someone who needed more time and reflection to better come to grips with the problem of finding new ways to see empire. These scholars included Jim Masselos, Geoff Sherington, both in Sydney, Dick Selleck in Melbourne, Clive Whitehead and Tom O'Donoghue in Perth, Richard Aldrich in London and Ruth Watts in Birmingham. They have been always willing to be my toughest critics, knowing that I have been able to hear their criticism because it was tempered through trusting bonds of scholarly community where many of their students are fortunate enough to belong. Robin Jeffrey, Peter Reeves and John McGuire then had much to do with the production of my first book, about male education in north India, and they could only be described as the most generous scholars in my field.

Deciding to write this book, *Learning Femininity in Colonial India*, with gender and India as its theme, as a white male, seemed a strange choice to some. As I picked up the threads of my story, Joyce Goodman, Stephanie Spencer and Camilla Leach at Winchester University gave me impetus to think about gender in ways that might align with colonial histories of women settler communities 'abroad'. While Gary

McCulloch at the University of London and Elizabeth Smyth at the University of Toronto were kind enough to offer new forums for testing my ideas. My Visiting Research Fellowship at the Georg-Eckert Institute in Braunschweig, Germany also gave me the time to reflect and write more on my themes under the inquiring mind of its Deputy Director, Eckhardt Fuchs.

The theoretical layers of this book have come to me through many productive conferences and workshops in the USA, India, Canada, Australia and Europe as I have worked with the acute observations of those patient enough to endure my halting explanations of where my work might be heading, and to offer suggestions to bring it into better focus. I was particularly interested in sensitising my research to Indian academic perspectives concerning the colonial era and I am grateful for the History Fellowship I was given by Jawaharlal Nehru University (JNU) to confer with leading Indian scholars in my field and for a demanding seminar I was invited to give at the Nehru Memorial Museum and Library, Teen Murti, where my ideas about racial hybridity took greater form. In 2013, as a visiting Professor at the Indian Institute of Advanced Studies in Shimla, and under the supportive Directorship of Professor Chetan Singh, I found the academic terrain especially rich in terms of engaging with Indian philosophical traditions, partly through its fine Tagore centre, and this has had a strong underlying influence on my book.

This book includes a selection of images that are an important part of my story. For the most part I have preferred more obscure images of women and girls in poses of interaction, admittedly staged mostly for Western audiences. The image of Mrs Elmslie in a zenana, but taken on the rooftop, was probably determined by the need to use outside photography (perhaps as the only technology available for relatively quickly staged photographs). This outside location, instead of inside the Indian household, may have been necessary anyway to gain the permission of the Indian women concerned. Again, *plein-air*, is the geography lesson, shown as the frontispiece of this book. This image depicts due displays of deportment (see how the teacher is sitting on her chair), student dress – West and East – and there are also displays of knowledge that are unequivocally Western, conveyed through the use of maps of England. The relational aspects of the girls as they interact with each other at Loreto, Darjeeling, and the display of intimacy in medical treatment of a Loreto woman religious (nun) at Morapai, as shown in the last two images of the book, also tell a richer story beyond mere words of text. As well, photography and publishing requirements produce other selectivity. There exist other images of Indian girls outside school and dispensary that I would very much liked to have included. Yet the very poor quality and blurred photography of these impoverished settings, usually just as groups of girls without displays of their learning, meant that it was not possible to include them in this book.

I am thankful for the permission Leprosy Mission International gave me to reproduce an image of Rosalie Harvey (an organisation that sadly still has work to do in the modern world); the British Library for permission to reproduce two images in its collection; the United Society and the Bodleian Library, Oxford for their permission to reproduce the three lantern slides of SPG women in chapters five and six; and for the permission of the Institute of the Blessed Virgin Mary (IBVM), Loreto and the Institute and the Irish Province Archives, Dublin to reproduce the final two images in the book.

Gaining access to archives has required much more exacting negotiation and for this I am deeply grateful to my friend Joseph Bara at JNU in Delhi and to the Brothers of the Cambridge Mission, also in Delhi. The Principals of Aitchison College and Government College in Lahore, Pakistan broke the stalemate of waiting for some days outside archives while my passport was meticulously translated into Persian Urdu. And Sister Cyril in Kolkata, Sister Kathleen and Judith Harford in Dublin, Robin Scott at Loreto in Ballarat, Lucy McCann at Rhodes House in Oxford and Rajesh Kochhar, Chandigarh University, India, did much to facilitate my access to key archives and interesting historical sites in those respective countries. My far too many calls on the time of archivists were always helpfully answered, particularly at the India Office Library at the British Library (BL) in London; SOAS, University of London; the Main Library, Birmingham University; Cambridge University Library, Cambridge; the National Archives of India and at the Nehru Memorial Museum and Library in Delhi.

I am grateful to Meera Kosambi, Ruth Watts, Elizabeth Smyth, Carey Watt and Jim Masselos who were kind enough to read parts of the book manuscript as it took shape, which also benefitted from more informal discussions with Professor Krishna Kumar, Kama McLean, Tamson Pietsch, Sanjay Seth, Jyoti Atwal, Peter Freebody, Devleena Ghosh and Nayantara Pothen. I am especially thankful to my anonymous readers whose timely and clever academic intervention showed me a degree of professional generosity, concerning the minute detail of my manuscript, that I have not experienced before. And also to Emma Brennan, my commissioning editor at Manchester University Press, for her patience as this book took better shape.

The writing of this book has been greatly assisted by the financial support of several small grants. I have needed to spend many hours in archives in expensive cities to build a story drawn from primary

sources and this could not have been achieved without the generous hospitality of my friends Clive Hedderly and Michael Andreatta
while I was researching in London. There was also the wonderful academic company provided by Piyush Mathur and Alex George that kept
me reasonably sane, or at least relatively so, after periods of solitude
immersed in my thoughts about how best to write the book.

I only wonder at my friends being still interested in this dilettantish
author labouring rather like George Eliot's character Edward Casaubon
in *Middlemarch*, never seeming to near the end of 'the project'. I am
grateful for their ongoing and precious companionship. Most especially, I owe much to my parents and to my sisters for their unqual-
ified love and support without which this book could not have been
written; and for Daniel, Toby, Thomas, Nicholas, Julian, Oliver, Liam
and Ashton who are the new generation in my life.

ABBREVIATIONS

AL	Angus Library, Regent's Park College, Oxford, UK
BL	British Library
BLO	Bodleian Library, Oxford, UK
CBMA	Cambridge Brotherhood Mission Archives, New Delhi, India
CML	Cambridge University Library
CMS	Church Missionary Society
CP	Central Provinces
DDA	Dublin Diocesan Archives, Dublin, Ireland
DPI	Director of Public Instruction
HMSO	Her Majesty's Stationery Office
ICS	Indian Civil Service
IES	Indian Education Service
IBVM	Institute of the Blessed Virgin Mary
JNU	Jawaharlal Nehru University
LAD	Loreto Archives Dublin, Ireland
LB	Main Library, Birmingham University, Birmingham, UK
LBA	Loreto Archives, Ballarat, Australia
NAI	National Archives of India, New Delhi, India
NMML	Nehru Memorial Museum and Library, New Delhi, India
NWP	North Western Provinces
OGA	Office of the General Assembly, Lombard Street, Philadelphia, United States of America
OIOC	Oriental and India Office Collections, British Library, UK
PSA	Punjab Secretariat Archives, Anarkali's Tomb, Lahore, Pakistan
PUC	Punjab University College, Lahore, Pakistan

LIST OF ABBREVIATIONS

RHL	Rhodes House Library, Oxford, UK
SLV	State Library of Victoria, Australia
SNDT	Shreemati Nathibai Damodar Thackersey
SOAS	School of Oriental and African Studies
SPG	Society for the Propagation of the Gospel

GLOSSARY

anjuman	voluntary association
anna	the sixteenth part of a rupee
Bangiya Mahila Vidyalaya	(BMV) school for Hindu women
bania	a Hindu of the trading class
bhadralok	Indian middle-class in Bengal
Brahmin	the priestly or highest caste of Hindus
chamars	leather workers
dais/dhaees	midwives
ghats	river bank steps
Gurmukhi	the script in which the Punjabi language is written
guru	religious teacher
halkabandi	lands and buildings belonging to a circle of villages
Hindustan	the country of the Hindus in India, north of the Narbudda and exclusive of Bengal and Bihar
Hindustani	the language of the people of upper India, which developed out of a mixture of Hindi, Persian and Arabic words
itineration	preaching journey
lakh	100,000
mofussil	outlying rural areas, away from the principal towns
pandit	Hindu teacher
pathshala	an elementary school, often in the village, especially for learning simple Arithmetic and book-keeping
pathshala gurumohashoys	elementary Hindu indigenous schools
patwari	tax collector, village accountant
purdah	the custom of veiling and secluding women

Purana	one of the eighteen collections of 'ancient stories' which preserve Hindu tradition, myth, legend and rite
Rajput	military caste or clan
Romanised Urdu	Urdu written in the English alphabet
sabha	an assembly
sahib	ruler, lord, especially a European government official
satyagraha	insistence on truth
Seva Sadan	home of service
Sharada Sadan	home for learning
swadeshi	anti-British self-sufficiency
tahsil	an administrative unit smaller than a district
tahsildar	chief revenue officer of each tahsil
vakil	agent
Veda	wisdom, knowing, the sacred literature to be revealed
zamindar	land-holder, often the head of the village
zenana	private part of the household for women (often on the rooftop)

The spelling of place names conforms to those adopted in the last years of the raj as used by the 'Atlas and Gazetteer Index', *Modern World Encyclopaedia*, vol. ix (London: Home Entertainment Library, 1935).

£1 approximates to Rs.10.12 in 1880.

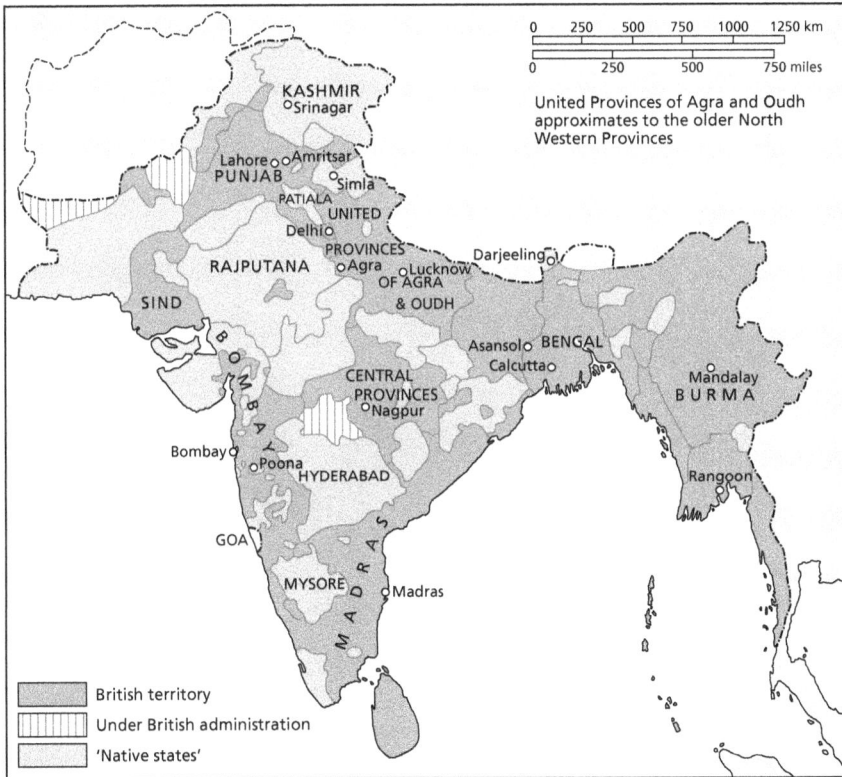

Map British India, 1915.

Legend:
- British territory
- Under British administration
- 'Native states'

Map labels:

0 250 500 750 1000 1250 km
0   250   500   750 miles

United Provinces of Agra and Oudh approximates to the older North Western Provinces

KASHMIR
Srinagar

Lahore Amritsar
PUNJAB
Simla
PATIALA
UNITED
Delhi
PROVINCES
RAJPUTANA
Agra Lucknow
OF AGRA
& OUDH
Darjeeling

SIND

BENGAL
Asansol
Calcutta

CENTRAL
PROVINCES
Nagpur

Mandalay
BURMA

Bombay
Poona
HYDERABAD
BOMBAY

Rangoon

GOA

MYSORE
Madras
MADRAS

Introduction: learning femininity in colonial India, 1820–1932

In 1888 Flora Annie Steel and Grace Gardiner published *The Complete Indian Housekeeper and Cook*.[1] This book, offering advice to European women on how to supervise their households in colonial India, proved very popular and ran to many editions. It contained the following guidance regarding the employment of Indian women to nurse European babies:

> As wet-nurses, none are better than the Cashmiri woman at Amritsar, although at Agra *dhaees* [midwives] have got a great name. The former are very amiable, get very fond of their charges, are simple in their ideas and unsophisticated, and not so grasping in their expectations. It is a great mistake to change the *dhaee's* habits beyond insisting on personal cleanliness and frequent change of clothes. The simpler and more familiar the food she gets, the better she will digest it, and the better will be her nourishment for the child.[2]

The modern reader is struck by the manner and content of Steel's counsel. It is expressed in emotionally remote and racially separate terms, suggesting considerable personal distance from the Indian women she employed. However, Steel was no mere European hostess. Four years earlier, in 1884, she had been appointed inspectress of girls' schools in the Punjab, in north India. In this role, she combined genuine interest in the lives of Indian women and their culture with strong support for British India.[3] Yet, the difference in her approach towards Indian women once they crossed the threshold of a European household is striking, both in terms of her detachment towards them within this domestic domain, and her perception that their biology was differentiated by their race.

Outside the European household, Steel's professional life required her to engage with the women and girls whom she administered. The colonial state's macro agendas around the education of females in India formed an indispensable part of its public rhetoric about its civilising mission. Steel's professional duties were part of this different landscape of female interaction in the colonial sphere – a scene that had a long history behind it. Unlike in the European household, the colonial classroom and, later, the colonial hospital and dispensary, were places in which the role of participating women of all races was subject to changing forms of scrutiny, driven by the strong organising agency of the colonial state. The state also responded to female professionals working on the spot in India, such as Flora Annie Steel herself, and to the women and girls whom she taught.

The official focus on female education in India is not significant so much in terms of specific educational outcomes, of which there were relatively few, particularly for Indian women. Rather this focus is significant as a way to better understand how female education initiatives indicated broader attitudes towards women of all races in India, attitudes held first by the East India Company and later by the raj. As in other colonial domains, these education initiatives were built upon contested pedagogical, institutional, politico-cultural and sociological perspectives. However, in addition, in colonial India, there were also idiomatic race, class, caste, religious and gender barriers that reflected distinctive and traditional cultural spaces on the subcontinent, which were only partially engaged by the interaction between official policy-making and females participating in the colonial sphere.

The story of how women and girls were constructed in colonial India is an important one – especially regarding the forces that drove changes in the educational contexts in which these females interacted. This interaction also had ramifications for other settler societies in the colonial era. In the early nineteenth century, colonial female education in India mostly concerned a few mission schools seeking to assert a Judeo-Christian hegemony in surrounding communities. By the early twentieth century, female education had become more politicised, culminating in unsuccessful inferences by the raj to be supporting Western feminist modernity, with all its uncertain relevance for an emerging India.

My book has an ambitious scope: it studies state-sponsored education for women and girls in colonial India over a 112-year period from 1820 to 1932, when the story was at its richest. Some earlier context is also provided. In particular, the book looks in detail at the changing influences and networks that operated around the female education dynamic in India, including those that applied to medical training. The book begins by building important context about how colonial narratives created official mentalities concerning the female body in India in the rich early orientalist period of the 1820s.[4] It ends in 1932, by which time the activism of women, including that of Loreto women religious (nuns), had built limited, but much more individualist, education enterprises in the context of a failing colonial state. Some additional survey commentary on the post-1932 period is also provided in the conclusion of the book.

The precursors of colonial education for girls were different from those for boys. Through this book I argue that the interaction between state and schoolgirl created a powerful and distinctive symbiosis that evolved over time. To trace this evolution, I have identified key periods, each with its own characteristics and imperatives. These periods are solidified by the aggregation of different interactive connections and networks; networks that drove education mentalities in India, not all of which were coterminous with empire. By examining these periods, this book offers context for other studies on women and India, by identifying the changes at work concerning women, even within the restricted colonial project. An understanding of these changes also better contextualises those studies on India and women that have concentrated on the later colonial period. Through this book I demonstrate that the colonial project remained capable of evolution, producing broader outcomes that both accentuated and reconfigured race and class and gender boundaries as they related to women and girls in India.

There are, naturally, some artificialities involved in this approach, particularly in the time frames that I have identified as marking elemental shifts in policymaking. There are also, within the vast educational vista of India, exceptions to the phenomena I identify. Powerful emerging scholarship offers deeper case-study analysis of specific locations and educational stratums, including detailed micro and regional studies concerning aspects of the female experience in colonial India. For example: Siobhan Lambert-Hurley examines efforts to reform women's health in Bhopal State in the early twentieth century; Nita Verma Prasad's work dissects the complex legal terrain of widow inheritance disputes in north India in the latter part of the nineteenth century;[5] and Jyoti Atwal explores the uncomfortable location of indigenous feminist practice within anti-colonial programmes in the North Western Provinces (NWP) in the early twentieth century.[6] These are just a sample of the regional and time-specific studies that relate to the diffuse and specific ways that mentalities about females can be seen in the colonial period.

However, the approach I have taken here is to attempt to understand different periods of colonial interaction within a broader view, and to seek to explore how these periods relate to each other. This approach develops my earlier work identifying key phases of educational change in colonial India.[7] While it is true that the history of the subcontinent from the perspectives of Indians does not lend itself to grand narratives permitting longitudinal analysis, it is the case that the superficial imperatives that drove European-predicated education were simpler and more unified across the subcontinent. They are, therefore, more capable of study across each period. Looking at these colonial imperatives, the state is usually paradigmatic, while women occupied many peripheries in the British colonial era.

The imposition in India of emerging Western conceptions of schooling and medical professionalism, as far as both related to women and girls, might naturally identify feminism as a key underlying feature. Yet here the picture is complicated and scholars have different perspectives. Kumari Jayawardena confronts the contentious issue of assigning 'feminism' to the subcontinent by seeing the term as best loosely applied to those women 'involved in projects to change the lives of women', including Western missionaries and social reformers who felt they had a 'moral duty to uplift, sanitize and modernize traditional societies'.[8] From the Indian side of the story, Padma Anagol identifies a second generation of Indian converts in the late nineteenth century who were feminists who used their ideology to critique Hinduism and its role, as they saw it, in the oppression and vilification of Indian women.[9] Their regional activism was variable, and was likely to have ranged from communities of activists in Bengal (east India) to more individually based effort in Maharashtra (west India). On the other hand, Geraldine Forbes suggests Indian feminism did emerge from behind the *purdah* (traditional seclusion), but not as a carbon copy of Western feminism in either ideology or goals, as the Indian social system bore little resemblance to European countries.[10] The complex issue of assigning feminism to the subcontinent in educational contexts is examined later in this book. It is certainly the case that, at least by the First World War, there was a strong feminist consciousness among the female Indian literati in the Hindu provinces.[11]

My approach in this book is primarily concerned with Western perspectives about femininity (rather than feminism) in tracing the agency of Western women and Westernised women in colonial India. This is because I explore the nature of mostly British-inspired female agency, where considerations of femininity, even at the level of state directives, remained at the centre of official rhetoric and racialised policies based on gender. Additionally, the international networks that fed into the activism of most Western-influenced nurses and women teachers (particularly for 'accomplishments', to be explained below) involved principally feminine, rather than feminist, constructs. As such, I have found narratives concerning femininity more productive in analysing

[4]

the thought and actions of European and Eurasian women in India, and the Indian women with whom they interacted. This is particularly apparent as the book mostly interprets changing Western perceptions, which were both generated by and imposed upon these women in their often-isolated colonial workplaces. Additionally, Western scholars such as Sonya Adnermahr, Terry Lovell and Carol Wolkowitz, drawing on the earlier work of Toril Moi, suggest there is also a direct academic tension between 'femininity' and 'feminism' that, in part, goes to the definition of both terms:

> feminine designates the set of cultural attributes assigned to the female sex, which the political discourses of feminism seek to critique ... [and that] theories of the feminine tend to present in one of two ways: something basically imposed on women from the outside either through direct or indirect means ... or as a psychosexual process involving the female unconscious.[12]

Although this tension is less visible in colonial India, and in the context of postcolonial research concerning colonial India, evidence of it does emerge – particularly in the context of medical care as practised by female missionaries and the competing later contributions of secular women physicians, as shown in chapters five and six of this book.

There is, of course, a much longer-standing story of Indian women who were not within the ambit of the raj. In the nineteenth century these women were undergoing other changes in identity formation, particularly within the Hindu polity and under reforming agencies such as Dayananda Saraswati's (1824–83) Arya Samaj in north India and Swami Vivekananda's (1863–1902) philosophy of *Vedanta* (new life based on individual freedom and opportunity).[13] However, it would be near impossible to systematise in some way the highly variable, and culturally different, receptivity and resistance of Indian women over the long time period of this book, using even a notional Indian perception or perceptions of favoured femininity in the colonial era as they might relate to female education.

───◆───

The book's female subjects

To study this topic effectively, my book confines itself to the constrained ambit of British India and some other spheres of European interaction. It offers thick descriptions of the work of key women and their contexts to illustrate broader theoretical issues. In understanding the fascinating intersections created by the vicissitudes of female education, the book examines some of the many women educators and schoolgirls (a professional divide easily blurred within this story) who actually worked *in* colonial India. This research is therefore distinct from other works that have looked at those middle-class women who wrote about female education, philanthropy and the empire from the distant vantage point of the metropole. This book also differs from research into Indian activists such as Rabindranath Tagore, Sarala Devi Chaudhurani and Rokeya Sakhawat Hossain, whose more abstract commentary on female education was part of their broader alignment to the rising national movement.[14] My work takes an intimate look at the labours of women educators and female learners operating in local school and medical domains in colonial India. Their voices inform the discussion in a more specific way than would be possible by relying on broad theorisation without mention of individual experiences. This book systematises and gives context to the work of these women by referring to the organising hand of broad raj policymaking, as well as to imported ideas from the West and other agencies both inside and outside India.

By the end of the nineteenth century, depending on province, the raj claimed coverage of only between 1 and 2 per cent of school-age girls in its schools, which nominally amounted to some 780,000 individuals. In 1892, more reliable government reviews estimated that only 0.4 per cent of these girls were in secondary schools, with only half of this tiny percentage being Indian girls, and with twenty-five times as many boys being in this category.[15] Unlike colonial boys' education, those who focused on colonial education for girls did not have pretensions to be overriding stronger pre-colonial educational traditions on the subcontinent. Proportionately speaking, very few Indian girls ever secured careers as a result of their education under the raj, despite an ongoing official discourse throughout the colonial period about the professional trajectories created by female education. Instead, the usual colonial image regarding girls' education was highly gendered and saw female education as important in diagnosing the cultural 'deficits' of Indians. The British in India were particularly energised when displaying Western stereotypes of child marriage, caste and widow customs as part of what they claimed to be a 'degenerate' Hindu polity. By the end of the nineteenth century, official female education policy was highly sensitised by race considerations to protect the moral body of a small group of mostly Eurasian women, and an even smaller group of Indian women whose families were closely connected to Western commerce.

The book's theoretical framework

This book's theorisation responds to recent powerful academic developments that provide potential for a deeper exploration of these issues. Since the publication of Vron Ware's *Beyond the Pale* in 1992, little cross-generational work concerning women educators in India, and their female recipients, has attempted to trace change over almost the entire British colonial period. Ware suggested that an analysis of race, class and gender configurations remained relatively unchartered territory for those studying Victorian imperialism.[16] Anne McClintock is one of a very small number of scholars who have elaborated on the relational aspects of these configurations: asserting that race, class and gender were not, in fact, distinct realms of experience, but came into existence *in* and *through* relation to each other in colonial contexts.[17]

This neglect by researchers can be explained by the almost insurmountable complexity and scope of such study, at least before the development of new models of analysis to refine and distil such configurations. Developing adequate theorisation has turned out to be a demanding task. Cecily Jones' *Engendering Whiteness* contributed by building new ways to interrogate largely colonial contexts where gender subordination, but class privilege, created conflicted domestic spaces for white women in Barbados and North Carolina.[18] Meanwhile, as far as colonial India is concerned, new research possibilities are now brought into play by the use of three traditions of scholarship that have been largely unconnected in the past fifteen years. These are elaborated upon in each of the three following sections.

The subaltern legacy and women in India

The highly influential Subaltern Studies Group (SSG) appeared in the 1980s under the leadership of Ranajit Guha.[19] It was rightly dismissive of earlier writing on India as being elitist and mechanical. By the early 1990s, these scholars had moved the raj out of the picture almost entirely, preferring, instead, an analysis of subaltern groupings themselves and of the input of Indian elites. Subaltern contributors came together to recover experiences, cultures, traditions and identities that had been lost or hidden by the action of a historiography that related mostly to elites.[20] However, despite their theoretical brilliance, at the time of Ware's writing subaltern approaches had become, uncomfortably, hegemonic. There was a reluctance, indeed an avoidance on the part of some scholars, to talk of the European in India. This led to a delay in works on European women operating in India – unlike research into other parts of the British empire. Subsequent revisionism concerning the subaltern tradition is particularly important for the purposes of this book. For example, Chris Bayly re-established the obvious importance of the European interaction, recasting it mostly in terms of gossip runners and information gatherers in the earlier nineteenth century.[21] Sumit Sarkar has written about the influence of the British in another way: as bringing with it clocks and the notion of linear time, as well as the ancient/medieval and modern schema established in a post-Renaissance West.[22]

The subaltern approach has influenced this book in terms of my interest in the consequences of policymaking and an emphasis on 'learning' rather than 'teaching', as indicated by the book's title. However, in the last decade, the decentring of subaltern scholarship itself also offers other realignments that I have found useful when researching the colonial period, especially when it comes to the issue of gender. As Jim Masselos suggests of more recent scholarship directions:

> Subaltern subjects have been lost in the theoretical and methodological structures erected over them and the academic agendas created around them.[23]

This very methodological ambivalence offers new theoretical possibilities. For example, new work on Indian feminism questions and appropriates subaltern historiography and its close use of Spivak's Marxist approach of rigid 'elite' and 'oppressed' categories.[24] Anagol's *The Emergence of Feminism* has placed subaltern approaches under examination in this way, particularly their earlier neglect of gender and the differentiated roles of women on the subcontinent, and how one group of women might, in fact, oppress other groups of women.[25] It is worth noting here, too, that Indian women fighting anti-caste crusades, and crusades against child marriage, embarked on truly radical activism within their own communities in a way not yet adequately acknowledged by Western scholarship. On the key question of education, current theoretical revisionism offers new possibilities for building a more differentiated schema of women of different social classes and races, particularly as they interacted with each other and with the state.

Writing this book has proved to be an uneven methodological enterprise, given what has gone before. For example, it is beyond the scope of a book of this kind to fully engage with the multiple narratives of feminist critique of the imperial interlude. Powerful subaltern analysis has, in a sense, overrun some gender narratives, such as contested notions of 'femininity' characterised here, even before these narratives could be established in postcolonial scholarship. However, new work, such as that of Roland Colomba writing about the gender colonial experience in the Philippines in the early 1900s, does reconfigure

Spivakian framing of 'white men saving brown women from brown men' to analyse 'white women … saving white men and brown women from each other'.[26] For much of the colonial experience in India, this framing reveals a more intricate entanglement of these groupings, particularly the groupings directed by white women.

Further, feminist critiques by Indian scholars have been concerned with the actions of groups of mostly unidentified women, whose learning and domestic space is defined mostly through the formulation of theories about their oppression, their cultural identity and their poverty. That is, the rendering of colonial-era feminism by Indian scholars mostly focuses on groups of women, and their social, political and household interactions, especially regarding social reform, rather than on the study of individual feminists *per se*.[27] This contrasts with Western scholarship, which, with mostly pan-imperial vistas in view, has been less productive in attempting to identify feminists, white or non-white, living in colonial India during the same period. Additionally, as Rosalind O'Hanlon suggests, conventional histories of women and gender relations have obscured the local activism of women in other ways: by assigning them to more limited domains of family organisation, reproduction and sexuality, rather than seeing this activism as part of larger political processes concerning the nation state and related social, secular and religious processes.[28]

It is also necessary to consider the critical issue of race and the colonial state, which hindered later Western feminist engagement with India in the colonial era. Before the 1790s, in the remote and manly world of colonial India, the East India Company encouraged racial intermixture between Indian women and Company officials, which was commonplace. When white relations with Eurasians occurred in the 1820s, this was again driven by Company macro policymaking, and not by the intervention of white women. Later in the nineteenth century, the writing and actions of white women at home in Britain often amounted to little more than a Western-oriented philanthropy that was rarely used to attempt to actually change the lives of Indian women in India. However, for those white women actually living in India, the terrain of their engagement with Indian women – the classroom and the dispensary – was not feminist inspired, but was mostly negotiated through the paradigm of femininity and the preservation of the female body according to prevailing Western moral norms; norms amplified by the rhetoric of the colonial state itself.

The attainment of these moral norms in the classroom and in the dispensary was also indicated by due displays of Western-conceived female professionalism. Key women figures in India, such as Annie Besant in the early twentieth century, subsequently rejected these brands of Western professionalism for the subcontinent because of the internal Western femininity values that mostly drove such Western professional mentalities as they related to women in India.[29] Furthermore, in the early twentieth century, the activism of white women was closely bounded and controlled by a superficial, but powerful, raj state authority; an official boundary that only really began to break down during the First World War. Before that time, these white women rarely acknowledged the discrimination inherent in decisions by the colonial state, based on race, that allowed only some women living in India to be the recipients of the Western civilising mission. This complicity was usually because the white women preferred a smaller group of more European-like Eurasians, whom they felt could more 'realistically' benefit from Western cultural 'redemption', as compared to their Indian sisters.

Gender, education and the 'white' empire

Scholarship on gender and empire, now well established, comes from a different tradition. This scholarship has made an important contribution to understanding the colonial world. It mostly concerns the experience of European women who were generally not part of power elites, but who were subject to distinctive oppression – operating under different social constraints, and experiencing empire differently from white men.

In the 1990s, writing about the empire gave greater attention to women: mostly those of the late nineteenth century and early twentieth century. Antoinette Burton's *Burdens of History* asserts that feminist writers, in the later nineteenth and early twentieth centuries, created images of 'needy' Indian women merely to encourage British women living in England to think of themselves as committed to a 'racial mother-hood' and part of an imperial civilising mission.[30] Claire Midgley, looking to other parts of non-white empire, sees the input of European women into the anti-slavery campaigns as part of the British feminist discourse 'in an imperial context'. Midgley argues that these women did not simply draw on imperial ideologies, but were active in gendering them.[31] These views regarding female activism, mostly about women resident in Britain, built on the perspective of Margaret Stroebel and others who examined how women functioned within the framework of 'masculine' imperialism, considering whether European women in India were, as Barbara Ramusack has posited, 'cultural missionaries', 'maternal imperialists' or 'feminist allies' of the Indian women they sought to help.[32]

[10]

Also significant is the work of scholars of the history of women's education. Their work has recast the way academics consider the European view of women's education in the nineteenth century, throughout the British empire. Joyce Goodman and Jane Martin show how leading feminist educators resisted gender roles and combined their public lives with private commitments.[33] Ruth Watts has interpreted the colonial divide concerning women travelling to India by studying the work of Mary Carpenter and her context of the 1860s and 1870s, both in England and in India.[34] These works add to Burton's view of the changing perceptions of British feminists, who, arguably, imagined that the Western women's movement, concerning empire, was one of imparting the products of a superior civilisation, almost as a commodity.[35]

Acknowledging this scholarship, I have endeavoured to be sensitive to the need to avoid taking stereotyped language from colonial writers and unselectively applying it to current theorisation about females. Looking at the economic and social condition of most Indian women today, earning a tiny fraction of global income and owning little if any property, McClintock argues that, for most of them, postcolonialism has in fact merely been a history of 'hopes postponed'.[36] Meanwhile, Raewyn Connell views femininity and masculinity in current and past contexts in highly relational sociological terms.[37] These views strongly suggest that scholars of colonial India need to engage more with the etymology of gender terms in the subcontinental context.

Colonial language also creates some inescapable ambiguities. 'Female education' is a phrase used unavoidably throughout this book, as in other works, and it relays, to some degree, the language of empire. Its use is necessary when referring to the mid-decades of the nineteenth century because girls as well as women were recruited to train as teachers. However, the frequent use of this phrase in colonial India is revealing as being indicative of a colonial state that was unwilling to recognise the distinction between Indian women and girls when they entered colonial classrooms. Official acknowledgement of the Indian mother, as a responsible adult, was also rare.

Gender, empire and education considerations in late colonial India suggest other hidden barriers to an imagined collective female activism. Both raj and Indian nationalist thinking about females was driven by unyielding patriarchies, which, by the early twentieth century, in different ways accentuated different roles for women compared to men.[38] This might have led, in this late colonial period, to the woman teacher and the schoolgirl being forced to belong, in a philosophical sense, to a broader schooling community of females pressing against gender-driven barriers created by males on both sides of the nationalist debate. Yet, antithetical patriarchies on both sides of the colonial divide were not about to enter into the conversation. As Partha Chatterjee contends, female emancipation disappeared from the public agenda of nationalist agitation in the late nineteenth century because of the refusal of nationalism to make the women's question an issue of political negotiation with the colonial state.[39] Conversely, the raj's veiled barriers of race and class regarding education enabled colonial operatives to retreat from the need to engage much at all on the issue of female education with leading nationalist figures in the twentieth century.

Knowledge transfer

Bridging the subaltern legacy and colonial gender narratives is a third school of scholarship that relates to the difficult issue of how best to characterise knowledge and cultural transfer as it related to the colonial education of women and girls in India. When taking a closer view of the educational link between Great Britain and India in the colonial phase, we can obviously see that there were strong transformational interchanges that most contemporaries – whether apologists for empire or not – were keen to acknowledge. However, centre-periphery approaches, which identify just one imperial centre and peripheries only in colonial domains, have been largely unsuccessful in tracing complex relationships of the kind explored in this book. This is particularly so if the colonial period is perceived, erroneously, as one relatively even enterprise of imposition upon settler societies and 'native' communities; and where the metropole itself has not been identified as a cultural space worthy of similar problematisation and subject to influence from colonies abroad. On this latter point the work of Catherine Hall and others is a welcome contribution.[40]

Furthermore, networks among colonies themselves – and ex-colonies such as the Indo/American relationship – come into play, creating a perplexing web of imperial and later international connections that are impossible to adequately map, but which also inform contemporary gender practice. In this frame, Muhammad Yunus' micro-credit Grameen bank conception (with groups of poor Asian women acting as cross-guarantors for small commercial loans) owes some provenance to Jonathan Swift's humanitarian rural Irish fund in the late seventeenth century and to the peoples' banks in the German states supported by Friedrich Raiffeisen and others a generation later.[41]

Recent theorisation about the problem of how to write about cross-border and cross-boundary influences, and the attendant rejection of simpler centre/periphery approaches, provides especially robust approaches that are also apposite to the gender themes of this book.

Ann Curthoys and Marilyn Lake proffer models of transnational history where analysis is based on understanding what happens to people and practices when they cross national boundaries.[42] Kate Darian-Smith, Patricia Grimshaw and Stuart Macintyre, in their study of Britishness as a global phenomenon, examine what happened to this Britishness in its diffuse forms as the empire declined. However, it is the network and circuit conception of empire that is most compelling for the purposes of this book.[43] Alan Lester poses this schema on multiple levels when analysing colonial practice, performance and experience as a more productive enterprise, rather than simply attempting to locate putative social, economic and political causes.[44] Additionally, the work builds on Tony Ballantyne's organising metaphor of an agglomeration of overlapping webs to explain the multi-sited history of empire.[45] While Chris Bayly's recent work underscores the receptiveness within the language worlds of Arabic and Hindi to vitalise Western theorisation such as Darwinism, and even Social Darwinism. As Bayly argues, this conceptualisation and translocation of theory from the West was carried out much more successfully within these language worlds than many Christian apologists were able to achieve, even given their discomfort with the creation story.[46]

Academics interested in comparative education are also feeling the impact of new work concerning networks, moving on in some cases from rather overused globalisation critiques and looking instead to historical context. Jürgen Schriewer and Carlos Martinez compare Spain, Russia/Soviet Union and China in their analysis of the variable dimensions of the internationalisation of educational knowledge at different stages between the 1920s and the 1990s.[47] Concerning an earlier century, Christina de Bellaigue's *Educating Women*, offers a similar schema of intellectual transference, this time between women educators in France and England, 1800–67,[48] while Tamson Pietsch's *Empire of Scholars* identifies networks that reconnected settler universities in the colonies with scholarship in Britain, particularly in the first half of the twentieth century.[49] Most especially, David Phillips and Kimberly Ochs suggest a useful approach for studies into predominantly non-white colonial domains. In this approach, perceptions of cultural and other 'deficits' in one domain 'externalise potential' to ostensibly warrant intervention from more powerful coloniser domains; and in the colonial world, the 'indigenisation' of Western-predicated policy is adapted to different socio-cultural contexts, making the intervention of European colonial powers possible and seemingly morally justifiable.[50]

These emerging theoretical frameworks have yet to be systematically applied to colony and empire, particularly concerning women. They offer new ways of understanding intellectual and cultural

[13]

transmission across state and colonial boundaries, including the raj. The frameworks also bring together and engage other academic traditions, including those that concern the subaltern approaches and gender paradigms referred to above. This theorisation directly informs this book. In colonial India, the nature of knowledge transfer differed in each period under study, being determined in different ways by active women and men in the field who, in turn, shaped and were shaped by state macro policymaking in each period. My book also understands that, while ideas and actions might be ascribed to particular networks of power and influence, often these ideas and actions were really driven by short-term, local motives that were conveniently camouflaged by claims of broader provenance and legitimacy.

It is evident that the networks that facilitated knowledge transfer over the long time span covered by this book operated differently in different periods. This difference was due to shifting imperial relations, particularly in the mid-nineteenth century. At other times, the specific arenas of interaction were at local colonial sites, and these sites determined the networks that came into play. Each chapter in this book therefore elaborates on the transformational interchanges of a particular period and the networks that drove these interchanges regarding gender and the colonial sphere in India. However, three patterns stand out. In the middle of the nineteenth century, in particular, and later in the century concerning the learning in India of Western scientific medicine, network interchanges were mediated via top-down Western power brokers of both genders. At other times, when British colonial women and men sought Indian influence and contribution, the network interchange was more nuanced and became situated and determined much more by individuals on the spot. A third pattern in play regarding networks, mostly towards the end of the colonial period, involved periphery-to-periphery connection. Chapter nine provides the strongest example of this, where the Irish foundation of Loreto interacted with very poor Indian girls, largely in defiance of the state preference for schooling Eurasian girls.

‒◆‒

Eurasians, accomplishments and the state

Three key themes recur throughout this work: Eurasians; the accomplishments curriculum; and the multifaceted and changing nature of colonial governance in India.

Eurasians

A key part of this story relates to the question of Eurasians, whose narrative engaged many networks within and without the British sphere. Anxieties about Eurasians began before the British raj and endured after its departure. The Eurasian story emerged strongly in the seventeenth century, when Portuguese coastal entrepôts and diplomatic forays to the old Mughal courts in north India offered possibilities for regular sexual encounters with the local population. At the other end of the colonial period, Eurasian women and girls provided some educational institutions with a favoured enrolment that was unofficially merged with Indian girls only in the 1920s. The merging of this enrolment was then executed in a way that even allowed some colonial institutions to transcend Partition successfully after 1947.

People of mixed race were powerful initiators of policy in many colonial domains. For instance, in Senegal, French West Africa, in the seventeenth century, *signares* (women of Afro-French descent) on the Isle St Louis acted as demi-official intermediaries: providing French traders with access to African commercial networks that engaged the brutal slave-trafficking trading posts of the new world.[51] In the Dutch East Indies, a century later, poor Eurasians troubled the Dutch colonial mind because of their lack of *innerlijke kracht* (moral strength), reckoned to come from the character frailty of the indigenous parent.[52] In the colony of Victoria, Australia in the 1860s, regulations banning 'half-caste' children from living on reserves with their pure-race Aboriginal parent were responsible for the near extinction of entire Aboriginal tribes.[53]

In colonial India, these ways of thinking about people of mixed race were exported from and imported to the subcontinent by global empire constellations; yet they were also separately applied within the raj. The term 'Eurasian' itself was slippery and its meaning unstable. For much of the nineteenth century, 'Anglo-Indian' was a label that guaranteed ethnic purity for those living in India of solely European descent.[54] Wealthy families of part-Indian descent also appropriated the term to falsely claim a purely European heritage. However, paradoxically, as official raj attitudes about inter-racial mixing hardened by the 1830s, the phrase 'Eurasian' became a useful term for the colonial state to use to justify new policymaking in the name of strategically placed philanthropy. This 'charity' mostly concerned a particular group of Indians of part-European racial lineage. These children were often the issue of redeployed soldiers and their Indian mistresses. The philanthropy was driven in part by a genuine affection felt by some of these soldiers for the children they had fathered but whom they could not parent. As an inadequate form of moral absolution, they sometimes provided modest funds for their child's basic schooling in India, as will be elaborated upon in chapter two of this book.

In the mid-nineteenth century, the question of Eurasians in India created, at times, moral fears at government level that then directed its educational policymaking. The prospect of vagrant children of part-European descent roaming the streets of the raj was not an attractive one for British administrators. In particular, there was a fear that miscegenated European racial lines, if not managed well in terms of macro statecraft, might reveal themselves to local indigenous elites not to be very superior after all.[55] This was especially so after the Great Revolt of 1857, when overly rigid state-imposed categories of race, ethnicity and caste became a more conscious domain of the newly reinforced raj *imperium*. In this middle period, 'Eurasian', while still a race designation, also became an identifier whereby mostly 'orphan' children might be targeted for philanthropic help. As shown later in the book, this racial category could be so broad as to include the children of rescued African slaves.

The state went through several iterations of attempts to put legal bounds around the term Eurasian. As the nineteenth century progressed, this legalese also served the purpose of racialising classrooms for schoolgirls. In the 1850s, partly out of embarrassment and partly out of a need for control, Eurasian girls were given preference over Indian girls in accessing colonial schools. By the end of the century, Eurasian girls had become the prototype schoolgirl to be taught accomplishments along with their European sisters.

Defining race by regulation could also produce extraordinary results underpinned by highly convoluted social histories – histories that British detailed record keeping has been good at preserving. For example, in 1915, when confronted by the dark-skinned 'Eurasian' girls attending Loreto Convent School in Calcutta, the visiting Director of Public Instruction (DPI) was satisfied to put their unusually dark skin colour down to a papal ruling three generations earlier. The Catholic Church in Calcutta, then made up mostly of Portuguese, had sought to swell its rapidly dwindling flock by purchasing consignments of slaves on the Hooghly river *ghats* (river bank steps) and selling them on to Catholic families for employment in their various business enterprises.[56] When slavery was abolished throughout the British empire in 1833, these families were obliged by Rome to adopt any domestically employed slaves. This automatically made them legally *Kiutal* (Eurasian) under the law of the province if they were baptised. As manumitted slaves without any European racial lineage, they were taught some basic literacy (to 'read, write and cypher'), which provided them with some kind of economic future. The DPI supposed it was the *Kiutal* descendents whom accounted for Loreto's, 'dark-skinned', seemingly racially aberrant, student enrolment in the early twentieth century.[57]

The term 'Eurasian' also had a strong socio-cultural bearing that was fluid and much more dependent on job description, geography and physical appearance than on formal government categorisation. For instance, most lower and middle-class Eurasian families worked as separate communities, employed by the railway company networks that defined the reach of British India. Yet, even towards the end of the raj, the benefit of a paler skin – if racial mixing was with lighter-skinned Indians such as the Pashtuns on the Frontier – could also win access to exclusively white social circles that excluded other Eurasians. As this passage from *Plain Tales from the Raj* retells:

> I knew an Anglo-Indian girl [here meaning Eurasian] in Peshawar [north India], white with blue eyes, who was known to be Anglo-Indian because her parents lived in Peshawar. She knew I used to go to the club because I used to talk about the parties there and she wanted to join. I asked a lady doctor who had influence to try and get Celia in and she told me it was no use trying: 'because everybody round here knows Celia is an Anglo-Indian'. I told this lady doctor, 'Well so am I', 'Yes, but people don't know it here. You have passed in the crowd, but Celia won't'. The club was taboo.[58]

These European-predicated distinctions also cut across class lines. Significantly, there was an even fiercer race distinction constructed by Eurasians themselves when quarantining their communities from Indians, who made up the vast bulk of the population.

After 1860, British colonial schools in India, particularly for Eurasian girls, came to strongly reinforce official racial mentalities concerning females. These mentalities explained why parents were keen to seek out Western schools as part of an attempt to win favourable racial recognition from Europeans for their Eurasian daughters. Additionally, those Eurasians who could pass as European often went to great lengths to hide any part of their Indian ancestry. For example, Anna Loenowen (of *The King and I* fame), who arrived in Bangkok in March 1862 to teach the children of King Mongkut (Rama IV) of Thailand, claimed that she was born in Wales and that, when her parents died young, and having gone out to India, she was brought up by 'an eminent Welsh lady'. In fact her birth was in India and her origins Eurasian, with a mother made destitute after her father met an early military death. Loenowen's brief formal education was in the local regimental school and her exceptional language skills, including Sanscrit, were learnt as she roamed as a child around the heaving, fetid and racially diverse military cantonments of Bombay.[59]

Eurasian girls taught in a good school with a European-based curriculum could also win European husbands from the lower ranks of the army or from the uncovenanted Indian Civil Service (ICS). This offered possibilities for naturalisation, and perhaps an eventual passage to England. Sometimes their husbands secured a posting first in one of the Near East protectorates, such as Iraq or Egypt, to obscure the racial transgression. Nonetheless, such intermarriage could still result in rejection by the rest of the family in England, even in the 1930s. It was not unknown for Eurasian wives to be hidden beneath strategically placed hats shading their faces in photographs sent to their all-white family resident in other colonies, who were unlikely ever to make personal contact.

Finally, Partition saw the departure of many Eurasian families from the subcontinent, and they then became part of strong diasporas in cities such as Toronto, Melbourne, Sydney and London. Even in India today, the minority Eurasian community is recognised by the Indian constitution; a community Norman Ivan Marshall has illustrated as adopting an amusing array of remnant Anglo-Indian etiquettes that are still visible as an amalgam of East and West custom, and a cuisine with its own separate lexicon.[60]

Accomplishments

The Eurasian interaction throws up a complex array of connections and networks that relate to empire, but that are not wholly parallel to it. A more immediate intersection that engaged the Eurasian political and socio-cultural dimensions during the time of the raj was the accomplishments curriculum that was transplanted directly from the metropole for middle and upper-class girls in India. This intersection was particularly strong during the second half of the nineteenth century.

Accomplishments in England encompassed a far broader curriculum than the one usually taught in India (where there were fewer available teachers) even in the rarefied circles of polite white society. At its broadest, in England, the accomplishments curriculum included geography, history and arithmetic, as well as the more commonly assigned elocution, music, needlework, modern languages, drawing and elements of the natural sciences. In India, its canon was usually this latter grouping only and generally excluded, as in England, middle-class boys' education in Latin, Greek and mathematics.[61]

As in England, the accomplishments canon in India was principally concerned with transmitting colonial moral and class codes, preferably signified by a marked Knightsbridge elocution. Jane McDermid's work shows that, even in the mid-nineteenth century in England, accomplishments was subject to revision in favour of more academic subjects for girls.[62] This feminine teaching and learning was still strongly associated with supposed mid-Victorian establishment norms of respectability and deportment. There were also curious oddities in this derivation smoothed over by powerbrokers who wished to invoke conformity in those females they wished to dominate. On the issue of language alone, it is likely that Queen Victoria spoke, at least in informal settings, with what her most recent biographer, A. N. Wilson, characterises as 'unreformed Regency English'; while, a generation earlier, Jane Austen (another quintessential agency for relaying English feminine codes of deportment and genteel sensibility through her novels) probably spoke with a broad Hampshire accent.[63]

These are perhaps trivial points, but accomplishments as a cogent educational philosophy is best seen as something that preceded the middle-class, mid-Victorian moral code that most of its proponents, in the Empress's India at least, assumed had given rise to it. Such Indian-based syncretism was probably a product of the strong social positioning that occurred on the subcontinent regarding female education in the late nineteenth century, and for the Eurasians who were its most favoured recipients. This was part of broader hankerings of the same time period by 'brown Englishmen' – Indians who wished to take up European ways.

In England, Erasmus Darwin's *Plan for the Conduct of Female Education* (1797) and Hannah More's *Strictures of a Modern System of Female Education* (1799–1811), among other treatises, delineate a much earlier time period for the genesis of accomplishments. Here English femininity was not defined by sexuality, but by purity and modesty. Femininity was a worthy character trait for man's inferior domestic supporter and consoler.[64] This mentality was also enshrined by the advent of new social ideas in later nineteenth-century Britain, especially Social Darwinism. Conservative ideas about the mother, breastfeeding and about maintaining a 'clean' and 'healthy' household were filtered and translated by fashionable Social Darwinism terminology about racial evolution and progress; and these ideas also made their way to colonial India.[65]

Accomplishments preserved female codes of self-image and deeper socio-cultural considerations that were distinctly European. For this reason, Marjorie Theobald sees the accomplishments curriculum, developing as it did in the same way in different national contexts, as evidence that there were common influences behind the push for female education, most particularly the rise of Protestantism. Protestantism emphasised individual responsibility for salvation through reading the Bible: this required literacy for both genders wishing to attain it. However, Theobald's work also accepts that the accomplishments curriculum owed its genesis to additional precursors in different domains: in Australia, as part of a female academy in the scramble for respectability by a 'thin' bourgeoisie in a convict society; in the USA it was more part of a reform ideology of 'Republican motherhood', where women took on an indirect political role as the first educators of male citizens.[66] Accomplishments in India presented few surface differences with what was happening in Europe and the USA. Yet, as a movement from 'without', accomplishments was embedded on the subcontinent by European power elites for a different array of racial and gendered reasons.

Understanding the historicity and positioning of accomplishments for women and girls in colonial India is assisted by first turning to the development of boys' education. In England in 1868 the Taunton Commission recommended a new secondary curriculum for the middle-classes, including one for girls. Yet in India, in the same decade, bifurcated syllabuses that were taught in English, and in one dominant Indian language, were introduced in each province, with some textbooks also prescribed. These syllabuses were for application in province-wide schooling systems that were supposed to grant access to all boys. They applied to village school, to district school, and to high school, for access then to colleges affiliated (under the original University of London model) to the first three universities (Calcutta, Madras, Bombay), established in 1857.

Building on this approach in India, creative educators, such as William Arnold (son of Thomas Arnold of Rugby) in the Punjab, encouraged limited educational experimentation concerning boys in the mid-nineteenth century. He wished to prevent class taking hold of college education in the way that it had in England. As a result, both Arnold and, earlier, Henry Reid in the North Western Provinces (NWP), attempted to establish a strong village base as an alternative first step to facilitate eventual access for most clever Indian boys to higher forms of education. However, the broader colonial education model across India, formally established by Wood's Education Despatch of 1854, did not turn out to even approximate to this ideal of inclusion. Engagement by education stakeholders over the next two generations established a tradition of circumvention by officials and exclusion of the poor instead, which was far greater than anything seen in Britain.

In different ways, this tradition of circumvention and exclusion also separated girls' education, away from the formal workings of state-directed schooling in India. As with their administration of boys' education, local authorities were complicit in this circumvention and exclusion, mostly by their neglect. Thousands of elementary schools for girls were on the books by the 1870s, yet their existence was defined mostly by sporadic reports into sanitation, building efficacy and enrolments, with little reference to pedagogy or curriculum. Many other girls' schools existed only as modest institutions reconfigured from earlier unrecognised indigenous *plein-air* schools adjacent to traditional Indian spaces, such as the *dharmsala* (resting place for travellers), the *masjid* (the mosque), the *antahpur* (female apartments) or the *zenana* (household female quarters). At the secondary level, very few state schools for girls existed at all. The separateness of these secondary schools was emphasised further by an unweaning raj attachment to the Cambridge local examinations that were made available to girls in England from 1863–4 onwards. These exams were imported to drive the accomplishments curriculum in India, particularly in the more dynamic and privately run female academies, at around the same time.

The visible separation of schooling for girls from the state might well have been ignored, relegating female education to a growing residue of unfulfilled raj promises and leaving its operation to private enterprise only. However, the problematic cultural connections that accomplishments made with India generally were of more immediate concern to state sensibilities. After 1860, female education was an important part of the colonial state's rhetoric, although the state's exclusion of most Indian girls from senior levels of colonial schooling kept this brand of European femininity safely limited to a small number of female recipients.

In England in the mid-nineteenth century, accomplishments subjects had nested within them two opposing socialising norms: one rejected by the Establishment; and one embraced by it. The 'blue stocking' who learnt in manly ways offended both patriarchal and matriarchal sensibilities as to what was a 'woman's place'; while proponents of 'accomplishments' were approved of as pursuing an appropriate deployment of women's intellect, biologically predetermined as different to men, and based on home domesticity constructed by the middle-class.[67]

This stark binary dissipated when applied to the subcontinent, with its smaller number of girls' schools, its more dispersed teaching community and, especially, its different cultural milieu. In India particularly, although certainly not exclusively in this age, teachers usually lacked a pedagogical language to critique their praxis. This meant that, when these teachers found time to reflect on their practice, their focus fell on broader cultural and gender issues. Additionally, the cultural setting of colonial India, and the crossovers that occurred between the European expatriate and indigenous resident societies, presented new cultural and gender parameters and inverted others. Accomplishments

[21]

subjects in England were partly about the adornment of the body, with fine lace, coiffure and tailored smocking kept in place by intricate needlework. Yet in the India of the sari, the British believed it was usually only the courtesan who sewed her clothes.[68] The barriers of purdah in the north, the 'civilising mission' for Eurasian girls, and the creation of refuges for the Hindu 'widow' were other Indian-based imperatives.

Separate to this, Theobald's nineteenth-century accomplishments still existed in India; that is, the European woman at the piano, in the parlour and not the concert hall, unequivocally belonging to the realm of culture.[69] In India, her territory was more constrained and her identity an untenable cultural isolate. She might occupy the restrained and temperate alpine and red-gravel terrain of the hill stations. However, the enrolment of her sister scholars, and perhaps even herself, in the schools, the parlours and the bungalows of India, also involved anxieties about race when she attempted to negotiate India's socio-religious terra firma. This was especially so as her education in feminine accomplishments remained mostly European middle-class predicated.

An inescapable cultural melange of East and West still lay beneath the Western façade that the accomplished female confronted in India, making her liable to occidental objectification by local Indian elites. Using Sylvana Tomaselli's broader construct, she had, as civiliser (though lower than man), the capacity to cultivate and refine, but also the ability to adulterate and corrupt.[70] However, in India, her agenda was liable to be written by others also. To this end, the accomplishments mentality troubled, to a limited degree, the thought and writing of the Hindu and Muslim intelligentsia and was viewed as something worthy of great suspicion by the late nineteenth century. This cynicism was sometimes expressed in the form of Bengali theatre farces, or in Indian social parodies concerning colonial women professionals, which presented the Westernised Indian woman as only fond of useless luxury and caring little for the well-being of the home.[71] Or, it could go to a deeper and subtle filtering. As Meredith Borthwick argues about the 1860s period, the conjugal relationship in the household in Bengal, at least, could extend to the permission of husbands for their wives to attend social and political gatherings, but mostly as a means to signify Indian male social 'progressiveness' to philanthropic English observers.[72] Influential local newspapers such as the *Brahmo Public Opinion*, or organisations such as the Simla Literary Society, placed an important proviso on colonial female education of this kind too. An educated wife was still provisionally approved of, even in acquiescent Western terms, but only if this meant that she was able to create a better Indian home.[73] However, accomplishments subjects, having a robust, European, middle-class outlook, might have also become a matter of fierce dispute had they ever permeated large stratums of Indian society. After all, the accomplishments canon directly represented a key concern of Indian nationalists: that colonial education, as a pathway to modernity, might also lead to a loss of Indianness by its recipients.[74]

Furthermore, an emerging India in the early twentieth century assigned social service, rather than Western forms of female professionalism (not in themselves a natural legacy of accomplishments anyway), to its women participants. As Sanjay Seth theorises, leading nationalist leaders saw Western education in its broader incarnation as a path to 'de-nationalising' and 'de-sexing' women, which was therefore to be resisted.[75] Instead, Indian women were considered by most nationalists as harbingers of the spiritual, protecting cultural identity, and in the domestic domain as a counterpoise to their husbands' material and cultural compromises in the external colonial world of commerce and work.[76]

Taking these considerations into account, this book does not examine female schooling and nursing in India as separate Western-predicated professional practices available and responsive to all women and girls in India. Instead, I view these two education endeavours as bound together by the raj's more powerful race and class imperatives: where the actions of colonial-inspired females more acutely exercised alternative femininity and moral values, in a way that mostly reinforced these imperatives.

Multifaceted and changing colonial governance in India

This book's use of overlapping periodisation illustrates the unstable conception of the state itself in India and its many layers of male oppression and direction of females. The East India Company was originally granted its charter by Queen Elizabeth I in 1600. Its business was commerce, trading with the subcontinent in tea, cotton, silk, indigo and opium. After the battle of Plassey in 1757, and with the use of its own private armies to annex territory and eject European competitors, the Company's power was still not strong in its early years. For its trading networks to expand, this powerlessness necessitated Governor General Warren Hastings and his successors to engage in clever accommodation and negotiation with well-entrenched local nawabs, maharajahs and tribals. New power then eventually came through the bureaucracy and Western rationalisation on which the new capitalism depended.

In Max Weber's terms, this Western rationalisation, where in many places it touched 'the local' in India, set up a new power ambivalence as it attempted to eschew traditional forms of Indian social organisation and to bring Indian religious activity to a new secular reality.[77] To disempowered Indian women, the state could also mean the *patwaris* (tax collectors) and *zamindars* (landlords). Generally, the more local these male authorities were, the more likely it was that their authority transcended the British period, reaching back in their structures of control to Mughal and even earlier times. As with other new work on empire, this book does not see 'the raj' in terms of territorial annexation on the subcontinent but, rather, in terms of British practices of control.[78] There are also other ambiguities of colonial governance in India, such as the examples Joseph Sramek provides in the early nineteenth century where the East India Company, rather than 'the British state', ruled India.[79]

The Great Revolt ended East India Company governance, and Queen Victoria's Proclamation of 1858 signalled Westminster's determination to take control of the administration of the raj.[80] The Governor General and East India Company directors in London were replaced by a viceroy in India and a secretary of state at Westminster. What remained of Mughal authority also was ended. In the 1870s a much more pressing imperial imposition was to follow, enshrined by an almost wholly Western-conceived governance mentality. The Empress of India era dawned as part of Victorian high imperialism and as a grandiose claim worthy enough to direct the *Great Game* popularised by Rudyard Kipling and others in the early twentieth century. Displays of the formal apparatus of the state in India were at their most visible regarding Indian women and girls when attempting their social amelioration at law, such as the Sati Abolition Act (1829), the Widow Remarriage Act (1856) and the Age of Consent Act (1891).

Just how much state governance of India really changed after the Great Revolt of 1857 remains a matter of conjecture, although the shock to the British of the Great Revolt was profound. Whatever the case, this book's characterisation of changing 'state' and 'official' mentalities is not intended to reflect these wider changes in a simplistic way. Even at the multiple levels of state governance in India (viceroy, provincial governments, commissioners, municipalities, residents in a princely states), there were important variations in the exchange of information. For example, Bombay, unlike the rest of the raj, communicated directly to the India Office in London rather than through the Viceroy's office in Calcutta. More critically, as Zoë Laidlaw's work shows, personal connections went well beyond the formal avenues of governance to influence what was identified by contemporaries as official policymaking: particularly the complicated networks of connection that eschewed hostile scrutiny at the metropole.[81]

Women teachers and the state

Throughout the period covered by this book, the role of the woman teacher in colonial India was part of a very active macro dynamic. Statecraft put her to work in the classroom, but subjected her to quixotic non-education agendas and dismissed her female students with similar capriciousness when broader power plays intervened. This was a story reactive to, but kept largely separate from, broader and developing political sensibilities of Indian communities towards the end of the nineteenth century. Conversely, these Indian communities mostly did not contest the pedagogic and knowledge constituencies of female education as they occurred in the colonial classroom, but saw their broader socio-cultural purpose, instead, in strongly antagonistic terms.

The very few women educators who were recruited by the state to provincial education services (separate to the ICS) were employed on pay rates that were about two-thirds those of their male counterparts. Even when the central Indian Education Service (IES) was established in 1910, only a tiny number of government-employed women teachers made it into its ranks. In 1913 there were just seventeen women IES officers, of whom twelve were inspectresses and five were superintendents of schools, with an average age of thirty compared to twenty-six for their male counterparts.[82] These women were more usually embraced through the missions and convents as part of the grant-in-aid provisions that paid half their salary. Many other colonial-sponsored women teachers struggled in remote locations and under very demanding conditions. They had to contend with antagonistic local school boards, or with demanding *vakils* (agents) in the princely states. Inspectresses travelled on camel *dâks* (carriages) to traverse inspectorate fields of responsibility that were sometimes the size of a small European country. In the main, their official brief was still directed by men, even by the time of the First World War, as it was in the West.

By 1900, Eurasian women and some Indian women were employed on racially calibrated pay rates, which were partly disguised by pinning these rates to the type of *alma mater* claimed by these candidates – school, college or university. It was, of course, virtually impossible in most cases for this *alma mater* to be in Europe. For example, even by 1917, a Eurasian woman teacher with an Indian college degree was paid Rs.158 per month; her female colleague who had graduated from a European university was paid almost double this at rate at Rs.300 per month; and their female Indian junior, who had access only to education at the local government or mission school in India, was paid just Rs.70 per month. In addition, the pay rates for new recruits from Europe who were women teachers were, by the First World War, only about 80 per cent of those on offer to them in England, despite the fact that they had to be prepared to endure the privations of the subcontinent. This remuneration was not adjusted either for escalating inflation that devalued the rupee, the currency in which they were paid.[83]

Recruitment of women to the central IES, set up in 1910, was far more rarefied and often for women of a higher social class. Patronage networks were used, rather than open advertisements, and these networks reached to Europe as well as to well-qualified Eurasian women already working in senior positions in elite schools in India. Recruitment patterns continued to reflect enduring state sensitivities about racial frailty, particularly where these concerned women, rather than the qualities of a teacher. For example, as late as 1907, an interviewing committee in England, when considering a candidate with an *ad eundumn* degree from Trinity College, Dublin concluded:

> A slight trace of Indian blood. In connection with this suspicion, together with her Indian upbringing, special enquiries were made as to a possible deficiency in energy and initiative but the result confirmed the impression she conveyed when she was interviewed, that she was lacking in neither of the necessary qualities mentioned.[84]

Such eugenic supposition remained operative at the metropole, as it did in India, well into the twentieth century.

Lack of state funding disabled most imaginative educational ventures for women and girls in India in the colonial era. However, other foundations were made. The Bethune school (Calcutta) and, later, the SNDT (Women's) University (Bombay) were important examples of a new educational configuration that embraced Indian women and girls, and which built powerful tertiary pathways for later generations of Indian women to follow in the late colonial and early independent eras. Women physicians, nurses and midwives, the only other forms of Western professionalism available to women in India (apart from very few in the law), also made some headway. This was particularly so under the auspices of the Lady Dufferin Medical fund in the 1890s.

This book does not presuppose that empire is the centre of the story. Instead, it identifies other points of interaction in the colonial period as multiple centres. I have also endeavoured to recover key features of the colonial past as they relate to female education, to reposition them using the new theoretical frameworks mentioned earlier, and to place this past in its broader setting of operative networks. The book's contribution, using a strong empirical base, is to build an understanding of how empire, through its networks of interaction, created increasingly constrained socio-cultural, race and class imperatives that reorganised and reshaped the colonial 'educated female'. I am particularly interested in showing how and why these imperatives changed over time within the otherwise limited remit of the raj. Western-predicated female learning in colonial India, as superficial as it often was, is a complex story to lay down in a linear and periodic manner. This complexity means there are overlapping features both within and between the chapters.

European women in India were also powerful influencers of racialised state policy, both through the club and through their husbands. In 1888 Flora Annie Steel and her co-author were happy to add a guarded qualification to the approach they recommended towards the Indian wet-nurse in the European household, and referred to at the beginning of this introduction. This qualification ran: 'within limits she should be allowed to see her friends, and she should not be treated as if she was merely an animated bottle'.[85] Yet despite this small humanitarian concession, at this time European women in India principally saw Indian women through a Western utilitarian perspective, in terms of their relationship to empire, and with little sensitivity to their Indian identity, race or culture.

⋅⋅◆⋅⋅

The book's content

The main content of this book is organised into nine chapters. Chapter one considers the nature of early European interaction with Indian females and how this intervention constructed early colonial stereotypes of Eastern femininity between 1820 and 1865. This chapter explores how fledgling Western education endeavours began to take hold, and how sporadic evangelical mission engagement established a low church Christian stereotype about the emotional deficits of Indian women, requiring remedy by the metropole. In competition with these stereotypes, advocates of orientalist-inspired experiments in Bombay, the NWP and in the Punjab were establishing a more profound connection with traditional Indian education for females. As part of these competing colonial agendas, which eventually saw a wholly Western-inspired model embraced by the raj, female education was viewed by the East India Company as having only a moderating Western social function. Here colonial projections of the 'moral' body of the educated Indian female – now detached from her own cultural space – were to mediate her less raj-amenable husband and brother. Colonial intervention also brought artificial codifications regarding language, as well as self-serving official crusades to rescue baby girls from female infanticide in the northern village.

Chapter two concerns a new turn in official attitudes regarding schooling for girls, which occurred between 1840 and 1867. This was partly overlapped with emerging tension between Bengal versus the NWP and Bombay regarding schooling for Indian girls that is discussed in chapter one. This new turn concerned Eurasian girls. The rearticulation by the Company of 'coloniser' and 'colonised' now engaged new networks, mostly independent of the missions. New social ideas about the need for the educated female in India began to focus instead on her racial phenotype. The emotional needs of one large European cohort in particular, the soldier, brought pragmatic responses by the Company to acquiesce in the sexual relations of soldiers with Indian females, and also some commitment to the education of the resulting Eurasian issue.[86] This new official racial agenda necessarily included girls as well as boys. Eurasian girls, in particular, often abandoned when their fathers were stationed elsewhere in India or retired back to England, were offered sanctuary in a new type of military asylum: the Lawrence Military Asylum. At these sites, their femininity was built around emerging forms of accomplishment education that were imported directly from Europe.

In the wake of the Great Revolt of 1857, chapter two also examines how British bureaucratic instrumentalism became more purposeful in reinforcing a threatened state power. With state-institutionalised education now the norm, its female participants, as a matter of routine, were organised by the raj to serve broader socialising agendas. This was a gradual process and it is traced in both chapters one and two. For those few participating Indian girls in mission schools by the 1840s, education was no longer contiguous with what they heard at the foot of the guru, or even in empire-created subaltern settings of learning in the NWP and Bombay. In 'school', if she could attend at all, colonial 'education' for the Indian girl became increasingly separate from her cultural and family background, and this separateness fragmented the basis of her learning. A new official female learning space was authorised instead. After 1860, stronger state surveillance garnered an emerging cultural role for female education that was both racialised in favour of Eurasians and predicated on European forms of middle-class schooling for girls.

Chapter three then looks at how official racialisation worked in favour of Eurasians in the form of the new schoolgirl prototype in the 1860s and 1870s. This new feminine prototype was made possible by a peculiar interlude in which the newly established relationship between statecraft and female education was taken over by a novel narrative concerning the teacher 'training' of women. This narrative now focused on accomplishments as the chief form of educational endeavour. It was supported by the growing number of European women travelling to India by the late 1860s. One European woman in particular, Mary Carpenter, generated the new narrative. Prompted by the powerful Carpenter lobby at the metropole, state intervention in India further perverted Indian educational evolution in the colonial sphere by putting teacher training (designed to produce women who were new guides of Western moral propriety) ahead of education for Indian schoolgirls. Carpenter's social theorist approach led her to emphasise the moral redemption of Indian females over their education as schoolgirls. Given the dominance of the Carpenter narrative at this time, this predication helped the state to obscure the serious lack of secondary schools for girls throughout the late 1860s and early 1870s. The state was still able to claim a moral superiority by promoting the 'training' of females as teachers, even though they had little formal school education first. Of more consequence was that, in the process, valuable orientalist-inspired educational initiatives in the NWP and in Bombay that included some Indian females were defunded to pay for the Carpenter scheme.

The new focus on the female teacher as a Western moral guide brought official anxieties about what turned out to be a frail model of colonial femininity. When a venereal disease scandal broke out in the normal (teacher training) school in Nagpur (central India) in 1872, the state responded by closing down most of its central normal schools throughout India by 1875. This was seen as necessary because, by this time, the official raison d'être of these institutions was too tightly defined by Western moral values, and not by more sustainable educational interchanges built up among Indian communities over several generations, as had been the case in the NWP and Bombay. The normal schools imposed in Carpenter's name were in danger of becoming sites for local political intrigue, where Indian intellectual elites could easily challenge British pretensions to be promoting a superior feminine morality. As a result, when the state abandoned the normal schools it had built in Carpenter's name, many of their former students were placed at risk, stranded between two cultures and without an educational future.

Chapter four considers the missions, to which the state turned after 1874 to carry forward its conception of the professional teacher within the safer confines of the Western-acculturated mission compound. By this time colonial teacher training was wholly Western constructed, and well supported by longstanding state rhetoric concerning female education. This rhetoric was an important plank in justifying a reinvigorated *Pax Britannica* now ruled over by an Empress of India. Female missionaries who were European began to emerge as identifiable individuals – activists pressing against the hostile authority of the bishops and their agents. State-directed mentalities that focused on the Eurasian teacher as a moral guide were preserved within mission compounds. However, outside these compounds, and away from the imperial gaze, female missionaries began to build new networks that were directed towards the conversion of Indian women and girls. As part of this work, the education site of the zenana became important and realigned the labours of these women missionaries. Outside the mission compound, their focus was Indian females, and not Eurasians, as they attempted to accommodate local Indian learning in new ways to facilitate conversion. The activism of these missionaries, eventually forced the raj to interact with these traditional Indian female domains.

The next two chapters examine how femininity, and limited forms of feminism, were built around emerging colonial-inspired female medical care initiatives in the later nineteenth and early twentieth centuries. These initiatives were built upon the female missionary footprint, established outside the mission compound for conversion purposes, which solidified in colonial India after 1872.

Chapter five examines how female medical care, most particularly females practising medicine, nursing and midwifery as emerging Western professions in India, began to break down race and class barriers concerning Indian women between 1865 and 1890. Engaging with new networks of medical professionalism emanating from Europe, but also procedural innovation regarding tropical sanitation and epidemiology developed on the subcontinent, missionary medical carers created a new terrain to connect with Indian women. Unlike the vagaries associated with assessing largely hidden pedagogy in colonial female classrooms, singular Western medical practices and professionalism gave missionary women an upper hand in having their agency recognised and funded by the state. This was because codification concerning disease, diagnosis and cure were readily externalised to British and global philanthropic agencies in a way that was powerful enough to redirect raj macro agendas concerning women. The filtering by Westerners regarding their perceptions of desirable character and disease treatment still organised the Indian female recipient. However, medical treatment by missionaries became robust enough, as an officially acknowledged female occupation, to even expose deficits at the metropole, where potential women physicians were still denied access to medical learning. On the subcontinent, more than elsewhere in the empire, female missionary carers framed the subsequent emergence of secular medical professionals. And these missionaries eventually dominated the new female doctor and nursing professions until the end of the colonial period.

Chapter six examines the colonial institutionalisation and categorisation of female medical training, and explores how missionary education feminised these learning outcomes between 1880 and 1927. This chapter looks at the funding bodies that were largely state driven, most notably the Lady Dufferin Fund. This fund set up hospitals and formalised other Indian sites for the medical treatment of Indian females. It also created institutions with new patriarchal barriers that female doctors who were feminists, in particular, found to be places of conflict in their struggle for equality in the profession. This chapter, like chapter five, takes an intimate look at colonial female interaction and at the treatment of India's most needy women and girls. In pursuing this interaction, these colonial women still maintained a largely unremitting Western feminine discipline. Enshrined in this discipline was a fierce belief in the sanitation procedures of the West, which offered remedies to an 'unclean' East. In this sense, feminist female physicians and nurses formalised earlier feminine missionary outreach by offering only Western types of medical treatment. They also kept their struggle against colonial men within the bounds of their colonial European communities, rather than attempting to instil a similar brand of feminism in their Indian female counterparts.

Chapter seven returns to the female colonial teacher in 1883. Unlike the medical care initiatives of female missionaries in the same period, class and race boundaries grew stronger as a different kind of femininity was projected by the state concerning the college and school classroom for women and girls. More European women teachers from Europe entered the subcontinent as a result of the opening of the Suez Canal in 1869. The earlier endeavour of female missionaries concerning medicine had inconveniently blurred raj race and class agendas, and a new official manoeuvre was decided upon regarding the teacher training of women to stem this racial and class shifting in policy application. Instead of the missions being left to oversee the production of female teachers as moral guides, the raj now looked to educational commerce to solve the problem. This new strategy centred on meeting an emerging middle-class parent demand in India for teacher training for their daughters. Private-venture schooling was appropriated and the law changed. A new education Code was introduced in 1883 that restricted nearly all secondary schooling for girls, and the funding for teacher training of women, to Eurasians and Europeans only. As a new generation of female professional teachers arrived from Europe with stronger networks to the West, accomplishment subjects were directly embedded in their teaching practice. These women also now had individual identity in their dealings with the raj, rather than having their praxis aggregated anonymously as a group, as had earlier been the case under Haileybury College reportage protocols.[87]

These new professional teachers, who were women, were now forced to negotiate a new feminine cultural terrain in order to satisfy market demand in India for British middle-class credentials in a way that was also sensitive to India's socio-cultural realities concerning females. New luminaries emerged within this new, self-aware, European teaching community of women. One such example was Elizabeth Brander in Madras. Using her training in Western pedagogical theory, particularly Froebel, she adapted it in effective cultural ways to teach Indian schoolgirls.

Chapter eight examines the work of the colonial teachers who were both European and Eurasian women, between 1870 and 1932. During this time this community drew apart from the raj in the face of the realities of an emerging India and hardening nationalist critiques. Within the restricted world of the woman teacher of Western feminine sensibility in colonial India, some of these teachers developed new agency when relating to the colonial state. Their activism led to some limited engagement as these teachers, now as learners, needed to negotiate with an emerging threshold consciousness of Indian women, in terms of a new Indian cultural awareness that directly challenged the West. Although it was usually elite Indian men driving the Nationalist movement after the First World War, who mostly articulated this emerging Indian female consciousness.

These colonial women teachers were still unrelentingly Western and usually sympathetic enough with the broader colonial project to happily participate in government inquiries into education: most particularly William Hunter's 1882 Hunter Education Commission, Austen Chamberlain's 1913 inquiry into the education of Indian females and Michael Sadler's Calcutta University Commission of 1917. Furthermore, at these commissions, the participation of these women teachers gave a false sense that their work represented a coherent Western professional relevance to the Indian schoolgirl without any race or class prejudice. The testimonials of these women teachers, by 1913, also introduced an element of Western feminism into the narrative contained within government reports, which allowed the colonial state to falsely imply a new Western modernity in its policy-making. However, chapter eight reveals that these women, scarcely a professional academy at all, were also no longer organised by state rhetoric and some of them quietly sublimated government imperatives as they responded to new, *ex officio*, education professional ideas emanating from Europe and the USA.

Two separate universes frame chapter eight, with the colonial state no longer being a central feature. Colonial men like Sir Phillip Hartog still clung to a myth of a coherent colonial policy when it came to educating Indian girls in the late 1920s. However, at a different level, there was M. K. Gandhi, a leader of the nationalist movement, who deftly stepped around the well-worn rhetoric site, and who refused to engage in any deeper discussion about British displays of female education policy because of its deep colonial origins. At a second and separate level were the colonial women teachers themselves. In the 1920s and 1930s, some of these teachers, at last, began making overtures to the largely neglected population of Indian girls by supporting un-gendered academic scholarship, away from accomplishments, ready for Indian female citizenship as they saw it. However, this was still largely separate from Indian intellectualism that drove emerging nationalist social service agendas.

Finally, chapter nine examines a thin but key aspect of Westerness in India in the high imperial age through to an era of retreating colonial power. This period spans 1890 to 1930. Networks of knowledge transfer remained just as important in this period, but these networks now strongly defined female education efforts outside the state sphere, particularly those run by strategically positioned Roman Catholic religious orders. The example of Loreto in Calcutta is examined to understand how a Western educational enterprise could flourish and eventually transcend Partition in 1947. The Indo-Irish connection, mostly inimical to the raj, offered new structure to Loreto's female education imperatives. Its women religious were also bound up in different patriarchal and matriarchal networks that emanated from the Roman Catholic Church itself. However, remarkably, the Loreto Christian ethic survived the retreat of the British as it embraced outreach programmes for impoverished Indians and attempted not to objectify Indian girls as Western learners, nor cut them off entirely from Indian ways of learning and teaching. Western ways of knowing remained the only ones available to Loreto's women teachers, but their capacity to embrace Indian poverty as committed and work-weary carers, rather than as teachers, repositioned the order as something more than a mere remnant of empire by the late 1920s.

———◆———

Through this book I offer a theoretical interpretation and a broad framework to understand the actions of many colonial women and their agents. The book also illustrates the nature of official raj engagement with them. The interactional features of the story change over the long time span under study. New and evolving networks from within and without the empire drove this change, and as networks became outdated, they quickly withered away. However, when operative, these networks were powerful enough to transfer knowledge and praxis and to shape raj mentalities. The women who engaged with these mentalities could also shape the networks as a result of their own activism. Making these processes explicit and illustrating their ramifications is an important goal of this book, particularly when examining women working *in* British India. In the raj, these women were more dynamic in their activism, and in their professional contributions, than their sisters who merely promoted philanthropy at the metropole. The book's illustrative approach gives voice to the rich experiences of many of these women, and to groups of women living in colonial India through the strong documentary record that remains: albeit in the dispersed depositories still available to scholars of gender in India and Pakistan, and at the old metropole, and in depositories located in other former colonies of empire.

Notes

1 R. Crane and A. Johnston (eds) of the reprint of F. A. Steel and G. Gardiner, *The Complete Indian Housekeeper and Cook* [first published 1888] (Oxford: Oxford University Press, 2010).

2 R. Crane and A. Johnston (eds), of the reprint of F. A. Steel and G. Gardiner, *The Complete Indian Housekeeper and Cook* ..., p. 162.

3 R. Crane and A. Johnston (eds), 'Preface' for the reprint of F. A. Steel and G. Gardiner, *The Complete Indian Housekeeper and Cook* ..., p. xiii.

4 The 'Orientalist' period in India is usually assigned to the first three decades of the nineteenth century up to the publication of T. B. Macaulay's *Minute of 1835* that mandated English as the medium of instruction in government-funded educational institutions. Orientalist scholars differed in their approach, but generally they were interested in the exchange of ideas and knowledge as a mostly even enterprise between East and West, where neither side could claim superiority. They believed local languages in India were worthy as the medium of instruction in schools with a vocabulary adequate to convey complex Eastern and Western thought and capable of the 'engraftment' of Western scientific knowledge. L. Zastoupil and M. Moir, *The Great Education Debate* (Richmond, UK: Curzon, 1999), pp. 1–25.

5 S. Lambert-Hurley 'Subtle Subversions and Presumptuous Interventions: Reforming Women's Health in Bhopal State in the Early Twentieth Century' and N. V. Prasad 'The Litigious Widow: Inheritance Disputes in Colonial North India, 1875–1911' chs 5 and 7 in A. Ghosh, *Behind the Veil: Resistance, Women and the Everyday in Colonial South Asia* (London: Palgrave Macmillan, 2008).

6 J. Atwal, 'Revisiting Premchand: Shivrani Devi on Companionship, Reformism and Nation', *Economic and Political Weekly*, 42:18 (May, 2007), 1631–7.

7 T. Allender, 'Learning Abroad: The Colonial Educational Experiment in India, 1813–1919', *Paedagogica Historica*, 45:6 (2009), 707–22.

8 K. Jayawardena, *The White Woman's Other Burden: Western Women and South Asia During the British Period* (New York: Routledge, 1995), pp. 8–11.

9 P. Anagol, *The Emergence of Feminism in India, 1850–1920* (Aldershot, UK: Ashgate, 2005), pp. 30–4.

10 G. Forbes, *Women in Colonial India* (New Delhi: Chronicle Books, 2008), p. 11.
11 For example, see V. B. Talwar, 'Feminist Consciousness in Women's Journals in Hindi, 1910–1920' in K. Sangari and S. Vaid, *Recasting Women* (New Jersey: Rutgers University Press, 1990).
12 S. Andermahr, T. Lovell, and C. Wolkowitz, *A Concise Glossary of Feminist Theory* (London, Arnold, 1997), p. 75; T. Moi, 'Sexual/Textual Politics: Feminist Literary Theory' in C. Belsey and J. Moore (eds), *The Feminist Reader: Essays in Gender and the Politics of Literary Criticism* (London: Macmillan, 1989).
13 The Arya Samaj was founded by Swami Dayananda Saraswati (1824–83) who was a scholar of Hindu ethics and of Sanscrit. This Hindu reform movement was particularly interested in establishing schools for boys and girls based on Saraswati's vision of reforming the Hindu polity and returning it to the philosophical and ethical purity of ancient Vedic teaching. Vedanta or 'the conclusion of the Vedas' was promoted by Swami Vivekananda (1863–1902) who reinterpreted ancient Hindu texts to urge a rejection of the evils of society and to actively meet the needs of contemporary Indian life as defined by the wisdom of ancient Hindu texts. See C. H. Heimsath, *Indian Nationalism and Hindu Social Reform* (Princeton, NJ: Princeton University Press, 1964), pp. 25–9.
14 See, for example, K. Dutta and A. Robinson, *Rabindranath Tagore: The Myriad-Minded Man* (New York: St Martin's Press, 1996); B. Ray, *Early Feminists of Colonial India: Sarala Devi Chaudhurani and Rokeya Sakhawat Hossain* (New Delhi: Oxford University Press, 2002).
15 A. M. Nash (Professor, Presidency College), *Progress of Education in India 1887–88 to 1891–92: Second Quinquennial Review* (Calcutta: Government Printing, 1893), p. 277 (OIOC). Even in 1919 the British estimated only 0.9 per cent of Hindu girls and 1.1 per cent of Muslim girls were receiving some form of education. J. A. Richey, *Progress of Education in India, 1917–22* (Calcutta: Government Printing, 1923), p. 126; G. Srivastava, *Women's Higher Education in the Nineteenth Century* (New Delhi: Concept, 2000), p. 13.
16 V. Ware, *Beyond the Pale: White Women, Racism and History* (London: Verso, 1992), p. 119.
17 A. McClintock, *Imperial Leather: Race, Gender and Sexuality in the Colonial Contest* (New York: Routledge, 1995), p. 5.
18 C. Jones, *Engendering Whiteness: White Women and Colonialism in Barbadoes and North Carolina, 1627–1865* (Manchester: Manchester University Press, 2007).
19 S. Amin and G. Bhadra, 'Ranajit Guha: A Biographical Sketch' in D. Arnold and D. Hardiman (eds), *Subaltern Studies VIII* (Delhi: Oxford University Press, 1994); P. Chatterjee, 'A Brief History of Subaltern Studies' in P. Chatterjee (ed.), *Empire and Nation, Selected Essays* (New York: Columbia University Press, 2010).
20 R. O'Hanlon, *At the Edges of Empire: Essays in the Social and Intellectual History of India* (Ranikhet: Permanent Black, 2014), p. 32.
21 C. A. Bayly, *Empire and Information: Intelligence Gathering and Social Communication in India, 1780–1870* (Cambridge: Cambridge University Press, 1996), esp. chs 2–4.
22 S. Sarkar, *Writing Social History* (Delhi: Oxford University Press, 1997), p. 8.
23 J. Masselos, 'The Dis/appearance of Subalterns: A Reading of a Decade of Subaltern Studies' in D. Ludden, *Reading Subaltern Studies: Critical History, Contested Meaning and the Globalization of South Asia* (London: Anthem, 2002), p. 188.
24 G. C. Spivak, 'Can the Subaltern Speak?' in C. Nelson and L. Grossberg (eds), *Marxism and the Interpretation of Culture* (Chicago: University of Illinois Press, 1988).
25 P. Anagol, *The Emergence of Feminism in India* ..., passim.
26 R. C. Coloma, 'White Gazes, Brown Breasts: Imperial Feminism and Disciplining Desires and Bodies in Colonial Encounters', *Paedagogica Historica*, 48:2 (2012), 243–61.
27 S. Nijhawan, *Women and Girls in the Hindi Public Sphere: Periodical Literature in Colonial North India* (New Delhi: Oxford University Press, 2012), pp. 12–15.
28 R. O'Hanlon, *At the Edges of Empire* ..., p. 78.

29 A. Besant, 'Annie Besant on the Type of Education for Indian Girls, 1904' in
    S. Bhattacharya, J. Bara *et al.*, *Development of Women's Education in India, a collec-
    tion of documents, 1850–1920* (New Delhi: Kanishka, 2001), p. 316.
30 A. Burton, *Burdens of History: British Feminists, Indian Women and Imperial
    Culture, 1865–1915* (Chapel Hill, North Carolina, 1994), pp. 8, 82–3.
31 C. Midgley, 'Anti-slavery and the Roots of "Imperial Feminism"' in C. Midgley
    (ed.), *Gender and Imperialism* (Manchester: Manchester University Press, 1998),
    pp. 161–6.
32 M. Stroebel, *European Women and the Second British Empire* (Bloomington, Indiana
    University Press, 1991), pp. ix–xi, 46; N. Chauduri and M. Stroebel, 'Western Women
    and Imperialism', *Women's Studies International Forum*, xiii:4 (1990), 290–1;
    B. Ramusack, 'Cultural Missionaries, Maternal Imperialists, Feminist Allies: British
    Women Activists in India, 1865–1945', *Women's Studies International Forum*, xiii:4
    (1990), 309–20.
33 J. Goodman and J. Martin, *Women and Education, 1800–1980* (Basingstoke,
    UK: Palgrave Macmillan, 2004).
34 R. Watts, Mary Carpenter and India: Enlightened Liberalism or Condescending
    Imperialism?' *Pedagogica Historica*, Supplementary Series 7 (February, 2001), 181–97.
35 A. Burton, *Burdens of History ...*, p. 11.
36 A. McClintock, *Imperial Leather ...*, p. 13.
37 R. Connell, *Gender in World Perspective* (Cambridge: Polity, 2009).
38 P. Chatterjee, *The Nation and its Fragments* (Princeton, NJ: Princeton University
    Press, 1993), pp. 116–34.
39 P. Chatterjee, 'The Nationalist Resolution of the Women's Question' in K. Sangari
    and S. Vaid, *Recasting Women* (New Brunswick, NJ: Rutgers University Press, 1990),
    p. 249.
40 C. Hall, *At Home with the Empire* (Cambridge: Cambridge University Press, 2006).
41 A. Fazli and Y. Kavyani, 'Evaluating the Performance of the Agricultural Bank in
    Allocating Rural Credits', *International Journal of Academic Research*, 2:6:1
    (November, 2010), 148.
42 A. Curthoys and M. Lake, *Connected Worlds: History in Transnational Perspective*
    (Canberra: ANU E, 2005).
43 K. Darian-Smith, P. Grimshaw and S. Macintyre, *Britishness Abroad: Transnational
    Movements and Imperial Cultures* (Melbourne: Melbourne University Press, 2007).
44 A. Lester, 'Imperial Circuits and Networks: Geographies of the British Empire',
    History Compass, 4:1 (2006), 124–41.
45 T. Ballantyne, *Orientalism and Race: Aryanism in the British Empire* (Basingstoke,
    UK: Palgrave, 2002).
46 C. A. Bayly, *Recovering Liberties: Indian Thought in the Age of Liberalism and
    Empire* (Cambridge: Cambridge University Press, 2012), pp. 252–6.
47 J. Schriewer and C. Martinez, 'Constructions of Internationality in Education' in
    G. Steiner-Khamsi (ed.), *The Global Politics of Educational Borrowing and Lending*
    (New York: Teachers' College Press, 2004).
48 C. de Bellaigue, *Educating Women* (Oxford: Oxford University Press, 2007).
49 T. Pietsch, *Empire of Scholars: Universities, Networks and the British Academic
    World, 1850–1939* (Manchester: Manchester University Press, 2013).
50 D. Phillips and K. Ochs, 'Processes of Policy Borrowing in Education; Some
    Explanatory and Analytical Devices', *Comparative Education*, 39:4 (November,
    2003), 451–61.
51 N. Hafkin and E. Bay, *Women in Africa* (Stanford, CA: Stanford University Press,
    1976), p. 7.
52 J. Cotè, '"The Sins of their Fathers": Culturally at Risk Children and the Colonial
    State in Asia', *Paedagogica Historica*, 45: 1–2 (2009), 137.
53 D. E. Barwick, *Rebellion at Coranderrk* (Canberra: Aboriginal History Inc., 1998).
54 There is an extensive literature on Eurasians and Anglo-Indians in Colonial India.
    See, for example, C. J. Hawes, *Poor Relations: The Making of a Eurasian Community
    in British India, 1773–1833* (Richmond, UK: Curzon, 1996); K. Ballhatchet, *Race,*

Sex and Class under the Raj: Imperial Attitudes and Policies and their Critics, 1793–1905 (London: Weidenfeld and Nicolson, 1980).

55 The extent to which the British were reliant on a perceived moral conduct, including the male domain in the army, to authorise their claims to racial superiority, see J. Sramek, *Gender, Morality and Race in Company India, 1765–1858* (New York: Palgrave Macmillan, 2011).

56 W. Hornell, May 20, 1915 Bengal Education Proceedings (OIOC) P/9640/60. The complex overlays of direct papal and episcopal authority structures in India changed as new European ethnicities intervened. This was particularly so as Rome attempted to accommodate declining Portuguese interest in the subcontinent and French missions declined in the south after the French and Napoleonic revolutionary wars. For a discussion of this complexity including after the rise of the British East India Company see K. Ballhatchet, *Caste, Class and Catholicism in India, 1789–1914* (Richmond, UK: Curzon, 1998), pp. 1–22.

57 W. Hornell, May 20, 1915 Bengal Education Proceedings (OIOC) P/9640/60.

58 C. Allen, *Plain Tales From The Raj* (Newton Abbot, UK: Readers Union, 1976), p. 104.

59 S. Morgan, *Bombay Anna: The Real Story and Remarkable Adventures of the King and I Governess* (Los Angeles, CA: Berkeley University Press, 2008).

60 N. I. Marshall, *The Anglo-Indian Absconder Soldier Daddy* (New Delhi: Marshall and Myers, 2011).

61 M. Theobald, *Knowing Women: Origins of Women's Education in Nineteenth-Century Australia* (Cambridge: Cambridge University Press, 1996), p. 15.

62 J. Mc Dermid, *The Schooling for Girls in Britain and Ireland, 1800–1900* (London: Routledge, 2012), pp. 69–71.

63 A. N. Wilson, *Victorian A Life* (London: Atlantic Books, 2014), p. 484 and D. Faye, *Jane Austen* (London: British Library, c. 2003).

64 E. Jordan, 'Making Good Wives and Mothers?', *History of Education Quarterly*, 31:4, (1991), 443–4.

65 C. Dyhouse, 'Social Darwinism Ideas and the Development of Women's Education', *History of Education*, 5:1 (1976), 41–58.

66 M. Theobald, *Knowing Women* ..., p. 16.

67 M. Theobald, *Knowing Women* ..., pp. 21–2.

68 See for example [DPI], incl. in Government of Central Provinces to Government of India, January 5, 1873 (OIOC), P/520.

69 M. Theobald, *Knowing Women* ..., p. 27.

70 S. Tomaselli, 'The Enlightenment debate on women' *History Workshop Journal*, 20 (1985), pp. 101–24 cited in M. Theobald, *Knowing Women* ..., p. 23.

71 P. Chatterjee, *The Nation and its Fragments* ... (Delhi: Oxford University Press, 1995), p. 122.

72 M. Borthwick, *The Changing Role of Women in Bengal* (Princeton, NJ: Princeton University Press, 1984), pp. 119–23.

73 S. Seth, *Subject Lessons: The Western Education of Colonial India* (Durham, NC: Duke, 2007), p. 140.

74 C. Gupta, 'Portrayal of Women in Prechand's Stories: A Critique', *Social Scientist*, 19, 5–6 (1991), 88, 101, 108–9.

75 S. Seth, *Subject Lessons* ..., pp. 142–4.

76 P. Chatterjee, *The Nation and its Fragments* ..., p. 6.

77 W. J. Mommsen, *The Political and Social Theory of Max Weber* (Cambridge: Polity, 1989), pp. 109–20.

78 J. Burbank and F. Cooper, *Empires in World History: Power and the Politics of Difference* (Princeton, NJ: Princeton University Press, 2010), pp. 3–4, 122 cited in T. Pietsch, *Empires of Scholars* ..., p. xii.

79 J. Sramek, *Gender, Morality and Race in Company India, 1765–1858* ..., p. 2.

80 *Proclamation by the Queen in Council to the Princes and People of India, November 1, 1858* (Allahabad: Government Printing, 1858) (OIOC).

81 Z. Laidlaw, *Colonial Connections 1815–45: Patronage, the Information Revolution and Colonial Government* (Manchester: Manchester University Press, 2007).

82 C. Whitehead, *Colonial Educators* (London: IB Tauris, 2003), p. 58.
83 A. Mercer, *Fifth Quinquennial Education Report 1912–17*, p. 37 (OIOC) V/24/4436.
84 Interview report concerning Ethel West quoted in C. Whitehead, *Colonial Administrators* ..., p. 59. As with many women of her generation West's *ad eundumn* ('courtesy') degree was taken out at Dublin University because she was unable, as a female, to have her actual degree conferred at Cambridge.
85 R. Crane and A. Johnston (eds), of the reprint of F. A. Steel and G. Gardiner, *The Complete Indian Housekeeper and Cook* ..., p. 162.
86 For a detailed discussion of the early Company attitudes towards Eurasians see A. D'Souza, *Anglo-Indian Education: A Study of its Origins and Growth in Bengal up to 1960* (New Delhi: Oxford University Press, 1976), pp. 1–32.
87 Opened in 1806, Haileybury College was a training college for the East India Company's civil servants where standardised reporting procedures, among other functions of civil governance, were taught. These standardised procedures contributed to agreed realities built by Indian civil servants that created stereotyped and overly rigid British categorisations concerning India. The college closed for this purpose in 1858 after the British government took over responsibility for the administration of India. A fascinating memoir compiled by former students of Haileybury College of the period, and others with experience of the College, including English social theorist, Harriet Martineau, was compiled at the end of the nineteenth century. F. C. Danvers *et. al.*, *Memorials of Old Haileybury College* (London: Constable & Co., 1894).

CHAPTER ONE

Finding feminine scholars, 1820–65

Pre-British India possessed vibrant, diverse and sometimes contested and exclusive female learning spaces for women that had evolved in culturally sympathetic ways over many centuries. In the Vedic age, but before 1,000 BCE, both girls and boys underwent *upanayana* (religious initiation), which entitled them to study Vedic texts. For elites in pre-Mughal times, in the early medieval period, ancient Hindu court poetry, as a projection of the soul, was seen as neither a male nor a female preserve and widowed queens actively served as regents for under-aged eldest sons.[1] Much later, in the mid-seventeenth century, Mughal ruler Jahangir fêted his most favoured wife, Nur Jahan, for the active role she took in the public affairs of his vast empire.[2] While emperor Aurangzeb's daughter, Zinat al-Nisa, was celebrated and recognised for her *naskh* calligraphy of the sacred words of the Koran.[3] Furthermore, female members of socially ambitious families in the north imitated the Mughal court by maintaining a *rishtahdar* (connection) of widows and spinsters, whose property rights were negotiated within this strictly private domain. Although, like Europe, aristocratic femininity and virtue was still seen as compromised by too much education.[4]

Away from these elites, and considering the broader population 3,000 years ago, pre-Aryan tribal custom permitted matrilineal authority. This was where women as priestesses and clan heads were custodians of religiously based epistemologies. However, in the middle of the first millennium BCE, the solidification of class and caste under patriarchal Brahmin authority gradually eroded this status and precluded the development of a women's movement in the following centuries.[5] Just how robust early female learning was in this very early period is unclear. Recent scholarship has shown that, even in the Vedic period (1500–500 BCE), women were not initiated into Vedic study, despite taking part in Vedic rituals alongside their husbands, and despite being the composers of hymns of the *Rgveda* (a sacred collection of Vedic Sanscrit hymns). Sanscrit etymology of words such as *upādhyāya* (female teacher) suggests that women directed at least some formal education settings. Many also received a limited co-education, along with their brothers, from their father or a close relative within the household.[6]

Concerning traditional Muslim women in the Middle Ages, there were female *muktabs* (Islamic schools) under the Delhi sultanate which taught girls a curriculum that incorporated military shield defence, wrestling, dancing, music and craft making.[7] In the nineteenth century Gail Minault recounts the actions of the upper-class mother of education reformer, Sayyid Ahmad Khan. She taught him to read the Koran, the Gulistan and some elementary Persian books that, in later years, he considered as forming the great moral force of his life.[8] Of course, a more general point can be made that the education of women and girls, mediating what Pierre Bourdieu might identify as social, cultural and symbolic capital, remained an ongoing aspect of Indian home life regardless of public patriarchal social roles in the village or the town.[9] Perhaps in part recognition of this, William Adam, writing of Indian village education in Bengal in 1836, concluded that *zamindars* (land-lords), when pursuing wealth and property through a good marriage for their daughters, educated them in writing and accounts so that they might withstand the potential predations of in-laws in the event of an early widowhood.[10]

Much of this rich and subtle heritage became obscured by the over-lay of European (particularly British) perceptions and reconstructions of Indian history. The Western educational orthodoxy of 'progress' and the 'schooling' of females eschewed representations by local Indian commentators, playwrights and artists, such as Hindu *pandit* (teacher) Gaurmohun Vidyalankar's 1822 Bengali pamphlet, *Stri Siksha Vidhayak*, on local female education. The range of perspectives on the social role of women previously conveyed by Indian artists had been an unusually diverse one, often communally aligned, and recognising women's unique roles as custodians of some Eastern forms of knowledge traditionally assigned to their gender.

By contrast, the East India Company's construction of Indian indig-enous heritage in the early nineteenth century hid much of this com-plexity by assuming a single narrative and by equating Indian history with developments in the West. For example, Western scholars used translations of Persian and Arabic literature, and the research of early British linguist academics (such as H. T. Colebrooke, William Carey and H. H. Wilson), to create a single fragmentary story that told of some well-educated women playing key roles in pre-British India. At a different level, while Sanscrit plays revealed that women of rank were traditionally taught to read and write, the British stereotyped their reputed drawing and music skills as 'accomplishments', thus normal-ising what the British saw as the Eastern exotic.[11] Using yet another provenance, formal government reportage of the Rajputs of central India depicted women directly participating in their government and gave accounts of occasions when the Delhi sultanate deferred to an elite cohort of highly educated women decision makers.[12] Somewhat ironically, this latter scenario overstated the case, and saw such gov-ernance in Westminster-like terms of administration, rather than as the fulfilment of a deeper social role for some Indian women. Indrani Chatterjee offers a more critical perspective on the colonial interven-tion and its consequences for Indian female identity. She sees elem-ents of the intervention as 'hypermodern' misogyny that impoverished women and disavowed their respected pre-colonial place in earlier monastic-based Indian societies, and a colonial state that also mislaid responsibility for this misogyny.[13]

The Indian household

The refuge of the traditional Indian household remained a powerful yet private domain throughout the British period. It encompassed finely networked and historicised relational spaces that were also highly sensitive to region. In Brahmin household communities in Maharashtra, for instance, the social universe was one where hierarchy was determined by gender and age: a man owed loyalty to other men in an extended family, while a woman owed loyalty to her husband as 'husband worship'. Losing caste by remarriage to a widow was a sin. Losing one's religion by conversion to Christianity meant the loss of household servants, who were otherwise threatened with excommu-nication by outside high-caste communities and who, when they did leave the converted household, were required to undergo purification ceremonies.[14]

In the Punjab (north India), in the mid-nineteenth century, the tal-ented yet abrasive Gottlieb Leitner (Principal of Government College, Lahore) worried about the potential destabilising effects of teaching his students, Indian males, the elite court language of Urdu. His con-cern was that, on return to their homes, they might teach their recep-tive wives, sisters and daughters a language that was traditionally the preserve of elite Indian men.[15] The concern here was what effect this teaching would have on the social fabric of local communities if this arcane language was made available to women. While, as far as Western knowledge was concerned, it was similarly unclear to the British as to how much intellectual transference occurred through networks of Indian females, carried first to them by the males that were educated in the government schools and colleges.

One aspect of these female household networks, apparent to the British, was that they were regionally sensitive. For example, the wild tribal regions of Ranjit Singh's Punjab seemed unlikely to provide strong cultural foundations for home learning that might assimilate Western knowledge.[16] There was more receptiveness in the Parsi communities of Maharashtra, the *bania* (trading) caste of bankers and commercial entrepreneurs in Gujarat (west India), and in the Tamil communities in the south.[17] However, the capacity of the British to infiltrate traditional intellectual communities in deliberate educational ways that embraced women, and in narrow colonial terms, was limited. Even when such infiltration did happen, Radhakant Deb argued, as early as 1851, that it was actually a force for disengagement, dislodging Indians from their traditional learning spaces, rather than offering a credible alternative Western forum of learning that could be an adjunct to these earlier learning modalities.[18]

The European household

In early British India, the Indian female was not yet defined through the East India Company's institutional schooling settings. Instead, the Western understanding of the Indian female body was negotiated in socio-cultural terms, mostly at the hands of a separated and expatriate European patriarchy employed by the East India Company and freshly arrived in India.

Georgian England in the eighteenth century was the world of *demi-mondaines* (such as Fanny Murray and Constantia Phillips), of Henry Fielding's *Tom Jones* and the poet Byron. It was a context that gave licence to sexual experimentation, eroticism and extramarital relationships for the upper classes, until the Victorian era imposed a new moral tableau. In the parallel universe of early British India, Georgian social freedoms were additionally differentiated by the dynamic of race and the allurement of a culturally different 'East'. In the mid-seventeenth century at Fort St George, Madras, the East India Company openly encouraged the marriage of European men to Indian women, partly to dilute the influence of Catholic Portuguese Eurasians, with Company payment forthcoming for any children from these marriages upon their Protestant baptism.[19] Company officials often lived in long-term concubinage with one or several Indian mistresses, without Western moral contest. However, for Indian women, formal or informal connection with Europeans was a powerful cultural signifier that separated them permanently from the caste or purdah restrictions of their traditional communities. Although, concubinage or marriage also carried the risk of destitution should their partner succumb, as often happened, to disease, war or a posting elsewhere in a rapidly expanding raj.

In this context, India offered new licence to men such as William Hickey, Attorney at Law, ruined at home for embezzling his father's fortune, yet able to give new expression to himself through the theatre and the sensuality of eighteenth-century European Calcutta.

> At the time I arrived in Bengal [1777] everybody dressed splendidly, being covered in lace, spangles and foil. I, who always had a tendency to be a beau, gave in to the fashion with much goodwill, no person appearing in richer suits of velvet and lace than myself.[20]

In a cultural sense, the India of the East India Company was a curious crossover between East and West. In Madras the avuncular Hickey found himself courted by competing officer-class Englishmen, largely through Western dining-room etiquette, but with the absence of European women. He endured 'tasteless' melons after dinner, offered because they were from England and 'entertainments' involving enforced walks through home gardens, their English outdoor furniture the victim of 'looties' and their 'grassless and wild' gardens comparing unfavourably, in Hickey's estimation, to even the most barren part of Hounslow Heath.[21]

The possibilities for Indian female companionship in the large villas with Georgian porticos proved much more attractive. In England, Hickey, like many of his class, had enjoyed the sexual gratification of tours to bawdy coffee houses and bordellos run by the likes of 'Mother Cocksedge' in Bow Street, Covent Garden.[22] Having freed himself from much Church influence at the metropole, and away from the moral scrutiny of white women and men of his class in England, long-term relationships with Indian women in the eighteenth century on the subcontinent were hardly a matter of contest, as demonstrated, by Hickey at least, in his unusually frank memoirs. Writing of his long-term Bengal *bibi* (respectable lady of the house), Jemdanee, who was a frequent hostess to his Calcutta male friends, and who bore him a son in 1796, he lamented upon her early death, 'As gentle and affectionately attached a girl as ever man was blessed with'.[23]

Hickey was not alone in forming genuine relationships with Indian women. At least 30 per cent of the European wills drawn up in Bengal in the 1780s contained substantial bequests to Indian female companions.[24] Possibly as many as 90 per cent of all lower-class British in India had formal marriages with Indians in the eighteenth century, with the East India Company actively encouraging a new generation of Westernised, mixed-race Company servants and soldiers by offering a Rs.5 christening present for any offspring.[25] Between 1767 and 1782, 54 per cent of baptisms at St John's Church in Calcutta were classified as Eurasian. These approaches, which encouraged racial miscegenation, were to continue until 1791, when the Company suddenly reversed its approach.[26] Alliances with Indian women permitted European men new emotional and sexual freedoms. However, these alliances also assigned the Indian female to a position of impermanence and relegation, contributors only to a private cultural domain of an Eastern exotic life for Western men.

There was another smaller group of women in India who were the direct result of several colonial interludes across two generations conducted by Portuguese, French and British men. These offspring were Eurasians. They were more powerful organising agents than their Indian sisters, largely because they were fewer in number – a fact made more apparent by the prohibition generally placed on European women travelling to the subcontinent in the eighteenth and early nineteenth century. Eurasian women were not obliged to accept extramarital relations, particularly if they were baptised and could speak English. They could therefore be selective of prospective marriage partners among the many British soldiers who flooded in to secure British India.[27] The solemnising of Eurasian marriage also admitted other Western-driven stratification. Lowly ensigns or second lieutenants often had to settle for poorer Portuguese Eurasians. These women were part of the remnant Portuguese Catholic Eurasian populations, which remained after Portugal's dowry gift of Bombay to Charles II of England in 1661 (upon his marriage to Catherine of Braganza) and Clive's seizure of Bengal almost a century later at the battle of Plassey in 1757. By the latter eighteenth century, the Company – whose soldiers required its permission to marry – preferred those of rank to marry Protestant Eurasian women who were mostly descended from earlier-serving English soldiers in India. Like their Indian sisters, these Eurasian women often provided genuinely intimate female companionship although, unlike them, they were almost wholly dependent on the soldier pool for husbands.[28]

Importing new evangelical mission-inspired femininity

In the 1820s, British conceptions of the Indian female moved from the household to the mission school. In this frame, it is tempting to see the beginnings of mission schooling for girls in the second decade of the nineteenth century as part of a broader knowledge and praxis transfer directly imported from Europe to an alleged *tabula rasa* in the Orient. However, new mission constructions of Indian 'deficits' that engaged some of the earlier Western gender narratives in India and inverted others, created a new sphere for action that appropriated Indian women in more abrasive and unremitting terms.

Cultural antipathy partly explains why the Company, still struggling to establish its own power base, resisted admitting the missions to its governance domain until it was forced to do so in 1813, when the Company Charter came up for renegotiation at Westminster. Influential directors of the Company, Major John Scott Waring and Thomas Twining, feared new evangelical missionary activity would create undue interference in Indian culture that might threaten the long-term stability of British India.[29] More particularly, rasping evangelism was seen as likely to disrupt the emotional settlement already in place between European males and some Indian and Eurasian females. By the early nineteenth century, new international and parallel empire networks were being built, based on an evangelical faith in providence and the reliability of divine promises that encouraged Christian self-sufficiency in overseas domains. Andrew Porter's work shows that these networks involved a new brand of missionary: one who saw secular and indigenous governance in these domains as limiting their actions and who therefore strongly resisted reliance on, or subservience to, such governance.[30] Insensitive evangelism also posed broader threats to the Company's commercial exploitation of the subcontinent. There were still powerful nawabs, tribals and Indian princes to consider who regulated, at key trading sites, the degree of European cultural intervention. Even at Fort St George, Madras the British and other Christian Europeans were required to paint their buildings white under a treaty with the local Nayak rulers.[31]

There were, of course, missions in India well before the nineteenth century. The mission claiming the earliest British Protestant presence in India was the Vepery Mission in Madras city, created in opposition to Roman Catholic missions in the south at Fort St George and the Portuguese settlement, San Thome (also in Madras). In 1727 the English Society for Promoting Christian Knowledge took over from an earlier Danish Protestant mission. The new English mission extended the sectarian conflict of Europe in its conversion discourse. While not gendered, this discourse aimed to carry out new Protestant conversion in a society corrupted, it claimed, by 'public whoredom with papist harlots' and amid a mass of 'unmusical' Tamil children.[32]

In the first decade of the nineteenth century, British missionary accounts of the cultural deficits of Indians began to emerge, particularly regarding Indian women. These were mostly concerned with stripping away Indian emotional legitimacy. For example, there were accounts sympathetic to the missions, especially in Bengal, of some Indian babies, which these accounts suggested Indian parents believed were possessed by demons, and were left by their mothers in baskets hanging from trees for ants and birds of prey to devour. There were stories of *Hûree* (local Hindu) rituals in Serampore involving the burying alive of widows with sweatmeats and sandalwood. Indian households controlled by females were reported to leave infirm males to die lingering deaths on the banks of the Ganges, ears and nose stuffed with mud, as its sacred tidal waters rose.[33] Lithographs in English-language newspapers in India also gave new visual literacy to these claims, including mothers throwing their infants to the crocodiles at Sagar Island adjacent to the Ganges delta.[34]

Though mostly apocryphal, and never relaying the privations caused by the colonial intervention itself, these stories encouraged new donations in England for missionary work in India. Accounts also began to appear in Company gazettes from resident bishops that conflated anxieties about a rapidly growing Eurasian population with new stories of privation that required a European missionary remedy.[35] Most particularly, these gazettes elaborated in salacious and mostly inaccurate ways pre-existing metropole knowledge about *sati* (burning of widows) among the Indian elite. The attention paid to this practice was mainly about Western characterisation of Hindu tradition, the 'civilising' role of missionary evangelism and the role of the East India Company, with the women who were actually burned being only a marginal consideration.[36] Atwal's research shows the colonial state, in the early nineteenth century, only concerning itself with determining whether widow immolation was 'voluntary' or 'involuntary'.[37] Not all Europeans living in India were likely to be responsive to this lobbying of Westminster for large-scale mission access. Experienced Indian-resident Europeans of William Hickey's stamp lived and worked in carefully tidied Western inner-city spaces within a closely connected European community. These salacious revelations must have appeared to them as little more than starkly bogus and joyless intercessions that dehumanised the Indian woman.

Before the formal admission of British missions to India in 1813, earlier missionary activity was of a different kind. Far from the corrosive force of cultural transfer and imposition that some missions became in the later nineteenth century, in the late seventeenth and eighteenth centuries mission agency, by contrast, provided a bridge that linked Western and Eastern intellectualism, using a common frame of monotheism. Exploring this, Hayden Bellenoit has traced Hinduism's monotheistic *bhakti* (devotion) and the way Indian mystics and gurus used it as a key reference point to foster deeper intellectual exchanges with those Europeans who made contact.[38] Portuguese Jesuits followed the military conquests of Alfonso Albuquerque in the south and were received at the Mughal court of Akbar in the north. Others such as Roberto de Nobili, also known as the 'white Brahmin' at the Madura mission in southern Madras, won favour with Hindu intellectuals by learning Sanscrit and observing upper-caste protocols. This tradition of cultural and intellectual transferral through theology and observance in both directions was in powerful contrast to the stark money-making enterprises of the Company. This transferral also authorised, perhaps paradoxically, the racial mixing and relaxed sexual codes of Europeans abroad in India pre-1800.[39]

Authorising the new missionary learning space

By 1813 the English missions were something new. The English Evangelical Revival led by John Newton, William Wilberforce and the Clapham sect worked to combat social ills at home and slavery abroad. They founded Bible and missionary societies throughout the empire that now powerfully, but artificially, projected a home domain whose cultural formation was stable and uncontested. In fact, the new Christian-based projection of a 'home' domain had only limited verac-ity, even though it was a crucial adjunct to missionary evangelism abroad. In this light, Mary Poovey sees the imagined 'home' domain as the product of new technologies, such as census and statistics gath-ering, transport and cheap publications. These technologies brought together diverse social groups in Britain that had rarely mixed before and increasingly presented them as an undifferentiated whole. They were codified, and the new rationality that resulted was then legiti-mised by new private and government institutions to justify policy-making based on this one new reality.[40]

In this tradition, Benthamite Utilitarian experimentation in India, and particularly the influential James Mill's view of a mendacious, venal and dissolute India, imagined an even more ambitious process of colonial regularising, notwithstanding India's vast linguistic, cultural and racial diversity.[41] The new missionary push unconsciously carried within it these regulating, codified assumptions as well, even though exclusive Judeo-Christian theology was at its core. In this frame of a regulated and codified 'home', the hybridity of mixed-race alliances in India was to be countered and remedied by missionary itineration, Bible classes and the control of the European classroom. For females of mixed race, new femininity was mediated, via the conduit networks

[47]

of empire, in the same Western unified way. These networks from abroad now embedded early stereotypes of female propriety and purpose, even before the advent of Western formalised schooling in India. These stereotypes, once established, were to be built upon by the West in India for the rest of the nineteenth century.

After 1813, Company fears reflected the new brand of missionary it knew was coming to India. However, the new missionaries did not begin to monopolise schooling for girls in India, as they would later claim. The missionaries found much more to contend with in India than in most other colonies of the period. The many European agents of conquest had already brought European schooling institutions to the subcontinent, which offered education for girls as well as boys. In 1821, the Company itself set up regimental schools, with attached garrison libraries, in its military cantonments. In these schools, the daughters of soldiers, as well as their brothers, were educated for up to four hours a day in a single room or on a house verandah. The schools were occupied by children of all ages who were taught basic reading, writing and arithmetic by an army sergeant, with the idea that such knowledge would be a marketable commodity for their future employment. The schools were for Eurasian as well as European children, who were already brutalised by living at close quarters with battle-hardened soldiers.[42]

These cantonments were hardly ideal environments for children, dispossessed as some of them were from any sense of filial belonging. The soldiers drank and frequently sought out the companionship of prostitutes, most of whom were recruited by the Company. The soldiers lived squashed into squalid clusters of semi-permanent tents or rows of mud-brick, thatched-rooved bungalows, together with their barbers, their gambling partners and their packhorses.[43] Rousseau's *Émile*, which understood the phenomenon of the child, had been published in 1762.[44] However, such scholarly thinking scarcely touched the fierce exigencies of empire. As at Waterloo, some of these children marched off to battle with their parents, including to the cruel Maratha campaigns, adjacent to Bombay, of 1817 and 1818. As was so often the case in similar settings throughout the empire in this period, these children also received the blame for the socialising consequences of such neglect by their regimental teachers, including Mrs Mary Sherwood: 'Many of my children were extremely wicked – in short ... there was nothing that some of them were not up to'.[45]

Paradoxically perhaps, with all of the imperfections of regimental schooling, it is likely that these girls and boys had more opportunities to learn than if they had been in the Ragged school or the Dame school for the underprivileged child in England, even by 1820. Against this background of existing schooling, the missions still had much work to do to establish their new education code, given the opposition of the resident European population who, established now in India for several generations, favoured the status quo.

An early setback for the missionary lobby regarding Bengali girls came when, in 1825, the missionary Calcutta Ladies' School for Native Females was unsuccessful in applying for a Rs.10,000 grant from the Company to set up an Indian girls' school. Expatriate European resistance emerged because leading Indian merchants, while beneficiaries of East India Company commerce, were suspicious of the school's proselytising purpose. This despite the fact that, four years earlier, its predecessor, the Calcutta School Society, had met with greater success (largely because it shrewdly attached a girls' school to David Hare's well-received Hindu College for boys[46]) and the fact that William Carey's Serampore mission in Bengal had begun admitting Indian girls in 1816.[47]

The very small European population made it difficult for early missionary enterprises to attempt to gain a broader foothold on the subcontinent. However, new agency from abroad after 1813, particularly via the evangelical, low church, Church Missionary Society (CMS), still attempted to impose a new agenda on India: an agenda that would require skilful negotiation if it were to be sustained on the subcontinent. The new approach began with a complex CMS administrative takeover of pre-existing Christian-inspired missionary organisations: organisations that had earlier been able to win local acceptance and Company permission to operate. These earlier organisations had succeeded because they had demonstrated a genuine sympathy with contemporary orientalist approaches that acknowledged the Eastern contribution to learning. The CMS now worked to appropriate this socio-cultural beachhead for its own evangelising purposes.

The new CMS female learner

The new missionary approach was facilitated by the failure of earlier Indian and European factions of the Calcutta School Society to agree on establishing Indian girls' schools taught by women teachers already resident in India (and presumably of at least part-Indian descent).[48] By 1828, in Bengal, the CMS had taken over much of this effort, mostly through the rather changeable agency of Mary Ann Cooke. The CMS favoured a stark form of schooling for girls that was scripture based and that began to import elements of accomplishments such as needlework and Western calligraphy handwriting.

Mary Ann Cooke (soon to be Mrs Wilson) was recruited by the more moderate Liverpool branch of the London Missionary Society at the behest of the Rev. William Ward of the Baptist Serampore mission.[49] She was thirty-seven when she arrived in India and her earlier employment, as the 'accomplished' governess in England of the Earl of Mulgrave's children, was a world away from what she would find on the mission field in India.[50] However, once in India, Wilson's theology seems to have been transformed to a lower church bearing by the opposition she encountered from local Hindu elites and by her marriage to a CMS missionary. Her fledgling educational method was also shaped by the patronage of accomplishment-educated European aristocrats, most notably the wives of two successive governor-generals, Lady Hastings and Lady Amherst.

A stipulation of Mary Ann Wilson's recruitment from England was her competency in the Lancaster schooling model of monitorial teaching. By 1828 she had instituted this model in the CMS Calcutta central school. However, another European woman, Priscilla Chapman, writing to an audience in England, characterised Wilson's approach in terms of European social rescue rather than teaching acuity:

> There was one class of teachers or monitors consisting of twenty-five native females; young as they were, they were all either widows or forsaken by their husbands: they had been educated in the schools of the Society, and when they became destitute, they had recourse to Mrs Wilson, who was thus able to employ them in the service of their country women.[51]

The cheap monitorial pedagogy relied on very few actual teachers, despite the size of the school. Widows and other abandoned Indian females, as less literate monitors, were likely, because of their circumstances, to be no less enthusiastic than their male counterparts a generation earlier at Andrew Bell's Asylum in Madras, where he had developed his monitorial method of teaching.[52] The CMS had a well-meaning Western social agenda attempting to rehabilitate these Indian women, although it underestimated the enormous cultural barrier the presence of these widows still posed to other prospective Indian girls who were wealthy enough to be able to afford the school fees.

The physical appearance of the central school itself symbolised its cultural separateness. Priscilla Chapman's book describes an imposing walled central institution of neo-classical architecture in a wide, swept street in an almost peopleless landscape. The only concession to the East was the inclusion of banyan and copperpod trees. The school cut off the possibility of mainstream Indian engagement, and Hindu girls of caste ceased to attend after 1824.[53] There were also other Western failures to embrace Indian schoolgirls in surrounding communities. For example, a mission school in Calcutta founded by a Ladies Society

Figure 1 Lithograph of Mary Ann Cooke's central CMS girls' school, Calcutta.

for Native Female Education was disbanded in 1834. The school had been a very ambitious experiment to educate Muslim girls, in which they were taught by Muslim male teachers but 'visited' daily by European women.[54] Mary Bird, inspired by a visit to New York to meet Scottish-American missionary, philanthropist and educator, Isabella Graham, also attempted, without success, to set up a school for illiterate Eurasians in Calcutta who could only speak Hindustani.[55]

However, Wilson's CMS school in Calcutta continued. Despite its limited potential to build enrolments, the school established a firm nexus in Bengal between Western education only and conversion that admitted no other spiritual code. Enrolments continued to be built through the socially separate, either through widowhood, or mission-designated 'orphans' (who might still have living parents or who were genuinely left as orphans as a result of famine or disease). With this remit, Wilson gathered girls, mostly from upper India, in thirty branch schools and, by 1826, had a total of 600 pupils under her charge.[56] A Bengal Ladies Society was set up as an umbrella organisation. Although, the CMS Christian bearing meant there was little to engage Bengali Brahmin elites, who owed none of their identity to steadily encroaching British commerce and the few European women who followed the commerce. Even Indian converts, such as Krishna Bannerjee, knew that these female students were not part of a strong connection with the broader stratums of Hindu society.[57] Furthermore, reliance on 'orphans' for enrolments, though worthy philanthropic work at a time of crushing cholera epidemics, was also symptomatic of a serious flaw now established in Bengal regarding female education. Designated 'orphans' could be detached from the cultural settings in which they had once belonged. Yet this very separateness accentuated the superficiality of mission schools such as these. Wilson eventually decided to deploy her teaching elsewhere where she felt it might be more productive, going to Syria, where she was to set up a new 'Arabic school'.[58]

Educational trading in 'orphans', and associated categorisation based on destitution, was not new territory for the British, even at the metropole. There were strong precursors in the way this kind of child was viewed by state authorities. For example, coming after the dissolution of the monasteries, Christ's Hospital in London (now relocated to Horsham) was founded by Edward VI in 1552 to educate some of the overflow poor and destitute children. Two centuries later, Sunday Schools conflated religion, moral training and the duties of the poor.[59] Beryl Bubacz argues that, in the eighteenth century, Charity Schools in England reinforced 'respectable class' perceptions about the different standing of children of the poor, even dressing them as 'charity children' to mark them out as different from other pupils. The evangelical John Pounds' humanitarian Ragged Schools movement sought, through some basic literacy education, to elevate 'destitute and outcast children of the streets' to a better life.[60] Reference to 'destitute' children in England by these early middle-class philanthropists, amid the urban chaos of the industrial revolution, was often without acknowledgement of living parents, particularly those already in the workhouse. Destitute children became synonymous with the phrase 'orphan', which then authorised their incarceration in stark institutional spaces for moral cleansing, social control and an 'industrial' education that was really about them producing goods and services – cooking, laundry and ironing – to pay for their keep. In Rudyard Kipling's India, two generations later, there was also a different kind of orphan characterisation. Kipling's *Kim* enjoyed the camouflaged freedom, 'burned black' by the sun, among the ash-smeared *faquirs* (holy men) of Lahore, where his love act was as *chela* (disciple) to his Tibetan *lama* (high priest) rather than any enforced enrolment at St Xavier's College.[61]

Somewhere between these two worlds, CMS Bengal missionaries in the 1820s collected scholars who were 'orphan' girls, imagining perhaps an improvement on practice in England, although still directed by the mentality of child difference based on child destitution. There was one essential difference: the participation of female orphans in the small number of available Western classrooms of the 1820s and 1830s hid deepening opposition from local brahminical networks to colonial education. This problem would not be recognised by the British in Bengal until the early twentieth century. In the meantime, with an unwavering belief that it would eventually convert India, the CMS saw their orphan scholars as the first step in the process of 'Christianising' India.

Another factor that set these early mission girls' schools apart was a parallel, but much more sophisticated, intellectual pursuit that configured the East/West intellectual link in other ways. CMS mission expansion was in the context of the founding of the Brahmo Samaj in Calcutta in 1829, led by Ram Mohan Roy.[62] Mohan Roy was from a wealthy Brahmin family and had worked for the Company. He opposed the founding of a Sanscrit College as a solely traditional Indian enterprise and rejected the Hindu notions of idol worship. He also established an Anglo-Hindu school, and later college (for boys), in Calcutta in 1822. Roy's erudite scholarship in both Sanscrit and Arabic and his visits to England and Paris established a credible connection with the West that authorised an Eastern intellectual and spiritual contribution. Unlike the CMS, Roy's intellectual contribution was complex, particularly his monotheist interpretation of Hinduism, which he then melded with Christian precepts and connected particularly with the Unitarian tradition in England. However, coming the other way, from Europe, the CMS in the early nineteenth century was not about ecumenism, even within the Church of England tradition, let alone any 'adulteration' with Eastern spiritualism and belief in Calcutta.

How to teach in Bengal

Networks concerning pedagogy also came into play in Mrs Wilson's mission schools in Bengal, particularly the monitorial system (referred to earlier), where one 'headmaster' imparted didactic knowledge procedures to senior students or monitors, which they then relayed to clusters of students arranged in rows according to age. Monitorial education for girls was complex educational terrain even in the early British period in India. Unlike Bell's experiments in Madras, Wilson's schools involved teaching Indian girls rather than Eurasian boys.[63] The CMS mission girls' schools had conversion as their chief agenda, but achieving this also necessitated deeper thought about how to teach when student literacy, in particular, was measured by their understanding of the 'meaning' of the words they learnt rather than just by rote recitation. The imperative was reiterated many times as Wilson adapted Bell's model to the reality of teaching Indian rather than Eurasian children.[64] Clearly, conversion through literal biblical understanding, even via parables, was heavily dependent on the intelligent teaching of the meaning of words. Wilson's tutelage continued into the evening:

> After dinner many of the children assembled and read Scriptures in English, translating them into Bengali as they proceeded, in a way which clearly proves their understanding of the sacred truths they read.[65]

This account suggests a naïve approach. However, even in this early period the CMS was aware that the mere use of monitors alone would not be effective to teach Indian students the complexities of language. More significantly, the issue made the CMS dependent on the available Indian intelligentsia, which then also imported additional gendered approaches to CMS schooling. To attract students, CMS personnel soon worked out that they needed to teach in Bengali rather than in English. In 1820, for their outlying boys' schools, which claimed an enrolment of over 1,000, the CMS was able to employ some complicit 'learned Brahmins' to circulate among these schools to examine student knowledge of key Sanscrit words. The resident Indian schoolteacher and his monitors then devoted their time constructing broader conceptual understanding of Western and Christian terms, using carefully codified primers that offered proximate ethical frameworks. For example, the first class (the highest class) studied the 1808 edition of *Beauties of History* from pages ten to thirty-two. The text organised European Ancient History into the Eastern moral code categories of: 'pride', 'revenge', 'treachery', and so on; while the third class was taught the more biblically constructed 'History of Joseph'.[66] These were heavily negotiated learning sites that laboured under an impossibly attenuated cultural transference between the East and Western understanding of an ancient Western historical past and also first-century biblical literacy. It was also the preserve of males to teach on both sides of the cultural divide.

This Brahmin philological mediation was only available to boys, and the missions themselves saw even this contribution as a necessary evil with few redeeming features. The CMS missionaries were popular in these boys' schools, yet were strategic enough to know they could not yet explicitly teach scripture. Parents were more interested in their sons being taught numeracy for the workplace and each school had to adjust its budget to employ a *sircar* (steward) to teach the *Devanagari* (Hindi/Sanscrit) script, particularly for student training in account keeping. However, the broader socio-religious business to hand was more closely watched by the CMS from outside and here the missionary stereotype of Eastern deficit was much more visible. As the Rev. Deerr claimed:

The boys are willing to accept instruction and show great affection when I come to them ... but the old wicked Idolaters chiefly the Bramens [sic] do spoil them. With the last mentioned we have a great deal of arguments. As long as one speaketh to them from morality they agree and accept everything; but as soon as our blessed Saviour is introduced they begin to contradict.[67]

For girls the scenario was different. As a mostly orphan population in CMS schools of the early nineteenth century, they were shielded by Europeans from this deeper Indian-based engagement. More separate than the boys from the broader Indian communities of Bengal, CMS girls' schools adopted the money-saving 'efficiencies' of the monitorial system that taught a crude accomplishments curriculum without additional teachers.

Despite the elaborate ploys of the CMS to proselytise India via the classroom, little could come of this kind of teaching of Indian girls. Leading educationalists such as Krishna Mohan Banerjea had decided by 1849 that the upper echelons of Indian society could never be enticed to risk having their daughters abandon their own culture and beliefs.

I do not think the respectable classes of the Hindus will at present suffer their females to attend any public schools where pupils may be indiscriminately received, without consideration to caste and creed.[68]

The cultural isolation of Wilson's girls' schools was verified, in retrospect, by Mary Carpenter's National India Association in 1871 to justify the Carpenter model of colonial state intervention and funding, which will be discussed in chapter three.

Not a single child of the middle-classes or decent poor ever attended these [Wilson's female CMS] schools, and as the distribution of coppers ceased, the number of pupils decreased, until the missionaries were obliged to confine their labour chiefly to the children of their own converts & destitute orphans sent to them by government.[69]

This reticence on the part of broader sections of Indian communities to participate in missionary schooling also had another cause. By the late 1820s, evangelical attitudes had infiltrated most levels of Company administration, and evangelical education in this period was really social reform aimed at undermining Indian students' attachment to their own culture and at inculcating a Western viewpoint, which included Indian redemption through Christianity.[70]

Yet, despite the highly restricted enrolment of Indian girls, the new CMS missionary female pedagogical approach dominated East India Company conceptions of female education in Bengal up until the 1850s. Few government schools competed with it, except the fledgling Bethune school, as discussed in later chapters. Macaulay's 1835 Despatch decreed that all government-funded education needed to be through the medium of English. However, by the late 1840s, even the Bengal provincial government recognised the need for a more culturally sensitive accomplishments curriculum for girls outside the learning of English, which had become too synonymous with conversion and Western cultural imposition.

> The course of study should be confined exclusively to reading and writing the Bengalee language, painting, drawing and needlework, with the proviso that English education should be imparted to such of the pupils, whose parents or guardians may desire it by written application.[71]

The 'orientalism' of the North Western Provinces and Bombay

The mannered approach of the early CMS mission in Bengal concerning female education ignored much richer developments in the NWP and in Bombay, provinces away from central colonial governance in Bengal. These developments actually reached back far earlier than the CMS in Bengal. Well before the official admission of the missions in 1813, early Company alignment with education was part of a deliberate strategy of reconciliation driven by early British colonial insecurities about its power base, and the need to better understand the sophisticated pre-existing social and political orders of the subcontinent. These factors gave rise to a series of education amendments to the younger Pitt's 1784 India Act. The first Governor General Warren Hasting's (1773–85) official policy of 'orientalism' fused this perceptive, but practical, strategy of accommodation and conciliation with Indians with a genuine fascination for Eastern learning and language.

Just as Thomas Acquinas and the Dominicans gained access to Aristotle's lost writings through the translation of Arabic texts in the Middle Ages, it had been long understood in Europe that languages of the East, particularly Persian and Sanscrit, had critical Eastern knowledge embedded within them. This sympathetic environment empowered 'orientalists' such as H. H. Wilson, H. T. Prinsep and J. C. Sutherland to recognise and study the intellectual integrity and communal significance of education traditions that had long been a cohesive force in indigenous communities. Away from the classical languages of Persian, Arabic and Sanscrit, there were also attenuated discussions about the capacity of local languages or 'vernaculars', including Hindi or Bengali, to have Western knowledge 'engrafted' onto them to create a robust and modern national literature.[72]

In Bengal, in this spirit, William Adam's extensive village school surveys in the mid-1830s showed an Indian literacy rate of 6.1 per cent for males and 3.1 per cent for females as a result of traditional Indian school teaching.[73] This early ethnography was intended to reveal to British colonial rulers the potential of an already vibrant and responsive Indian intellectualism; and these literacy rates for females were never to be surpassed by the British, even by the 1920s. Away from the CMS strictures of Bengal, the views of Bombay civil servant, Lancelot Wilkinson, in particular, found resonance in the NWP in the early 1850s under a reforming Lieutenant Governor James Thomason and his imaginative DPI, Henry Reid.[74] Here an experimental schooling system called *halkabandi* (circle of schools) had achieved considerable success in eight experimental districts.

This system appropriated existing Indian village schools and their teachers and, in so doing, tacitly recognised the veracity of pre-British learning traditions and practices.[75] By early 1857 many halkabandi village schools were co-educational and in Agra, one of Reid's eight experimental districts, there were almost 5,000 girls in 288 schools. Reid was enthusiastic about these developments regarding the schooling of Indian girls because they represented, as he saw it, the start of a 'social revolution'.[76] For this intelligent man the revelation at hand was that building an education nexus between East and West was no longer an insurmountable task; and, more than this, education of Indian females, if managed properly, could lay the foundations for a felicitous imperial future in India for all. The chief contributor to his vision was an inescapable and genuine responsiveness Reid thought he could detect in local Indian communities to the idea of schooling for girls, even when taught by men, so long as these teachers were local village-based pandits (Hindu teachers).[77]

More significantly, the potential of these schoolgirls to shift the social frame in his province was reinforced to Reid by simple, and to his mind, irrefutable evidence. Many of these Indian village schoolgirls were actually from poor agricultural backgrounds, or were the daughters of traditional artisans and weavers, rather than the daughters of *patwaris* (tax collectors) or the trading classes directly involved in Company commerce.[78] Reid's 'ground-up' village schooling endeavours for girls were also showing strong signs that supposed purdah seclusion barriers could be breached if Indian parents were afforded some control over the school itself; this was made clear enough to Reid by the age range of these students, extending as it did well beyond the purdah boundary of puberty.

All these factors were highly significant to Reid by 1858, and worth fighting for in the face of sceptical district officers, who were angry and frightened at what had just transpired in the province during the Great Revolt, when all the major colonial educational institutions in the province were destroyed. Eighteen months after this violent turmoil and retribution, Reid wrote enthusiastically of the degree of Indian participation in his schools, where girls were taught.

> The schools were attended by scholars of all classes of Hindoos [sic], including a considerable proportion of Brahmins; and of the girls, the age of some of these exceeded 20 years, the remainder being from 6 to 20 years. The masters were selected by the parents of the scholars, and committees of respectable native gentlemen were formed to exercise a general supervision over the schools, and to arrange for their visitation.[79]

There were even more remarkable revelations in the neighbouring Punjab. This province also had adopted the halkabandi experiment, where girls were traditionally taught up to the age of ten before they were secluded. However, much older pre-British schools had a different agenda for them. In the 1850s the DPI, William Arnold, employed a large number of Indian sub-deputy inspectors.[80] Without any known connection with the British, these pre-British girls' schools followed a curriculum with features that resembled those in the West.[81] The resemblance indicated the organisation of knowledge for young girls using a graduated syllabus that was not just a Western invention. What was distinctly Eastern was the overarching agenda of these syllabi, which were principally an enterprise designed to educate Indian girls so that they could cross class boundaries for employment involving more than just menial tasks in elite Muslim households. Most specifically, in this non-colonial domain, 'low-caste' Muslim girls, daughters of barbers and shoemakers, were learning the elite language of Persian Urdu through traditional texts, including *Tahsil-ul-talim* and the *Ahmud Kalikburi*.[82]

In Bombay, another longstanding strategy was in play that again entertained the possibility of stronger engagement of female education efforts with local communities. The patronage offered by 'high' company officials, namely Thomas Munro, Montstuart Elphinstone and John Malcolm, resulted in native education societies being set up in Madras and Bombay in the 1820s and 1830s. These societies aimed at encouraging learning by building dictionaries publishing cross-translated Eastern and Western scholarship in vernacular (local) languages.[83] At least one society in Bombay founded a teacher training institution for Indian, non-colonial schools using Bell's monitorial model as a unifying, yet now Indian, local endeavour.[84] In this city in particular, Elphinstone's reputation and longstanding sympathy for traditional Indian education allowed him and his immediate nominees to gain access to Indian girls' schools, even in his capacity of Governor of Bombay. This was a privilege denied his successors. Unlike in Bengal, Indian benefactors were encouraged by Elphinstone to set up girls' schools in cities such as Ahmedabad, Poona and Dharwar. Strong Parsi communities, who had always encouraged education for their daughters, continued on as well. Additionally, the Secretary of State, Edward Stanley, at the India Office in London, even hypothesised that these efforts would eventually result in the breaking down of a gendered curriculum in India. He also ventured:

> The prejudices against female education are fast disappearing ... there will be no more difficulty found in establishing female schools than there is in those for boys.[85]

What to teach the girls?

The curriculum for girls was itself also up for negotiation more generally among orientalist thinkers. Earlier orientalist experiments deliberately let the curriculum evolve as an emerging connection between East and West. The proponents of these experiments, both European and Indian, were wise enough to know that any solidifying of the curriculum could not be orchestrated by the favoured colonial route of administrative regulation.

In India in the 1820s and 1830s, the work of orientalists borrowing from Western thought developed powerful new discourses, this time concerning secular knowledge. For example, in the 1830s, Lancelot Wilkinson's work with the pandits of Sehore had produced lively scholarship where comparisons were made between the twelfth-century Sanscritic Siddhantic systems of astronomy with the one offered by Copernicus.[86] Such formal connections between Eastern and Western women were not possible in this early period, although the intermingling of Eastern and Western ways of knowing that concerned females was still part of the educational vista of mid-nineteenth-century India. For example, school textbook committees for girls and boys attempted to support language-bifurcated curriculums that fragmented Eastern knowledge along the continuum of Western-constructed epistemologies. In addition, Western disciplinary procedure divided and organised school subjects in much the same way as happens today, even though elemental ancient Eastern texts had long directed the thought processes of both females and males in other ways. The verses of the Hindu *Puranas* (ancient Hindu texts) conflated history, cosmology, geography, genealogy and ethics; while the Eastern poetry and literature of Saadi's Persian *Bostan* and *Gulistan* had itself influenced European thought in the Middle Ages.[87]

These different knowledge constellations were not considered to be insurmountable, even by Indian educational reformers, despite British assumptions on the issue. Nor was education for girls seen as a threat to their chastity or their femininity, if carefully and sensitively managed. For example, even two generations later, Indian reformer and Brahmin, Kandukuri Veeresalingam, set up a school for Telugu women in Madras in 1875. He argued:

> education is for enlightenment and cultivation of the mind, as it should be. It is as essential for women as for men. It is an equally indefensible proposition that girls would be exposed to ... sex-laden poetic classics of old, if they are to be educated ... the traditional scholars are [already] most exposed to it ... On the other hand, our women are sure to benefit from a study of the spotless lives of the chaste women of our *Puranas* ... The statement that ancient Hindu women were not educated is not credible. Female education was not frowned upon by the *sastras* [ancient Sanscrit rules] ... It was not banned by any of the *srutis* [Sanscrit sacred texts] ... There is little doubt that female education had the sanction of *srutis*, *smritis* [Hindu religious scripture] and *Puranas*.[88]

Like other orientalists, Veeresalingam supposed that a negotiable curriculum terrain for girls was possible if only both Western and Eastern educators would put their minds to it.

Many centres

Gender-based power relations concerning the British educational space varied across the subcontinent and invited a variety of British responses. For example, in Burma many women and girls of all castes were free to direct their public and private lives because of their unique economic position. They operated 75 per cent of the busy bazaar trade in timber products, cotton, sugar and semi-precious stones under the control of the British. This context was one in which Burmese women and girls did well under Western commerce, which also made them freer from traditional patriarchal control. As a result, the raj felt confident to establish some exemplar schools on the Western model for these females.[89]

However, in places such as Oudh, in north central India, women were heavily secluded, at least within the wealthier classes whose power and influence continued to interest the British the most. This secluded status inclined the raj to think only in terms of winning the cooperation of husbands or fathers, so that the colonial education of females might be extended. Furthermore, refusals by pupils 'to come out from behind the curtain' resulted in many early raj girls' schools being 'closed' in Oudh by the British, leaving them to continue as before, under sole indigenous custodianship.[90]

In Assam there was yet another scenario. Indian tea merchants were offered financial inducements to send their daughters to mission schools. When these tea enterprises failed, local gurus refused to have these girls back into their *pathshalas* (elementary schools), where they had previously been taught Eastern scholarship in coeducational classes.[91]

These highly regional outcomes failed to alert the British to the need to accommodate such variability regarding the education of females. Instead, raj regulation was through one centre, defined by strenuous efforts put into the gathering of statistics, census reports and one Hailebury bureaucratic model of regulation. Certainly ICS district officers should have been alerted to the problem of girls being rejected by local intellectual elites once they crossed over and joined complicit raj institutions. Less powerful education department personnel wrote frequently in their reports about this fine detail. However, district officers were too occupied with issues of colonial governance concerning sanitation, trade regulation, military affairs and the prevention of another Great Revolt, to delve too much into local cultural affairs and how these might differently direct schooling for girls.

Of most significance was the fact that the raj's understandings of social formation, as they related to the education of Indian females, continued to be built around the paradigm of broad cultural deficits. As far as macro statecraft was concerned, the official response to such deficits was normalised into one model by the 1860s. 'Female education' became 'regulated', as a matter of Western routine and subject to colonial modes of bureaucratic compliance. Most of the deeper cultural and intellectual interchanges of two generations earlier, which had been led by local Indian community networks, and which had also embraced female learning, were bypassed by this time. Instead, the government now promoted a new type of intervention that it claimed was about transformational change based on large school enrolments of girls.

For example, by the mid-nineteenth century, a new generation of government officials viewed most mission schools as comfortably full through orphan enrolments, even though most of these schools remained limited enterprises confined to the largest cities and towns.[92] At a government of India level, Western statistical precision in compiling data on colonial girls' schools also seemed to add credence to a picture of rapidly expanding enrolments of Indian girls from the broader community. Fallacious student numbers of Indian girls claimed by the raj reached 84,995 in 1882, although 97 per cent of these girls were listed as being only in 'primary schools'. These figures were speculative enough, and included girls of part-European racial lineage, but the Hunter Commission of that year also noted that zenana (household) teaching of whatever kind was responsible for 277,207 girls, who were not at school, but who were able to read and write anyway.[93] Official categorisations of caste, class and linguistic profiling of the students also lent a semblance of credibility to the enrolment claims of girls' schools. However, this was not the whole story. In rare candour, A. M. Monteath, Undersecretary of the Home Department of the Viceroy's Council, explained the statistical devices to hand that produced these bogus official claims of large school attendances of Indian schoolgirls.

> When we compare the total number of female pupils on the rolls in Government Schools, namely, 1,036, with an average daily attendance, namely, 695.3, the unsatisfactory character of most of these Institutions must be at once inferred. The first characteristic of our Girls' Schools is extreme irregularity of attendance; the second, is that they are in reality Infant Schools, in which it appears to me that the great bulk of the children, being very young, sit looking on, while a few girls at the top of the School receive a little instruction.[94]

Female 'infanticide' in north India

This kind of official licence with the truth concerning the colonial schooling of Indian girls allowed for other excursions by ambitious senior colonial officials. Their actions were much more visible and ham-fisted. By the early 1860s some of them had grown frustrated by the refusal of Indian elites to back girl schooling enterprises. Earlier in their careers, these European males, as junior administrators out in remote district postings sometimes only had survey officers and merchant agents for European companionship. They also saw hapless missionaries on itineration tours trying unsuccessfully to drum up support for the establishment of a local mission school. Local Indian resistance offended the sensibilities of these officials, who were convinced of the integrity of the Western 'civilising mission'. Faced with Indian patriarchal non-compliance, it was easy for these European males to rehearse in their low-level reports earlier raj anxieties about Indian female degeneracy that was manifest, as they saw it, through the cultural oppression by recusant Indian males.

The most public case of this kind occurred in the Punjab and is sufficiently illustrative of British colonial mentalities of the 1860s to merit brief recount here. At this time the province had a newly appointed Lieutenant Governor Robert Montgomery. He was a man of Irish family background who had built his earlier career in the ICS from the early age of seventeen. (He was also the grandfather of Field Marshal Bernard 'Monty' Montgomery of Second World War fame.) Montgomery's early career was built upon his skills in using Western codification and statistical gathering to reveal one 'congenital' Indian phenomenon in particular: female infanticide practices in the Punjab. Female infanticide had been banned on pain of death under the British as early as 1847, but the British suspected that it persisted among some Muslim groups in the north and east of the province. Montgomery had 'found' the practice particularly endemic among Sikh tribal group called the Bedis in the Gurdaspur district (central-north Punjab). They were known as the *Koree Mar* (daughter slayers).[95] In their stronghold town of Dera Baba Nanak, he estimated that female infanticide had resulted in there being only sixty-one girls compared to 450 boys under the age of four.[96] Accounts of the burial alive of baby girls, with ceremonial *gur* (sugar and molasses) between their lips and the accompanied recitation of ritual poems, were confrontational. This observation confused much earlier ancient, eleventh-century *Mitākṣarā* legal Indian rites, already known to the British in the north India, that prescribed this ritual for baby corpses less than two years of age.[97] Montgomery's accounts were strongly redolent of the evangelical-inspired mission characterisation (mentioned earlier in this chapter) of the emotional degeneracy of the Indian female 'condition' a generation earlier in Bengal.

Since the arrival of the British, the Bedis had seen their wealth decline rapidly, mostly as a result of the revocation of their *jagirs* (rent-free lands), which had sometimes been held for several centuries by these families. This had enabled the British to free up property rights in favour of more complicit elements of the surrounding Indian communities. For the Bedis, their wealth loss made them more fearful of baby girls, given the subsequent cost of dowries when these daughters reached the age of twelve or thirteen. As a junior officer, Montgomery's first ploy to monitor the 'social evil' of infanticide was to count the number of *alhwahan* ceremonies (celebrated after the completion of the eighth month of pregnancy) and then compare the tally with the number of girls who reached their tenth birthday.[98] Given the obvious cultural insensitivity of this approach, his superiors rejected his suggestion. He then fathomed that another way of 'counting' the daughters of the Bedis was by enrolling girls in nominal schools funded by the British.[99]

It was not long until administrative distortions emerged as local power brokers, who were Indian males, saw their chance to make a quick rupee in the wake of what seemed to be rare and unsupervised government largess. As a result, monies were soaked up by households masquerading as 'schools' and husbands acted as teachers to 'educate' their wives, receiving pay at almost five times the going rate for other Indian men already teaching large classes in government schools.[100] The entire Punjab education department almost went bankrupt as a result of this scheme, with funding outgoings reaching four times the monies coming in from available taxes.[101] The Viceroy, John Lawrence, who had been Montgomery's predecessor in the Punjab, soon understood the financial unsustainability of the entire initiative and put a stop to it by executive decree in 1868. Cooperative Indian intermediaries in Montgomery's venture lost their jobs, and this loss of face stopped most other female education initiatives coming from the Punjab for the rest of the century.[102] The episode demonstrated just how fraught premature official intervention could be when high-handed British self-assurance, justified on seemingly solid philanthropic grounds, was implemented without any genuine educational foundation.

Funding and language

Finally, some plainer colonial interventions mid-century also influenced the course of education for Indian females for the rest of the nineteenth century and undermined its broader implementation. The first was the way the British used the revenue base that it had secured for education. The second was the language barrier the colonial state itself had created. Both had a direct bearing on how the state framed the possibilities for female education, particularly after the Great Revolt of 1857.

The colonial state was nimble at what it valued most: administrative regulation, standardisation and control. Part of this control was securing revenues for education, which were wrapped up in the collection surveys conducted in the mid-1850s and early 1860s. How this revenue was secured was cleverly hidden. One per cent of land tax (in most northern provinces at least) went to the education of boys and a smaller number of girls. The land tax itself was derived from a careful survey of revenue sources in each village.[103] The actual method of collection of land tax dated back to the time of Sher Khan in the sixteenth century, and was carefully preserved by the British.[104] In good seasons, careful British calculations showed that these new monies were large enough to approximate to Rs.4 per month per child. This was a considerable sum, being the equivalent of the three-shilling rate that only the most ambitious education reformers hoped for as a funding base when William Forster presented his Elementary Education Act in England two decades later in 1870.[105] However, the problem was that this taxation was borne by the agricultural, rather than the urban, population, despite most colonial girls' schools being in the towns and cities.

The second issue of language placed even stronger restrictions on the development of education for Indian females. A fierce Anglicist/Orientalist controversy had seen Macaulay's Despatch of 1835 'decide' the question in favour of the Anglicists and English-medium teaching in government-funded schools. However, the new unbending linguistic barrier removed a vital conduit for intellectual transference at lower schooling levels for both poor girls and boys. This was because most students at this level spoke only the local language of their village or their urban shanty community. Furthermore, the linguistic barrier meant that building a Western-style institutional schooling hierarchy for Indian girls – school to college – was something of a sham, even with a modified accomplishments curriculum in place.

As a result of these two barriers alone, village uplift of Indian girls through a Western-predicated education was structurally very difficult to achieve even after 1857. Using Chandra Mohanty's interpretation, the products of empire were more to do with the practices of ruling rather than a general colonial condition itself.[106] Communal and linguistic trajectories of local communities were cut off and it was not surprising that local council authorities had their faith shaken as to the veracity of the British educational mindset in post-Revolt India. The upshot was that, by the 1860s, local Indian councils, who knew their local communities intimately, preferred to fund local sanitation projects and local industry projects than speculative local schools for Indian children.[107] These difficulties remained unacknowledged by the state, because schooling for Indian girls was not the core education business of the colonial state mid-century, despite its rhetoric to the contrary. Instead, as will be shown in the next chapter, race and the moral body of a much smaller group of females were to become the key drivers of Western educational intervention for much of the rest of the century.

Colonial engagement with Indian schoolgirls in the first half of the nineteenth century was part of a broader colonial process of closing down earlier networks of sensitive Western and Indian orientalist educational interaction. To the colonial mind, Indian females moved from being potential partners, household custodians and emotional refuges for some European men to being classroom participants of a younger age. Evangelical mission imposition after 1813 cut these participants off from their Indian community connections in a different manner to that effected by concubinage or marriage to Europeans a generation earlier. 'Orphan' schoolgirls of the next generation were relatively few in number, but the schooling enterprise they represented distracted Company officials from the much stronger and longer-standing local traditions of education for Indian females; traditions colonial officials in the NWP, the Punjab and in Bombay had begun to identify and accommodate. Western social codification and commodification practices, which had emerged in Europe in the early nineteenth century, saw only one female education project emerge to 'remedy' the social and emotional condition of the Indian female in general. However, even this idea was to become too ambitious for the colonial state to implement, especially after the Great Revolt of 1857, even in a rudimentary form, and this perception justified official inaction on the education of Indian women and girls. Instead, officials turned to earlier stereotypes developed by the European missions about supposed Indian cultural backwardness and the reluctance of the Indian female to learn.

Notes

1 P. Mukherji, 'Sex and Social Structure' in K. Chanana (ed.), *Socialisation Education and Women: Explorations in Gender Identity* (New Delhi: Sangam Books, 1988), pp. 35–6.

2 A. Eraly, *The Mughal Throne* (London: Weidenfeld and Nicolson, 2003), p. 277–8.

3 This 1670 copy of the Koran is now part of the Nasser D. Khalili Private Collection, London.

4 G. C. Kozlowski, 'Muslim Women and the Control of Property in North India' in J. Krishnamurty (ed.), *Women in Colonial India* (Delhi: Oxford University Press, 1989), p. 121.

5 G. Omvedt, *Feminism and the Women's Movement of India* (Mumbai: SNDT Women's Unversity, 1987), pp. 9–10.

6 H. Scharfe, *Education in Ancient India* (Boston: Brill, 2002), pp. 199–205.

7 L. C. Nand, *Women in the Delhi Sultanate* (Allahabad: Vohra, 1989), pp. 199–200.

8 G. Minault, *Secluded Scholars* (Delhi: Oxford University Press, 1998), p. 14.

9 P. Bourdieu, *Language and Symbolic Power* (Cambridge: Polity, 1991), pp. 61, 78.

10 W. Adam, 'Second Report on Vernacular Education in Bengal' in S. Bhattacharya, J. Bara *et al.*, *Development of Women's Education in India ... Documents, 1850–1920 ...* (1836), pp. 3–6.

11 A. Howell, *Education in British India Prior to 1854 and in 1871* (Government Printing, 1871), section xi.

12 A. Howell, *Education in British India Prior to 1854 and in 1871...*

13 I. Chatterjee, 'Monastic Governmentality, Colonial Misogyny, and Post Colonial Amnesia in South Asia', *History of the Present: A Journal of Critical History*, 3:1 (2013), 57–98. Her larger work greatly elaborates these themes. I. Chatterjee, *Forgotten Friends: Monks, Marriages, and Memories of Northeast India* (New Delhi, Oxford University Press: 2013).

14 M. Kosambi, 'The Home as Social Universe' in I. Glushkova and A. Feldhaus (eds), *House and Home in Maharashtra* (Delhi: Oxford University Press, 1998), pp. 82–101.

15 G. Leitner, 'History of Indigenous Education in the Punjab Since Annexation and in 1882' in U. Sharma and S. Sharma (eds), *Women's Education in British India* (New Delhi: Commonwealth Publishers, 1995), p. 2.

16 As shown by the unusually detailed Indian sub-deputy commissioner reports to William Arnold, DPI in the Punjab, 1854–9. These reports, located in the Secretariat Library archive in Lahore, are largely unselfconscious in their language, not being required to deliver colonial, pre-determined findings. 'Abstract Statement of Indigenous Village Schools Existing in the Punjab in the Year 1857–58' incld. in the Education [Report], July 31, 1858, no. 131–58, Punjab Secretariat Archives, Anarkali's Tomb, Lahore.

17 'Note by Mr A. P. Howell, Undersecretary of State, Home Department, on the State of Education in India, 1866–67', pt. ii, pp. 110–11 (OIOC) P/434/31.

18 J. C. Bagal, *Radha Kanta Dev, 1784–1867* (Calcutta, 1957), p. 47.

19 E. Chatterton, *The History of the Church of England in India* (London: SPCK, 1924), ch. 2.

20 A. Spencer (ed.), *Memoirs of William Hickey* (London: Hurst & Blackett, 1948), vol. i, pp. 22–3.

21 A. Spencer (ed.), *Memoirs of William Hickey...*, vol. i, pp. 22–3, 71–2.

22 A. Spencer (ed.), *Memoirs of William Hickey ...*, vol. i, pp. 22–3, 71–2, 168–9, 173, 175.

23 A. Spencer (ed.), *Memoirs of William Hickey ...*, vol. iv, p. 141.

24 T. R. Barrett, *Calcutta: Strange Memoirs-Foreign Perceptions* (Kolkata: Sankar Mondal, 2004), p. 233.

25 R. Hyam, *Empire and Sexuality* (Manchester: Manchester University Press, 1991), p. 116; V. Brendon, *Children of the Raj* (London: Phoenix, 2006), p. 43.

26 In 1791 Eurasians, or 'Anglo-Indians' (meaning in this sense people of mixed race) were banned from holding civil or military office in the Company, a policy so effectively enforced that by 1808 there were no Eurasians left in the British army (separate from the India army) in India. New work on the building of railways was where many Eurasians were subsequently employed. R. Hyam, *Empire and Sexuality ...*, p. 116.

27 T. R. Barrett, *Calcutta: Strange Memoirs-Foreign Perceptions ...*, pp. 245–54.

28 T. R. Barrett, *Calcutta: Strange Memoirs-Foreign Perceptions ...*, pp. 243–8; A. A. D' Souza, *Anglo-Indian Education: A Study of its Origins and Growth in Bengal up to 1960* (New Delhi: Oxford University Press, 1976), pp. 10–15; C. Hawes, *Poor Relations: The Making of a Eurasian Community in British India, 1773–1833* (Richmond, UK: Curzon, 1996).

29 J. Marriott, *The Other Empire: Metropolis, India and Progress in the Colonial Imagination* (Manchester: Manchester University Press, 2003), p. 93.

30 A. Porter, *Religion Versus Empire: British Protestant Missionaries and Overseas Expansion, 1700–1914* (Manchester: Manchester University Press, 2004), pp. 116–35.

31 C. S. Runganadhan, *History of the City of Madras* (Madras: Varadachary & Co., 1939), p. 17.

32 Rev. A. Westcott, *Our Oldest Indian Mission: A Brief History of the Vepery (Madras) Mission* (Madras: Madras Diocesan Committee Publishing, 1897), pp. 8–9.

33 T. R. Barrett, *Calcutta: Strange Memoirs-Foreign Perceptions ...*, p. 282.

34 T. R. Barrett, *Calcutta: Strange Memoirs-Foreign Perceptions ...*, p. 285.

35 Bishop Heber in T. R. Barrett, *Calcutta: Strange Memoirs-Foreign Perceptions ...*, p. 248.

36 M. Lata, *Contentious Traditions: The Debate on Sati in Colonial India* (Berkerley, CA: University of California Press, 1998), *passim*.

37 J. Atwal, 'Foul Unhallow'd Fires: Officiating Sati and the Colonial Hindu Widow in the United Provinces', *Studies in History*, 29:2 (2013), 229–72.

38 H. Bellenoit, *Missionary Education and Empire in Late Colonial India, 1860–1920* (London: Pickering and Chatto, 2007), pp. 14–16.

39 P. Spear, *The Nabobs: A Study of the Social Life of the English in Eighteenth-Century India* (London: Oxford University Press, 1963), p. 105.

40 M. Poovey, *Making the Social Body: British Cultural Formation, 1830–64* (London: University of Chicago, 1995), p. 4.

41 J. Mill, *History of British India*, 3 vols. (London: Baldwin, Cradock and Joy, 1818). James Mill was the founder of classical economics along with David Ricardo. More importantly for this story, he was an influential politician at Westminster and was

appointed in 1819 examiner of correspondence at the East India Company where he was influential in reforming the system of government in British India for the next seventeen years.

42 M. Sherwood, *Stories Explanatory of the Church Catechism* (Baltimore, MD: Protestant Episcopal Female Tract Society of Baltimore, 1823), p. 276.

43 S. Morgan, *Bombay Anna* ..., p. 23.

44 J. Rousseau, *Émile: or A Treatise on Education* (1762).

45 Mrs Mary Sherwood quoted in S. Morgan, *Bombay Anna* ..., p. 47.

46 This college was recognised locally because its founders Rammohan Roy, David Hare and Radhakanta Deb, while favouring English instruction and an education that better placed young Bengalis to participate in Company commerce, built this institution on the earlier *tols* (small individually run traditional Indian schools) education of Sanscrit, metaphysics, logic and Eastern literacy. The attached Female Juvenile Society School was for poor Bengali girls.

47 R. Seton, *Western Daughters in Eastern Lands: British Missionary Women in Asia* (Santa Barbara, CA: Praeger, 2013), pp.117–19.

48 W. Adam, 'First Report on Education ...' (1835) in J. A. Richey, *Selections from the Educational Records* (Calcutta: Government Printing, 1922), part ii, p. 40.

49 P. Chapman, *Hindoo Female Education* (London: R. B. Seeley and W. Burnside, 1839), p. 76.

50 Mrs Weitbrecht, *The Women of India and Christian Work in the Zenana* (London: James Nisbet & Co., 1875), p. 153.

51 P. Chapman, *Hindu In Bengal Female Education* (Surrey: L & G Seeley, 1839), p. 92.

52 A. Bell, *Sketch of a National Institution for Training up the Children of the Poor in Moral and Religious Principles, and in Habits of Useful Industry* (London: J. Murray, 1808). Andrew Bell was a Scottish Anglican priest. There had been a strong controversy between the competing Lancaster system and Bell's model, the latter having the unique provenance of being developed in Madras for orphan Eurasian boys. While both systems purported distinctive strategies, their distinctiveness was more about sectarian ownership of the model itself: Bell of the established Church and Lancaster a Quaker. It is probable both these schooling approaches drew partly upon earlier models in the Spanish South American colonies and also in North America. Jana Tschurenev even sees links with Francke's pietistic pedagogy as practised by German missionaries stationed at Tranquebar (near Madras, southeast India). J. Tschurenev, 'Diffusing Useful Knowledge: The Monitorial System of Education in Madras, London and Bengal, 1789–1840', *Paedagogica Historica*, 44:3 (2008), 260.

53 P. C. Mitra, *A Biographical Sketch of David Hare* (Basumati Sahitya Mandir, 1877) in J. A. Richey, *Selections*, ii, p. 35.

54 J. Long [CMS], *Handbook of the Bengal Missions in Connection with the Church of England* (London: John Shaw, 1848), pp. 439–40.

55 Mrs Weitbrecht, *The Women of India and Christian Work in the Zenana* (London: James Nisbet & Co., 1875), p. 167. Bird was a sister of an East India Company official.

56 A. Howell, *Education in British India* ... in J. A. Richey, *Selections* ..., ii, p. 46.

57 Rev. Krishna Mohan Bannerjee in J. A. Richey, *Selections* ..., ii, p. 45.

58 This new venture happened after the death of her husband in India. Mrs Weitbrecht, *The Women of India and Christian Work in the Zenana* (London: James Nisbet & Co., 1875), p. 163.

59 B. Simon, *The Two Nations and the Educational Structure 1780–1870* (London: Lawrence & Wishart, 1974), p. 183.

60 B. Bubacz 'The Female and Orphan Schools in New South Wales, 1801–50'. PhD thesis, 2007, University of Sydney, p. 11.

61 R. Kipling, *Kim* (London: Macmillan & Co., 1901). 'St Xavier's' was a fictional institution based on a La Martinière school, to be discussed in chapter seven.

62 The *Brahmo Samaj* was founded in 1828 by Ram Mohan Roy. Based originally in Bengal, it held to a universal monotheistic creed that aimed to reform Hindu medieval practices, particularly *sati*, caste and child marriage, that were not seen to be

consistent with the Vedas (sacred ancient Hindu texts). Suffering from much faction-
alism, the organisation grew during the British period and continued on after 1947.

63 'Report of the Commission Appointed to Inquire into the Constitution and Working
of the Lawrence Military Asylums in India' [1871], Appendix, vi. p. 8 (OIOC) L/
Mil/17/5/2295.

64 'General Index' [1824], CI2/O/237/96 CMS Archive, Birmingham (LB).

65 Mrs Weitbrecht, *The Women of India and Christian Work in the Zenana* ..., p. 162.

66 L. M. Stretch, *The Beauties of History or Pictures of Virtue and Vice Drawn from
Real Life* (Paris, 1808), Bodleian Library, Oxford (BLO).

67 Rev. William Deerr to the Secretary [CMS] July 7, 1820 CI/O/88/2 (LB).

68 Banerjea to Bethune (n.d.) in S. Bhattacharya *et al.*, *Development of Women's
Education ... Documents* ... (1849), p. 7.

69 *Journal of the National Indian Association* (November, 1871) no. 11 (OIOC).

70 E. M. Collingham, *Imperial Bodies: The Physical Experience of the Raj, c. 1800–1947*
(Cambridge: Polity, 2001), p. 51.

71 Report of the Bengal Council of Education, 1848–9 in J. A. Richey, *Selections from
the Education Records* (Calcutta: Government Printing, 1922), ii, p. 48.

72 L. Zastoupil and M. Moir, *The Great Education Debate* ..., pp. 39–45.

73 W. Adam, 'Reports on the State of Education in Bengal 1835 and 1838 ...'
reprinted in A. Basu, *Reports on the State of Education in Bengal 1835 and 1838*
(Calcutta: Government Printing, 1944), p. xxiii.

74 See, for example [L. Wilkinson] *A Brief Notice of the Late Mr Lancelot Wilkinson of
the Bombay Civil Service with his Opinions on the Education of Natives of India
and on the State of Native Society* (Cornhill: Smith, Elder and Co., 1853).

75 T. Allender, 'William Arnold and Experimental Education in North India,
1855–59: An Innovative Model of State Schooling', *Historical Studies in Education*,
16:1 (2004), 63–83.

76 H. S. Reid, 'Education Report NWP 1859/60', p. 46 (OIOC) V/24/908.

77 H. S. Reid, 'Education Report NWP, 1858/9', pp. 46–55; H. S Reid, *Education Report
NWP, 1860/1* pp. 29–33 (OIOC) V/24/908.

78 NWP Provincial Evidence, *Hunter Commission* ..., 1884, p. 34.

79 Secretary of State, Despatch, April 7, 1859 Collections to Despatches (Home) 1870
no. 4 (OIOC).

80 Their reports survive in the Punjab Secretariat Archive in Lahore; a converted building that was originally a tomb built by a remorseful Emperor Akbar for his executed
mistress, Anārkalī. Akbar had reputedly had Anārkalī, a favoured member of his
harem, buried alive after falsely accusing her of having an affair with his son.

81 'Abstract Statement of Female Schools Established in the Punjab 1857/8' Punjab
Secretariat Library, Anarkali's Tomb, Lahore, Pakistan. See also in this archive E. H.
Paske to W. Arnold, March 3, 1859 and for 'indigenous' boys 'Education', July 31,
1858 nos. 131–58, as well as various other correspondence between Arnold and his
sub-deputy inspectors.

82 W. Arnold, 'Abstract Statement of Female Schools Established in the Punjab in
the Year 1857/8', incld. in 'Education [Report]', July 31, 1858, no. 131–58, Punjab
Secretariat Archives, Anarkali's Tomb.

83 'Native Education Articles', Elphinstone Papers, Oriental and India Office Collections,
British Library (OIOC) MSS Eur F 87/109; George Jerves, Native Education Society to
the Government of Bombay, December 14, 1827 (OIOC), P/346/43.

84 A. Howell, *Education in British India, Prior to 1854, and in 1870–71* (Calcutta,
Government Printing, 1872), pp. 62–3.

85 Secretary of State, Despatch, April 7, 1859 Collections to Despatches (Home) 1870
no. 4 (OIOC) P/434/35.

86 C. A. Bayly, *Empire and Information* ..., pp. 257–60.

87 The *Bostan* and the *Gulistan* are two critically important texts written by Sheikh
Sa'adn in the twelfth century. Together they constitute the primary textbooks for any
child learning Persian from the age of five years of age upwards. They were also considered by many Indians to be the primary textbooks for training in ethics and morals.

88 Veeresalingam in his Telugu monthly *Viveka Vardhini* (February, 1875) in S. Bhattacharya *et al.*, *Development of Women's Education ... Documents ...* p. 68.
89 A. M. Monteath, 'Note on the State of Education in India, 1865–66' in S. Bhattacharya *et al.*, *Development of Women's Education ... Documents ...* pp. 50–2.
90 'Report on Public Instruction, Oudh, 1877' in S. Bhattacharya *et al.*, *Development of Women's Education ... Documents ...*, p. 71.
91 C. A. Martin, 'General Report on Public Instruction in Assam, 1877–78' in S. Bhattacharya *et al.*, *Development of Women's Education ... Documents ...* p. 71.
92 T. Allender, 'Anglican Evangelism in North India and the Punjabi Missionary Classroom: The Failure to Educate "the Masses", 1860–77', *History of Education*, 32: 3 (May, 2003), 273–88.
93 W. W. Hunter, *Report of the Hunter Commission* (Calcutta; Government Printing, 1884), pp. 536–7.
94 A. M. Monteath, 'A Note on the State of Education ...', Government of India Proceedings, June, 1867, no. 37 in S. Bhattacharya *et al.*, *Development of Women's Education ... Documents ...*, p. 48.
95 E. B. Wace and F. C. Bourne, 'Montgomery District, part A', *Punjab District Gazetteers*. Lahore: Government Printing, 1935 [1933 revised edition], vol. xviii, p. 107. The community contained the lineal descendants of Nanak, the putative first Sikh guru, and they commanded notable loyalty among Sikhs in this and adjacent districts.
96 Sec. of the Chief Commissioner to R. Montgomery, September 19, 1853, no. 263, 'Minute on Infanticide in the Punjab', Lahore: *Chronicle Press*, 1853, no. xvi, p. 404 (OIOC) V/23/335.
97 R. C. Temple, *Panjab Notes and Queries: A Monthly Periodical* (London: Trubner & Co., n.d.), vol. ii, Cambridge Brotherhood Mission Archives, New Delhi (CBMA).
98 D. McLeod to R. Montgomery, April 15, 1854, no. 99; R. Montgomery, 'Selections of the Records ...' (OIOC) V/23/335.
99 A brief and inaccurate account of provincial attempts to deal with female infanticide can be found in L. J. Trotter, *Lord Lawrence: A Sketch of His Public Career* (London: Allen & Co., 1880), pp. 35–7.
100 Director to the Sec. to the Government of the Punjab, July 31, 1865, no. 20 (OIOC) P/239/39; Fuller, A. R. 'Education Report for the Punjab ... 1863/4' (1864), p. 35 V/24/929.
101 In the month the Lieutenant Governor retired, the paymaster general could not approve any more funding from the fund for female schools for this reason. Director to Sec. to the Government of the Punjab, January 23, 1865 no. 14 (OIOC) P/239/39. By June 1865 even recurrent expenditure was proving a problem for the overburdened fund, with outgoings for female and town schools increasing to three times normal incoming revenue. In this month outgoings had leapt to Rs.60,059 while monthly incoming revenue was just Rs.21,382 'General Journal and Ledger (Punjab)' (OIOC) P/442/56.
102 T. Allender, 'Robert Montgomery and the Koree Mar (Daughter Slayers): A Punjabi Educational Imperative, 1855–65', *South Asia-Journal of South Asian Studies* (2002), 97–119.
103 T. Allender, *Ruling Through Education* (New Delhi: Sterling, 2006), pp. 35–43.
104 Sher Khan's administration in north India represented a brief interregnum in Mughal rule after his defeat of the Mughal emperor Humayun in 1540.
105 J. S. Hurt, *Elementary Schooling and the Working Classes*. (London: Routledge, 1979), pp. 10–15.
106 C. Mohanty, 'Cartographies of Struggle' in C. Mohanty, A. Russo and L. Torres (eds), *Third World Women and the Politics of Feminism* (Bloomington, IN: Indiana University Press, 1991), pp. 14–15.
107 See, for example, 'Review of the Reports on Municipal Administration [Punjab] ... 1876–77', May, 20, 1878 no. 87 (OIOC) P/1146.

CHAPTER TWO

Shaping a new Eurasian moral body, 1840–67

Female schooling took a new turn in the mid-nineteenth century, driven primarily by concern about the education of Eurasian females. This change imperfectly connected and fragmented Western paradigms about female education, moving them away from the early missionary focus on Indian female scholars. State anxieties regarding the Eurasian female body were responsive to new imperial mentalities about the educated female in India. This focus on Eurasian education would serve to direct other networks to the site of the raj female classroom and orient it towards a new recipient Eurasian cohort for the rest of the century.

This development did not produce a 'policy' change by the East India Company, because there was little earlier cogency, which could be called 'policy', in Company determinations concerning its attitudes towards Indian females regarding their interaction with Europeans. As already discussed, between 1813 and 1854, colonial education of Indian girls, although differentiated by gender, was placed at the edges of other centres newly built by new forms of colonial intervention. Such centres included the CMS proselytising agenda in Bengal, and the very different orientalist-inspired village school experimentation in north India and in Bombay. However, in the late 1850s, the question of Eurasian females configured 'female education' as a new official focus and, as a consequence, it began to be scrutinised as a facet of state policy.

By the 1850s, the East India Company, new missionaries, and officials at Westminster, had already assigned the rich and differentiated Indian female learning heritage to a Western-conceived periphery. In the 1820s and 1830s these colonial agencies had failed to follow the only likely avenue of success: namely, to engage Indian communities and their intellectual stakeholders and encourage them to follow earlier orientalist overtures into a shared and negotiated female learning space. The NWP and Bombay approaches would finally be set aside in

the 1860s. While British and other colonisers in India had imposed artificially rigid delineations around language and caste, which then contributed to the British view of the inaccessibility of the Indian female.[1]
To cover over this simplified view, the colonial state identified 'local
prejudice' and the 'barriers of purdah' as convenient administrative reasons for relegating education for Indian girls from its funding regime.
Such phrases litter the formal communications of the 1850s, including those sent back to London. This stereotyping was indicative of a
broader impasse first marked out by the missions in both Bengal and
Madras two generations earlier. It was also symptomatic of a new colonial state mindset that refused any more to acknowledge local practice,
or what the East India Company had earlier, crudely, identified as some
kind of unacceptable 'Brahmatical' intellectual custodianship over the
education of Indian females.[2]

A deeper conceptual but unrecognised difficulty also confronted the
British mid-century. Overarching imperial social formation ideas had
emerged from the ongoing colonial relationship. Shared conceptions
had solidified around new English/Indian categorisations concerning
key phenomena such as the 'middle-class'.[3] For the Indian middle-class,
known as the *bhadralok* in Bengal, education was now identified as an
essential part of social reform. Mrinalini Sinha's analysis of the binary
'effeminate Bengali' and the 'manly Englishman' illustrates another key
aspect of this powerful new imperial social formation. As she asserts, the
formation was a response to new political and economic realities of the
latter half of the nineteenth century that were part of the ongoing relational rearticulation between 'coloniser' and 'colonised'.[4] The evangelical missions also played their part in establishing a new European social
separateness from most Indians by the 1850s, one that ignored deeper
Indian socio-cultural and gender complexity and diversity. The missions directly linked the European moral body and its supposed physical
decline to cohabitation with Indian mistresses and the over-stimulation
of India's heat, with resulting overpopulation borne from a lack of moral
restraint.[5] With this new perspective, educational questions, particularly
regarding females, were now problematic for the colonial state, if viewed
only in Indian terms. To compensate for this, new state socio-cultural
configurations were applied, well before developing models of European
schooling for girls had a chance to make their mark on the subcontinent.

Soldier fathers

There was one significant qualification regarding this development.
In the 1850s a key rupture occurred within the new shared language
between European and complicit Indian participants in the colonial

interchange. It was around the issue of race. Put briefly, at this time Company disquiet about Eurasian children stemmed mostly from a concern that, if they became vagrants, or aberrant in other ways, Indian elites would blame it on their miscegenated European 'blood'. If this happened, it would damage any English claim to be racially superior or to be pursuing a valid colonial mission. As a polemic concerning race rather than gender, this was one of the few issues that compelled the colonial state to later consider girls as well as boys in its policy declarations. The race issue also had a long history that involved the likely paternity of fathers who were soldiers. This story is important because it laid another foundation for female education in India and would eventually justify the very strong, but unpublicised, Eurasian racial boundary placed around female education in the early 1880s.

The first part of the story of Eurasian female education is the dispossession of this entire raj-based racial grouping. In the late eighteenth century, employment of Eurasian males by the East India Company had steadily become more restrictive as a result of directives from the Court of Directors in London. For example, in 1780 all Company postings were open to Eurasians, but in 1792 employment in the European branches of the civil and marine services was barred to them. In 1795 this restriction was extended to the army, except for 'pipers, drummers and bandsmen'. Furthermore, in the 1820s the CMS in Calcutta discouraged Eurasians from joining its ranks as pastors, perceiving this population to be 'cantankerous' and unconditioned to the verities of European biblical revivalism.[6] Even so, this evangelical mission was concerned about the social consequences of the clumsy salary distinctions now being made by the Company, which put Eurasians on much lower pay rates than Europeans.[7] Such distinctions bred resentment, especially among those Eurasians who had been brought up in expensive European households with fathers who had 'accustomed [them] to the same comforts'.[8]

As part of the move to disassociate itself from Eurasians, in 1786 the Court of Directors turned its attention to education. It banned graduating Eurasian 'orphan' school children from travelling to England to further their studies.[9] Eurasian daughters of high-ranking Company officials had previously done so to further their prospects, although at least some then returned to India as the only means of securing a European husband.[10] The mentality behind this ban sat uncomfortably with the Eastern cultural gifting emblematic of late Georgian and Regency England, where sanitised 'oriental' motifs adorned the great houses of the aristocracy, not least the Prince Regent's pavilion folly in Brighton.

Not all Europeans in India were a party to these regressive racialised Company policies. European soldiers serving there in the first half of the nineteenth century were a strong countervailing agency. Many of them naturally developed strong attachments to the Eurasian children they fathered, living at close quarters with their mistresses in the squalid cantonments of the large towns and other travelling military outposts. Most soldiers knew these arrangements were likely to be temporary: if they were not killed, they were often redeployed elsewhere in India and sometimes their service took them to other parts of the empire or even back to a new married life in England. Leaving the children they had fathered in India to uncertain futures could be a wrenching experience and generated emotion at a personal level, rather than from a broader social conscience.[11]

The fate of the children of soldiers remained precarious, as they were left to eke out an existence by tapping into irregular through trade in the town markets and bazaars. Christian orphanages, such as Mary Sherwood's institution in Cawnpore, took pity on abandoned Eurasian girls on the grounds of the neglect of their European fathers. Sherwood saw such neglect as especially culpable, given that these same fathers had earlier, presumably, been conditioned by the feminine Christian benevolence of their own mothers and sisters.[12] The emphasis here was not on the masculinity of these soldiers, but rather on a failure of their actions in adulthood to truly reflect the transmission of feminine moral virtue. Company 'orphanages' were also set up in Calcutta and other major urban centres, where children could receive shelter while they were organised according to the rank of their fathers: Upper Orphanages for the children of officers and Lower Orphanages for the children of 'other ranks'.[13] However, without education and with new and largely hidden racial bars in place in favour of Europeans for government and colonial employment, such children still had poor prospects.

The problem of Eurasian children led the military generally to strongly lobby the Company to provide a more systematic approach for their support. In addition to any token monies that soldiers might thrust into the hands of their Indian or Eurasian partners, was the possibility of providing these Eurasian children with some kind of elementary education. An education might at least allow them to use basic literacy and numeracy skills to get ahead in a world that, because of their parentage, necessitated some degree of attachment to the raj, since they could not belong to the surrounding Indian communities. The only possibility for these fathers was to send their children to the mission schools, but these schools needed to be nearby and the missions were selective as to which prospective scholars might be most ripe for conversion. Mission fees were also relatively high, because most such schools needed to subsidise their captive famine orphan students who were Indians.[14]

The military philanthropy lobby also worked to overly simplify and rigidify colonial conceptions of race, a typical product of the British and other empires. Adrian Carton describes racial hybridity as a key component of race making along gender, religious and citizenship lines as early as the eighteenth century in French, Portuguese and British India.[15] The British and Indian armies in India, themselves, were sites of increasingly rigid racial categorisations.[16] And what followed, partly in response to the lobbying of the military regarding 'Eurasian' schooling, was an eventual official racial stratification based on which girls might have access to colonial female schooling.

Building asylums

Against the backdrop of gradual Company disassociation from Eurasians, new possibilities for the education of some Eurasian children were offered by the development of asylums. In their pursuit of profit, Company officials rarely acted out of philanthropy in this period. However, these officials knew that offering even very meagre funding for soldiers' children could act to uphold regimental morale; morale already sorely tested by the privations and dangerous diseases associated with the usually long periods of service in India. This exigency eventually produced in some asylums a unique institutional site, developed from the basis of the military asylum, within which Eurasian inmates were not only constructed by race, but also by an arms-length military, as well as fatherly connections of affection and quasi-responsibility. Although the resulting benefaction was very limited, the asylums did create a significant social dynamic that was to produce some unanticipated educational outcomes.

Asylums had strong precedents in both India and England. It was in the Military Asylum at Madras that Bell's monitorial teaching of Eurasian boys had been based in the late eighteenth century. Eurasian girls had in fact been enrolled at this institution a year before the boys in 1788, although they were not 'taught' by this method.[17] The model of the military asylum in India was also powerful enough to prompt the Duke of York to found the Royal Military Asylum thirteen years later at Chelsea in England in 1801 for the destitute families of dead soldiers, and there were subsequent educational outcomes when this institution developed into the first schooling enterprise to receive government funding for elementary education in England in 1812.[18]

As the early nineteenth century progressed, powerful lobbying by the British army resulted in a more structured and a better funded system of asylums in India. With the Company in the mood to cut loose the Eurasian population, the female and male asylums in Madras were amalgamated in 1826 to save money. In the previous twenty years, between 1788 and 1818, funding had tripled to Rs.2,55,849 (£25,584) for the 350 'wards' in residence by 1818; a very large sum by the standards of the day for the Company to provide for any educational institution. Public lotteries were launched to meet these costs, but, even with favourably termed government bonds, there was still a shortfall of just under a third of the total budget. By 1830, across India, asylums were losing their intended philanthropic edge and the Company was tempted to close them all down. However, instead, it was forced to accede to military demands for direct donations from soldiers to keep them afloat. To this end, by 1849, a scheme was provided giving a sliding scale for contributions based on an individual soldier's pay: an officer £5 a year, an ordinary soldier £2 per year per child if they had children in asylum care.[19] This scheme helped the Company out of a difficult financial position, but the arrangements had an uncomfortable downside for Westminster and its missionary lobbyists: the additional financial subsidy carried with it acknowledgement of actual paternity by the soldiers concerned. As financial supporters, soldiers were now given Company permission to acknowledge their children and also to be in regular contact with them while they were still stationed in India. Although, these unusual joint Company-soldier funding arrangements did not, at first, do much for Eurasian female schooling.

Company marginalisation of Eurasians in the early nineteenth century had seen attempts to reconfigure Eurasian girls in socio-cultural terms, especially in its military asylums, by attempting to connect them with their part-Indian heritage. This was not so much the case for the boys, who still had good prospects for employment, particularly in building railways and administering private and public commerce. For Eurasian girls before the 1840s, all the asylums scattered on the edges of British India were little more than orphanages, imitating the bleak poor houses of England. The Company's strategy was to use these institutions as a means for social assimilation of Eurasian girls with Indian communities, by weaning them from their European heritage and then decoupling official responsibility for their future conduct and social situation. A chief signifier of this attempt at assimilation was not the education of these girls but what they were given to eat. For example, in 1826, it was recommended by one superintendent that their diet of bread, milk and tea should be substituted by rice and pepper water. This was done so that

> the children ... would be fed in a manner, both more wholesome and better adapted to their condition in society. It seems evident that the children of the Asylum, in consideration equally of the climate in which

it is their lot to live, and of their prospects in life, should be fed like Natives rather than Europeans, and that a … culpable injury is done to them if in their early years they are led into habits as to diet, which afterwards must be abandoned, or cannot be gratified except with much inconvenience.[20]

To reinforce the hardening racial barrier, the girls were also forbidden to marry European soldiers.[21]

With this official agenda in play, the education of Eurasian girls in military asylums before 1849 was almost completely neglected. One government report observed of one asylum that female education was conducted by 'two Portuguese women, destitute of education, and without knowledge of the world'.[22] At best it was assumed that these Eurasian girls could only be 'trained' as servants, having received an education that even inspecting officers admitted was 'perfectly useless'.[23] Furthermore, this form of social engineering, bereft of education, might well have seen these children relegated to even more impoverished futures as the Company strove to recoup even more of the costs during their time in the asylum, particularly by the 1840s.

State anxieties

One key realisation made mid-century changed the fate of at least some Eurasians and, in doing so, attracted new forms of educational practice to some military asylums in India. It related to changing Eurasian demographics, which alarmed Westminster and those conducting central governance in Calcutta. The Company continued to recognise, in cold terms, that the Eurasian population was a collateral social consequence of its own occupation of the subcontinent. However, after the Great Revolt in 1857, and perhaps as a direct consequence of it, the raj saw new alarm in the potential of the Eurasian population (mostly outside the asylums) to grow to numbers that could threaten the very power base of the raj itself.

The Eurasian population was increasing at what the colonial state supposed to be almost twice the rate of the European population; and it was the demographic of child populations that created most official concern. Statistics compiled from Company records before 1865 and presented to parliament at Westminster showed an 'Indo-European' population in each of the two presidency towns of Bombay and Calcutta that comprised many more children than did their European counterparts. For example, Bombay had only a tenth of the Eurasian population in India, but 32 per cent of these Eurasians were children under the age of fourteen, compared to just 13 per cent for the European population.

In Calcutta, the Eurasian population under the age of eleven was 25 per cent of this population, compared to 16 per cent of children of the same age in the European population. There was one other portent regarding the future demographic: while the adult gender balance among Eurasians at this time was roughly equal, for Europeans, even in the 1860s, the ratio of males to females was still almost three to one in Calcutta and over five to one in Bombay.[24]

These figures suggested to the Company that a potentially uncontrollably large future Eurasian population would require some kind of social regulation based on a codified and unified Western education remedy. New official concern in post-Revolt India about what were considered to be ever increasing numbers of louche and vagrant Eurasians led the Viceroy, Lord Canning, to issue a key despatch in 1860, which read in part:

> If measures for educating these children are not promptly and vigorously encouraged and aided by the Government, we shall soon find ourselves embarrassed in all large towns and stations with a floating population of Indianized English, loosely brought up, and exhibiting the worst qualities of both races ... I can hardly imagine a more profitless, unmanageable community than one so composed ... it could be called a class dangerous to the State.[25]

The government envisaged the future of educated Eurasian boys, 'acquainted with Native languages' to be as much needed employees for British planters 'to extend the commerce and manufactures of Great Britain and Europe in the East'.[26] However, the future for Eurasian girls lay as teachers of 'good character and training', badly needed, according to Canning, '[to] bring their talents to so uncertain and ... so discouraging a field of labour'.[27]

The Lawrence military asylums

The turnaround in official attitude regarding Eurasian girls was relatively sudden. It was not driven by Western eugenic thought, which was a later development, although the Eurasian governance experience in India may have influenced the thinking of Herbert Spencer and others at the metropole. The argument in India about the social control of Eurasian girls through education was drawn from actual experimental practice at another institutional site that was also known to government through its military arm: a special type of the asylum, the Lawrence military asylum.

Lawrence military asylums were a special form of institutionalisation for European and Eurasian children. They were established from

1847 onwards and, like the asylum model before them, were only for the children of European soldiers and not for all Eurasians. These institutions were set up by Henry Lawrence, partly funded by his benefaction and partly by direct imperial grant. Lawrence became famous throughout the empire, mostly because of his death at the siege of Lucknow in 1857.[28] His brother was John Lawrence, Viceroy of India, 1864–9. Both brothers were known for their sensitivity, by contemporary British standards, for Indian affairs in the prickly business of consolidating the north after the two Sikh wars (1845–6, 1848–9).[29] The four asylums established in Henry Lawrence's name were in north Indian hill stations: at Sanawar (adjacent to the north Indian city of Patiala); Mount Abu in present day Rajasthan; Murree (now in Pakistan, just north of Islamabad); and at Lovedale (in the state now known as Tamil Nadu) in south India. Their purpose was to remove children from 'the debilitating influences of a tropical climate and the demoralising effects of barrack life'.[30]

These institutions were contained within impressive buildings, but were run with an air of the regiment about them. At a superficial level they appeared close to Western models of schooling, yet they inherited, and then reconfigured, the earlier socio-cultural bearing of colonial female education in India. For example, in 1849 the Lawrence asylum establishment at Sanawar was described as:

> A large upper-roomed building of stone, with a shingle roof containing a spacious school room used also as a chapel, 5 other rooms of similar dimensions capable of accommodating another 200 children and rooms for pupil teachers.[31]

Each older boy and girl was responsible for the personal cleanliness and neatness of the younger children and the girls were given a uniform of 'English print, cambric bonnets and pelerines [short capes]'.[32]

These were important steps towards realigning Eurasian education with the forms of European, rather than Indian, education. New funding from soldiers also made the reconfiguration possible. In a photograph taken for Western consumption, the new European order is clear, although the girls' shaded faces suspiciously veil the true racial makeup of much of the enrolment.

There is also strong evidence that personal attachment between parents and their children was acknowledged and encouraged. Fathers who were soldiers, and Eurasian or Indian mothers, were able to stay at these asylums in adjacent bungalows for up to two weeks, provided they brought their own bedding, food supplies and were willing to share accommodation with other parents.[33] The parental links and more sympathetic superintendence by institutional managers also

Figure 2 Lawrence Military Asylum, Sanawar. Eurasian girls in the shade. © The British Library Board, Photo 703/(32).

encouraged filial connection. Furthermore, this was a powerful new context for learning, particularly given the marginalisation of girls in earlier asylum institutions.

The 'Lawrence' asylum now became a metaphor for combined Company 'efficiency' with a quasi-Western domesticity. For example, in 1853, the Fourth Report described the Sanawar Lawrence Asylum as:

> very much that of a well ordered regiment, modified to meet the peculiarities and imperfections of childhood, by an infusion of the milder sway of the domestic hearth.[34]

Official recognition was tempered by the condition of the child, still not as 'learner', but as worthy of protection without a religious, commercial or broader social purpose. There were also children of entirely European origin in the Lawrence asylums. Their mixing with many 'illegitimate' Eurasian children revealed a new raj capacity, by the latter 1850s, not only to accommodate cultural hybridity but also to transcend moral boundaries concerning racial intermixture, as well as illegitimacy, in a way that was not yet possible in Europe.

What eventually developed out of this institutional site was a new form of education for girls. Fathers who were soldiers and European parents wanted futures for their daughters that went beyond their child's time in the asylum. As a result, a differentiated European curriculum was introduced that taught more than basic literacy and numeracy. Girls, along with the boys, now began studying formal academic subjects in co-educational classes at least three days a week.[35] These subjects included English history, geography, arithmetic and geometry. Senior girls also learnt Urdu in the two most northern Lawrence asylums, a language still only the preserve of upper-class males in traditional Indian societies.[36]

The mixed curriculum of overlapping boys' and girls' instruction was not yet about gender scholastic equivalence. It was mostly driven by an institutional necessity to combine classes given a shortage of staff. However, it was significant that this learning formation for Eurasian girls, like their diet, was now on European and not Indian terms. The new curriculum also replaced the 'sewing' and 'laundry classes' of earlier asylums, which had been dull fare mostly about female child exploitation and the need to provide external 'orphanage' income.

Now, instead of sewing and laundry, there were new female subjects. On the remaining two days of the week girls learnt 'needlework' and 'drawing', seemingly following European accomplishments, although 'accomplishments' was yet to be formalised as a feminine academic approach across raj India. These additional 'subjects', though more rarefied than before, were still utilitarian, but now the focus was on institutional, rather than commercial, benefit. For example, needlework included mending school clothes. Other female student time was taken up with classes on 'neatness' and on tending to the infants also 'enrolled' in the Lawrence asylum. Furthermore, the boys learnt 'cooking' as a similar institutional service, which again illustrates that a gender curriculum boundary had yet to be fully formalised.[37]

There was something immediately attractive about the Lawrence asylums when compared with what had gone before for institutionalised poor children, and what was still happening elsewhere in India. The likes of the doughty and long-serving Mr and Mrs Mellor at Sanawar, and their assistant schoolmistresses recruited in India, ensured that the Lawrence asylums were relatively commodious and well-run institutions; they were receptive spaces that allowed the focus to be on teaching. The Lawrence asylums were also about community building, based on socio-cultural inclusion, and were refuges from a world in which colonial commerce was particularly aggressive in robbing children of their identity and dignity, often as slave labour in the cotton, tea and indigo plantations. Such community building was perhaps the most valuable contribution of these new institutions.

In educational terms, the Lawrence asylums were distinguished by the pedagogy they imported into their community context which will be elaborated upon in the following pages. In contemporary government reports, 'monitorialism' gave way to increasing mention of female teachers, designated with some formal training and often warranting identification by name. These positions were still mostly based on marriage and personal patronage, rather than qualifications, although the husbands of these teachers, also recruited by the asylums, usually had some teaching experience in government and mission colleges.[38]

The school classes of the women teachers in the Lawrence asylums still comprised strong elements of mechanical exposition and teacher didacticism, particularly concerning the learning of mental arithmetic and Roman copperplate writing style. However, their stronger discipline-specific teaching in English history, European geography and Western-derived geometry softened this form of schooling. Most significant was an emphasis on new pedagogy, which is remarkably apparent through the imperfect filter of contemporary inspectors' reports, which usually ignored such detail.

> When a question is proposed by the teacher, the children prepared with an answer hold up their right hands and the teacher then calls upon another and so on until the correct answer is obtained. The incorrect answers are made useful by being analysed and proved to be ridiculous or imperfect, thus suggesting further explanation by the teacher ... The principles are fully explained before any riddles are given. Everything is clearly demonstrated on the blackboard ... The children work the exercises on their slates, and take part in the work of investigation by giving simultaneous answers to questions. The lowest classes are taught to count and calculate with abacus. The whole of the classes are well practised in mental arithmetic, adapted to both English and Indian currency &c. These exercises do not consist of mere rules and sums, but embrace all the principal properties and relations of numbers.[39]

Looking through the window of the raj classroom in this way was exceptionally rare in government reportage throughout the whole British period. That government inspectors elaborated at all about this new pedagogy is testament to the impression that such new teaching made upon them. The voice of the child learner may still have been stilted, but these institutions understood the significance of teaching innovation enough to attract the attention of inspectors who usually only concerned themselves with school building conditions, the composition of enrolments based on age, religion and gender, and examination results. The Lawrence asylum at Sanawar, in particular, melded innovative pedagogy with more clearly defined disciplinary procedure, with girls and boys actually sharing a large part of the curriculum. Furthermore, the element of learning through deduction and reasoning was a clear departure from the earlier monitorial method.

The early powerful force for pedagogical innovation in the Lawrence asylums came directly from England via two separate avenues of army connection. The first of these was Edwin Rodgers, an influential custodian appointed as headmaster of the Lawrence asylum at Sanawar in the northern Punjab. Rodgers had the unusual career profile of an earlier education at the Chelsea Normal (teacher training) College in England, then becoming a schoolmaster of the 87th Fusiliers in India.[40] Other headmasters and their wives also had teacher training and military backgrounds.

The second avenue promoting innovation was the direct recruitment of young teachers by the Lawrence asylum at Sanawar from a key teaching institution in England: the Norwood school for 'pauper' children in London, which had a teacher training branch attached to it.[41] The decision to recruit from the Norwood Normal school was no accident. A generation earlier, James Kay-Shuttleworth, first Permanent Secretary of the Education Office in London (1839–49), had elevated the normal school, through hard-fought-for government funding, to supply workhouses with trained teachers for the destitute. Kay-Shuttleworth saw the authority of the state as the best means to protect society from moral evil. Destitute children in the workhouse were still classified in England in highly pejorative terms – the offspring of 'felons', 'cripples', 'idiots' and 'bastards'.[42] Through Norwood, Kay-Shuttleworth sought to encourage teaching in England according to new Scottish, Prussian and French practices. Classes of forty or fifty were created based on age, suitable desks were provided and separate partitions constructed. Norwood teaching was recognised by government reports as bringing pupils 'gently and smoothly to understanding' and 'to sound moral values' by not burdening the memory with ill-understood facts nor subjecting pupils to corporal punishment or other unnecessary forms of coercion.[43]

Norwood's female clientele, despite Kay-Shuttleworth's pessimistic description of them as being almost all 'plain' in appearance, had qualities that were attractive to army officers seeking to recruit teachers to the Lawrence asylums in India.[44] With the status of 'pauper', rather than 'poor', these teachers, some as young as seventeen, had an ongoing 'poverty' status themselves. Furthermore, their need for work as newly 'trained' teachers with limited professional avenues meant that at least some of them were willing to endure the poor professional conditions of India. Their impoverished backgrounds did not equip all Norwood teachers for the giant social leap involved in relocating to India. At least one prospective Norwood female teacher was sent back to England upon landing at Bombay because of her exhibiting 'so unpromising a disposition during her voyage'.[45] However, the new pedagogy that these very young teachers brought with them was probably a direct reproduction of the manner in which they themselves had been recently taught.

Rodgers and his army teacher colleagues already knew the value of the application of the new educational practices developed at Norwood. In the Indian Lawrence asylums, these new young teachers and experienced army personnel now worked in effective combination for the first time, sharing a staff common room and willing to try new teaching approaches together. The noteworthy ideas of Thomas Tate and Johann Pestalozzi were also directly applied within the Lawrence classrooms.[46] Thomas Tate's Forgotten Philosophy of Education, published in 1857, was one of the first works to view the principles of teaching as a philosophy of education that was theoretically based.[47] Tate's approach applied the seventeenth-century philosopher Francis Bacon's idea of 'induction' in science to education settings in all academic subjects. This encouraged student inquiry by the proposing and 'testing' of hypotheses.[48] Tate's work was applied across all academic subjects in the Lawrence asylum at Sanawar at least as early as 1859.[49]

A second teaching philosopher, also explicitly referred to at this time by government inspectors regarding Sanawar, was the prominent eighteenth-century Swiss educational reformer, Johann Pestalozzi.[50] His philosophy, more influential in the USA than in England in the nineteenth century, was that children learnt in individual ways and that a child's education was central to their character formation and their capacity to reason. This necessitated, according to Pestalozzi, child-centred pedagogy. His work at the orphanage at Stans in Austria further commended this approach to those teachers presiding over similarly institutionalised children in India.[51]

No doubt these theories were applied in imperfect ways within the Lawrence asylums. However, their transferred application elevated the Eurasian girls, as well as the boys, as being worthy recipients of such theories in India in the late 1850s and early 1860s. These methods of teaching, particularly their heuristic elements, were also a radical departure from anything previously known in colonial India. Further, they placed the child at the 'centre' of the teaching and learning process and vested in him or her a capacity to learn intuitively, using their own reason.

In practice, greater numbers of the recipients of these new approaches turned out to be girls rather than boys. For example, at Sanawar in 1861, the female enrolment exceeded the previous limit of

200 and was raised to 500.[52] This was made possible because many of the boys found early employment in the survey, sub-medical and telegraph departments as the British consolidated their rule in north India. To cater for the change, all four Lawrence asylums recruited the very few single Eurasian teachers who were female, in their late twenties or early thirties, and available in India at this time. Younger female Eurasian assistants assisted their work, these assistants being willing to be married off quickly to available husbands of officer rank in the nearby barracks.[53]

In essence, the significance of the Lawrence asylums was to codify pedagogy for some Eurasian girls that would then become a yardstick for all female education in India. Institutional approaches to these girls were no longer just in terms of their bodies and concerned with their sanitary or moral rectitude. In a sociological sense, the Lawrence asylums brought these Eurasian girls back into the European fold, linking them with the opportunities available to European girls and not the restricted fare the raj offered to their Indian sisters.

The dynamic of the Lawrence asylum was also powerful enough to place the Eurasian female scholar at the centre of new state policy, with curriculum at its core for the first time in British India. As part of this process, the deficits of the Eurasian scholar 'condition' in India were scrutinised and made ready for 'remedy' from the metropole. This remedy set a different direction for the conception of female education that was now racially based (favouring Eurasians over Indians). The outcome also had embedded within it a new pedagogy with trajectories that would influence curriculum development in colonial schools in India for the rest of the century. Significantly, too, the Lawrence asylums enforced class boundaries within the Eurasian female population itself. Canning's 1860 Despatch prescribed education for all Eurasian girls, although, as drivers of new female education practice, the Lawrence asylum prism restricted this to only the daughters of soldiers who were able to pay for it. Additionally, the state confirmed the Western class distinction applicable to Eurasians. As the Punjab Education Report of 1867 asserted, the Lawrence asylums were not for the

> the children of Sadr Bazaar who are of the class which Ld Canning's Minute had in view, because the general style and arrangements [of the Lawrence Asylums] are unsuited to the requirements of persons of humble circumstances.[54]

These asylums were now new touchstones in terms of teacher praxis, racial grouping and class distinction for Eurasians and they excluded all Indian girls. Networks of soldiers who were fathers reinforced these boundaries, because their patronage and surveillance was limited to warranting better futures for their own daughters and sons.[55] More particularly, as part funder, the state was complicit in these new inclusions and exclusions as to who were the beneficiaries of female education, and its policy formation was now directed by the new categorisations.

By the 1870s the Lawrence asylums lost focus, largely because Henry Lawrence's benefaction began to be eaten up by over-spending and inflation of the rupee. Other agendas also intervened by this time to take the state conception of female education, which the Lawrence asylums had earlier reconfigured, in other directions. These state conceptions are examined in later chapters. However, at the time of Canning's Despatch in 1860, the female classroom at the Lawrence asylums had more or less solidified in its form and subject disciplines along Western lines. While other schools, such as the Anglican Bishop Cotton School in Simla and the Roman Catholic Jesuit St Joseph's College at Darjeeling, both for boys and founded soon after Canning's Despatch, instead imitated the public school ethic in Britain, with European, rather than Eurasian students, being preferred as part of the rising ruling class in India.[56]

Impoverished Eurasians and the Indian female poor

While the Lawrence asylums offered educational possibilities for some Eurasian children, dispossessed and poor Eurasian and Indian female scholars remained ripe for abuse and exploitation. In the second half of the nineteenth century, for poor Eurasian girls, 'Railway' schools were the most likely destination. These were co-educational and managed by local committees under the control of a government officer of the railways.[57] By the 1860s an additional unhealthy arrangement emerged concerning Indian girls in Bengal, which emanated directly from the colonial state itself. Under the direction of the Lieutenant Governor, Sir John Grant, 'night schools' for some 2,500 Indian girls were set up, where fees in kind were paid by female inmates in the form of child labour during the daytime to provide local businesses with cheap raw materials, mostly derived from agricultural products. The state made the local 'gurus' of some *pathshalas* (elementary schools) complicit in this trade by making their salaries dependent on village recruitment of girls in their local areas. The state simultaneously compelled these same 'gurus' themselves to enrol in poorly resourced normal schools so that they could create maps of India, and other basic classroom materials, for more senior schools to use.[58]

Such bogus self-sufficient schemes were justified by the colonial state in India as necessary forms of famine relief. In practice, their distortion of traditional Indian female educational ethics did damage in confirming to Indian elites and village *zamindars* (landlords) the avaricious and exploitative aspects of Western-imposed female educa-tion. The many more anonymous girls and women who found them-selves in 'prison schools' on the subcontinent must have felt this also, although the situation of Britain's own industrial poor children at this time was probably every bit as bad.[59]

Governance from the metropole: Wood's Education Despatch, 1854

By the mid-1850s it was not within the capacity of the India Office in distant London to engage with, understand and appropriate the com-plex, racialised and local developments concerning female education in India of the past half century. Instead, at this central official level in London a more general education policy for India was announced. The following Education Despatch of 1854 resulted in Charles Wood (Secretary of State for India) being lionised in colonial bureaucratic cir-cles for his authorship of this document, even though the uncertain and unsystematic implementation of this Despatch was delayed until the mid-1860s. By the end of the century Wood's Despatch was officially promoted as the most important macro education policy document of the nineteenth century, yet its actual importance in the development of female education was comparatively less than Canning's later 1860 Despatch issued in India. The relevant institutional features of Wood's Despatch will be discussed in the next chapter, although its contrast with what was actually happening in India regarding the education of females in colonial India could not have been more stark. For the first time, through this Despatch, the state did address the institutionalisa-tion of 'female education' as an instrument of socialising policy:

> The importance of female education in India cannot be over-rated ... by this means a far greater impulse is imparted to the educational and moral tone of the people than the education of men ... Government ought to give native female education in India its frank and cordial support.[60]

However, this was Western discourse, and it ignored the already racialised colonial schoolgirl. Wood's Despatch contained pedagogy-free language and the Indian female pupil was only mentioned as a pos-sible future aspiration. Furthermore, the sociology of the Despatch understood little of the female learning space in India, even as it had developed under East India Company rule. The difference in approach regarding female education: Bengal versus NWP and Bombay, as well as Eurasian versus Indian, also went unnoticed. More significantly, however, Wood's Despatch began to promote the role of 'female education' only as mediator of English middle-class moral norms. This promotion now placed the 'native' Indian girl away from the cultural benefits of her own traditional Indian education, even if she had been able to subsequently enter the colonial classroom. These omissions left the field open to new networks of European women, based mostly in Britain, to build other Western philanthropic perspectives; and to an even smaller number of European women activists who were willing to travel to India to engage directly with what was to be actually found on the subcontinent.

Notes

1 N. Dirks, *Castes of Mind: Colonialism and the Making Of Modern India* (Princeton, NJ: Princeton University Press, 2001), *passim*.
2 The best examples of early discursive official Company constructions of the traditional Indian education landscape come from Madras. See, for example, 'A Memorandum of the Proceedings of the Madras Government in the Department of Public Instruction' (OIOC).
3 K. Sangari, 'Relating Histories: Definitions of Literacy, Literature, Gender in Early Nineteenth-Century Calcutta and England' in S. Joshi (ed.), *Rethinking English: Essays in Literature, Language, History* (New Delhi: Trianka, 1991), pp. 32–123.
4 M. Sinha, *Colonial Masculinity: The 'Manly Englishman' and 'the Effeminate Bengali' in the late Nineteenth Century* (Manchester: Manchester University Press, 1995), pp. 1–32.
5 E. M. Collingham, *Imperial Bodies ...*, p. 75.
6 Rev. Deocar Schmid to the Corresponding Committee [CMS] 1826, CI 1/O/255/37 (LB).
7 Rev. Deocar Schmid to the Corresponding Committee [CMS] 1826, CI 1/O/255/37 (LB).
8 Rev. Deocar Schmid to CMS Corresponding Committee, Calcutta 1827, CI 1/O/255/37 (LB).
9 For a more detailed discussion of hardening Company attitudes towards Eurasians in the period see V. Brendon, *Children of the Raj ...*, pp. 43–4.
10 Hornell to Government of Bengal, May 20, 1915, no. 60. Bengal Education Proceedings (OIOC) P/9640.
11 *First Report of the Lawrence Asylum in the Indian Hills for the Orphan and Other Children of European Soldiers Serving or Having Served in India* (Delhi: Gazette Press, n.d.[1849]), p. 29 (OIOC).
12 S. Kelly (ed.), *The Life of Mrs Sherwood* (London: Darton & Co., 1854), p. 427.
13 V. Brendon, *Children of the Raj ...*, p. 44.
14 Rev. Andrew Jetter, Calcutta 'List of CMS Boys' and Girls' Schools in Calcutta', January 20, 1823. CI 1/O/153/23 (BL).
15 A. Carton, *Mixed-Race and Modernity in Colonial India: Changing Concepts of Hybridity Across Empires* (London: Routledge, 2012).
16 H. Streets, *Martial Races: The Military, Race and Masculinity in British Imperial Culture, 1857–1914* (Manchester: Manchester University Press, 2004).
17 A. Bell, 'The Report of the Military Male Orphan Asylum at Madras with its Original Proofs and Vouchers' (London, 1812) (OIOC).
18 A. White, *The Story of Army Education, 1643–1963* (London: George Harrap, 1963), pp. 24–6.

19 *First Report of the Lawrence Asylum in the Indian Hills for the Orphan and Other Children of European Soldiers Serving or Having Served in India* (Delhi: Gazette Press, n.d. [1849]), p. 1 (OIOC).

20 'Report of the Commission Appointed to Inquire into the Constitution and Working of the Lawrence Military Asylums in India' [1871], Appendix, vi. p. 9 (OIOC) L/Mil/17/5/2295.

21 'Report of the Commission ...', Appendix vi. p. 8.

22 'Report of the Commission ...', Appendix vi. p. 8.

23 'Report of the Commission ...', Appendix, vi. pp. 8–10.

24 *Statistical Abstract Relating to British India from 1840 to 1865 (as far as particulars can be stated)* London: Her Majesty's Stationary Office, 1867, p. 3.

25 'Minute by the Governor General, October 29, 1860,', no. 2. Government of India Proceedings (OIOC) P/188/75.

26 'Statement by the Bishop of Calcutta on the subject of Schools for European and Eurasian Children in India for Circulation in the United Kingdom, July 30, 1860,' no. 1, Government of India Proceedings (OIOC) P/188/75.

27 'Minute by the Governor General, October 29, 1860,' no. 2, Government of India Proceedings (OIOC) P/188/75.

28 H. B. Edwardes, *Life of Sir Henry Lawrence* (London: Smith & Elder, 1873).

29 C. Bruce, *John Lawrence: Saviour of India* (Edinburgh, 1893).

30 R. Nathan, *Progress of Education in India 1897/98* (Calcutta: Government Printing, 1904), p. 327 (OIOC) V/24/4430.

31 *First Report of the Lawrence Asylum in the Indian Hills for the Orphan and Other Children of European Soldiers Serving or Having Served in India* (Delhi: Gazette Press, n.d. [1849]), p. 1 (OIOC).

32 *Fourth Report of the Lawrence Asylum in the Indian Hills for the Orphan and Other Children of European Soldiers Serving or Having Served in India* (Sanawar: Institution Press, 1853), p. 6 (OIOC).

33 *First Report of the Lawrence Asylum in the Indian Hills ...*, p. 29.

34 *Fourth Report of the Lawrence Asylum in the Indian Hills ...*, p. 6.

35 R. Nathan, *Progress of Education in India 1897/98* (Calcutta: Government Printing, 1904) p. 358, V/24/4430.

36 R. Nathan, *Progress of Education in India 1897/98 ...*, p. 358.

37 R. Nathan, *Progress of Education in India 1897/98 ...*, p. 358.

38 'Punjab Education Report 1868/9', p. 133 (OIOC) V/24/930.

39 'Inspectors Report' W. Holroyd to Captain Paske July 29, 1859, *Fourth Report of the Lawrence Asylum ...* Appendix III.

40 *Fourth Report of the Lawrence Military Asylum* (Sanawar: Institution Press, 1853) (OIOC).

41 *Fourth Report of the Lawrence Military Asylum ...*

42 R. J. W. Selleck, *James Kay-Shuttleworth: Journey of an Outsider* (London: Woburn Press, 1994), p. 141.

43 'The Training of Pauper Children', Second Report (1839), p. 97. James Phillip Kay to Poor Law Commission, Poor Law Commission Papers, 32/49 cited in R. J. W. Selleck, *James Kay-Shuttleworth ...*, pp. 140–1.

44 R. J. W. Selleck, *James Kay-Shuttleworth ...*, p. 141.

45 *Fourth Report of the Lawrence Asylum ...*, p. 12.

46 *Report of the Lawrence Military Asylum (Sanawar) 1859* (Sanawar: Lawrence Military Asylum Press, 1859), Appendix III, pp. xxvii–xxxiv (OIOC).

47 T. Tate, *The Philosophy of Education or the Principles and Practice of Teaching* (New York: E. L. Kellogg & Co., 1885 [first edition preface dated 1857].

48 J. Chambers, 'Thomas Tate's Forgotten Philosophy of Education', *Educational Theory*, 13: 4 (1964), 309–13.

49 'Report of the Lawrence Military Asylum (Sanawar) 1859' (Sanawar: Lawrence Military Asylum Press, 1859), Appendix III, pp. xxxviii–iv (OIOC).

50 'Report of the Lawrence Military Asylum (Sanawar)..., Appendix III, pp. xxxviii–iv.

51 K. Silber, *Pestalozzi: The Man and His Work* (London: Routledge and Kegan Paul, 1965).
52 *Report of the Lawrence Military Asylum (Sanawar)1861* (Sanawar: Lawrence Military Asylum Press, 1861), p. 2 (OIOC).
53 *Report of the Lawrence Military Asylum ...*, pp. 5–6.
54 'Punjab Education Report 1867/8' p. 57 (OIOC) V/24/930.
55 *First Report of the Lawrence Asylum in the Indian Hills ...*, pp. 1–29.
56 D. E. Dewan, *Education in the Darjeeling Hills: An Historical Survey: 1835–1985* (New Delhi: Indus, 1991). See also E. Buettner, *Empire Families ...*, pp. 77–8.
57 A. Croft, *Review of Education in India in 1886* (Calcutta: Government Printing, 1888) p. 345 (OIOC) V/24/4429.
58 J. Long, 'Introduction', *Adam's Reports on Vernacular Education* (Calcutta: Secretariat Press, 1868), pp. 39–40 (OIOC).
59 See S. Williams, *Poverty, Gender and Life-Cycle under the English Poor Law, 1760–1834* (Suffolk: Woodbridge, Boydell and Brewer, 2011).
60 Charles Wood, 'Despatch from the Court of Directors of the East India Company to the Governor General of India in Council dated the 19th July, 1854' in J. A. Richey *Selections from the Education Records ...*, pt. ii, p. 388.

CHAPTER THREE

Mary Carpenter and feminine 'rescue' from Europe, 1866–77

The 1860s brought new horizons to the subcontinent. Company rule was replaced by direct ministerial responsibility from Westminster. A Secretary of State in London now directly governed India, like Ireland, with a viceregal agency directing central governance *in situ* 'abroad'. The apparent equivalence in procedural authority between India and Ireland seemed to equate both domains. For the British, this justified colouring India pink on the world map, along with the rest of Victoria's Empire, which was pleasing for those who wished to equate territory with imperial power. This tableau was reproduced on durable canvas maps hung in schoolrooms throughout the empire, impressing the new conformity upon a rising generation.[1]

In the 1860s, as a result of the changing nature of contact between the metropole and the subcontinent regarding females generally, a new scene emerged in India that was conducive to a new spirit of Western uniformity regarding the education of women and girls. It was now much easier for European women to travel to the raj – to follow a husband, to seek one out, or to become a part of mission or professional communities. In addition, the opening of the Suez Canal in 1869, and the invention of the telegraph (sea cables running from Cornwall to Bombay), made communication with 'home' much faster.[2] In 1867, just before the opening of Suez, statistics did not discriminate between European females born overseas or in India, and there was no distinction made in the overall tally between women and children.[3] Twenty-four years later, Denzil Ibbetson's 1881 Indian census provided a breakdown of European women born in the UK. By this time there were 1,829 women in Bengal who had been born in Europe, with 2,264 in Bombay and 1,240 in Madras. This was equivalent to 17.23, 16.36 and 21.07 per cent of the adult males born in Europe and resident in each of these provinces, respectively.[4] There were also other women of purely European descent resident in India who had been born in

India, in the USA or in other parts of the empire or Europe. The influx of European women, and the increasing ease of communication with Europe, facilitated greater European cultural transmission to India. This was particularly the case within elite colonial circles regarding English middle-class sensibilities about the woman's relation to the domestic home and to education.

Earlier European enclaves in all the major Indian cities now gave rise to broader social networks through the club and through the domain of the family bungalow. New women's networks of power and influence in colonial female spaces could be directly transferred from England, at the hands of individual women who were in India through choice or for family or other reasons. The new European women arrivals were often married to self-made men of low birth in Britain, who had taken up the opportunity India offered to build their status. Rapid social mobility was made possible by the employment of these European males in carefully ranked official raj positions.[5] As an adjunct to this, their wives, as memsahibs, presided over the home and acted as hostesses, working at building class status for their family that might also lead to future promotion for their husbands. These women were not in India as menials, but were in control of protecting and promoting their family's social standing.[6] Displays of accomplishments were an important part of their work as custodians of European etiquette and middle-class form. Building European social networks in India in this way also had class currency for their eventual permanent return to Europe. Their husbands often retired in their mid-to-late forties, with a lifelong pension and a retirement in Britain that could therefore last for many decades.[7] The price these women paid for this relatively comfortable retirement was spending their younger years in what was often lonely isolation in India, within a very closed white expatriate society.

By 1866 the emerging European social mosaic in India was yet to connect with official developments in education for girls. By this time, new avenues were opening for greater Western transference around girls' schooling. A decade earlier, in 1854, the India Office in London published Charles Wood's Education Despatch, which decreed, in almost formulaic fashion, a bureaucratic apparatus for each province to follow, with only a minimal rationale for the new Western-oriented organisation of education.[8] While the Despatch provided detail to Indian Civil Service (ICS) and Education department personnel in each province, it resulted in over-governance for schooling in general in India.[9] ICS men on the spot now had a bureaucratic formula to enforce, as a matter of routine, that required little spontaneity or responsibility on their part for decision making. The new rigidity meant local sensitivities were more likely to be ignored, even when influential Indian elites or freer

thinking Westerners objected to this formulaic approach.[10] New official standardised approaches emerged that took little account of local
differences at the provincial level. For example, grant-in-aid regulation
was applied to all mission schools with little regard for local circumstances.[11] A uniform linking of village school, *tahsili* (district) school,
college and university education was developed across all India. This
institutional hierarchy was regulated and controlled by scholarships,
school inspection and building grants.

Unitary education departments were established or confirmed in
each province. Among the newly Western-conceived 'duties' of these
departments, a key requisite for each was to tie school inspection and
teacher training closely to the normal (teacher training) school – an additional institution recognised by Wood's Despatch.[12] This development
was significant for the education of women and girls in the new social
context for Westerners in India. In the 1860s Wood's Despatch applied
largely to boy's schooling. However, an important part of it set up a
strong official nexus between teacher training and government inspection that elevated teacher training as a cornerstone of female education
for the rest of the century. Normal schools for boys were ineffective,
largely because they didn't accommodate local language barriers and
because parents found more lucrative occupations for their sons. The
development of normal schools for women and girls was a different
matter, because their purpose resonated with the socio-cultural agenda
the raj had identified for female education by mid-century, most particularly through Canning's more recent 1860 Despatch with its strong
class and race basis.

The new agenda, which fused considerations of schooling for girls
directly with women teacher training, allowed the raj to begin sidestepping altogether the whole business of the schooling of Indian girls.
This was an unplanned consequence. Attempting to embrace Indian
girls in the 1860s would have brought the raj back to the acute cultural
and political difficulties of building Western education for girls from
the bottom up. Such possibilities were no longer available given the
withering away of earlier orientalist approaches to education and the
monopolisation of scarce funding by Eurasian and European schooling that had begun to follow the pattern of the Lawrence asylums.
As a result, demi-official correspondence became concerned with the
importance of teacher training instead.[13]

The new narrative around teacher training was opportune for the
British, because it hid the gap that had, in reality, developed between
the Indian schoolgirl and unofficial raj funding priorities. Now the priority became the selection of 'suitable' young women to act as social
mediators, bringing a semblance of safe feminine propriety, in Western

terms, to the subcontinent. This choice was made at a time of cutbacks in funding in the raj in the wake of declining revenues.[14] The class and race of these young women was central in their selection as trainee teachers, even when most had received only basic primary education. The raj now saw them as potential Western role models in terms of 'character', and not as teachers imparting academic knowledge, even of the kind considered suitable for girls.[15]

For the raj at least, the teacher training of women displaced school education. Government control was to be ensured via central government directed and organised inspection of girls' schools by European women. These new arrangements looked impressive in terms of embracing the new European female vista in the India of the 1860s. The employment of women inspectors could be promoted as innovative and progressive – and well ahead of developments in England. In addition, the new direction of teacher training of women was premised on the stereotyping of Indian schoolgirls as supine, dull and mendacious, thus justifying their exclusion from the education agenda of colonial India. In this, Bengal education inspectors again readily obliged, as one of their reports articulated:

> The [Indian] Female Schools which I have seen consist in general of three to six infants sprawling about and inking their fingers in copying letters on strips of leaves. Sometimes one or two could attempt a very little reading.[16]

Adding to the negative views that marginalised Indian schoolgirls in favour of Western 'trained' female teachers, most of the Bengal inspector reports framed a more general racialised case, arguing that until Indian girls were amenable to Western discipline they could not expect more funding. The fault was seen to lie, not with the state, but with the Indian girls themselves as products of an inferior civilisation.[17] This form of racial and cultural retrenchment overlooked the cultural capital and learning needs that these Indian girls brought to school, which differed from those of their European, and even many of their Eurasian, sisters.

From England

The case for female teacher training in the 1860s and 1870s in India was also powerfully built in England, although the imperatives for doing so, and the networks that facilitated them at Westminster, were of a distinctly different genesis. Though presented as the voice from the 'mother country', this was not a unified voice. In England ideas about women teacher training, as they related to colonial India, developed from three distinct but overlapping corners: a distortion of Indian scholarship; feminist critiques; and, lastly, the Unitarian, Mary Carpenter's influential narratives, on which this chapter concentrates. However, the distinction made in India in favour of Eurasians was not a part of any of these three approaches.

The first of these three imperatives, a seeming hybridity of Indian scholarship, was constructed by the utterances and writings of several Indian intellectuals travelling in Europe. The most significant example was Keshub Chunder Sen, formerly a member of the Brahmo Samaj, who visited England for six months in 1870.[18] He urged further expansion of colonial education in the fight against *sati*, child marriage and caste. Like much of the Brahmo Samaj ideology, this Indian aspiration concerning Indian women was framed in terms of the confluence of West and East.[19] Sen's lecture tours and brief stays in the houses of European patrons were not sufficient to protect his arguments from being skewed by philanthropically interested English audiences receptive to his view. This distortion objectified Indian woman in ways that Sen did not endorse. After his visit to England, Sen was discouraged by how little the English were interested in the capacity of the Hindu reform movement – still distinct from an unreformed Christianity as he saw it – to embrace monotheism in order to embark on its own reform project in India.[20] While networks of interested European women in Britain did not attempt to renegotiate the Christian ethic of empire, they began to think about how the learning space for Indian females might be refined using an explicitly Western 'remedy' for what they saw as Indian deficiencies.

The more sophisticated British narratives about the deficiency of the Indian female fed into a growing British enthusiasm for popular imperialism. Articulating these deficiencies by reworking the ideology of the Brahmo Samaj, in particular, proved a new approach for English philanthropists in Britain. This produced a view on Indian women that rankled with some politicians at Westminster, who were increasingly obliged to receive well-meaning deputations from the burgeoning committees of women based in Britain that organised around aspects of empire. The European hybrid perspective on Indian women, which used the views of Indian reformers selectively, also meant that Western deliberations with Indian reformers could not now really deepen beyond the superficial contours of thought already established by the missionary lobby.

The second imperative, formed around feminist critique, concerned the views of English and American feminists such as Elizabeth Adelaide Manning, Josephine Butler, Elizabeth Andrew and Katharine Bushnell. These women saw the 'uneducated' and secluded Indian

woman as labouring under both oppressive Indian and colonial patriarchies.[21] While emerging Western feminist arguments such as these
about gender power relations held little sway in a still largely separate
India, they did provide useful vignettes 'at home' to build a broader
case of female oppression and inequality around the world. As Ware
argues, such ideas helped to consolidate feminism in Britain.[22] For the
Indian women resident in India, however, they merely served as distant obfuscation, because they built on a perspective that was still only
germane to Britain and the West and that justified, as Burton argues, a
metropolitan-based 'professional authority' over Indian women.[23] For
the Indian schoolgirl, however, what was applicable was the way in
which she was ignored by a raj that was engaged in a different struggle
based on its own race, class and moral objectives.

Mary Carpenter

If interested women were prepared to travel to India, there was scope
to take arguments about female education further. Actual experience
in the field could deepen their understanding about the 'condition' of
the Indian female, even though this travel was still mostly for consumption at the metropole. As chapter one shows, women evangelical missionaries had distorted some of this understanding as part of
their evangelising agendas in India two generation earlier. By the late
1860s, however, relatively high-profile European women travelling to
India, as part of a new influx of European women to the subcontinent,
could achieve something new. In a spirit of conveying 'one racial motherhood', the individual identity of these high-profile women could also
suggest forms of agency to other women active in education in India;
forms that were separate from the state, particularly when responding
in India to raj policymaking.[24]

One key woman whose work mostly lay outside the regular missionary agenda was Mary Carpenter. Belonging to the generation before
Annie Besant, Carpenter was to prove one of the most influential of
all European women concerning colonial female education on the subcontinent in the mid-nineteenth century. She was also to be one of the
most disruptive: eventually, but unintentionally, forcing the state to
return custodianship of female education to the mission compound
after 1875.

Carpenter's influence was powerful. Her father's friendship with Ram
Mohan Roy, and her own association with Satyendranath Tagore and
Keshub Sen, gave her a sense of entitlement when writing and speaking
publically on Indian affairs.[25] Yet she ignored Sen's criticism of evangelism in India and his representation of the materialism and corruption – a

modern Sodom and Gomorrah as he saw it – of Christian England.[26] Carpenter made a total of four visits to the subcontinent between 1866 and her death in 1877, with her first being at the age of fifty.

In England, Carpenter had not been educated in accomplishments but in her father's Unitarian boarding school, along with the boys, in the sciences, mathematics, Latin and Greek. She was active in the anti-slavery movement and later supported female suffrage in Britain.[27] Both these facets of her life in England suggest an activism that went beyond the safe bounds of polite middle-class committee work. Carpenter's strong Christian views, her own ethnicity as an English woman, and her brand of cultural imperialism are also illustrated by Ruth Watts as important precursors to any work Carpenter later attempted in India.[28] In this sense she was little different to other women of her generation who saw females as a philanthropic project to pursue in India. However, her Unitarian beliefs, like those of other Unitarians of her generation, led her to adopt egalitarian views by the standards of her day concerning women and their education.[29]

Carpenter's book *Last Days in England*, published just before her first visit to India in 1866, illustrates her European-oriented world view. It concerned Mohan Roy's visit to England in 1833. By the time of its publication, Roy's ideas were well known to orientalists and to the Asiatic intellectual community. These ideas involved a deep intellectual enterprise of genuine Eastern and Western orientalist intellectual interchange. Yet Carpenter chose to characterise Roy's ideas regarding females, at least, as a response only to a generally superior European cultural mindset, and not as something where both East and West could make a contribution. In Carpenter's estimation, Roy's writings were about a 'regeneration' of India drawn from 'the wise and good among … [Britain's] citizens'.[30] She also claimed Indians visiting England did so to participate in what amounted to a form of social cleansing, ready to imitate, and then transplant in India, superior English household domestic procedure and law.[31]

Something powerful and different lay behind Carpenter's European-oriented determination to help the women of India. This was her theorisation about underprivileged females in England: theorisation that she ultimately saw as readily transferable to the subcontinent. For many years Carpenter managed her own school for underprivileged girls in Bristol, funded in part by Lady Byron. In 1853 she published a 388-page book, entitled *Juvenile Delinquents: Their Condition and Treatment* which encapsulated this earlier work.[32] Carpenter's observations during this time also built upon her first-hand experience of Ragged schools and of underprivileged females in England's jails.[33] Carpenter was a social theorist, like many of her fellow Unitarians in mid-Victorian England, although there were limits to this in her writing and teaching.[34] Her ideas were based on her experience supervising and teaching underprivileged children in England, and they took her into the realms of what amounted to amateur anthropology. Carpenter was not alone here; there were strong causal links between colonialism and the emergence of anthropology.[35] In this frame she drew upon the observational data gathered by other like-minded philanthropists in cities as diverse as Hamburg, Dublin and Hobart.[36] Like her self-confident mid-Victorian contemporaries, Carpenter's theorisation about social reform had an element of certitude and verification about it that promoted a case for general human application.

Women and girls were Carpenter's particular interest and they, rather than males, were at the centre of her emerging agenda of social reform. In a captivating commentary on the contemporary scene in England, Carpenter's *Juvenile Delinquents* ..., (1853) developed what was, by the standards of the time, an explanatory framework for the behaviour of females among the 'perishing classes', where their behaviour would determine future social outcomes.[37] For Carpenter, mothers and daughters were harbingers of deep-seated household and maternal instincts that, once disrupted, were much more difficult to restore than was the case in the reformation of delinquent boys.

> The little girl early serves apprenticeship to future maternal duties, by bestowing motherly cares on her doll, and in a lower class becomes a little nurse of a younger child ... her affections and young powers are thus called forth ... but in the arms of the drunken or mendicant mother ... feminine delicacy there is none, nor ... anything to call out the higher parts of her nature.[38]

Carpenter argued that, unless aberrant mother behaviour was rectified, daughters could only drift downwards into a form of irredeemable social malignancy that would rob society of their nurturing, domesticating, social role. This social theory, grounded in Carpenter's own observations in underprivileged English institutions, authorised her thoughts to range seamlessly from girls in prison to girls in Ragged school educational settings. Her conclusion was based on the depressing outcomes that she experienced after many arduous hours spent attempting to reform some of England's most obdurate women and girls. Her attempts at social theory provided a rationale as to why the task was so difficult: a rationale that was already articulated by others in England by this time. Like other Unitarians such as Harriet Martineau, Carpenter was willing to engage with emerging secular knowledge on the topic that was formed well outside the bounds of her religious beliefs.[39] Carpenter also offered one key solution: only the woman teacher, with right-minded social conditioning and the ability to model good feminine behaviour, could rectify the transgression that had resulted from childhood neglect.[40]

It is striking that in Carpenter's formal writing underprivileged females were not always the objects of compassion. She did not always study them through a prism of patronage and kindness. Rather, Carpenter's dominant thoughts were expressed in terms of the supposed threats that such underprivileged girls posed.[41] She thought that these girls could disrupt, rather than reinforce, social cohesion unless women teachers intervened to model 'proper' feminine behaviour to correct the neglect of 'mothers'. In this sense the moral feminine teacher was to provide the antidote to non-nurturing feminine domestic households.[42]

Carpenter's early writings provide important context for her later work on the subcontinent. The philosophical beliefs that drove her forays into teacher training in India were not readily apparent, even to most of her closest confidents or to those pursuing an apparently similar agenda. The broader European female community that was establishing itself on the subcontinent in the late 1860s had shared little of Carpenter's life experience in England among the very poor. Carpenter's social reformist approach helps to explain her wish to promote women teachers as individual agents, rather than as part of Christian communities as the missions did. It also drove her insistence that only women could teach females effectively.[43] Her ideas embraced only the lowest classes, which resulted in Carpenter treating Indian schoolgirls, unlike their teachers, as a social aggregate rather than as individuals located within separate racial or communal spheres. Her approach reflected a similar process at the metropole a generation earlier where the official making of an aggregated underprivileged social body was part of new cultural formation that then authorised official, broad strategies of 'cure' for the ills of this new, largely anonymous social body.[44]

Carpenter's long years of teaching experience, and her frank approach, cut across established myths about how girls learnt as compared to boys. On this topic she argued:

> the deficiency in intellectual power and activity in girls as compared with the boys ... is not universally true, as all who have had an opportunity of comparing the youth of the two sexes under *equally favourable circumstances* [Carpenter's italics] will readily admit.[45]

This observation came from her experience of education in England, where the lack of resources for single-sex schooling for the poor often enforced a shared curriculum for both genders. However, for Carpenter, as for most of her generation, the moral frailty of the girl remained firmly in view. Without the benefit of the better understanding of ado-lescent behaviour that developed later in the century, underprivileged girls remained 'the problem'. Citing her 1840 Ragged school experience Carpenter argued:

> There is much more difficulty in interesting ... girls in their lessons than the boys; these [the boys] require only to be restrained, and show an eagerness to acquire knowledge, while the girls manifest an indolent listlessness from which it is very difficult to rouse them. When the mas-ter gives a general lesson to the school, the boys are generally attentive, and evidently taking in ideas, but the girls are bold, and keep noticing the boys even without encouragement from them.[46]

This rather cold, even Dickensian, narrative does not reflect Carpenter's humanity in devoting many hours to poor girls in her home town of Bristol, nor, for that matter, her sometimes perilous for-ays in middle age across British India. At the core of her beliefs lay anxiety about the frailty of females, whom she believed were best pro-tected, in India as in Europe, by the corrective of the woman teacher. Her attitudes towards underprivileged girls were driven more by her socio-cultural anxieties than by concerns about their intellect. Her views were to cut across the race agendas of empire that were already in place by the time of her first visit to India in 1866.

Travelling in India

Given Carpenter's earlier experiences with institutions and educa-tion in England, and her reflections on and theorisation about them, it is not surprising that her visits to India sat uncomfortably with the European colonial establishment there. In India, Carpenter took advan-tage of the hospitality of the many European communities she visited. She was obliged in the process to observe government schools and bet-ter resourced mission schools. However, when she was able to way-lay provincial officials, she also ventured down side alleys to witness traditional Indian schooling that remained outside the control of the government. In Bombay, Carpenter was particularly impressed by the calibre of the schools funded for Parsi girls by wealthy Indian benefac-tors. The two largest of these claimed an enrolment of 1,900 and 1,600 girls, respectively, and taught the 3Rs and Persian history.[47] She also cited six girls' schools that taught in Parsi, Marathi and Gujarati. These had been established by the Bombay Students' Literary and Scientific Society and collectively taught 308 girls Eastern geography, astronomy and advanced 'arithmetic', as well as classes in ethics.[48]

Carpenter's favourable assessment of the vitality of these schools catering for subsections of the Indian population was well removed from seeing them as mere enforcers of the Western accomplishments curriculum. When she visited Bengal, she also confronted the issue of race. There she toured the Bethune school (a unique school for Hindu girls supported by private European patronage), and this and her visits to other Hindu girls' schools led her to conclude:

> Young native girls are quite equal in intelligence and quickness in learning to their Western sisters, if properly instructed and trained.[49]

This was not the vision being promoted by Bengal provincial officials or those of the Viceroy (in the same city of Calcutta). As such, it was not surprising that Carpenter's enthusiasm roused a rather awkward official response in India.[50]

Unlike government, Carpenter's work in respect to the education of women and girls was designed to ameliorate, in Western terms, the social condition of females; and in doing so to transcend colonial race, if not class, barriers in India, if this became necessary. To this end, moulding the underprivileged female on the subcontinent, as in England, was to be placed in the hands of Western women teachers who would direct a new array of female normal schools.[51] For Carpenter, the vitality of indigenous girls' schools could only be properly harnessed if a socio-cultural mediation occurred first, through teacher training, that would turn women of any race into good moral guides ready to shape the next generation. Although Carpenter herself initially saw Indian girls as being just as worthy as recipients of her agenda as Eurasians and Europeans, the institutional arrangements and funding of her plan also carried with these arrangements and funding much of the stamp of Haileybury and Western organisation that continued to shape and project official ICS mentalities about women in India.[52]

As a form of social rehabilitation, Carpenter's initiatives were reinforced by her broader agenda that also took her into Indian jails. This approach reflected her earlier work in England, which theorised about social remediation through the agency of moral and emotionally nurturing women acting as role models. In Indian jails, Carpenter observed up to thirty-two boys and men in a single cell, tried and untried, huddled together in leg irons, where, she believed, 'it was difficult to preserve decent order, and impossible to prevent great moral evil'.[53] More speculatively, she theorised that the inadequate development of girls through education, and the resulting lack of the moderating moral influence of women, was the cause of social breakdown for men.[54] Carpenter's narrative conflated sociological issues concerning prison welfare with her argument for the recruitment of women teachers.[55]

[101]

She assigned the training of women teachers as a higher priority than the reform of education for Indian girls, the accommodation of local languages in the classroom, or the barriers of race that directed state policymaking by the time of her first visit to the subcontinent in 1866.

Foreshadowing her plan

Carpenter's plan of action was relayed to senior education officials in India after her first visit in 1866. Her connections at Westminster, and with the Queen herself, were never fully known to even her closest contemporaries, but her influence with the Secretary of State for India, Stafford Northcote (part of Disraeli's Conservative Government), gave her unprecedented influence as a woman in the male domain of raj governance.[56] Carpenter astutely expressed her plan in ICS bureaucratic language. Her female normal schools were to have two purposes that chimed directly with her earlier theorisation on destitute children who were girls.

First, normal schools were for the physical and moral redemption of Indian girls 'that can be given only by trained female teachers'. Here, again, she meant Western-trained teachers, but their function was to be more important than their role 'merely in the acquisition of a knowledge of reading and writing'.[57] To Carpenter, 'training' of the female teacher in India was really about 'character', which she saw as more important in the classroom than knowledge of pedagogy or of knowledge itself.[58] For this reason she regarded monitorialism, though outdated by that time, as a permissible approach to increase the influence of what she knew would be a restricted number of teacher trainers. She also accepted that orphaned girls who were acclimatised Eurasians could swell the ranks of 'suitable' female teachers 'if their attention could be directed to this work'.[59]

Second, Carpenter's Western women teachers were to act as individual agents supported directly by government, rather than relying on communities of women missionaries and other friends already resident in India.[60] This was a strong element of her thinking. Sidestepping the missions in this way seems at variance with her Judeo-Christian ethic, and Carpenter had acknowledged effective female education work in cities such as Dacca (Eastern India), where missions were already deploying women *byraginees* (teachers) whom they had graduated to work in surrounding Indian schools.[61] Nonetheless, it was to government that Carpenter looked for joint funding of her teacher training project in India. She believed that this funding source, rather than the missions, would best protect her distinctive social reform approach for educating underprivileged girls.

New visibility

State funding in India was not as neutral as Carpenter supposed, how-ever, and this issue would lead to significant problems in the imple-mentation of her plan. Carpenter was not really cognisant of the race barrier already partly embedded in official funding policy for female education. She questioned even less her own assumptions about the frailty and complexity of Indian communal moral and ethical codes. An additional problem was the pragmatics of dealing with male ICS personnel, whom she needed to rely upon, but whose neglect of female education was driven by their beliefs about what they supposed was the 'unresponsive' Indian schoolgirl. Most significantly, the robust nature of official rhetoric regarding female education after 1860 also served to undermine Carpenter's influence. This was especially so once she had achieved a significant profile within India in colonial circles.

Carpenter's difficulties began in the British press in October 1867 and fed into India shortly afterwards. In this month an article enti-tled 'Miss Carpenter and our Mission Work in India' appeared in the *Edinburgh Evening Courant*, a conservative tri-weekly eager to pro-mote both Scottish benefits and contribution to the British imperial project. The broadsheet used Carpenter's views to promote a wider missionary agenda that identified India as fertile ground for action. The *Courant* created an approximation of India as part of the 'human family' whose 300 million people were already provisionally recruited by the state, ready for Western mission work, to remedy the 'charac-teristic' 'feeble' faiths of the East. Carpenter lent her name to this mes-sage in an open letter of support. She did so to magnify the impact on British audiences of her own project on female education on the sub-continent via the agency of Westernised women teachers. The India Office then circulated a simplistic representation of Carpenter's views as expressed in the *Courant* article to all provincial authorities in India,[62] who immediately took offence at her deductions, particularly as they were an implicit criticism of their own inaction concerning female education over several decades.[63]

The press in colonial India, more attuned as they were to the Indian cultural milieu, had already built on Carpenter's public profile, which seemed to challenge past government policy. Against the background of a generation of official rhetoric presenting the state as active in edu-cating girls in India, Carpenter was held up in public colonial forums as leading a new approach, in opposition to the reality of state inaction. Her various comments on the condition of Indian females played into an emerging critique of government policy that was more related to Indian cultural realities.

Reporting on a soiree in support of female education, attended by Carpenter at the Asiatic Society in Calcutta, *The Englishman* (a British Calcutta newspaper) surmised that Carpenter's promotion of female education was a matter of public health, social economy, prison discipline and moral protection.[64] The *Bombay Gazette* reported her meeting at the Students' Literary and Scientific Society by publicising Carpenter's view of the wasted resource of Indian widows, spending their lives secluded, with shaved heads and dressed in white, sometimes from the age of fourteen.[65] The *Gujarat Mitra* (west India) relayed Carpenter's view that government was too timid in broaching the religious and communal sensitivities around schooling for Indian girls.[66] The *Madras Times* reported Carpenter's approval of schools for Indian girls whose visual literacy and use of Indian music 'refresh the heart and refine the mind'.[67]

It is difficult to gauge the accuracy of these accounts or to judge to what extent they were the products of editors wishing to stir government into action concerning the education of Indian women and girls. It is significant that Carpenter, herself, took up these arguments advocating her work and published them in England after her visit in 1867.[68] Her personal crusade for teacher training to produce a Western-inspired moral schoolgirl who was Indian soon created new barriers. The Madras governor, embarrassed by Viceroy John Lawrence's questions as to why there had not been more action, banned Carpenter from his province altogether.[69] Other provinces reluctantly attempted normal schools, inspired by Carpenter's lobbying. Ultimately, it was only Bombay that allowed her to set up her teacher training institutions in person. Even in this key province, however, it was clear to the DPI in Bombay, Alexander Grant, that there were troubling cultural aspects to Carpenter's plan if it focused on highly sensitive Indian communities who had otherwise shown a willingness to participate in some form colonial-funded education:

> It is clear she [Mary Carpenter] will not be satisfied with aiming at merely the intellectual improvement of women of this country ... she underrates all of this compared to the influence on manners and character ... she wants to modulate their voices to sit in an upright and energetic attitude, to adopt the cheerful music of England, to practise plain sewing and, if possible, to give up wearing bangles.[70]

Implementing her scheme

Carpenter faced insurmountable difficulties when attempting to build broader acceptance and applicability among the Indians she encountered when travelling from one Indian town to the next. The state's contribution to the expansion of Carpenter's scheme beyond central colonial sites had been to divert funding from other limited education initiatives concerning colonial-sponsored schooling for Indian girls that were of longer standing and which had begun to win support from local Indian elites. The Viceroy, John Lawrence, a Carpenter supporter, promoted a central normal female school in each major city centre. However, provincial governments suspected that Carpenter was attempting to appropriate their authority and resisted a further spread of her normal schools. The only other avenue of hope for future expansion was a reliance on the, by now discredited, filtration theory (a precursor to modern-day 'trickle down'), whereby it was supposed that education provided first for the wealthier might eventually 'filter down' to benefit the lower classes. In a similar way, it was supposed that Carpenter's central urban normal schools might somehow achieve a similar outcome in the future.

In the face of this adversity, Carpenter came to rely on the patronage of local princelings and other elites, including the Rani of Jamkhandi (southwest India).[71] These elites were unaware of Carpenter's Western social reformist agenda. They were impressed by her donations of schoolbooks and paintings and by her courage in attempting to implement what they erroneously saw as a form of village uplift for Indian females.[72] Carpenter continued to insist on working outside existing missionary spheres of influence. When resolved to work mostly in Bombay, she publically signified this determination not to rely on the missions by agreeing to be taught the local languages of Gujarati and Marathi by local pandits (Hindu teachers), rather than from Eurasian 'mistresses' from the missions.[73]

Western India was probably the worst province for Carpenter to be working in given its traditions regarding state-assisted Indian female education. Here, three key female normal schools were her focus: one each in Bombay, Poona and Ahmedabad. Carpenter met opposition from longstanding Indian patrons of local education, who were also connected with the raj. This opposition emerged when it became clear that Carpenter did not intend to begin preparing Indian women teachers immediately using earlier native society traditions in Bombay, where British and Indian intellectuals had worked together a generation earlier.[74] Instead, Carpenter turned to Parsi schooling communities and their networks, which were more receptive to her idea of building female teacher training led by European and Eurasian women.[75]

Ultimately, Mary Carpenter's influence did indeed change the direction of female education in colonial India, but not as she had originally envisaged. Her powerful patrons at Westminster, and the sympathetic reception she received from Viceroy John Lawrence in Calcutta, were a good counterpoise to provincial government resistance to her ideas.[76] As a result, European-directed female teacher training became entrenched as the only active arm of government policy for the education of girls in India's key cities. This took state focus even further away from the more basic provision of school education for Indian girls.

India's colonial schoolgirl

Carpenter's intervention finally ended a deeper conversation between province and central government over whether schooling for Indian girls should be embraced, or whether female teacher training should dominate state discussion of girls' education, when disbursing very scarce funding. Teacher training for women became the mantra. In the later 1860s, Mary Carpenter's lobbying forced provincial authorities to cut drastically the little money they had at their disposal to spend on schooling for Indian girls. This was instead used to fund female normal schools and, later, women inspectors of teacher training. In the vast province of Punjab, funding for schooling for Indian girls was reduced by 53 per cent to just Rs.2,688 per month; this was typical of other parts of India. At the same time, funding for female normal schools was increased to almost double that amount.[77]

Few in India accepted Carpenter's sociologically based premise that only women could teach girls because of the need to transmit feminine virtue and affection. Even John Lawrence observed of the Indian educational landscape and the practice as he knew it at the metropole:

> I don't see myself anything much more shocking in the fact that Hindu girls are taught by an old [morally safe] Pundit [teacher] to spell and write, than in the fact that half the young ladies in England learn music, singing, and modern languages to a great extent from male teachers.[78]

Local Western-oriented practitioners now openly challenged Carpenter's prioritisation of Western-oriented teacher education for girls in India, for good reasons that went beyond the initial personal resentment they had felt towards her. The state's setting aside of the Indian schoolgirl was clearly not Carpenter's intention; but the funding choices central government made in favour of her normal schools hastened this process and became the main cause of opposition to her plan among provincial governments. The dedicated work of some earlier Westerners had resulted in at least some negotiation with the East, at the schooling level, for girls. This work included that at the Lawrence Military Asylum at Sanawar, as discussed in chapter two, and especially the village school experiments in north India, to be discussed later in this chapter. Regional responses, critical of Carpenter's broad approach, also revealed India's complexity and the longer-standing experimentation by other Europeans, who were already reflecting on their practice and whose work offered greater potential in educating Indian girls.

For example, princely states such as Mysore (south India) had seen only limited Western assimilation, even among the trading classes.[79] Poor Indian girls attended schools provided they were taught by learned Brahmin males, who were superintended by 'a committee of respectable gentlemen'. Resident missionaries at the court of the Maharajah of Mysore, such as Miss Anstey of the non-denominational London Missionary Society, had carefully negotiated these arrangements. Anstey openly challenged Carpenter's view concerning women teachers only. According to Anstey, who was considering educational outcomes only (and not sociological ones), recruiting male teachers (the only teachers available) to teach girls was already working well.[80]

> I have been a frequent visitor and teacher … in the best infant and common Schools in Edinburgh, and I must say that I think the children trained at Bangalore would stand a fair examination if compared with children trained for equal number of years in the best Schools in England and Scotland.[81]

Anstey's European middle-class status no doubt underpinned her appointment to the magnificent Maharajah's court, in much the same way that Anna Leonowens gained access to the court of the King of Siam at about the same time. Anstey was experienced enough in India to be critical of what she saw as Carpenter's 'impractical scheme' of European middle-class social and moral reproduction. Anstey pointed out that normal schools for the training of female teachers were premature until schooling for girls was first consolidated. For Anstey, it was not gender, but learning 'the art of teaching' that made the 'very good' teacher of females, and men could carry out this role just as well as women.[82]

In the province of Oudh (north central India), DPI Currie opposed Carpenter's scheme because it was predicated on building stronger English-oriented education first. The ambit of the raj in this province consisted of Indians made wealthy from global trade, whose cultural identity was still firmly in place. Material affluence was unlikely, in Currie's estimation, to induce them to embrace Carpenter's Western conception of the 'trained' woman teacher. Having already confronted the barrier of not enough colonial female teachers, he had turned to poor rural communities instead. Again, for him, schooling for girls took priority over teacher training. The poverty of these communities, distant from any connection to the raj, made them amenable to Western-funded education, however minimal, so long as girls' schools were established spontaneously first and contained teachers and pupils of good 'character'. In Currie's estimation, resistance from communities was best broken down by carefully negotiated payment for the attendance of girls in these poor villages.

> About 20 schools for Native girls are at this moment at work with from 10 to 20 pupils each, their origin is in all cases much the same; a Missionary, or some Officer or friends of this [Education] Department, finds a teacher who undertakes to collect pupils from among her friends and neighbours; she has to satisfy us of her own character, and engages to secure respectable pupils. I believe the pupils *are* respectable, but they are, for the most part, poor.[83]

In Berar (central India), the education of Indian girls was positioned through yet another orientation. As a legacy of the Mughals, this province had a traditional Muslim ruling class, although its general population was mostly Hindu. Berar was administered by the British after 1853, but the Nizam of Hyderabad still claimed formal sovereignty. To counter his powerbase, it suited British interests to direct their efforts to the lower stratums of the Hindu population. This uncharacteristic bottom-up approach by government also gave traditional Hindu communities access to Western schooling in ways that Carpenter could not have considered, given the rigidities of her scheme.[84] Female education had a part to play in this kind of power politics. As a result, Hindu village and tribal patriarchies were permitted to carry out their own kind of social filtering and character 'testing' based on Hindu traditions rather than on Western middle-class sensibility. One outcome of these arrangements seemed to be that local superintendence built more effective bridges with communities. This was particularly the case where parents were given the opportunity to understand just what raj-funded education for girls meant, and also to become comfortable with male teachers only teaching their daughters.[85]

Carpenter's formulaic approach of 'supplying' India with trained female teachers, at the vanguard of an endeavour to rejuvenate girls' education across India, was never sufficiently adaptable to these different local trajectories. These trajectories were imperfectly connected to the state in other ways under the Western-conceived paradigm of 'female education'. Most significantly, Carpenter's influence with the Viceroy and senior officials in the India Office in London damaged more profound orientalist-inspired girls' schooling endeavours of the NWP and Bombay that had remained largely intact up until the 1860s.

The NWP and Bombay: continuing schoolgirl endeavours

The raj also faced ongoing tension between Bengal in opposition to the NWP and Bombay over rhetoric about female education and over where to locate the Indian schoolgirl in the new state agenda. This was part of a much longer-standing tension – different to the one set up by the Carpenter intervention. It emanated from 1813, over fifty years earlier, when the missions had been granted access to India. As discussed in chapter one, it was orientalist practice in the field over several decades in the NWP, and in Bombay, that had created distinct philosophical views on schooling for Indian girls. These views were not racially based, unlike Canning's 1860 Despatch, and they were not about imposing Western forms of social remediation as Carpenter pre-scribed. Advocates of the NWP and the Bombay approach continued to hold out against both the simpler CMS approach in Bengal and the later approach of Mary Carpenter. Two European male intellectuals, who were not necessarily given to pragmatic ICS colonial education agendas, also encouraged their lobbying.

In the NWP, the DPI, Simon Kempson (1861–70), had been recruited to build on DPI Henry Reid's earlier orientalist-inspired *halkabandi* village schooling work. He was an expert in Indian history and in ori-ental languages, which he had read at Caius College Cambridge. With these credentials, and with the NWP's earlier educational history, he posed an opposing macro view to the ones emerging at the Viceroy level in Calcutta. Kempson argued that, even after ninety years of rule, Europeans were still, for the most part, ignorant of modes of 'native' thought; and more particularly of how this thought made sense within the domestic Indian household.[86] As far as the British were con-cerned, Kempson turned Carpenter's argument regarding female edu-cation on its head. Adopting an Occidentalist viewpoint, he simply argued: '[Indian] distrust of the moral character of the ruling race ... is not unnatural in a country held by a body of soldiers'.[87]

By the early 1860s, native societies also emerged in the NWP along the Bombay model that supported schooling for Indian girls. These societies were small, loosely organised groups of local Indian leaders and intellectuals. A generation earlier they had been encour-aged by European orientalists to build intellectual bridges with the West without the direction of the colonial state itself.[88] These societies were particularly strong in the city of Agra, where the Taj Mahal stood as evidence of an earlier era of more cultural inclu-siveness between Hindus and Muslims under the Mughal emperor Shah Jahan, and particularly his grandfather Akbar. One of these societies, the Sath Sabha, led by Pundit Bansi Dhar, was especially vigilant about any signs of new initiatives around girls' education that might undermine local religion. To win parental acceptance for their daughters' education, the NWP government used district-level committees comprising sympathetic Europeans and Indians.[89] This important groundwork in building community consensus was still to be fully developed. In the NWP Reid had observed, as early as 1852, that parents were very apprehensive about sending their daughters to school in the 'iniquitous' local town, just five miles from the village.[90] Instead of Carpenter's approach, Bansi Dhar convinced the NWP government to fund twenty modest, Indian-run, normal schools for girls that were responsive to micro local religious and language sensitivities.[91]

Kempson understood the possibilities the halkabandi village schooling model offered for building long-term local community consensus around schooling for girls, based on the orientalist philological approach of Western knowledge 'engraftment' through local languages first. Many Indian girls had already enrolled in these village schools in co-educational classes. By the 1860s this tradition was longstanding enough to be focusing on a new generation of female scholars: urged to enrol at the modest *alma maters* of their mothers.[92] Even by 1859, DPI Reid was aware that the Viceroy's government in Calcutta was reluctant to do more for Indian girls. For this reason he knew that his discovery of the potential of local communities to embrace at least elementary schooling for Indian girls was unwelcome news to the central authorities in Calcutta. If the state encouraged these new Indian endeavours around schooling for Indian girls, rather than continuing with its excuse that 'native prejudice' was in fact the chief obstacle to such schooling, a new direction could be launched in favour of these school children. This new direction was unlikely to win long-term support in Calcutta at this time because it was clearly at variance with the new central raj priorities favouring Eurasian schoolgirls and Westernising schoolgirls as conceived by Miss Cooke's Bengal CMS and fostered since that time in Bengal. Reid attempted to hide from the Viceroy's Council the extent to which Indian girls were participating alongside boys in his provincially funded halkabandi village schools.[93] However, with Mary Carpenter taking up nearly all the available scarce funding for her female normal schools in the 1860s, the axe wielded by Calcutta was to finally fall in the NWP in 1867, cutting central funding for most schools for Indian girls, with only some provincial funding still available.

By the 1880s, in the NWP, official neglect resulted in a decline in the school enrolment of Indian girls (even as measured by the dubious official figures available) from 6,593 in 1870 to only 3,465 girls in 1882.[94] By 1882 the only indication left of the potential for Reid's abandoned scheme, which had showed so much promise in the first half of the century, was that many of the remaining schoolgirls were from families not already dependent on the raj. Of those Indian girls still in colonial-supported schools, only 10 per cent had fathers who were directly employed by colonial enterprises. Most other fathers were cultivators, carpenters or weavers whose family connections had been made initially with Reid's imaginative village schooling experiments thirty-five years earlier. It is possible that, had these experiments been supported in the latter part of the nineteenth century, they would have been able to deliver long-term community-based schooling for Indian girls.[95]

In Bombay, the Canning Despatch in favour of Eurasian girls, and Carpenter's female teaching approach, were confronted by another Oxbridge-educated official appointed by the Bombay provincial author-ities to carry out the specialised education work there in the 1860s that had been under development for at least two generations. Sir Alexander Grant was a political economist and historian, born in the West Indies and educated at Balliol College, Oxford. (Upon retirement from India, Grant went on to become Principal of Edinburgh University.)[96] Grant was less opposed than Kempson was to Carpenter and to the central Viceroy authorities in Calcutta. Grant had ties to C. E. Trevelyan, the leading Anglicist[97] in India thirty years previously, and he was elit-ist in terms of who should direct local education matters. He lacked Kempson's Indian linguistic expertise. Yet, as a successor of Montstuart Elphinstone, even Grant knew that Carpenter's plan was too simplistic for Bombay.[98]

Grant saw Carpenter as an interloper because, in Bombay, as in the NWP, a longer-standing story around education for Indian girls had been built over several generations. As a result of these earlier endeavours, Grant already knew that, in Bombay, caste (at least as the British cat-egorised it) and region were strong discriminators as to which families were likely to send their daughters to part-government-funded schools.[99] Understanding this had required careful intelligence gathering. The Brahmins of the Deccan were the most hostile, but the Bombay provin-cial government had been successful in recruiting girls of *bania* (trading) castes in urban commercial centres.[100] There were better opportuni-ties to collect funds in Bombay than there were in the NWP, because of the province's strong native education societies. By 1866 three distinct societies in particular (the Students' Literary and Scientific Society for Girls' Schools; the Parsi Girls' School Association; and the Sir Jamsetjee Jeejeebhoy Benevolent Institution) were responsible for raising over Rs.248,000, which gave local government the justification to ask Calcutta for further funding to build normal schools for Indian girls.[101]

This was a considerable sum of money that approximated to the cost of building a premier college for men in any province at this time.

The Viceroy, responding to pressure from the Secretary of State Stafford Northcote at Westminster in favour of the Carpenter approach, refused to grant matching funds through grant-in-aid to these societies alone.[102] This unusual refusal left Grant with a potentially explosive provincial situation to deal with, as these merchants also funded many other government-approved projects. Grant had to appear to accommodate Carpenter at Bombay (where most central government money from Calcutta was made available for Carpenter's normal schools for women), while also attempting to keep most of the disbursement of these funds in the hands of Bombay benefactors of girls' education.[103] Carpenter played into his hands here, partly because of her disputes with her women teachers and because she was only resident in the province for brief periods during her trips to India. It was not long, however, until the Viceroy's government in Calcutta excavated old stereotypes about Indian women, concerning purdah and Eastern 'superstition'. This was in an effort to prove that schooling for local Indian girls was an endeavour still unworthy of funding, despite the fact that such schooling was already flourishing in the Parsi communities in Bombay.[104]

Carpenter's philanthropy, based on her model of social remediation, was now appropriated to accentuate official stereotypes in Calcutta that represented the Indian woman as supine and culturally degenerate, especially when dealing with the NWP and Bombay.[105] The official imperial mission repeatedly emphasised these 'deficits' of Indian women to solidify the racial and class agendas of the raj concerning female education: agendas that grew stronger as the age of high imperialism and the Empress' India emerged in the next two decades.

Surveillance by inspectresses

One way that central government could extend its surveillance over the girls' schools it did fund (using the revenue it collected from Indians) was by employing one or two inspectresses in each province. The state never built upon the partial responsiveness of Indian communities in the NWP and in Bombay in the 1860s to imaginative schooling schemes (which occurred despite their still being in the hands of a colonial master). Instead, women inspectresses now reinforced the Western moral domain. Raj administrators responded with more Western regulation, which demonstrated the widening cultural and intellectual gulf.

In all provinces there was suspect behaviour, on both sides of the classroom door, regarding new regulations implemented by inspectresses. The schools for Indian girls that the inspectresses observed had student numbers that fluctuated wildly day-to-day. This represented accommodation on the part of local teachers to parental wishes around girls' household obligations, as well as parental fears about too much Westernisation of their children. For those Indian parents who still wished to send their daughters to government schools, even in the 1860s, it was not Carpenter's insistence on female teachers that was most important to them, but the mechanisms of cultural scrutiny by the British. The extract below from a government report in the Punjab illustrates just how far apart the agendas of government and of Indian parents had moved by the mid-1860s.

> The great difficulty is to exercise proper supervision over them [Indian female pupils]. Although it would be obviously preferable to employ female Teachers, and the want of them is felt by some District Officers to be a great impediment to the progress of Female Education, yet the people do not seem to object to male Teachers for their daughters, so long as they are allowed to make their own selection. And, strange to say, the selection not unfrequently [sic] falls upon young men, as well as old – occasionally a mere lad, one of the senior scholars in the neighbouring Town or Village school.[106]

Surveillance by inspectresses created additional problems. The few employed in the 1860s and 1870s were usually the wives of European officials and, because they had little formal education, they were forced to make their assessments based on students reading aloud in English and on students' calligraphy using Roman script. To secure funding, Indian teachers in the government's pay had little choice but to submit to these superficial criteria as the means by which government measured their teaching 'proficiency'. In reality, the function of most inspectresses in India, who operated as loose departmental agents for the rest of the century, was to externalise to colonial authorities the supposed deficiency of the Indian side of an imagined partnership in the enterprise of schooling Indian girls. Unlike the 'home' domain a generation later in England, these inspectresses were never a collective force contributing to the elevation of the teaching profession in India.[107]

There was also considerable impropriety at the hands of non-compliant Indian teachers of Indian girls who believed the whole inspectress system was one of inescapable superficiality. For example, Mrs S. Macintosh, employed part-time to superintend thirty-six Hindi female schools in the Lahore district, was observant enough to suspect that the Indian teachers she was inspecting 'assisted' one another with a ready supply of girls who could read English. She complained that her *duli* (carriage) was delayed by a 'band of girls' as she travelled from one school to the next, and that when she arrived she realised that the girls before her reading

were the same ones she had seen in the previous school, these girls having travelled via a faster back *veethi* (alley) route.[108] Macintosh's distrust
of Indian women teachers and their 'noisy' classrooms was so great that
she was forced to rely upon nearby missions to keep accurate enrolment
numbers of the schools for Indian girls that she inspected.[109]

Such arrangements were hardly resonant of an idiomatic professional collaboration between inspectress and Indian women teachers
in girls' schools, even at a basic level. The dysfunction, exacerbated
by there being so few European women in India interested in a professional role in the administration of girls' education, only grew worse as
the century progressed.[110] This was particularly the case when inspectresses imagined that they were part of a coherent state education
strategy that had any potential to cut through a vast population with
strong non-Western cultural interconnections.

Fanny Ann Francis, the first European inspectress imported from
England employed in north India in 1889, was just one such case in
point.[111] Her accounts are rare in terms of their length and detail.
Writing for an audience at the Maria Grey College in London, she
recorded the cultural separation she felt when viewing schools for
Indian girls in starkly objectified terms. Seeking out impropriety in
outlying Lahore suburbia, the self-assured Francis sought to stamp
out the effeminacy of Indian male teachers of girls: an effeminacy she
saw as manifesting itself in their inability to follow a Western curriculum.[112] The Indian aesthetic Francis viewed from her bungalow
verandah – of gold-coloured turbans, 'olive' faces and dust-coloured
garments – held considerable appeal to for her. She regarded the teaching of literacy through the Koran in this densely Muslim populated
region as being tolerable enough if it taught girls ethics.[113] Both these
sympathies reflect some professional merit in her thinking.

Yet primary knowledge, to Francis, was to be had only through
primers following a 'Western pattern' and through a satisfactory grasp
of English. She gave summary notice to those male teachers whom she
judged as unable to deliver this form of learning: 'the sharp faced cruel
looking Brahmin' whose pupils were 'unclean'.[114] Francis regarded good
teaching as linking Western hygienic habits with the formation of the
female citizen, as was typical in many empire domains of the age.[115] For
Francis, her certitude was simply a matter of Western self-discipline,
and was without any local knowledge, little deeper cultural awareness,
or any regard for the teacher's need for employment.

> One of the dismissed masters came to beg pardon and being sent away
> sat under a tarnarisk [sic] tree and wept for some hours. He had fair warn-
> ing so I hardened my heart and let him weep on.[116]

Francis' judgements were part of what she saw as a policing role in what she regarded as the 'moral torpor' of the Indian school for girls. She imagined these judgements would stamp out nepotism in the appointment of teachers by newly empowered, but 'corrupt', Indian municipal authorities. It is perhaps surprising, given her audience at Maria Grey College in London, that Francis' accounts also included descriptions of the physical attractiveness of the male teachers over whom she had power and they may reveal her own personal moral struggle in relating to them.[117]

There were deeper aspects to these broader Indian education communities into which neither Francis, nor Carpenter, ventured. The Indian teacher, as counsellor, as an adjunct to the Hindu pandit or Buddhist monk, or to the local Imam, fed streams of consciousness to their students about calmness and centeredness in the face of daily poverty. There were Eastern dimensions to teaching, particularly regarding rich Indian philosophical traditions, about which Francis could not theorise in the tight epistemological territory of her Western-conceived classroom, which demanded regimen and compliance through Western-based examination. The sight of the local pandit happy to beg to supplement income, as a signifier of his giving to the local community, offended her sensitivities about teacher professionalism. It was for these reasons, and because of the cultural insistence on teaching only a Western curriculum, that the colonial divide became more broadly defined – a divide that most British educators in India still thought it was possible to bridge in the later nineteenth century. The endeavours of women like Francis, inspecting schools for Indian girls, were legacies remaining from Carpenter, who had completed her last visit to India a decade before Francis began her professional career in India.

In all of this, Mary Carpenter can be seen as a transformative figure, not so much in attempting to establish normal schools and a role for women inspectresses, but in locating Western constructions of the Indian female learner within them. Ramusack's 'maternal imperialist' tag could easily be applied to Carpenter, driven as she was by a Western orientation calling for more 'trained' women teacher educators for India.[118] Carpenter's vulnerability, however, was that she and the other arriving European women teachers in the raj of the 1860s did not together project a single Western project, but rather several projects, all of which had their genesis in Europe and not in India. Conversely, the state was obliged to keep its education discourse about girls' education active, not only through its champions in Britain, but also through the increasing number of European women living in India. Expatriate European women in India could read the English-language Indian newspapers over *kalewa* (breakfast) and could see and communicate among themselves about the consequences of the mismanagement of schooling for girls. The many Indian girls who were not participating in colonial schooling could also be easily ignored. Once these girls were in a Western classroom, however, the raj was on show and under scrutiny from many angles as to its imperial ruling ethic.

Despite these obvious shortcomings and restrictions, Carpenter's intervention did bring about important structural change in the way the state saw its role in educating women and girls in India. In 1868, scarce government funding was diverted to building female normal schools in urban regional centres, including Surat, Broach, Ratnagiri and Nagpur. Carpenter would later visit all these centres, even though most of the work she personally directed was restricted to Bombay.[119] The expensive salary now needed for her 'trained' European mistresses to head each normal school quickly absorbed any extra monies that might have been otherwise available for employing many more Western-trained Indian teachers, or for supporting the building of Indian girls' schools on the earlier NWP or Bombay experimental models. Carpenter's call for female teacher training in new normal schools forced the Viceroy's hand and resulted in attention moving away from the education of Indian girls at school level. In terms of consistent policy, Carpenter's voice was loosely compatible with that of Wood's Despatch of 1854, which had already established a firm connection between female teacher training and inspecting of girls' schools by women.[120] Although it was not her intention, Carpenter's views could also align with the internal state logic established by Viceroy Canning in 1860 that saw female education as really building a strong moral female body based on Western constructions of race and class across India, as discussed in chapter two.

Scandal at Nagpur

These tidy Western equivalences in policy direction could be made on paper on the office desks of the raj. But they had little connection with Carpenter's underlying theorisation about the social remediation of females, nor with the approach of inspectresses, such as Francis, who would follow a decade later. Sprinkling female teacher training institutions lightly across the subcontinent, with little or no actual connection with local populations, was to invite communal trouble in the early 1870s that would be of far greater state concern. This was especially if these normal schools were made up entirely of Indian girls.

The problems these institutions faced exemplify how tenuous raj governance really was when promoting its rhetoric about female schooling to some Indian communities that were dispersed, but politicised enough even in the 1870s to resist the British even on the question of female schooling.

For example, the location of regionally based female normal schools, away from European and more affluent Eurasian populations, meant that they escaped much attention from the central authorities in Calcutta. One of these regional normal schools was established under Carpenter's scheme in Nagpur (central India). Carpenter personally visited this school in 1869. Her visit was mostly taken up with the hospitality of the *bhonsles* (who were the dispossessed ruling Maratha clan of the region) and their Persian poets.[121] The school established in her name seemed to be flourishing, although under heavily negotiated local conditions. Government women school inspectors were encouraged to give up their supervision in favour of local Brahmins. This was justified on the basis that the school's narrow walkways and *raastas* (passages) prevented visits from European women in their mid-Victorian hoop dresses, unlike their sari-wearing Indian colleagues.[122] In this school early British attempts to filter enrolments, and to exclude more academically promising female candidates, had resulted in an early enrolment that was a quarter Brahmin, of which more than one-half were widows.[123] These girls were mostly between twelve and fifteen years of age and their desperate economic position induced them to attend, so that they could receive a generous 'scholarship'.[124] Carpenter supported these different arrangements partly because she was not in a position to change them, and partly because they afforded the chance to establish another school under her scheme that the government was prepared to part fund but not control.[125]

The school's curriculum and the attainment of its students were considered satisfactory throughout the late 1860s and in 1870–1.[126] The government anticipated that, as elsewhere in India, it would soon send out teachers, as moral guides, to surrounding schools, even if their education was not entirely complete. Carpenter's visit to the Nagpur normal school even resulted in the introduction of a differentiated accomplishments curriculum of needlework and music.[127]

There were other good portents. The headmistress of the Nagpur normal school was a Mrs Young, the wife of the head CMS missionary in the city.[128] The government had not been prepared to finance teachers from England for these regional schools in urban settings, as Carpenter had prescribed. However, Young was energetic and enjoyed her teaching, and in this relatively remote schooling site her mastery of the local language of Marathi facilitated her encouragement of a degree of cross-cultural learning.[129] However, despite these promising aspects, Western patriarchal constructions of the morality of the Nagpur normal school students would eventually bring the school crashing down, and with it the whole Carpenter experiment of direct state-sponsored female teacher training in India.

Carpenter's idealistic approach might well have been different if she had known more of local politics and of the simmering cultural antagonisms that had built up in Nagpur in response to broader abuses by British rule in this region of central India. In 1872, the school became the focus of these antagonisms because of the Indian girls recruited in the name of government. Additionally, from the British side, when things went badly, acute colonial racial sensibilities melded with Carpenter's narrative regarding its 'educated' women as Western moral guides could easily be disrupted.

The difficulties at Nagpur began with growing antagonism from local Indian elites who resisted the normal school. These included the influential Brahmin Wamun Rao, who began to infiltrate the institution by arranging for its widowed students to take up the Nagpur custom of forming non-marriage 'contracts' with Indian males who were pre-selected by him because they were already hostile to British colonial rule.[130] The British could hardly oppose this action, given the strong colonial campaigns under way to remove the stigma of Indian widowhood. However, as Wamun Rao's initiative began to affect the school, government officials began to see that this school site might provide unwelcome opportunity for local Indian opponents to British rule. Uppermost in British minds was the possibility that the Nagpur accomplishments curriculum might even be projected by these opponents as a Western colonial agenda of feminine immorality. As the DPI of the Central Provinces ventured:

> I thoroughly understand how impossible it is for a Maratha to dissociate our schools in which reading, writing and sewing are taught, from the courtesan who, until the British government interfered, was the only woman who read and wrote and wore sewn clothes.[131]

Mindful of the broader political dangers that Carpenter's school at Nagpur presented to colonial rule, local ICS officials also began to question its raison d'être – that of operating on the ideological terrain of Carpenter's female teacher as moral guide. Then a school inspector claimed that he had been propositioned by one of Wilson's trainee teachers, 'forward and pert', while on an inspection visit.[132] No Indian official could be found to corroborate the accusation, nor could any other similar moral 'flaws' in Mrs Young's trainee teachers be identified. Nonetheless, military officers stationed at the nearby cantonment were abruptly called into Young's school, as were the Infectious Diseases Police. The discovery was then made that one of the teacher training scholars was suffering from venereal disease, with most of the other girls suspected of being equally 'vicious' with the disease.[133]

Accurate or not, this reported discovery resonated with a broader public concern in the province regarding the spread of syphilis and gonorrhoea. Government dispensary reports already showed a steady annual increase of 16 per cent in cases among Indians to 50,733 confirmed cases.[134] It is probable that these figures resulted from an increase in European investigation at around this time, and perhaps from some misdiagnosis, rather than much actual recent real change in prevalence. These diseases were well documented in earlier, pre-British, Mughal times.[135] Of much greater concern to the colonial authorities was the fact that, by the 1870s, an annual average of 19 Europeans and 310 Eurasians around the military cantonments of the city were also contracting these incurable diseases.[136]

Locating the moral panic at this schooling site appears suspicious. However, it was extremely effective in discrediting the fragile ideology enshrined in the training of Carpenter's moral female teacher and, therefore, the rationale for the school's existence. (It may also have resulted in Young's early death.) What troubled both the official mind and the antagonistic Nagpur Hindu community leaders the most about the Nagpur normal school were the problematic connections that it was beginning to make with the local Indian community.[137] To counteract this, an apparent lack of feminine 'modesty' in the school was equated with teaching incompetence. Middle-ranking ICS officers who were unsympathetic to Carpenter's scheme were now able to claim that isolated trained women teachers out in such schools alone could not succeed. According to these officers, the reason for this had nothing to do with teaching ability, but was the inescapable vulnerability of women teachers when alone in Indian communities, a presence that they considered would inevitably create local political problems.

> Women in the position of school mistress in a small town could hardly escape scandal. If she remained perfectly chaste, the head of the village (who ... looked on her as his *haq* [property]) resenting her chastity, would give her a bad name; whereas, on the otherhand, if she responded to his advances, she secured the censure of her less successful suitors: her greatest safety would lie in indiscriminate incontinence.[138]

These narratives, and the frenzy that followed the Nagpur scandal, fed into earlier debate about the Indian Contagious Diseases Act that went into operation in many parts of British India in the later 1860s, following on from similar projects elsewhere in the empire. The act was designed to preserve the health of soldiers, by 'protecting' them from the moral 'risk' of 'infected' Indian women, by assigning these women to lock (prison) hospitals.[139] The discrediting of the Nagpur normal school was underscored by a broader gender double standard of the era regarding epidemics of venereal disease, which attributed blame to local Indian women and which rationalised the non-examination of European men.[140] (Only towards the end of the century would the undercover work of American missionary feminists Katharine Bushnell and Elizabeth Andrew, in army barracks, reverse this gendered view and identify female victims and male oppressors instead.[141])

As a direct result of the Nagpur scandal, in 1874 all of the newer government-run female teacher training schools in India were quickly closed down and their work handed over to the missions. This shut down came at the urging of provincial governments, which feared a repetition of Nagpur in their own domains where a new combination of 'religion and education', through 'moral' female teacher training, presented unacceptable political risks to broader colonial governance.[142] As a state-sponsored co-initiative, the Carpenter approach was now denigrated by the raj almost entirely in terms of Indian feminine prurience.[143]

Perhaps the most extraordinary aspect of this affair was the way that male ICS officers rationalised the stereotype of Indian female rather than European male sexual culpability, despite Mrs Young being earlier commended for her energetic approach to teaching. The episode left these ICS officials in no doubt that 'naturally in the future all female schools will be viewed with suspicion and narrowly watched'. This last statement was not about the moral pedigree of these Indian female teacher trainees – these officers were quite happy for the daughters of courtesans to be educated before they 'grew up to adopt the immoral profession'.[144] Rather, their view was it was the cultural frailty of Indian communities themselves that made them not yet ready for Western training as teachers in preparation for a professional life of Western moral guardianship.[145] The liberal Viceroy Lord Northbrooke, in a rare missive directly from the Viceroy's office on female educational matters, put the matter even more bluntly in a confidential memo to all provincial authorities:

I communicate to all of you the perilous nature of any experiment which may be prematurely placing women in a position of independence beyond that which the opinion or practice of their own class or country would assign to them. [We] need greater vigilance and caution in the employment of adult women in the profession of teaching ... with the safeguards by which they are surrounded according to the strict usuages [sic] of Native Society.[146]

The Viceroy's summation seemed not to recognise that most students in female normal schools up to that time were girls under the age of 16.[147]

The Nagpur scandal also reflected a broader malaise in the 1870s. In the eyes of indigenous elites, only imperfectly linked to the British by a rising colonial print culture and benefitting from some elevation in literacy, the early tentative connections of female education with the colonial state had broken down.[148] On the other hand, informal systems of knowledge among Indian women through the household were assumed by the British to be weak and inconsequential. Instead, the raj believed that the influence of thought in education circles reflected the power of its authors.[149] Such authors in India were almost exclusively male. The different colonial embodiment of these unfortunate Indian girls of Nagpur normal school, and other similar government schools, meant that they could have no such voice. Whether or not the girls of the school had been trafficked for sexual gain was of only passing interest to the imperial state: an attitude Philippa Levine identifies as one typical across the empire at large.[150]

By mid-1874 the Nagpur scandal had ended the pretence of a holistic British system that was ready to elevate those Indian women, of whatever caste or race, who were considered to have acquired appropriate feminine knowledge in the Westernised classroom. Instead, the girls of the closed Nagpur normal school, caught between two cultures and at risk, were now abandoned to their fate.[151] They were anonymous, except when identified as morally 'deficient', and their treatment could not have been in sharper contrast to British attitudes towards their own children in India at this time.[152]

The Carpenter idea of an array of female normal schools, state backed as individual enterprises, seen as sites for the social reproduction of Western feminised teachers, and ready to recondition India's female young, was easily swept aside in the wake of the Nagpur debacle. More pressing broader state anxieties regarding Eurasians – a consideration around race that did not form part of the Carpenter normal school agenda – were just too strong to allow her experiments even begrudging continuation among Indian communities. Sporadic female normal school forays that connected with hostile Indian activists in politically damaging ways, even at a local level, were seen by the British as simply too dangerous.

The mission compound, with its financial backing from well-established networks of tithing from parent bodies in Britain and elsewhere, offered an attractive alternative: particularly as government only had to find half the funds through grant-in-aid. For nervous provincial officials this alternative seemed safest, and nearly all provincial governments quietly redirected funding for female teacher training to their grant-in-aid budgets for the missions in the latter part of the 1870s.[153]

Towards the end of her life, Carpenter came to terms with the hard experience she had confronted in India. Writing to Lord Salisbury (Secretary of State for India) from her home in Bristol in 1876, she contended that only Europeans and Eurasians with a very strong English predication could now run her scheme, in much more restricted and racially constrained terms.[154]

Compared to Carpenter's high hopes in the mid-1860s, this was a prescription for a much more controlled agenda that was galvanised by her sporadic but direct experiences of India. The race and class predications decided upon earlier by the government were not a part of Carpenter's agenda. Nevertheless, these predications did intervene strongly, particularly from the 1880s onwards, even while Carpenter's influence was still in place, as will be shown in chapter seven.

The networks that drove the genesis of the Carpenter initiative were almost wholly European inspired, and included the response of women philanthropists in England to the reformist ideology of the Brahmo Samaj. For the first time, this powerful genesis overrode longer-standing, sensitive and locally inspired connections – connections that had been built up by careful East/West orientalist-inspired negotiation regarding Indian female education, as part of a broader approach for both Indian girls and boys, particularly in the NWP and in Bombay. Carpenter was resisted by provincial authorities not only because of her seemingly audacious claims pointing to earlier inaction by these provincial authorities, but also because they were aware of other valuable and sensitive local efforts, mostly concerning village-level education, which were beginning to be productive in embracing Indian schoolgirls. In the late 1860s, however, raj perceptions of scarce funding for education meant that choices had to be made. At a time when more communities of European women began to emerge in British circles, and starker cultural equivalencies were made across the empire, the raj chose mostly in favour of what the state chose to define as Carpenter's scheme. The raj then deployed Carpenter's social reformist imperatives from Europe to facilitate its own racial priorities in favour of Eurasians, as will be shown in chapters seven and eight. Women inspectresses, as discussed in this chapter, were also part of the process of officially denigrating the capacity of Indian girls to learn, and further reinforced existing official stereotypes about race, caste and widowhood, which the state argued prevented these girls from learning.

Some of the female teacher training schools established under Carpenter's plan had shown a very limited capacity to attract Indian female enrolments. However the Nagpur scandal demonstrated that networks of Indian males, opposed to British rule, were aware enough of colonial rhetoric to attempt to subvert it by challenging Carpenter's Western social reformist agenda of using female teachers as Western moral guides. Indian activism was still highly specific to particular Indian localities, but this activism seemed prescient enough to potentially challenge more longer-standing British pretensions to be 'remedying' the customs around Indian widowhood and child marriage. This latter consideration of child marriage, driven by an accompanied Western view of under-age child abuse, seemed under another potential challenge too in that Carpenter's normal schools often enrolled under-aged children to train as teachers without an adequate education first. These factors encouraged the state to change strategy and to look to the safer space of the mission compound where the colonial education of females, particularly Eurasian and European females, could be better protected as part of the British civilising mission. The mission compound, even with an apparently stronger and consolidated cultural presence on the ground, was to encourage new networks of female activism. These networks would evolve to shape women's engagement in colonial India in a different way in the coming decades, first regarding Indian female education (as will be shown in the next chapter) and particularly regarding female medical care (as will be shown in chapters five and six).

Notes

1 V. Brendon, *Children of the Raj* ..., p. 146 gives an account of just this vista in the Army schools in India.
2 D. A. Farnie, *East and West of Suez: The Suez Canal in History, 1854–1956* (Oxford: Clarendon, 1969).
3 *Statistical Abstract Relating to British India from 1840 to 1865* (as far as particulars can be stated) London: HMSO, 1967, p. 3. For this set of statistics Madras is even more difficult to discern as the data combined Europeans and Eurasian numbers, which are listed together under the same category 'European'.
4 In the Punjab and the NWP the numbers of women born in Europe were actually slightly higher, but the ratios compared to men born in Europe were slightly lower, being 12.63 and 15.27 per cent, respectively. This was because there were a larger number of European-born men in these last two provinces. For a breakdown of these figures across India, see D. Ibbetson, *Census of India* (Calcutta, Government Press, 1883), vol. ii, p. 153.

5 T. Allender, *Ruling Through Education: The Politics of Schooling in the Colonial Punjab* (New Delhi: New Dawn Press, 2006), pp. 268–71.
6 A. De Courcy, *The Fishing Fleet: Husband Hunting in the Raj* (London: Phoenix, 2013), ch. 19.
7 For a detailed discussion of the professional trajectories of Europeans in government service in India in the Indian Education Services, see C. Whitehead, *Colonial Educators* ..., ch. 2.
8 'Despatch from the Court of Directors of the East India Company to the Governor General of India in Council, June 19, 1854' in H. Sharp, *Selections from the Educational Records* (Calcutta: Government Printing, 1920), pt. ii, p. 368.
9 T. Allender, 'Learning Abroad: The Colonial Educational Experiment in India, 1813–1919...', *Paedagogica Historica* ... , 707–22.
10 Mr Monteath, 'Note on Education in India, 1865–66...', pp. 99, xxxii–xxxiv (OIOC) L/P&J/3/1159, f. 7.
11 T. Allender, *Ruling Through Education* ..., p.42.
12 'Despatch from the Court of Directors of the East India Company ... June 19, 1854' in H. Sharp, *Selections from the Educational Records* ..., pt. ii, p. 368.
13 This correspondence refers to the enormous education correspondence generated by this issue, particularly between the Viceroy's Council and Provincial governments and then additional correspondence in each province between DPIs and Deputy Commissioners, which were the two arms of governance that mostly directed colonial education administration.
14 A. Mitra, *The Financing of Indian Education* (London: Asia, 1967), p. 189.
15 For examples of the imbalance between females in teacher training compared to those actually receiving any secondary school education see 'A note on Female Education submitted by Dadabhai Naoroji to the Indian [Hunter] Education Commission, 1882' in S. Bhattacharya ... et al., *Development of Women's Education in India ... Documents, 1850–1920...*, p. 139.
16 Home Office Proceedings, May 1868, p. 374 (OIOC) P/434/31.
17 Home Office Proceedings, May 1868 (OIOC) P/434/31.
18 Keshub Chunder Sen (1838–84), Theist, later leader of the Brahmo Samaj and social reformer, combined Christian doctrines and the devotional practices of Hindu Vaishnava cults in his writings. In touch with other leading reformers of the age in India, such as Dayananda Saraswati, founder of the Arya Samaj, he advocated education for women and railed against the status of 'untouchability'.
19 S. Collett, *Keshub Chunder Sen's English Visits* (London: Sophia Dobson, 1900), p. 199.
20 M. Borthwick, *Keshub Chunder Sen* (Calcutta: Minerva, 1977), pp. 153–69.
21 A. Burton, *Burdens of History* ..., pp. 127–69.
22 V. Ware, *Beyond the Pale* ..., pp. 119–20.
23 A. Burton, *Burdens of History* ..., p. 98.
24 'One racial motherhood' is Antoinette Burton's phrase referred to in the introduction.
25 Satyendranath Tagore (1842–1923), the elder brother of Rabindranath Tagore, likewise belonged to the tradition, particularly the part that focused on the rights of women. His wife gave up the veil at home and she was the first Indian woman to enter Government House at the invitation of the Viceroy.
26 C. A. Bayly, *Recovering Liberties* ..., p. 39.
27 C. Hartley (ed.), *A Historical Dictionary of British Women* (New York: Routledge, 2003), p. 84.
28 R. Watts 'Mary Carpenter and India ...', pp. 193–210.
29 R. Watts, *Gender, Power and the Unitarians in England, 1760–1860* (London: Longman, 1998), p. 198.
30 M. Carpenter, *The Last Days in England of the Rajah Rammohan Roy* (Calcutta: The Rammohan Library, 1915), first edition preface pp. iii–iv, third edition, pp. 104–5.
31 M. Carpenter, *The Last Days in England of the Rajah Rammohan Roy* ..., p. vii.
32 M. Carpenter, *Juvenile Delinquents: Their Condition and Treatment* (London: W. and F. Cash, 1853).

33 M. Carpenter, *Juvenile Delinquents* ..., pp. 88–90.
34 R. Watts, *Gender, Power and the Unitarians in England* ..., p. 87.
35 R. O'Hanlon, *At the Edges of Empire* ..., p. 25.
36 M. Carpenter, *Juvenile Delinquents* ..., pp. 84–5.
37 M. Carpenter, *Juvenile Delinquents* ..., pp. 86–7.
38 M. Carpenter, *Juvenile Delinquents* ..., pp. 86–7.
39 For the most recent exposition of the secular thought of Harriet Martineau, for example, see R. Watts, 'Harriet Martineau (1802–77): A liberal Protestant/secular educationalist', a paper delivered on June 26, 2015 at the International Standing Conference
   for the History of Education (ISCHE 37) Istanbul, Turkey.
40 M. Carpenter, *Juvenile Delinquents* ..., pp. 87–93; 'Mary Carpenter to the Marquis
   of Salisbury, Secretary of State for India' in *Letters to the Rt Hon the Marquis of
   Salisbury, Secretary of State for India on Female Education in India, Prison
   Discipline and the Necessity of a Factory Act in India* (Bristol: L. Arrowsmith,
   1877); M. Carpenter, *Addresses to the Hindus Delivered in India by Mary Carpenter*
   (London: Newman & Co., 1867).
41 M. Carpenter, *Juvenile Delinquents* ..., p. 91.
42 M. Carpenter, *Juvenile Delinquents* ..., pp. 86, 348.
43 Mary Carpenter to Stafford Northcote, October 8, 1867, Education Proceedings, 1877
   (OIOC) P/1000, pp. 100–1.
44 M. Poovey, *Making the Social Body* ..., chs 1–3.
45 M. Carpenter, *Juvenile Delinquents* ..., p. 90.
46 M. Carpenter, *Juvenile Delinquents* ..., p. 88.
47 M. Carpenter, *Six Months in India* (London: Longmans, 1868), vol. 1, p. 151.
48 M. Carpenter, *Six Months in India* ..., vol. 1, p. 150.
49 M. Carpenter, *Six Months in India* ..., p. 186.
50 'Extract from the Proceedings of the Government of India (Home Department,
   Education) April 20, 1868 (OIOC) P/434/31.
51 M. Carpenter, *Six Months in India* ..., pp. 150–1.
52 Mary Carpenter to Northcote, October 8, 1867 in M. Carpenter, *Six Months in India*
   ..., pp. 157–65.
53 *Edinburgh Evening Courant*, October 15, 1867 incl. in Government of India to
   Government of Madras [and to other provincial governments] January 17, 1867
   (OIOC) P/434/31.
54 'Memorandum' Government of India to Provincial Governments, January 18, 1868
   Home Proceedings (OIOC) P/434/31.
55 'Memorandum' incld. in Home Office Proceedings, May 30, 1868 (OIOC) P/434/31,
   p. 716.
56 N. Sargant, *Mary Carpenter in India* (Bristol: A. J. Sargant, 1987), p. 72.
57 Mary Carpenter to Stafford Northcote, October 8, 1867, Education Proceedings, 1877
   (OIOC) P/1000.
58 M. Carpenter, *Six Months in India* ..., p. 161.
59 M. Carpenter, *Six Months in India* ..., p. 162.
60 M. Carpenter, *Six Months in India* ..., pp. 156–7.
61 M. Carpenter, *Six Months in India* ..., p. 163.
62 Government of India to Government of Madras [and to other provincial govern-
   ments] July 30, 1867 (OIOC) P/434/31.
63 'Extract from the Proceedings of the Government of India (Home Department,
   Education) April 20, 1868 (OIOC) P/434/31.
64 M. Carpenter, *Addresses to the Hindoos Delivered in India by Mary Carpenter*
   (London: Newman and Co., 1867) p. 12.
65 M. Carpenter, *Addresses to the Hindoos* ..., pp. 58–9.
66 M. Carpenter, *Addresses to the Hindoos* ..., p. 53.
67 M. Carpenter, *Addresses to the Hindoos* ..., pp. 48.
68 M. Carpenter, *Addresses to the Hindoos* ...
69 A. M. Monteath, 'Note on the State of Education in India, 1865–66', p. 59 (OIOC)
   V/27/860/5; Home Office Proceedings, May, 1868, p. 376 (OIOC) P/434/31.

70 Sir Alexander Grant to Government of Bombay, April 14, 1867 (OIOC) P/434/30.
71 N. Sargant, 'India, My Appointed Place: An Account of Mary Carpenter's Found Journeys to India', pp. 86, 91 (OIOC) MSS Eur Photo Eur F 147.
72 N. Sargant, 'India, My Appointed Place ...', pp. 86–92.
73 N. Sargant, 'India, My Appointed Place ...', p. 84.
74 'Note of A. P. Howell [Undersecretary Home Department, India] on the State of Education in India for 1866–67', pp. 110–12 (OIOC) P/434/31; 'Journal of the National Indian Association', November, 1871, no. 11, p. 230 (OIOC).
75 N. Sargant, 'India, My Appointed Place ...', p. 85; Mary Carpenter, *Six Months in India* ..., pp. 164–5.
76 N. Sargant, *Mary Carpenter in India* ..., pp. 73–4.
77 Officiating Commissioner, Lahore to Government of the Punjab, November 10, 1967 (OIOC) P/442/25 no. 438.
78 'Memorandum' Government of India to Provincial Governments, January 18, 1868 Home Proceedings (OIOC) P/434/31.
79 Commissioner of Mysore to Government of India (Foreign Department), February 13, 1868 (OIOC) P/434/31.
80 Commissioner of Mysore to Government of India (Foreign Department), February 13, 1868 (OIOC) P/434/31.
81 Memorandum by Miss G Anstey, Female Missionary for the London Missionary Society, August 19, 1867 (OIOC) P/434/31.
82 Memorandum by Miss G Anstey, Female Missionary for the London Missionary Society, August 19, 1867 (OIOC) P/434/31.
83 F. Currie to Chief Commissioner of Oude to Government of India, January 3, 1868 (OIOC) P/434/31.
84 R. S. Sinclair (DPI) to First Assistant Resident (Hyderabad), February 7, 1868 (OIOC) P/434/31.
85 R. S. Sinclair (DPI) to First Assistant Resident (Hyderabad), February 7, 1868 (OIOC) P/434/31.
86 Simon Kempson, 'Memorandum', April 14, 1868 (OIOC) P/434/31.
87 Simon Kempson, 'Memorandum', April 14, 1868 (OIOC) P/434/31.
88 L. Zastoupil and M. Moir, *The Great Indian Education Debate* ..., pp. 1–31.
89 Simon Kempson, 'Memorandum', April 14, 1868 (OIOC) P/434/31.
90 H. S. Reid, 'Report on Indigenous Education and Vernacular Schools' (Agra: Orphan, 1852), p. 102.
91 Simon Kempson, 'Memorandum', April 14, 1868 (OIOC) P/434/31.
92 Simon Kempson, 'Memorandum', April 14, 1868 (OIOC) P/434/31.
93 H. Reid, Education Report NWP, 1858/9, p. 57 (OIOC) V/24/908.
94 *NWP Provincial Report: Hunter Commission 1882* (Calcutta: Government Printing, 1884), pp. 33–4 (SLV).
95 *NWP Provincial Report: Hunter Commission 1882* (Calcutta: Government Printing, 1884), pp. 33–4 (SLV).
96 *Dictionary of National Biography*, p. 375.
97 Anglicists were proponents of teaching in English in government funded institutions and some were supporters of the study classical languages of Persian, Arabic and Sanscrit. They were putative opponents of the Orientalists who supported government funding learning in the local languages and who believed complex Western ideas were capable of 'engraftment' onto these local languages.
98 A. Grant to Government of Bombay, December 21, 1867 (OIOC) P/434/31, May, 1868.
99 A. Grant to Government of Bombay, April, 14, 1867 (OIOC) P/434/30.
100 'Female Schools in India', pp. 55–6 (OIOC) L/PJ/3/1159.
101 Mr Munguldass Nuthobhoy and others, inhabitants of Bombay, to Sir Alexander Grant, November 5, 1867 (OIOC) P/434/31.
102 Government o f Bombay to Government of India, October 5, 1867; reply December 7, 1867 (OIOC), P/434/30; A. Grant to Government of Bombay, December 21, 1867 (OIOC) P/434/31.

103 A. Grant to Government of Bombay, December 21, 1867 (OIOC) P/434/31.
104 'Resolution' Government of India (Home Department), April, 24, 1868 (OIOC) P/434/32.
105 See, for example, among many others, Government of India to Government of Bombay, July 20, 1867 (OIOC), P/434/31. Some government inspectors of schools, especially in Bengal, also built the stereotype. Home Department May, 1868, pp. 374–81 (OIOC) P/434/31.
106 Government of India Proceedings, June, 1867 in S. Bhattacharya *et al.*, *Development of Women's Education ... Documents* ..., pp. 46–7.
107 G. Sutherland, *Elementary Education in the Nineteenth Century* (London: Historical Association, 1971), pp. 18–26.
108 Mrs S. MacIntosh, Inspectress of Female Schools, Lahore Circle to the Inspector of Schools, Lahore Circle, January 18, 1875 no. 3 (OIOC) P/139.
109 Mrs S. MacIntosh, Inspectress of Female Schools, Lahore Circle to the Inspector of Schools, Lahore Circle, January 18, 1875 no. 3 (OIOC) P/139.
110 For a fuller discussion of the role of women in colonial education service circles in India see C. Whitehead, *Colonial Educators* ..., ch. 4.
111 History of Service (OIOC) V/12/323 p. 545.
112 F. A. Francis 'Some Municipal Schools in the Punjab' in the *Maria Grey College Magazine* (London: Baines and Scarsbrook, 1891), p. 9 (OIOC).
113 F. A. Francis 'Some Municipal Schools in the Punjab ...', pp. 10–13.
114 'Fourth School' F. A. Francis 'Some Municipal Schools in the Punjab ...' pp. 11–14.
115 See, for example, A. Knapp, *How to Live: A Manual of Hygiene* (New York: Silver, Burdett and Company, 1902).
116 'Fifth School' F. A. Francis 'Some Municipal Schools in the Punjab ...'
117 F. A. Francis 'Some Municipal Schools in the Punjab ...'
118 B. Ramusack, *Cultural Missionaries, Maternal Imperialists, Feminist Allies* ..., pp. 309–20.
119 Mary Carpenter to the Marquis of Salisbury, August 30, 1876, pp. 94–101 (OIOC) P/1000.
120 'Despatch from the Court of Directors of the East India Company ... June 19, 1854' in H. Sharp, *Selections from the Educational Records* ..., pt. ii, p. 368.
121 M. Carpenter, *India, My Appointed Place* [unpublished manuscript], p. 110 (OIOC), Photo Eur 280.
122 'Report of Education in the Central Provinces, 1866–67', p. 12 (OIOC) V/24/996.
123 'Education Report, Central Provinces for the Year 1871/2', p. 29 (OIOC) (Nagpur: Office Press, 1872), V/24/996.
124 'Education Report, Central Provinces for the Year 1871/2' (OIOC) (Nagpur: Office Press, 1872), V/24/996.
125 This was after the school was initially closed down and relocated with her consent when, in her words, 'serious evils' had emerged. She did not elaborate upon these, but they probably related to an enrolment not likely to fulfill her prescribed Western moral outcomes. Carpenter to Northcote, October 8, 1867 (OIOC) P/1000.
126 'Central Provinces Education Report, 1869–70', p. 49 (OIOC) V/24/996.
127 'Central Provinces Education Report, 1869–70', p. 49 (OIOC) V/24/996.
128 'Central Provinces Education Report, 1869–70', p. 49 (OIOC) V/24/996.
129 'Memorandum Concerning the Nagpur Female Normal School' incld. in Chief Commissioner, Central Provinces, October 4, 1872 (OIOC) P/520.
130 'Report on Education in the Central Provinces, 1873/4', p. 65 (Nagpur: Office Press, 1874) (OIOC) V/24/997.
131 'Memo. regarding the Nagpur School by Mr Pedler' [DPI] incl. in Government of Central Provinces to Government of India, January 5, 1873 (OIOC) P/520.
132 Government of Central Provinces to Government of India, January 5, 1873 (OIOC) P/520.
133 'Memorandum Concerning the Nagpur Female Normal School' [n.d. 1873] incl. in Chief Commissioner to Government of India, January 5, 1873 no. 377 (OIOC) P/520.

134 Report on the Working of Government Charitable Dispensaries in the Central Provinces, 1874 (OIOC) V/24/764.
135 A. Eraly, *The Mughal World* (New Delhi: Penguin, 2007), p. 4.
136 Report on the Working of Government Charitable Dispensaries in the Central Provinces, 1874 (OIOC) V/24/764.
137 Education Report of the Central Provinces, 1871–2 (OIOC) V/24/996.
138 'Memorandum Concerning the Nagpur Female Normal School' [n.d. 1873] incl. in Chief Commissioner to Government of India, January 5, 1873 no. 377 (OIOC) P/520.
139 G. Forbes, *Women in Colonial India: Essays on Politics, Medicine and Historiography* (Delhi: New Chronicle Books), p. 103.
140 P. A. Kramer, 'The Darkness that Enters the Home: The Politics of Prostitution during the Philippine-American War' in A. L. Stoler (ed.), *Haunted by Empire: Geographies of Intimacy in North American History* (Durham, NC: Duke University Press, 2006), pp. 373–96. The 'hospitals' were later given the disingenuous title 'voluntary venereal hospitals' by the British.
141 E. Andrew and K. Bushnell, 'Cantonment Life in India' in P. Tuson (ed.), *The Queen's Daughters* (Reading, Ithaca, 1990), pp. 176–199.
142 Government of India to all Local Governments and Administrators, March 17, 1873; Major General William Hill to the Viceroy, March 3, 1874; Resolution no. 3, pp. 100–12, March 9, 1874; Secretary of State to Government of India, July, 1874, Government of India Proceedings, 1874 (OIOC) P/520.
143 Chief Commissioner, Central Provinces to Government of India, January 5, 1873, India Education Proceedings (OIOC) P/520.
144 'Memo. regarding the Nagpur School by Mr Pedler' (CP DPI) incl. in Government of Central Provinces to Government of India, January 5, 1873, India Education Proceedings (OIOC) P/520.
145 'Memo. regarding the Nagpur School by Mr Pedler' (CP DPI) incl. in Government of Central Provinces to Government of India, January 5, 1873 (OIOC) P/520.
146 'Confidential' Government of India to all Local Government Administrators, March 17, 1873 nos. 110–18 (OIOC) P/520.
147 See, for example, regular references to these age groupings in Proceedings of the Government of India (Home Department) (OIOC) P/434/31.
148 For a contemporary view of this phenomenon, that is antagonistic towards the British, see G. Leitner, 'History of Indigenous Education ...'
149 M. Foucault, 'Two Lectures' in N. Dirks, G. Eley and S. Ortner (eds), *Culture/Power/History: A Reader in Contemporary Social Theory* (Princeton, NJ: Princeton University Press, 1994).
150 P. Levine, 'Sexuality, Gender and Empire' in P. Levine, *Gender and Empire* (Oxford: Oxford University Press, 2004), p. 137.
151 'Memorandum Concerning the Nagpur Female Normal School' [n.d. 1873] incld. in Chief Commissioner to Government of India, January 5, 1873 no. 377 (OIOC) P/520.
152 E. Collingham, *Imperial Bodies* ..., p. 90 cited in E. Beuttner, *Empire Families* ..., p. 30.
153 Grant-in-aid regulations, technically available to all approved private enterprises, were almost entirely monopolised by the missions, where half the cost of their contributions, including salaries of missionaries, were provided by government.
154 Carpenter to Salisbury, Bristol, August 30, 1876, pp. 94–101 (OIOC) P/1000.

CHAPTER FOUR

Both sides of the mission wall, 1875–84

The missions offered something far less speculative than lone ventures such as the Carpenter-inspired Nagpur Normal school. By the mid-1870s, the missions were communities built around central solid-walled compounds, which the state unquestioningly assumed were Western-cultured spaces, by virtue of their Christian foundation. This assumption was true when looking internally, as the state almost invariably did, to the central mission community, including the mission's education work. As discussed in chapter one, a good example of such Western orientation was Mary Ann (Cooke) Wilson's Church Mission Society (CMS) girls' school in Calcutta in the 1820s: a key driver of Company female education directives in the first half of the nineteenth century. For uninitiated Europeans, these sites seemed stamped template-like across the subcontinent: central compound in the city; branch schools in the suburbs or in the *mofussil* (outlying areas).

However, the relationship between mission and secular governance had matured during the years since the 1850s. There was a strict official insistence on religious neutrality in government schools after 1858; although, through a series of compromises, a succession of Indian customs most objectionable to the missions, such as *sati*, had been struck out by legislation. These compromises also aimed at greater balance between preaching, proselytising and English-language instruction in schools. Such compromise was designed to achieve greater consensus between missionary bodies at home, missionaries in India, British officials in India and at Westminster, and Indians themselves.[1]

Looking beyond the central mission, at how these missions projected outwards to the subcontinent, matters were very different. The roots of this projection lay in knowledge transfer and other network interactions that long predated the formal admission of the missions in 1813. Even before the time of British India, key male missionaries had interacted with leading Hindu intellectuals interested in equable knowledge transfer with the West, via the exploration of shared theological precepts. Even after the Great Revolt, theological fluidity of this kind continued, conducted by Indians heavily influenced by Western as well as Eastern scholarship.[2] This was despite most head missionaries resisting such intellectual confluence in the 1850s, partly because this interchange of ideas sat uncomfortably with their own theological rigidity. As one Baptist missionary contended:

> It is much more difficult to argue with the Mahammadans then [sic] with the Hindus. Amongst the former, the more intelligent are well acquainted with the Unitarians at home; and although ignorant of the general contents of our Scriptures, exhibit an acquaintance with most of those difficult passages which have reference to the Trinity. Some display considerable Socratical mode of disputation viz means of question and answer and by this means sometimes lead us into a subtle and profitless discussion before we are aware.[3]

Attempting to argue the doctrine of the Trinity, even to receptive monotheists was one issue. However, there was also the principle of 'fulfilment', which was adhered to by many missionary educators in the latter part of the nineteenth century. This principle claimed that all the world's faiths could be fulfilled through Christianity. Brajendranath Seal, and other Brahmo Samaj intellectuals, turned this view on its head, arguing that Christianity itself could only be 'fulfilled' by contact with the world's religions.[4] Such elite intellectualism, although mostly separate from the plainer exigencies that head male missionaries faced in their central compounds, was part of a longer-standing and spontaneous tradition of missionary outreach to Indians beyond these compounds that took place even before formal mission admission in 1813. Even in the 1870s, the interchange still offered possibilities for directing British rule away from its race agendas, at least where the interaction of European and Indian women was concerned, and when this interaction occurred beyond the imperial gaze itself.

This chapter looks at both sides of the mission wall, and at how female missionary educators, in particular, operated in different ways on either side of the divide. As a preliminary, it is important to briefly examine the mindset of two levels of male missionary governance within which these women missionaries operated: the bishops, and the male missionaries who directed central mission compounds. Then, more substantially, this chapter explores how female education developments within the mission wall connected with state imperatives after Mary Carpenter. Finally, it examines the way in which, outside the mission wall, female missionary agents operating within Indian households began writing new agendas which avoided the annoying state directives that otherwise ignored Indian female learners.

The mission network

By the late 1870s events had moved on from the generally bleak agendas offered by CMS female classrooms in Bengal in the 1820s. In the second half of the nineteenth century there was instead a complex array of missions in India, with various constellation networks in Europe, the USA and other empires. The British Church of England Zenana Missionary Society alone sent 214 women to India between 1887 and 1894.[5] In the USA, in the same period, Protestant missionary organisations formed the largest women's organisations in that country.[6] Territory was important, with each mission occupying a part of India that was both strategic to its interests and far enough away from other missions as to enable it to sell a separate mandate to its benefactors in India and abroad. The sectarian divide was strongly projected in mid-century India: not just between Catholic and Protestant, but also between different liturgical traditions within denominations, particularly the High and Low Church of England. German and Belgium Jesuits were active in schools in the east and south, while American missions fed important intellectual property back to emerging American universities, which were developing an intellectual tradition separate from that of Europe. The American universities strongly enforced the separation between Church and state, which additionally telescoped a distinctive type of secular education back to the American missions in India.[7]

At the macro state level, in the middle of the century, there were still the usual missionary problems. The CMS had got into trouble with the government for its evangelising agenda, which had sometimes resulted in it abandoning regional schools for the itineration trail. In particular, its insouciant forays to the market bazaars of highly politically sensitive Punjabi villages had resulted in serious riots in the 1850s.[8] Furthermore, at the time of the frenzied 'home' response to the 1857 Great Revolt, the CMS had leaked secret government despatches concerning controversies over Bible classes in government schools to the British press.[9]

By the mid-1870s, however, the state viewed the mission as the safest possible depository for its limited implementation of female education directives. This was with the aim of producing teachers who were Western, moral guides, the need for which the state had been active in articulating in the previous decade. Female normal schools, which might be operated by the missions, were a credible avenue for the state to use so it could continue to justify its official rhetoric on this topic.

The state's engagement of the missions also brought into play the ideas of senior churchmen; ideas which remained unbending throughout British rule and which mostly focused on Eurasians. For example, the Anglican bishops of Calcutta, Bombay and Madras kept an uncompromisingly strong line on Church policy that generally embraced only Eurasian 'orphans' as the most fruitful ground for conversion. Holding court in their Indo-Georgian city mansions, they enjoyed direct access to major state powerbrokers in India, as their brother bishops did in England. Their dioceses were enormous, with that of Anglican Calcutta including even the Australian colonies until 1836. This 'reach' invited the bishops to hold confident, but grotesquely overly simplistic, attitudes to education that only included females as part of their larger 'orphan' Christian strategies. More critically, these were men with an unyielding abhorrence of Eastern religion, who could therefore only offer remote philanthropy strategies that rarely included Indians. As they peered across the vast subcontinental expanse, they consequently saw a mostly Eurasian racial vista. They believed that it was here that the work of conversion could best be done, unhindered, as at least one bishop viewed it, by Hindu Gangetic purification beliefs that took the fear out of God's 'terrible' final judgement.[10]

There were also good financial reasons for the bishops to concentrate on Eurasians: wealthier Eurasian families could afford to donate. Mission coin was also to be had from Railway Company shareholders. These companies contributed large sums (£13,000) to the relatively High Church Society for the Propagation of the Gospel (SPG), in particular, for its work among the predominately Eurasian railway workforce, including funding for girls' education. In short, the money trail concerned mostly Eurasians and Europeans, rather than Indians, and this consideration, in turn, determined the focus of many missions. As these senior churchmen saw it, therefore, even as late as 1879, it was the 'European' (including Eurasians of European habit) demographic that mattered.

> The European population has increased rapidly and is distributed in comparatively small stations over the whole country. Their condition is similar to settlers in New Zealand, Australia and Canada, except instead of being separated by miles of uninhabited country they are separated by miles of country densely populated by Hindoos and Mahummedans.[11]

Dehumanising comparisons to the Canadian tundra, or the Australian desert, showed an obvious disconnection from India's large population. Anglican bishops from the 1840s onwards took a direct role in encouraging their female missionary subordinates to enrol Eurasians, rather than Indians, in central mission schools, although, unlike in the

Lawrence asylums, famine, rather than the conscience-bound soldier father, was the chief driver of the recruitment. For example, in Cawnpore (central-north India), a city in which seven regiments were stationed in 1840, the SPG 'harvest' was 150 Eurasian female orphans fully abandoned by their parents.[12] Many of the larger-scale mission networks swung into operation in a similar vein. As late as 1876, the famine in Bombay saw many desperate parents on the streets willing to sell their children.[13] The resident bishop's response to this tragedy was to counsel good forward planning for a new orphanage that concentrated chiefly on conversion, which might eventually see these children segregated into 'industrial' schools ready for Western-recognised, adult 'work'.[14]

However, in the India of the 1870s it became clear that another missionary approach was also needed. This realisation was not apparent to the patrician bishops, but to the middle-ranking male missionaries and some of their wives who were actually working 'the field'. For many of these middle-ranking missionaries the different purpose of state education was clear enough.

> Education pressed forward on Government terms means larger grants, honourable mention in Educational Reports, distinction in exams, & perhaps Government employment for distinguished scholars. Therefore the subjects that pay best must be taught and English is well paid for. But this is not a sufficient reason given the style of education by the Missionary body.[15]

Various issues concerning belief were central to the thoughts of these missionaries as they struggled to accommodate their experiences in India. Indulgent discussions about the thirty-nine articles of faith, or esoteric musings about the nature of the Holy Trinity, seemed somehow remote from India's daily agenda; an agenda that could reify, in non-European ways, the earlier theological training many missionaries of this period had received in London, Birmingham or in Boston. For example, R. R. Winter, head missionary of the Society for the SPG at Delhi for thirty years, yielded his high churchmanship to simpler forms of worship towards the end of his long career, in response to the stark realities he met on a daily basis of what he regarded as a needy India.[16] A close Cambridge Mission colleague working with him, the acerbic George Lefroy (later, Anglican bishop of Calcutta), described the phenomenon in exaggerated form to his mother back in England:

> [Winter] dislikes rules and formalities of any kind – the old story – he began as an extreme churchman – was unstable – then fell away utterly into the opposite extreme of disallowing all sacramental teaching, all church teaching.[17]

Others, such as the CMS's Vincent Harcourt at Madras, attempted to work within caste networks such as the Nairs to build schools of joint foundation, even sometimes using their religious texts, accompanied by *Sistrums* (Indian percussion instruments), rather than the Bible when teaching ethics.[18] In the far south, German Jesuit missionaries took over the work of Sir Thomas Munro in establishing village schools that mostly taught secular Indian knowledge.[19] Even as late as 1882, the Baptist missionaries were singled out by antagonistic Indian nationalists as worthy of Indian recognition because of their secular education work among the lowly *chamars* (leather workers) of Bengal.[20] Informal shifting of the liturgical and theological setting in this way was an inevitable consequence of long missionary careers spent in India. Careers required extraordinary energy, on a daily basis, to meet the difficult economic and social circumstances of surrounding communities. This was in an environment where heat and disease readily consumed fair-skinned Europeans. These shifting settings also allowed considerably more flexibility for women missionaries seeking new ways to reach Indian female scholars.

Significant barriers, however, still remained to education provided by women missionaries for Indian girls. In the 1860s Indian enrolments in branch mission schools could halve overnight as anxious Hindu parents responded nervously to even one Indian baptism.[21] Good cultural knowledge was needed to circumvent such resistance: knowledge that could enable the deciphering of local Indian power structures so that debacles like that suffered at Nagpur could be avoided. Building operative local knowledge of this kind usually took a lifetime, and to this end long-serving missionaries in the field were attentive to learning local languages and the village patois.[22] They also needed to find less formal ways to assimilate the Christian ethic, even if this meant building a connection with Indian teachings as part of the uncomfortable cohabitation.

As it was, women missionaries and their sister sponsors in Britain found themselves operating between the arch policymaking of the bishops and the practices of the, usually more adaptive, male missionaries whom they worked beside in the missions. Conversion imperatives continued to drive most of these women in the 1870s, although official rhetoric about 'female education' was still robust. Despite the failures of Carpenter, it was the women missionaries who were able to find new avenues for activism within this perspective of conversion. The new avenues, particularly as they related to Indian females, turned out to be of primary significance for the colonial education of females and colonial 'training' of female medical carers that developed in the last two decades of the nineteenth century.

[134]

Inside the mission compound

For women missionaries located in the central mission compound, there was an uncomfortable binary of action concerning their female students. This binary resulted in flagrantly cruel practices, such as public humiliation and sexual exploitation, on the one hand, while, on the other, also providing a functional Western learning space for the students.[23] This part of the central mission compound, preconceived and reserved by the missions for intensive conversion work, was equally attractive to the government, which saw its potential as a refuge for Western feminisation as well as for communal sanitation. The central mission compound was also sturdy enough to carry forward official female education rhetoric in the increasingly politicised India of the latter 1870s. However, it was only a short-term vision. Even when these girls graduated as newly minted teachers, they were not destined to join an imagined professional community. Instead, they were seen by the state, at best, as mere operatives at the mission periphery: a periphery that might filter their actions, in Western terms, without a repeat of the Nagpur scandal.

As directed by the bishops, 'orphan' Eurasians were the priority in the central mission compound, particularly for the dominant Anglican missions. The other missions followed a similar plan of action, as they were forced to compete for state grant-in-aid funding on similar terms. Eurasian girls who were orphans were, after Canning's 1860 Despatch, now the official priority in girls' schooling, partly because of the funding preference and partly because of their seeming Western orientation. These girls were brought to the mission compound for conversion but they were also subjected to physical and sometimes sexual abuse, with the direct knowledge of government well before the 1870s. For example, between 1863 and 1871, the CMS female normal school at Benares (NWP) operated mostly as a drop-off centre for Eurasian girls, in much the same way as the Lawrence military asylums were filling their classrooms at this time. The girls coming to this mission were without any attendant parents to modify potential abuse. They came from outlying areas, singly, as the illegitimate issue of Europeans and possibly some of the missionaries themselves. The girls only stayed for a few months at the central Benares mission normal school, and their education in accomplishments involved learning only basic sewing skills so that they could then be deemed a 'teacher'.[24] The details provided by the list of 105 Eurasian girls concerned, all with Anglo-Saxon names, makes for poignant reading, and shows the degree to which their futures were manipulated under the banner of mission education and the very limited self-actualisation available to them.[25]

In the mid-1860s most of these girls entered the mission at the age of twelve or thirteen (with some as young as ten) for 'teacher training'. This was probably a response to the Carpenter narrative. Only one or two years after their admission to the mission, many of these girls, now Eurasian 'converts', married missionaries. As a result they were destined to live out solitary lives accompanied only by their much older husbands in the lonely outposts of upper India.[26] Here their role, as 'female teachers', was to teach scripture, using the inducement of needlework lessons to attract local Indian girls interested in using this skill for commercial advantage in the local bazaar. The practice was designed to keep the mission community strong and self-supporting via the agency of the teacher who was female. The early death of a husband could mean further isolation, and some of these Eurasian female 'teachers' later graduated to lonely piecework in market places using their own sewing machines to ply their trade. Others did not live very long at all, dying of smallpox shortly after their first mission posting.[27] The one-way view of the world taken by the missions is demonstrated by the fact that the early marriages of these young Eurasian 'teachers', at just thirteen or fourteen years of age, to catechists seemed morally safe to them despite these same missions being vocal against the 'degeneracy' of child marriage among Hindus.

Harrowing accounts also exist of the mistreatment of Eurasian girls in the central mission, again with government knowledge. One, in particular, concerned the mission school at Nasik, Maharashtra in 1862. It is illustrative of how moral blame for the loss of perceived feminine virtue, particularly sexual virtue, could be easily apportioned and how closely this was related to professional outcomes for teachers who were female at the time. The head missionary account reads as follows:

At 8pm when all the girls were being locked up in their bedrooms, Rosemary was missing ... At last the girl returned to the Orphanage, but in a condition that excited suspicion, and led to an examination by Lala's wife, by which sad discovery was made that she had been ravished ... The girl was locked in the clothes room ... The girl ... opened her heart to Miss D[owman], and startled her with disclosures which showed ... such intercourse was kept up, between the elder orphan girls and several of the Karkhann [village] boys ... The [superintendent's] apprentice Paulos ... when he was feverish ... [also] took her into his room through the window where he lay down on his couch, and she had to shampoo him. She ... received intoxicating sweetmeats, which made her giddy, and he then cohabitated with her ... one of the girls (Isabella) not 13 years old, after having confessed to the same thing ... has been found to be in the family way ... the midwife thinks that she must have done more than one abortion.[28]

Much about this lurid account suggests that the mission staff already knew about the behaviour. As with other parts of the empire, ignorance of sex and sexual abuse were commonplace. Even European children in India learnt the facts of life through informal storytelling, and sometimes manikin making of miniature animals with erect penises, by the *Ayah* (family maid), rather than from embarrassed parents.[29] However, as in other cases in British India, the mission staff at Nasik, including the male abusers, were also protected by British law. The government Assistant Collector advised that as there was no violation of property, the only charge available was 'breach of trust'. Even this could not be tested in court because the girls concerned refused to testify.[30] There was no recourse for these very young girls who were mission educated. It would be another generation before the likes of Bombay journalist Behramji Malabari launched his campaign to raise the age of consent in India and when more emphasis was put on the need to protect the sanctity of girlhood ready for a full adult life.[31]

Within the bounds of the central mission compound, it was the girls themselves who could be made to pay a high price for the abuse they had suffered. In this spirit, the head missionary, the Rev. Isenberg, reported on the solemnity of the punishment procedure with all its ghoulishness and humiliation:

> When consulting with Messrs Appagi and Rutttongi ... & Miss Dowman [Mistress of the Girls' Orphanage] we all agreed in the propriety and suitability of cutting their hair and shaving their heads altogether ... During the whole process I spoke to them reminding them of the crown of thorns which Jesus had borne for the crimes they had committed and exhorting them whilst throwing off their hair, to root out their pride.[32]

At least one of these girls, classified as 'Eurasian' and considered ripe for conversion, had in fact been rescued by the British from an Arab slave ship (plying its way from Zanzibar, East Africa to the Persian gulf) and she had been brought to Bombay.[33] Rescued slaves from Africa was another avenue to recruit 'orphans' for educational institutions in Maharashtra which, after 1853, contained a significant community of rescued Abyssinian and Somalian female slaves.[34] Though having little dialogue with the Muslim world in Africa, the British were particularly active in negotiating with the Ottoman government to limit the slave trade by other European nationals in Africa and to ban it from Egypt.[35] However, to this former African slave in the mission school at Nasik, now deemed 'Eurasian', the sexual violation and humiliation must have seemed a continuation of what she had endured in her earlier life. Most importantly, the European-identified moral 'turpitude' of all these girls additionally had professional consequences that reflected the heightened European sensitivity against any Western compromises concerning the moral character of graduating teachers who were female.

> Ribka, Salome & the other (guilty) girls who were ... engaged in teaching, have been put more to grinding and cooking ... if they sincerely repent we may ... find suitable husbands for them, though the Karkhana boys are [not] as yet sufficiently up in their trades to support a wife and coming family.[36]

It is impossible to decipher just how widespread these and other abuses were across the missions in India. The systemic approach to recruiting, and then farming out of very young girls as female teachers as practised at the Benares mission female normal school, was likely to have been repeated elsewhere. Missions competing in the same field, with similarly meagre funding, were forced to employ similar strategies to staff an ambitious over-reach of trial branch schools in the contest with other missions to 'convert' India.[37] In the CMS at least, the strategy of recruiting very young Eurasian girls was designed to build missionary capacity, and the European adults who directed the trade in girls viewed it as an unremarkable practice.[38] As for the treatment of girls who had 'transgressed' in the normal school in Nasik, Maharashtra, it is obvious that, when this episode came to the notice of local government, such treatment was not objected to and, perhaps more significant, these Eurasian girls remained beyond the limited reach of English Common Law in India.

For women missionaries in direct daily contact with these orphan Eurasians there was also an odd juxtaposition. On the one hand the Eurasian female orphan was to be held to account for the consequences of her enforced institutionalisation. On the other hand, women missionaries were preparing the same girls, through teacher training, to exercise discretion and judgement as adults in the classroom in which they would supposedly teach. This latter professional discretion, however limited, was inescapably internal to the whole Western idea of teacher 'training' of females by this time, where teaching and learning outcomes were not the priority. Yet such professionalism was immediately compromised in the mission in India because these Eurasian trainee teachers were not yet adults as the West understood the term. Furthermore, the abilities of the available women who were heading teaching in missions were also liable to be brought into question by the men in charge of the missions. For example, Mary Dowman at Nasik, referred to above, was considered lacking in aptitude but not in work ethic, the latter being what really mattered as an extension of her moral authority:

> accomplishments not splendid, but quite sufficient for the post that she occupies and while she makes good use of them she seeks to improve them by diligent study.[39]

The men in charge of the missions continued to view education as a kind of moral and disciplinary training, rather than one of attainments, even when deploying an imperfect gendered curriculum for females. Furthermore, women missionaries could also find their own morality brought into question if they were too vocal in opposing the viewpoints of male missionaries, particularly on matters of Christian theology and the subcontinent. One such case was that of Miss Mary Pigot who, in 1870, offended Rev. William Hastie by supporting the opposing views of one of her staff members, Babu Kali Charan Banerjee. In retaliation, Hastie sent accounts of rumours of Pigot's immorality back to head mission office in Scotland, which he calculated was the best way to discredit her.

> After retiring from the dining room into the living room Miss Pigot, without any invitation or suggestion from her host, flung herself upon a sofa, and threw up her legs in a way that I have never seen a lady in such circumstance do before.[40]

Hastie's jealousy was inspired by Pigot's friendships with Indian men, and Pigot was strong enough to bring legal proceedings in Scotland. However, after a gruelling public trial she had to be content with just one anna (one sixteenth of a rupee) in damages and the requirement to pay her own costs.[41]

New communities

Wealthy European women, not directly part of any mission in India, were also reinforcing the racialised directives of the bishops in prioritising orphan Eurasians in the central mission compounds. By the 1870s the expatriate communities of European women in India's biggest cities were sufficiently large and affluent to begin part-financing the Eurasian racial outcome in the missions throughout India. In this decade various Ladies Auxilliaries in Calcutta were active in raising money for Eurasians in mission boarding schools.[42] Their motivation was simple: to provide viable Eurasian female enrolments for schools in which their own wholly European daughters could also be educated, without the expensive prospect of sending them back to Europe and away from family life. These racially distinct classrooms also avoided the possibility of their daughters being educated in mission classrooms, whose academic orientation had to somehow accommodate impoverished Indian girls who had no need of an accomplishments education.

The oversight of European parents reassured a government that remained fearful of a repeat of the Nagpur scandal. In Rangoon, Burma, one such auxiliary, working with a sister organisation in London, even worked to close a flourishing Burmese female mission school so that it could be moved to the 'white' part of town, where there were no Chinese Joss houses.[43] Female missionary supporters in Britain were still clinging to the more ambitious idea of converting Indian girls through schooling instead. They rightly criticised the 'reckless' actions of the Burma-based memsahibs.[44] However, the money in the gift of these secular European women living in India, in the context of very little available government funding, was difficult to resist. The networks of European women in India were strategically placed, not only in the 'club', but also through other white racial enclaves such as Women's Institutes, postnatal clinics, the Red Cross and later the Young Women's Christian Association.[45]

The central mission compound also projected a complex educational domain that was conveyed directly through the differential learning of its female scholars. Powerful directives by senior churchmen, mostly *in situ* in India, made for unstable intakes of girls in fluctuating numbers and of different ages. This instability required mediation by local agents, usually the wives of missionaries, to create classrooms in which it was possible for girls to progress in their learning.[46] In the 1870s there were usually separate living quarters and separate sections of schools where Eurasians and higher-caste Indian girls were educated, to satisfy parent sensibilities. This was even though there could be great family wealth differentials within these two groups of students, with the European and Eurasian students mostly making up the boarding school in relatively well-resourced mission schools. In addition, nearly all had a day school that kept separate any enrolled Indian girls of lower-caste status. This difficult learning environment was also accentuated by chronic shortages in staff. Furthermore, Western missionaries who understood the wealth discriminator – as in Europe – were engaged in ongoing tensions with poorer Indian parents, who insisted that their higher-caste status must also be respected if they were to enrol their daughters.

Three key female missionary sites: Delhi, Palamcottah and Lucknow

By the 1870s this very difficult educational task was addressed by at least three mission sites. The success of these missions on this issue was enough to persuade the government that the missions offered a viable alternative, when the Nagpur scandal finally scuttled the

Carpenter plan as far as state funding was concerned. These missions were already showing themselves as communities of educators ready to safely enshrine and protect the modesty and the femininity of the accomplished teacher who was female, which the Viceroy's government now wished to promote.

The wife of the head SPG missionary at Delhi, Priscilla Winter, built a successful normal school for females in Delhi, founded in 1864. Like her husband, she has been largely overlooked by institutional histories, perhaps owing to disagreements with the later Cambridge Mission over the nature of SPG mission outreach in the 1880s. Her influence over colonial female education in north India in the 1860s and 1870s was significant, being even greater than that of Mary Carpenter. Although her career was to stretch for some twenty years in the same mission, Winter's initial educational experience did not go far beyond Sunday-school teaching. The Sanawar Lawrence Military Asylum, in the same province, competed in staff recruitment with the SPG mission; however, it also offered Winter a fairly detailed plan as to new pedagogy and accomplishments, which she could develop in her own institution.[47] Winter's salary drew matching funding from government under grant-in-aid, although she was content for her mission to use this for other purposes as well.[48] However, the government soon offered more generous funding for this and other key missionary schools that were prepared to be recognised as 'training' institutions of women teachers.[49]

Unfortunately, this additional government funding immediately accentuated local racial tensions. Apart from its Eurasian and European pupils, Winter's normal school also actively recruited Indian girls of 'high' caste, which necessitated another division being made for girls of inferior rank in the day school.[50] Winter's strong belief in the accomplishments curriculum for Eurasian girls brought her into conflict with the women teachers of nearby Railway schools for Eurasian girls; schools that offered a basic form of literacy and numeracy education. The conflict deepened when Winter's sense of ownership of the education of the Eurasian female community was transcended by women teachers in other nearby schools who were not graduates of her own institution. On one occasion these disputes became so heated that a visit by the Lieutenant Governor of the province was required before he could authorise a severance of the cross-subsidy arrangements between the SPG and some Railway schools for girls (schools that were in preponderance in the bustling railway hub that was Delhi at this time).[51]

This was difficult work in India. By the end of the 1870s seventeen Eurasian teachers who were women were offering assistance in the mission school. Winter and her husband recruited them in India where they could 'judge character' first, rather than footing the bill for recruiting expensive European mistresses from Britain as Carpenter had urged.[52] However, provincial DPIs did not trust the Winters to do this alone, directly intervening on the grounds that 'it is very necessary that the character of women applying for admission should be most carefully enquired into before their applications are entertained'.[53] In 1868 Winter suffered the death of a baby daughter, but she was still expected to superintend an institution whose enrolment had grown to fifty-five women trainee teachers.[54] However, there was also strong educational consolidation at this site. Winter justified the work of her normal school to the government in terms of the accomplishments curriculum and also offered her students a thorough course that lasted for five years, which included good experience in practising teaching in nearby schools. Winter's normal school was one of the few that offered an education to her students that was separate from their subsequent teacher training. However, the state, despite its prioritisation of women teachers who were acculturated into Western feminine ways, began contesting Winter's costly curriculum, which it part subsidised, arguing that adequate teacher training could be despatched in just two years.[55]

It was only when Mary Carpenter took up the cause of Winter's normal school directly with the Viceroy that the school facilities began to rapidly expand.[56] By 1877, as a result of this intervention, Winter's school enjoyed new central quarters and became associated with twenty-three nearby girls' schools, teaching 840 pupils a curriculum that also conveyed credible literacy standards. These schools were taught by fifty-three teachers, many of whom were themselves graduates of Winter's normal school.[57] Most significantly, the example of this normal school showed government that the mission compound was a powerful enough cultural agency to direct education communities along lines deemed to encompass an appropriate morality for women, and in ways that the state's counterparts, mostly single-teacher schools, could not.

While Carpenter's normal school model had relied on complete government subsidy, Winter's normal school offered teacher training of females on the cheap. The missionary compound also mostly maintained the race and class bar regarding females that was so important to the raj by this time. Winter's normal school was appealing to the state, too, as another example of the kind of raj governance that it preferred, because it appeared to be a self-perpetuating educational site where the dependency of women was inculcated.[58]

Another exemplar of successful missionary custodianship was in south India at Palamcottah, the site of one of the oldest British military

Figure 3 Mrs Priscilla Winter, SPG. © United Society and Bodleian Library, Oxford.

cantonments in India and at that time in the province of Madras. Regiments from this town were used in the Maratha wars (1775–1805), in the third Anglo-Mysore war (1789–92) and, later still, even in the Boxer Rebellion in China (1899–1901). In this strategic centre of raj control and influence, the CMS mission-sponsored Sarah Tucker Institution was established for girls. It was an institution run by men; but by the end of 1874, under the tutelage of the Principal, Augustus Lash, and his first wife Alicia, it had developed a fully fledged normal school of eighty-three girls, with a Eurasian cohort that aspired to a teachers' certificate newly instated in the province.[59] As with Canning's Despatch its aim was to train Eurasian teachers who were females as:

> intelligent, well-informed, earnest minded [teachers] who shall go forth to various spheres of usefulness among their fellow country women and exercise a decided and irresistible influence for good, by their example, no less than by their work of teaching.[60]

[143]

The Tucker Institution, like Winter's in Delhi, also instituted an accomplishments curriculum that copied that already in place in the Lawrence asylums. The regime for women and girls was convent-like:

> rise at 5, 5–5.30 domestic duties, 7 to 7.45 morning meal, 7.45 morning prayer, until 10.30 go on with their studies, recreation until 11, 11–12 study, 2–3 given a second meal & their needlework until 4.45, recreation and domestic work until 6 p.m., evening meal 7, prayers, private study till 8 p.m. then retire.[61]

With so few women missionary teachers in the institution, this schedule must have been both tedious and exhausting to enforce. Like most mission schools in India, the central institution's cloistered nature did not allow for much engagement with the local community as an alternative educational institution, and the school term was punctuated by long interim vacation breaks.

Tucker's chief organisational structure, again like Winter's central mission school in Delhi, had teacher training at its core and was also supposed to be self-perpetuating, although Henry Lash based his plainer classroom praxis on simple imitation, rather than more sophisticated heuristic approaches. He described his approach in these terms:

> The theory of teaching is simply explained, and a few plain rules are given, but we rely most upon forming good habits of teaching by setting good models before the students & constantly practising them, correcting their faults ... [and] the day school is used as a practising school.[62]

The Madras government instituted separate examinations (along the lines that operated in Europe) for teachers who were females and their monitors at the Tucker Institution. It also offered school subsidies based on the proficiency of student teachers in needlework: first standard 'hemming on calico'; fourth standard 'cutting out and working on fine cloth, either a finely made European shirt, or a native man's jacket, or a female's plain dress and petticoat'.[63] The school was divided into a senior and a junior school: the senior for trainee teachers; the junior as a model and practising school for the trainee teachers to practice their art at least twice a week under the principal's supervision.[64]

The building of Eurasian female knowledge and skills at the Tucker Institution was probably inferior to that on offer in the Lawrence asylums or even in Winter's classes in Delhi. It is unclear just how much the school relied on the only text it cited, John Murdoch's *Hints on Education*. This textbook was the most starchy and Western-predicated missionary schoolbook on offer in nineteenth-century India.[65] Yet Tucker's attention to pedagogy was just as developed as that in Winter's normal school, with critiques of teaching and 'practice lessons' on random subjects chosen by the principal, which formed a large part of the school day for senior girls.[66]

A third influential missionary normal school for females in the key decade of the 1870s was newly established by Isabella Thoburn. This normal school was also particularly influential in persuading the state to hand over its project regarding teacher education to the missions. Thoburn initially saw herself as an individual Christian agent in India, rather than as part of a broader missionary effort. However, her thirty-year career on the subcontinent was to become heavily dependent on the American Methodist Episcopal mission. This American background differed from that of the two British Anglican missions in that Thoburn's work was articulated in more formal academic terms than that of most British women missionaries at this time. Formal missionary training in the USA was available to Thoburn, well before she travelled to India, as a female at the Wheeling Female Seminary in Virginia.[67] Her sponsors in the USA were also working towards founding Boston University at this time.[68] These were important precursors that help to explain the distinctive Thoburn College curriculum later in the century, particularly in attracting Muslim women.[69] However, in the 1870s, Thoburn also was influenced by the unremitting realities the raj presented regarding female education that was racialised, and which favoured European feminine sensitivities. Like Winter in Delhi, and the Lashs at Palamcottah, Thoburn set about establishing a boarding school mostly for Eurasian girls as the centrepiece of her school. She taught an accomplishments curriculum, but with stronger academic merit, with nature study, for example, taught in more formal academic ways under the label of 'physiology'.[70]

All three female institutions at Delhi, Palamcottah and Lucknow eventually gave rise in the 1890s to academic colleges for women. Yet their earlier forms, as essentially normal schools first, even before being schools for girls, was a distortion encouraged by targeted government grant-in-aid funding in the mid-1870s as the sites most conducive to the narrative around teacher training for women and girls. As normal schools, these institutions were to be models for other missions, which had mostly been given custody as well of teacher education for women and girls across India. Their enrolments in the central compound rapidly expanded as a consequence.

However, attempting to motivate Eurasian student teachers in the central mission compound, even when instructing the accomplishments curriculum, remained a fairly joyless teaching enterprise. This was partly because the emphasis in these schools was on Western moral and feminine character building, rather than on academic learning focused on future employment. An additional factor was that power relations could be inverted within these classrooms: these learning spaces were made desultory places by the mission teachers' fears that a withdrawal of support by Eurasian parents might lose them precious fees. This fear demotivated teachers in the classroom, and gave their students some discretion over how much study they were inclined to undertake. For example, the Sisters of the Community of St Mary the Virgin, an Anglican order based in Wantage, England, established a mission house school in Poona, Maharashtra in 1866. By 1879, the Sister Superior was describing her main in-compound, fee-paying class to her London-based SPG brethren in these terms:

> They are mostly what is called the 2nd class – they correspond to English Middle Class but have much less idea of making themselves useful & they are an indolent and do nothing class as a whole.[71]

Outside the mission compound

Central mission normal schools were generally considered central sites in which the state could find at least some solid manifestation and application of its female education rhetoric in the latter 1870s and early 1880s. Official funding strategies helped to hone this conformity, and the agenda was aided by a seemingly parallel missionary strategy of converting the 'heathen' partly through its style of education via literacy in biblical parables. However, the imperative of conversion also drew the work of missionaries who were women outside the mission compound, in directions that would prove very uncomfortable to the state. This was because, when many women missionaries moved their work outside the mission compound, they crossed state-established racial divides and renegotiated education for girls based on accomplishments.

In some respects this loss of control by the state over the direction of actual female education was inevitable, given the sheer scale of territory the missions claimed as their loose operational field. For example, Rev. R. R. Winter claimed a 'field' 75 miles north, 110 miles west and 54 miles south of Delhi, with the only real restriction being travelling time along the unwieldy and pot-holed trunk roads between sympathetic European safe houses.[72] Here the agency of female missionary educators, away even from male control in the hierarchies of their own institutions, could navigate a more fluid teaching and learning tradition, which was mostly only anchored in conversion outcomes. Teaching Indian girls and women, rather than Eurasians, in this 'outside' context was also very different. A broader sense of community with other missionary teachers also developed among these women teachers. Furthermore, travelling women missionaries developed a professional educational space that uninitiated women, even those from Europe, could not enter.

This new missionary educational territory outside the central mission wall in India solidified as the nineteenth century drew to a close. Burton has argued that feminist writers living in England at the time created images of 'needy' Indian women merely to encourage British women to think of themselves as committed to a 'racial mother-hood' and as part of an imperial civilising mission.[73] In the 1870s and 1880s this modus operandi drove a burgeoning industry of women's committees and organisations in Britain with India in view, but from afar. Paradoxically, however, European-based initiatives that stayed 'at home' in Britain could be used very effectively by Indian-based missionary educators to justify *ex officio* learning action for Indian girls that was both beyond the missionary compound and also the agenda of the state. 'Home' committees, not fettered by raj imperatives regarding Eurasian females, also embraced Indian female recruits to the mission – with parental consent – but outside the central mission compound. This usually involved an adaption of the Western accomplishments mentality into something that mostly only encouraged reward through prize giving. For example, outside the Sarah Tucker Institution, its sponsors, unable to gain access into neighbouring Indian households to teach, moved to take advantage of the Madras government's needlework subsidy instead:

> Each little girl and big girl too, as some of them are, has been furnished with a pretty little working bag containing a thimble, needle and thread and strips of calico. The mistresses have received strict orders to allow them to take them home to patch and darn. In my last examination rounds I also gave every child who could sew half a yard of pretty chintz to be converted by the children into little money bags such as Tamil children like to wear ... We have very recently introduced spinning for the very little ones ... whilst their mothers peer in with delight at the windows or through the door of the village school or church to see which child will be the happy possessor of the prize – only 4 annas but a considerable sum to them.[74]

Many in the missions were not as enamoured of sensibility and refinement as a result of an education in accomplishments, if they thought about it at all. When there was no outside market demand for knitting and 'fancy work', except in the military cantonments, this curriculum was met by regression in some mission schools for females, where teaching became only about instruction in crude and menial sewing, mending and the making of palm leaf place mats.[75]

[147]

Eurasians and lower-class Europeans were the only groups available to the mission and other female educational institutions at this time who were prepared to pay fees. Teacher training had a strong vocational focus, and these students could be motivated to eventually become superintendents of their own female classrooms, either in the mission model (practice teaching) school or in the surrounding mission branch schools. Yet untrained women missionaries struggled most in teaching these same student teachers basic secondary school education, which most of these women missionaries lacked. This struggle was probably responsible for these same women missionaries wishing to move at least some of their conversion work to surrounding Indian communities.

Women missionaries also had important barriers to overcome that directly related to state policy. By the latter 1870s government focus was firmly on offering missions favourable matching funding for teacher training of women that concentrated on character building for women along feminine lines for Eurasians.[76] This was despite women missionaries not being keen on the tight racialised and class strictures that this type of female teaching placed on their conversion activities.[77] Additionally, employment opportunities for mission teacher graduates were severely limited in India, beyond what the missions themselves could offer; and the government was not prepared to add to its own very few secondary schools, which might have otherwise expanded the job market for the graduate teacher who had an accomplishments education.[78]

The zenanas

Outside the mission compound, another avenue of teaching was much more appealing to woman missionary teacher operatives: *zenana* (household female quarters) teaching. This avenue was mostly free from state control and regulation because, as Gail Minault contends, governments throughout India found zenana teaching too expensive and were happy to delegate it to missionaries.[79] In response, Muslim delegations, particularly in the Punjab, established their own Islamic-based girls' schools in the later nineteenth century in very rare examples of colonial part funding for education that was not state, European or mission directed.[80]

For activist missionary women, however, there were countervailing incentives to enter the zenana domain. Most especially, the fact that antagonistic male missionaries, who were inclined to see the zenana – as one Bombay male missionary put it – as merely 'barricades of caste and of the mother-in-law', were mostly excluded.[81] Of course, the overlay of the intervention of these women missionaries was still a more basic Western imperative around conversion, in which the mother or future mother might become a facilitator for the conversion of their sons.[82] However, as Anagol asserts, new missionary work in the zenanas also saw the locus of the female missionary activity partly move from an agenda of conversion to one that more broadly concerned the 'plight of Indian womanhood'.[83]

Abuses against captive Eurasian orphan 'converts' could not be replicated in the zenana domain. In the zenana it was the woman missionary, rather than her student, who crossed a cultural threshold; the power structures surrounding this learning were more comfortably inverted in favour of students, and this change in power relations offered a deeper teaching challenge. If the female missionary was to be granted access, it was she who was required to display convincing cultural sensitivity and academic acuity as to how best to reach young Indian female scholars.

The zenana learning site gave women missionaries licence to be creative and strategic as they navigated a fragmentary but broader curriculum. This curriculum was grounded on building academic access to the highly sensitive Indian space in the household where female learning took place: a space also hidden from macro raj policymaking. These missionary women mostly lacked a strong formal Western education, but as they were compelled to respond creatively to local realities using their local language skills, they also became learners. There were other freedoms too. The zenana offered teaching opportunities beyond the stifling constraints of colonial education for women and girls: colonial education that was taught to only a select few and enmeshed within an overweening ethic concerning the Western teacher training of females.

Most major missionary settlements had some form of zenana teaching. Government DPIs dutifully acknowledged the work in superficial and uncommitted terms. Yet parent missionary bodies at the metropole gave their female agents in India permission to pursue the work in a way that fulfilled 'at home', at the metropole, non-racialised conversion aspirations. Furthermore, these British-based mission aspirations demonstrated little awareness of the complicated heritage in India that bounded official raj rhetoric about women and girls by the late 1870s.

There were different classes of zenanas. By the mid-1870s access to an elite family household was a glittering prize to be held onto at all costs, including any forthcoming fee revenue. Yet there were also zenanas inhabited by impoverished females, as one woman missionary recounted in the following terms:

> All pupils seemed to have clever bright faces ... only three appeared, one by one, in the little prison-like bedroom, with its walls which age and dirt had made all shades of brown to black, and which some pictures, and would be decorations, tried in vain to adorn.[84]

These women missionaries gathered another kind of professionalism around them, disciplined by zenana-based realities. In pursuing this professionalism their teaching perspectives soon lay partly outside the colonial mindset of the previous two generations about the limited learning capacity of Indian females. Accomplishments, and the pedagogical developments imported and developed at the Lawrence asylums and elsewhere, were not a core interest for these women missionaries. Instead, genuine piety and conversion first involved some knowledge transmission, across Indian language divides and household thresholds, which involved more than just the use of the catechism.

It was true that not all of these women missionaries had the erudition or the sensitivity to achieve a deeper connection through teaching. Crude attempts at Western assimilation in the zenana could also be counterproductive in sensitive parts of the raj at least. In 1868, the Peshawar CMS girls' school (North West Frontier) suffered an invasion by some 100 'noisy and ignorant women' threatening vengeance on its assembled pupils. CMS work in the zenanas of the homes of Muslim elites had been the provocation, while government schooling in the city had concentrated on the Hindu merchant classes that had a material interest in Western education.[85] However, without such colonial economic interventions, zenana teaching of elite Indian women could involve deeper discovery and reflection about what Indian women actually wanted from their secular education. Unwittingly, perhaps, as will be shown in the next two chapters, the dynamic of female missionary networks also created avenues for Indian women to pursue nursing and medical careers; both of which were well away from official state rhetoric around the accomplishments curriculum for Eurasian girls of the period.

Furthermore, as part of the new work for the Anglican missions at least, beyond the central mission compound, there were extensive female networks that offered support for informal Indian normal schools in local villages. The CMS's Indian Female Normal School and Instructional Society gathered an extensive array of patrons across Britain, raising in 1874, for example, £5,400 (the equivalent at the time to the total cost of building a major district school in India). The society attempted to run its operations out of the CMS central mission in Calcutta, and then to all of India using either missionary women from England, graduates from the CMS normal school in Calcutta, or educated Indian women converts.[86] Mrs Helen Tompkins directed the CMS female mission in Calcutta at the time; and under the influence of visiting American Unitarians she had become more receptive to education work with Indian females.

Missionary women working outside individual missions also had greater intellectual impact on at least some Indian females compared to most other colonial women teachers at this time. Levels of enthusiasm in the central local missions were also high regarding zenana teaching work, particularly in north India, where the zenana tradition was strongest. The work began to take up much of the teaching week. Even by the late 1860s, Priscilla Winter's SPG Delhi 'outside' mission teaching extended to 120 Hindu and ninety-three Muslim girls scattered among sixty zenanas in the city. A decade later the work, which required twice weekly visits to these zenanas, was demanding enough to occupy a staff of seventeen women teachers who were converts, under Winter's direction, and who were females from the central mission compound.[87] The traditional designation 'zenana' applied to upper-class Muslim families and, later, to wealthier Hindus. However, the missions, in search of converts, broadened the term to include poorer classes and lower castes. By 1882 the Baptists of Delhi also claimed strong outreach to 108 upper-caste Hindu zenana girls and eighty-four wealthy Muslim girls scattered in receptive households, although they also counted in this number sixty-five *chamar* (leather worker) girls at the bottom of the caste hierarchy along with the *dalit* (untouchable) female learners.[88]

CMS zenana work was most active in Amritsar (north India) under the direction of Margaret Elmslie, wife of the medical missionary Dr William Elmslie. Her work was usually on the rooftop zenanas of the city and, like the Baptists, much of this work was with poor families rather than with elites.[89]

The picture of Elmslie is a staged photograph probably produced for home consumption in England. Elmslie chooses the pose of a pastoral carer, rather than didactic teacher, bent over what is likely to be a book illustrating the gospel, and is shown capturing the interest of her nearest scholar.

Amritsar was a more politicised city than Delhi in the 1870s, and government educators chose the safer ground of educating children of the merchant classes, who were predominantly Hindu and who had a vested interest in a Western education.[90] The CMS conversion strategy was also more pressing than that of the SPG and the Baptists in Delhi. Attempting to teach poorer girls in the zenana had limitations, because their illiteracy offered little reaction at an intellectual level to the educational agenda of well-meaning missionary women, such as Elmslie. As a consequence, these missionary women could only offer Bible stories, gardening, cooking and dress making to try to build connections with their very poor and malnourished pupils.[91]

Figure 4 Mrs Margaret Elmslie and her rooftop zenana class.
© The British Library Board, Photo 793/(18).

Yet, for a smaller group of European women missionaries, the zenana offered a more intimate and revealing insight into the thought of elite Indian women. These few prescient missionaries, when visiting market settlements and *girja* (temple) precincts, knew that there was a different kind of female intellectual vibrancy that lay behind the demure and distrustful glances they received as out-of-place Westerners intruding into an ancient social landscape.

This was uncomfortable work whose success was denoted more through the level of acceptance these missionaries managed to achieve from their Indian hosts, in accordance with household protocols, than it was by the academic achievements of their female pupils. It tested the unerring pride of many of the women missionaries of this period, who often reacted badly to being disempowered in this manner. Indian feminine acceptance was supposedly to come with the female missionary's 'charitable' offer of Western scholarship, but this coupling of 'acceptance' in return for 'service' was not how many Indian women viewed the missionary visit. Wounded by the lack of such reciprocity, the inexperienced Miss Boyd, one of Priscilla Winter's European zenana teachers in Delhi, wrote in frustration:

Unfortunately these women are so imbued with prejudices that they do not like coming in contact with Europeans. Though they profess great affection for me, they [are] never willing to trust me, and if I happen, when correcting their mistakes, to dip my pen into one of the inkstands they are using, they will not use of it again, till the ink has been thrown away, and the inkstand washed and refilled.[92]

Experienced Baptist missionaries in the same city offered another view to that of the novice Miss Boyd. Their mission had been responsible for beginning zenana teaching in India several decades earlier, and so they were more knowledgeable about the detail of protocol in Indian households and more ready for the usual rebuffs. When visiting zenanas for the first time they accepted the obligation to stand for the entire time, and the need to endure the initial 'sullen dislike of our coming'. However, they also understood that it was they who were the real social misfits, with their voluminous Western dresses and whalebone corsets (which nearly all Western women refused to surrender in this period in India).[93] Nonetheless, after many visits, acceptance could be signified with reward. Such acceptance could be as subtle as the purchase of cane chairs by their Indian hosts to cater for the needs of these Europeans.[94]

Thus the intimacy of the zenana in the mid-1870s was reinforced by strong power structures, which the visiting female missionary was forced to acknowledge. This gave pause for thought, but such power delineation also encouraged some focus by missionaries on their views of the zenana as a learning space in the household, amid the corbelled ceilings and the jarokha balconies of the private living quarters of Indian females.

Minault describes a lively discourse among Muslim women, in particular, through women's magazines and newspapers in Urdu, as part of an overall rising print culture in colonial India. This discourse remained almost totally ignored by the British administration, unlike its assiduous surveillance of political comment in these mediums.[95] However, the more intelligent and receptive female missionaries detected the robust learning of Indian females that was gendered, and sometimes already partly influenced by Western thought, even within the zenana. This learning also lay outside the contours of education for women and girls within the raj that was now mostly available only to Eurasians and Indian converts. The zenana revealed that at least some secluded Indian women were not cultural isolates, but were active learners reacting to the outside world as they may have always done. For example, in Lucknow, females in joint Hindu households were learning Romanised Urdu as an alternative to raj English as the lingua franca of world knowledge. Missionaries who visited twice a week were relieved to follow this scholarship, rather than spending tedious hours teaching emblematic 'needlework'.[96] In

Lahore and Delhi, the learning in the zenanas was Urdu, Persian, English and Arithmetic. While in elite Bengal zenanas, it was Indian husbands, married early, and away in England reading Law at an English university, who were the chief motivators for their wives embarking upon formal academic study.[97] Even in this latter setting, when teaching biblical parables, the teaching and learning still could not be based on Western contextualised analogies, which were unknown to most female scholars of whatever class who were confined to the zenana.

Furthermore, the Baptist missionary women in Delhi remained attentive to the caste interconnections of each street they visited. They were as transfixed by the great wealth of Hindu families as the CMS was with the merchants of Madras. These commercial families that the Baptists viewed as 'rolling in money' included the Tata family of Bombay, who were later responsible for the building of the Taj Mahal Hotel in that city in 1903.[98] Lazily perhaps, the Baptists ventured further to teach a large proportion of the government boys' curriculum to secluded girls. This was because they found access to many elite households made difficult by resistance from men of these households to the teaching of what appeared to be only basic literacy based on English vocabulary. However, this more Western gender-neutral school curriculum still imported to the household the problematics of teaching Shakespeare, Milton or Dryden to an Indian audience and it involved treading wearily when teaching geography and astronomy, given the strong Eastern religious precepts attached to these epistemologies.[99]

The actions of women missionaries outside the mission wall remained bounded by the co-imperatives of piety and conversion. Unlike secular colonial education in India, their actions needed to operate within the restrictive patriarchal networks of the churches, mostly built in Europe, while importing attitudes of parent bodies at 'home' to raising money that were not generally racially based.[100] The work of these missionaries also partly disaggregated the raj education agenda for women and girls; an agenda handed over to them after the Nagpur scandal in the interests, as the state saw it, of protecting the exemplar Western-educated teacher who was female acting as a moral guide. Such female missionary work also set up new avenues of female learning for Indian females, again outside raj racialised and class agendas, but this time concerning Indian female medical care. As the next two chapters will show, at this periphery, professional connections of nurses, midwives and female doctors were much more powerful even than female missionary zenana teachers in taking a reluctant raj to new Indian female terrain.

Notes

1 A. Porter, *Religion versus Empire* ..., pp. 176–7.
2 H. Bellenoit, *Missionary Education* ..., *passim.*
3 Mr Parsons, *Missionary Herald*, June 3, 1857, p. 583, Angus Library, Regent's Park College, Oxford (AL).
4 B. Seal, *Comparative Studies in Vaishnavism and Christianity with an Examination of the Mahabharata Legend about Narada's Pilgrimage to Svetadvipa and an Introduction to the Historico-Comparative Method* (Calcutta, 1899). For elaboration on this issue see H. Bellenoit, *Missionary Education* ..., pp. 28, 132–4.
5 P. Anagol, *The Emergence of Feminism* ..., p. 23.
6 L. Flemming, *Women's Work for Women* (Colorado: Westfield, 1989), p. 1.
7 A. Nelson, 'Empire of Knowledge: Nationalism, Internationalism, and the Origins of the American University, 1770–1830'. Paper delivered at a Faculty of Education, University of Sydney Colloquium on August 8, 2011.
8 T. Allender, 'Anglican Evangelism in North India and the Punjabi Missionary Classroom ...', p. 278.
9 T. Allender, 'Anglican Evangelism in North India ...', pp. 275–6.
10 Bishop of Calcutta, January 11, 1838, Rhodes House Library, Oxford (RHL), CLR1.
11 Baly to Tucker, March 14, 1879, p. 473 (RHL), CLR51.
12 Bishop of Calcutta, December 16, 1840, p. 150 (RHL), 'East Indies' CLR2.
13 Bishop of Bombay, October 30, 1876, p. 299 (RHL), CLR4.
14 Bishop of Bombay, October 30, 1876, p. 299 (RHL), CLR4.
15 M. Rose Greenfield, 'An Address to the Conference of Lady Missionaries Held at Amritsar, Punjab, 1888' (RHL) BZM Papers.
16 Rev. T. W. Hunter, 'Three Months in the SPG Mission, Delhi', n.d., 1877 (RHL) E32, F. 145.
17 Lefroy to Mother, April 28, 1880 (RHL) 'Letters of G. A. Lefroy to his Mother and Sister' (RHL), Miscellaneous Series X 1240.
18 Vincent Harcourt, Journal, July, 1853 (LB) CI2/O/111.
19 A. Howell, *Education in British India Prior to 1854...*, pp. 68–9.
20 'Evidence of Sahib Singh ..., Delhi' in W. W. Hunter, *Report of the Provincial Committee for the Punjab of the Hunter Education Commission*, p. 427.
21 C. Alexander to A. Fuller, 'Report on Popular Education in the Punjab ... 1866/7', p. 43 (OIOC).
22 T. Allender, *Ruling Through Education* ..., pp. 192–4.
23 C. W. Isenberg, April, 1862 (LB) CI3/0/80/8L. Other accounts are to be found throughout the available missionary records.
24 'Pupils of the Benares C M Normal Female from January 1863 to January 1871' (LB) CI1 O 10/16.
25 'Pupils of the Benares C M Normal Female from January 1863 to January 1871' (LB) CI1 O 10/16.
26 'Pupils of the Benares C M Normal Female from January 1863 to January 1871' (LB) CI1 O 10/16.
27 'Pupils of the Benares C M Normal Female from January 1863 to Januaray 1871' (LB) CI1 O 10/16.
28 C. W. Isenberg 'Statement of Lala's case laid before the Assistant Collector and Magistrate of Nasik (somewhat modified), April 16, 1862' (LB) CI3/0/80/8L.
29 V. Brendon, *Children of the Raj* ..., pp. 165–6.
30 C. W. Isenberg 'Statement of Lala's case laid before the Assistant Collector and Magistrate of Nasik (somewhat modified), April 16, 1862' (LB) CI3/0/80/8L.
31 R. Phillips, *Sex, Politics and Empire* (Manchester, Manchester University Press, 2006), pp. 63–71.
32 C. W. Isenberg to Mr Weatherhead, April 20, 1862 (LB) CI3/0/80/8L.
33 G. Campbell, 'The East African Slave Trade, 1861–1895: The Southern Complex', *The International Journal of African Historical Studies*, 22:1 (1989), 1–26.
34 *Bombay Education Report*, 1858/59, p. 52 (OIOC) V/24/861.

35 D. Robinson-Dunn, *The Harem, Slavery and British Imperial Culture: Anglo-Muslim Relations in the late Nineteenth Century* (Manchester: Manchester University Press, 2006), p. 32.
36 C. W. Isenberg to Mr Weatherhead, April 20, 1862 (LB) CI3/0/80/8L.
37 The competition was particularly marked in the Punjab between the low-church missions. See T. Allender, *Ruling Through Education* ..., ch. 6.
38 Pupils of the Benares CM Normal Female School from Jan 1863–Jan 1871' (LB) CI 1 O 10/16.
39 'Papers Relating to the Case of Miss Mary Dowman, 1861' (BL) CI3/0/61/140C.
40 Account in the *Indian Daily News*, September 5, 1883 cited in Ballhatchet, *Race, Sex and Class under the Raj* ..., p. 114.
41 Ballhatchet, *Race, Sex and Class under the Raj* ..., pp. 112–15.
42 Bray to Bullock, July 16, 1878, p. 424 (RHL) CLR18.
43 Bray to Bullock, July 16, 1878, pp. 373 (RHL) CLR18.
44 Bray to Bullock, July 16, 1878, p. 424 (RHL) CLR18.
45 R. Hyam, *Empire and Sexuality* ..., p. 120.
46 Bray to Tucker, December 20, 1878, p. 460 (RHL) CLR18.
47 R. R. Winter to Bullock, July 28, 1868 D31 f. 371, SPG (RHL).
48 Tara Chand to the Sec. of the Calcutta SPG, April 24, 1864 (RHL) E15 f. 1263.
49 Tara Chand to the Sec. of the Calcutta SPG, July 7, 1864, 1864 (RHL) E15 f. 1271.
50 'Society for the Propaganda of the Gospel Report for the Year 1863' (RHL) E13 f. 781.
51 *NWP Education Report, 1872–3* ..., p. 103 (SOAS).
52 Winter to Bullock, July 28, 1868 (RHL) SPG D31, f. 371.
53 *Punjab Education Report, 1873–4*, p. 93 (OIOC) V/24/932.
54 'Civil Surgeon' Delhi, May 13, 1865; Winter to Bullock, October 10, 1865; Smith-White to Vallings, December 17, 1866; Winter to Bullock, March 8, 1867 (RHL) D21 ff. 660, 835, 1609, 1707; Archdeacon John Pratt to Bullock, March 23, 1868 (RHL) E22 f. 235; 'Annual Return for Yr Ending September 30, 1867' (RHL) E21 f. 795; 'Report of the ... Mission of Delhie [sic] by R. R. Winter, December 29, 1863' (RHL) E13 f. 707; 'Return of All Educational Establishments in Delhi & South Punjab', November 1, 1876 (RHL) D43.
55 Director to Sec. to the Government of the Punjab, March 31, 1875 no. 56 (OIOC) P/139.
56 Carpenter to Lord Mayo, September 24, 1869; October 27, 1871 Mayo Papers 1869–72 (CML) Add 7490 no. 12.
57 'Rev. T. W. Hunter, 'Three months in the SPG Mission, Delhi', n.d. 1877 (RHL) E32 f. 145; see also R. R. Winter, 'Report for January 1 to August 31, 1872' (RHL) E27 f. 2067; Tara Chand to (?) May 30, 1877 (RHL) E32 f. 287.
58 R. R. Winter, SPG Mission, February 26, 1873, E27 f. 2067, SPG (RHL).
59 'A Proposed Plan for Promoting Female Education in the Native Church and Among the Hindu Population of Travancore, January 5, 1878', LB CI2/0/48/25.
60 Report of the Sarah Tucker Institution, Palamcottah, December 31, 1874 (LB) CI O/143/6.
61 Report of the Sarah Tucker Institution, Palamcottah, December 31, 1874 (LB) CI O/143/6.
62 Henry Lash, Annual Letter, November 24, 1868 (BL) CI/0/151.
63 *Madras Education Report, 1872–3* ..., pp. 79–80 (SOAS).
64 *Madras Education Report, 1872–3* ..., p. 87 (SOAS).
65 J. Murdoch, *Hints on Government Education in India with Special Reference to School Books* (Madras: C. Forster and Co., 1873).
66 Report of the Sarah Tucker Institution, Palamcottah, December 31, 1874 (LB) CI O/143/6.
67 M. Nalini 'Gender Dynamics of Missionary Work in India and its Impact on Women's Education: Isabella Thoburn (1840–1901): A Case Study', *Journal of International Women's Studies*, 7:4 (2006), 268.
68 D. L. Robert, *American Women in Mission: A Social History of Their Thought and Practice*, 4th Edition (Georgia: Mercer University Press: 2005), pp. 142–4.

69 M. A. H. Taylor, *The Education of Women in India* (St Albans: Bamford, 1910), p. 9 (CBMA).
70 M. Nalini, 'Gender Dynamics of Missionary Work in India ...', pp. 273–4.
71 Elizabeth, Sister Superior, St Mary's Mission House Poona, April 20, 1879 (BL) CLR4.
72 R. R. Winter to Secretary of SPG, London, March 28, 1863 (RHL) SPG E13.
73 A. Burton, *Burdens of History* ..., pp. 82–3.
74 Vincent Harcourt to Rev. C. C. Fenn, April 18, 1871 (BL) CI2/0/111.
75 Girls' Boarding School, Chota Nagpur, Committee of Women's Work, p. 87 (RHL) CWW 47.
76 A survey of the provincial education reports for each province in the 1870s shows imperial monies being strongly directed into mission Eurasian female schooling.
77 See, for example, the commentary of the *Twenty-Third Annual Report of the Indian Female Normal School and Instructional Society* (issued April, 1875) (Birmingham: Josiah Allen, 1875) (OIOC).
78 Compared to the growing number of teacher training institutions for females, the very small number of female secondary schools across all provinces remained relatively static in the 1870s.
79 G. Minault, *Secluded Scholars* ..., p. 171.
80 G. Minault, *Secluded Scholars* ..., p. 172.
81 Rev. T. K. Weatherhead, March 31, 1864 (BL) CI 3/0/80/259.
82 See for example, Rev. J. Harrison (CMS), Bezwada, Bengal, Annual Letter, December 26, 1874 (BL) CI 2/0/115.
83 P. Anagol, *The Emergence of Feminism in India* ..., p. 23.
84 'January 27, 1873' *The Twenty-Third Annual Report of the Indian Female Normal School and Instructional Society* (Birmingham: Josiah Allen, 1875) (OIOC).
85 'Seventh Report of the CMS Mission to the Afghans at Peshawar, 1868–69' (LB) CI 1/O/20/10.
86 *The Eleventh Annual Report of the Indian Female Normal School and Instructional Society* (London: Suter and Alexander, 1863); *The Twenty Second Annual Report of the Indian Female Normal School and Instructional Society* (London: Suter and Alexander, 1874); G. W. Cooke, *Unitarianism in America* (Gutenberg: Steiner, Lund and Franks, 2005), pp. 212–9.
87 'Return of All Educational Establishments in Delhi and south Punjab', November 1, 1876 (RHL) SPG D43; P. Winter to Rev. J. Browne, June 1, 1869 (RHL) SPG D31 f. 603.
88 Baptist Annual Zenana Report, 1882 (AL).
89 J. Deed (ed.), *Church Work: Mission Life* (London, Wells, Gardner & Darton & Co., 1885), p. 374 British Library (BL); E. Stock *The History of the Church Missionary Society* (London, CMS, 1899), vol. iii, p. 145 (BL).
90 'Seventh Report of the CMS Mission to the Afghans at Peshawar, 1868–9' (LB) CI 1/O/20/10.
91 Mrs Elmslie to (?), March 31, 1875. See also 'Annual Letter', November 14, 1877 (LB) CI 1/O/101/2 & 3; E. Stock ...' vol. ii, p. 145 (BL).
92 Report of Miss Boyd [n.d.] November 1887, in Priscilla Sandys (Mrs Winter) 1867–91 (RHL) SPG X1168.
93 B. Cohn, *Colonialism and Its Forms of Knowledge* (Delhi: Oxford University Press, 1997), pp. 136–43.
94 Mrs Smith, Delhi, February 24, 1872, Baptist Zenana Mission Annual Report 1871–2 (AL).
95 G. Minault, *Secluded Scholars* ..., ch. 3.
96 Miss Hamilton's Report, *Lucknow in the Twenty-Third Report of the Indian Female Normal School and Instructional Society* (Birmingham: Josiah Allen, 1875).
97 Report of Miss Boyd [n.d.] November 1887, in Priscilla Sandys (Mrs Winter) 1867–91 (RHL) SPG X1168.
98 Mrs Harriot-Smith, March, 13, 1882, Baptist Zenana Mission Annual Report 1882, AL; Rev. W. T. Sattianadhan, Chairman of the Native Church Council, July 11, 1865 (LB) CI 2/0/211/2.

99 Miss Wells, Baptist Zenana Mission Annual Report 1882, AL. See also T. Allender, 'Closing Down an Intellectual Interchange: The Gifting of Text to a Colonial India', *Comparativ*, no. 1 (January, 2012), 15–32.
100 For examples of the deliberations of missionary parent bodies in Britain concerning India see the Church Mission Society, 'Annual Reports of the Indian Female Normal School and Instructional Society, …1863–75, …1876–79', reels 57 and 58 (OIOC).

CHAPTER FIVE

Female medical care: a new professional learning space, 1865–90

Colonial responses to the emergence of the female medical carer turned out to be a radical departure from those constructed by the state for the female teacher. By the late nineteenth century, traces of the official discourses concerning the femininity and morality of women physicians and nurses are apparent, which had earlier directed the state modus operandi regarding its women teachers. However, the practice of female physicians, and particularly female nursing and midwifery, were also professional sites where colonial barriers of race, and even class, were more easily broken down. The reason for this went to the essence of female agency itself. From the 1860s onwards, medical networks were less compliant with top-down raj racial agendas than were those networks that drove women teachers. This was because medicine for Indian females was effectively built upon the conversion activity of women missionaries outside the central mission compound and on a different type of interaction between participating females themselves. There was also greater colonial accountability to the West concerning the treatment regimes of women medical carers.

Rather than the slate and the chalkboard in the classroom that conveyed often unadapted Western knowledge, the more compelling imperatives of sanitation and cleanliness lay at the centre of the female medical profession. The white starched uniforms of its practitioners suggested a fierce conformity to European propriety and procedure, and there was unquestioned deference to a singular Western medical ontology that contrasted with the halting, yet plural, curriculum and moral features displayed in female teaching. As will be shown in this chapter and the next, paradigms of disease treatment and cure were powerful enough to compel European women in India to be effective and interactive within Indian female communities: an interaction that obviated and even directed raj macro agendas. Furthermore, the immediacy of this interaction with Indian women could not be, even unofficially, prohibited by the state on racial grounds, mostly because statistics showing 'results' in terms of medical treatment and healing could be more easily quantified and externalised to the scrutiny of the West than could those for female teaching.[1] Just as codification and regulation were the hallmarks of a Utilitarian-inspired raj, coming back the other way, from India to Europe and the USA, 'tropical' medicine on the subcontinent also bred new colonial responsibilities.

As early as the 1830s, statistics gathering had shifted official approaches to famine by virtue of the collation of crime statistics – these were seen as directly related to famine, and were of concern to Company officials.[2] In the same way, quantifiable medical results, available from the 1860s onwards, based on diagnosis, prognosis and 'cure', raised the question of the accountability of ICS officials to philanthropic agencies in India, to the metropole and, later, internationally.[3] Two generations later, in the early twentieth century, when the moral ascendancy of the British, in most other areas of colonial governance was breaking down, colonial medical outreach was at its most effective.

The different story about gender within the medical setting, as compared with the educational setting, established a paradox. European women and their agents were authorised to be in control of the Indian female body, unlike women teachers, who needed to contend with the vagaries of pedagogy and an esoteric connection between Eastern and Western classroom knowledge. Although the 'treatment' contact between 'trained' medical women and subaltern recipients was usually brief,[4] such brevity built capacity for the female practitioner to interact with many more individuals than the schoolteacher, who ministered to a smaller and less transient classroom cohort. Another feature was that female medical professionalism came to be more fiercely justified in terms of gender, even than teaching, by the end of the century, as female medics responded to a female Indian client base that refused, on strong cultural grounds, to accept male-administered examination and diagnosis. On this basis, highly gendered medical professionalism burgeoned in India in order to facilitate the cultural permission needed for the intimate clinical treatment of Indian females: the cornerstone of an otherwise anonymous relationship between medic and patient.[5]

Male medicine

Crossing the gender barrier regarding medicine in raj India carried even more significance than it did in Europe. From the early years of colonial rule, medical matters were strongly aligned to both masculine and military agendas. The 1840s saw the cultural transmission of magic when medical officer, James Esdaile, set up a hospital in Calcutta researching mesmerism with mostly males as his subjects.[6] Officers of the Indian Medical Services were mostly European military surgeons selected in England. They were then required to serve two years in the army before they could transfer to the civil service. Their brief almost entirely concerned the health safety of European males, particularly those in the army.[7]

Most of these early male doctors had received some training in Europe. However, the treatment schedule in Asia proffered 'tropical' medical bona fides – colonial knowledge that was longstanding and partly separate from Europe. Importantly, this colonial medical tradition later formed a distinctive knowledge context for the professional training of medical woman in India. European physicians visiting India as early as the late 1600s, such as physician François Bernier, suggested that the 'tropical' climate made sexually transmitted diseases 'less virulent' for those who contracted them in India.[8] Over two centuries later in the mid-1920s, Dr Grace MacKinnon, former superintendent of Patna Hospital in India, published beliefs that living in India brought forward the average age of menarche for European and Eurasian girls by about a year and contributed to their adverse sexual function.[9]

Before this tradition developed, the masculine, colonial state organised the early cohort of female patients in ways that ensured Indian female marginalisation. In this early period, a cross-racial patriarchal collaboration emerged between the European military and the Indian, male classes who collaborated with the raj. This collaboration powerfully rejected 'diseased' Indian and lower-class Eurasian women as morally or hygienically repugnant within the limited confines of the early raj.[10] Rejection of Indian women was at its starkest when they were seen as a medical threat to European men. Curiously, the magnitude of this feminine threat was calculated by the raj principally by how easily these females had caught illnesses from European men, especially in the case of sexually transmitted infection. As part of the colonial male defence mechanism, 'lock hospitals' were eventually established as coercive and punitive state institutions to regulate women who fell foul of the Indian Contagious Diseases Acts of 1864 and 1868. The *lal bazaar* (brothel area) consisted of grouped houses, caravanserai-style, that stood to accommodate what regiments viewed as the inevitable 'continence' of soldiers, with a ratio, by the 1860s, of one prostitute to forty-four soldiers.[11]

Keeping soldiers free from infection and also away from the likes of Captain Kenneth Searight (who documented 129 male Indian and European sexual partners while in India) was seen purely in terms of male physical and moral welfare.[12] Prostitutes were seen as performing an almost redemptive role in preserving the masculinity of the military, but only in terms of the European men with whom they inter-acted.[13] As late as the 1880s, salacious official accounts emerged in Madras, in particular, showing infected soldiers escaping moral blame for their medical condition, even when they pointed to registered and uninfected prostitutes as the source of their disease. Police responded by rounding up any unregistered prostitutes 'hovering around' army barracks 'in the rocks and other places of concealment'. The state assumed, solely because of their lack of registration, that these prosti-tutes were of particular malignancy and always in a more 'frightfully diseased state'.[14] However, not all was bad for these women, at least not for those confined to lock hospitals, which provided unintended opportunities for some of their female inmates. Astute and successful prostitutes incorporated compulsory registration and regular imprison-ment into their business practices, and destitute women turned such 'hospitals' into places where a subsistence living was possible.[15]

Even by the 1840s, tentative state expansion of medical education, beyond the central European encampments remained a masculine and military-oriented enterprise that mostly only treated men. When expansion did occur, it was directed towards Eurasians, as racially identifiable and separate enclaves distinct from surrounding integrated Indian communities. The racial identity of these 'Eurasian' recipients of medical care was not so targeted to those of part-European lineage as was the teacher training of females. 'Eurasian' was a brand broadly applied. For example, in 1842, Afghan 'orphans' in Assam were given stipends for medical instruction on camp sanitation by senior European medical students. These were Afghani boys earlier seconded by relo-cated Indian battalions of the Army now serving in Eastern India.[16] In the same province, other relocated racial groups, entirely without European racial lineage, were appointed as 'drill sergeants' to military orphanages to supervise adequate diets and exercise in the school play-ground.[17] This raj health policy, while well ahead of developments in Britain, nonetheless carefully kept these health agents separate from the surrounding Indian communities.

At the centre of colonial governance in India, early medical care was organised institutionally on a race and a caste basis. Elite hospi-tals were reserved for Europeans, run mostly like their counterparts in England: usually with civilian male wards outnumbering those for females by at least two to one. This ratio persisted even after the influx of European women to India upon the opening of the Suez Canal. There were then hospitals of lesser quality for Eurasians, and finally those reserved for Indians. These latter institutions were an unsatisfactory mix of dispensary and hostel for the very sick, and in times of ser-ious famine or epidemic only served those few who were able to gain admittance.[18] Even early medical treatments were racially organised. For example, Waltraud Ernst's work on lunatic asylums in India reveals the institutional spacial expression of madness, where 'mad' Europeans were sent home, while caste, class and communal barriers determined institutional places of confinement for insane Indians.[19] David Arnold's analysis frames these fierce European medical constructions further. He sees the expansion of Western medicine in India as being really one of plural dialogue, of occidental therapeutics, between India and Britain and as inescapably dependent on the political, economic and cultural forces at work in British India.[20]

Curing for Christ

Turning this pressing patriarchal and racial scenario around provided activist women in India considerable space in which to locate a countervailing professional ethic. With so few European personnel, early forays into Western medical care for females were, in fact, often just an adjunct of the classroom. In the 1840s in Bengal, teachers in girls' schools were required to monitor and administer medicines. These drugs were provided by the Company to keep students healthy and to prevent the death of teachers. The strategy was directed from the metropole by donor 'lady' organisations in Scotland, in particular, where research into infectious diseases was already beginning to captivate post-Enlightenment intellectual circles.[21] Even in the 1860s, European teachers who were female were pressured to provide medicines to their students when needed. They did so willingly; although they worried that their non-preferential dispensation of these scarce drugs might encourage new caste tensions to develop within classrooms of female Indians.[22]

As part of a more complicit interaction than took place within teaching, European and Indian missionary women broadened the 'caring' base, starting at new locations on the periphery of the raj that were of a deeper connection with Indians. By the First World War, this broadening had given female medicine more impetus than female teaching. In Britain, in the middle of the nineteenth century, missionary representations of 'native' women across the empire continued to show them as victims, suffering because of husbands and because of 'native' society itself.[23] However, the actions of missionary women resident in India regarding medical care created connections with Indian females that were built on far more sophisticated ground. Furthermore, the greater medical impetus was principally the upshot of earlier action by women missionaries, which unconsciously brought the raj reluctantly to otherwise marginalised traditional Indian communities.

[163]

Missionary zenana work outside the central mission compound, particularly in the 1860s, built up connections with local communities that were largely uncontrolled by the raj. In this context, racialising state action in favour of Eurasian females (in the manner that afflicted state policy regarding teachers who were female) was less possible when it came to nurses and *dais* (midwives). The medical imperative more easily cast aside frail state pretensions to be protecting any one morally threatened racial group. There was also the power of the metropole, which ran a separate 'benefaction' enterprise. As Burton identifies, the 'sunless, airless' zenana was a strong organiser of British medical philanthropy back in England.[24] The zenana was also an ongoing object of European fascination with the Orient.

The deployment of Western medicine also galvanised local missionary community action in the second half of the nineteenth century. George Lefroy, with characteristic frankness, claimed that rarely did an Anglican missionary 'lay his hand on a single one of the great band of catechists or readers & say this man's heart is really and evidently in his work'.[25] Yet medical work, with tangible results stemming from accurate diagnosis and effective treatment, had the advantage of keeping missionary agents committed, unlike the superficial exegesis of biblical text and evangelism in bazaars.

Within this sphere of action, and away from the gaze of the raj itself, lay a role for women missionaries, whose connection with the medical 'needs' of Indian females was the strongest bridge to conversion available to Westerners by the late 1860s. From the early 1860s, most mainstream missions knew the capacity of medicine as a potential tool for evangelism. At Delhi, Priscilla Winter began the SPG's female medical mission on the banks of the Yamuna river and expanded the work by forming the White Ladies Association for dispensary work, which eventually helped to found St Stephen's Hospital in the city. She had arrived in India at the age of just sixteen in 1858, and in 1867 she was able to seek the financial support of other Europeans.[26] Winter's apparent cultural awakening was also clever and intuitive strategy.

> Mrs Winter began by her use of a medical chest (without even quinine) & no medical qualification but stirred by the misery around her. She therefore availed herself of the unique opportunity the bathing ghats afford a meeting of all classes of Hindu women, the majority of whom, if they go nowhere else, yet go down every morning to the river both to make their vows and to dip in the sacred stream.[27]

Other large missions adopted a similar strategy, and the American Baptists were also involved in the new enterprise. American Baptist

Clara Swain was, in fact, the first accredited woman physician to be sent to missionary India. She arrived with fellow countrywoman and missionary, Isabella Thoburn, in early 1870, and just five years later claimed a practice of 2,000 patients with a further 5,000 prescriptions written annually at her dispensary.[28] Swain's approach also encouraged a broader reach than earlier permitted by the raj and British-oriented mission patriarchies. Her work opened up new connections with New York medical philanthropy. Rather than reside in mission quarters, she lived as a single women on the medical institution campuses in which she worked. Often her own anaesthetist, surgeon and compounder, she made home visits to zenanas and other Indian households. At her base in Bareilly (north India) in the 1870s she began medical classes in anatomy and physiology at basic certificate level, although it would be another two decades before Edith Brown, a British medical missionary, was to found the Ludhiana Medical College for Women, where formal physician classes could be held.[29]

Unclean heathens

Despite its impressive range, compared with other European endeavours in India, the reach of those missionaries who were medics concerned with females was every bit as paternal in this era as it was for female teaching. At Amritsar, the CMS's Dr William Elmslie, perhaps the most experienced physician in north India in the 1870s, was happy to put the case of Indian women carers in these terms:

> Besides native ... Hakims (male doctors), there exists a numerous class of native nurses, who are virtually all the sick women of India have for doctors in their own homes. And these native nurses are generally very ignorant, meddlesome and immoral.[30]

Such views externalised to the West an Indian female 'need' that melded established domains of zenana education work with dispensary work, resulting in the founding of new 'zenana medical schools'. Committees of missionary women abroad adjusted to this new reality by subtly changing their identity as sponsors of mission outreach. For example, the non-denominational 'Indian Female Normal and Instructional Society' was to transform itself in the early 1880s into the 'Zenana Medical and Bible Mission'.[31] In this way the primacy of the missionary conversion field authorised a blurring, and was even an amalgam, of the professional space for women teachers and women medics who were in India: unlike the rigid and separate parallel professional boundaries emerging in Europe.

Furthermore, the missionary orientation towards the medical care of Indian women only became possible when women missionaries in the 1870s began to work beyond the zenanas. This new work included engaging with networks of traditional Indian male apothecaries, well off the main trunk roads. Local Indian receptiveness to women missionaries emerged when these apothecaries were unable to treat seriously ill relatives and community members. In desperation, the apothecaries responded to the clarion call of new Western treatments. This patchy outreach was dangerous work for European women to undertake, but it also bred confident and paternal attitudes in them because of the seeming catalysing effects such work could have on the broader conversion landscape. The basic arrangement was free Western curative drugs in exchange for ideological and religious compliance. A CMS female missionary recounted one such engagement in these remote terms:

> Went on a drive to Thakurpookur [a rural area in Bengal near Calcutta]. The first house that of a native doctor ... the house a hovel really 'about forty minutes' walk from the road, through a rather jungly [sic] district, where in the rainy season many a snake crosses the narrow and almost impractical path. Dog rushed barking after us, cows turned their heads wonderingly, and the natives stared at us as if we were supernatural beings ... When there we stood outside a small dirty room which was decorated with shelves on which labelled old wine bottles stood – 'the Dispensary'. The doctor is very anxious for his wife to improve. She is a promising pupil and allows the Bible to be taught to her.[32]

Other agencies in conversion bridging work that combined evangelising with medical treatments for poor Indians were 'Bible women', who were also operative in Britain at this time. They were usually the daughters or wives of Eurasian or Indian converts, and their joint Christian medical vocation softened the internal racial barrier sensitivities, that were otherwise still typically strong between Indians and Eurasians. In the 1870s these women were only identified by an assumed European first name, as a signifier of their conversion. They were usually directed by the wife of the senior European missionary, who checked 'their' Bible women's visiting lists to Indian households at the end of each long day. Furthering the missionary focus on selected communities, Bible women such as 'Mary' worked with the Armenians in Peshawar (North West Frontier) and others used medicine and evangelism to infiltrate emancipated African slave communities in Maharashtra.[33]

Female medical missionary work of this kind was not yet constructed as a new form of professionalism for women in the West, responding to a distinct Western scientific knowledge. As Rosemary Seton points out, medical missionary William Elmslie did not see the need for formal medical qualifications for women missionaries engaged in therapeutic work with Indian women. For him, these women missionaries simply required courses in training in Indian female maladies, including obstetrics and diseases of the eyes and skin. They ought to be taught by a 'refined Christian medical man', according to Elmslie, but certainly not in mixed classes with trainee male medical missionaries.[34] Mission attitudes to medicine also still rehearsed strong colonial messaging concerning the bereft and emotionally inadequate Indian female, as depicted two generations earlier in Bengal regarding schooling for girls. However, unlike with early colonial schooling, Indian communities demonstrated some responsiveness to Western medical intervention. Supriya Guha argues that female missionary medical outreach prompted a small but influential group of Indians to desire new medical techniques in childbirth, which created the climate for later more widespread work.[35] Strong Indian cultural barriers remained in the north well into the twentieth century, although, in the south in Kerala, limited Christian Indian communities established by missions were more amenable to the idea of nursing as a noble female pursuit. The husbands and brothers of very poor Indian females organised their enrolment in nursing establishments for simple financial reasons, first as stipend recipients and then as wage earners.[36]

Women missionaries undertaking medical work were not necessarily close personal allies of the Indian women they treated. In the 1860s impressive underground sewerage systems built for London and other major British cities were hailed as great public works necessary to keep the surging metropole populations 'safe' from the ravages of cholera and typhoid. At Crossness, Charles Driver's pumping station – part of the London system – was heavily decorated with Islamic motifs.[37] However, in India at the same time, missionary sanitation discourse was located more around the Indian female body itself, as both victim and perpetrator of her own condition, rather than as a product of her broader social context. False dichotomies were built around the lack of Indian cleanliness that conveniently confused a supposed racial languor with the tragic results of grinding and unrelenting poverty. As one Protestant medical missionary related of her work in 1873:

The poor woman lay on a pile of clothes, which I presume, had never been washed since they were first brought into use. Her wasted body was partially covered with rags, as dirty and filthy as rags ever become. She had been ill for more than a month … and owing to the barbarous treatment she had received, was too far gone for anything I could do to help her.[38]

However, these attitudes also spurred on other medical activism by female missionaries. Una Saunders was the daughter of a well-to-do father who was a lawyer in England. New to India as a missionary, she was given first-hand experience in 1898 of the, by then, well-established mission dispensaries in western India. Her visits to these dispensaries were organised within safe striking distance of the local zenana 'mission house' in the town of Ahmedabad, yet they were still hair-raising forays for a genteel apprentice like Saunders. What she witnessed was, again, more skilful melding of conversion work with industrial-scale triage medical treatment that only the hardiest of European women could have endured for any length of time.

> This morning I drove off at 7.30 with Dr Nell [Montgomery] to her native dispensary, which she holds daily from 7.30 to 10.30 in a native house in town. Two rooms with mud floors & staircase like a ladder with no handrail, furniture nil, except for a table for dispensing & her own writing table and chair, form the scene. The big room is used for the waiting room & dispensary, and a tiny back room with no light but the little that comes down between the wall of another house & this window just gives the Dr sufficient light to see patients by. Air nil!
>
> Women & children soon begin to arrive & squat on the floor, getting a ticket given them to show the order they go in, no one being allowed to go away till after the service at 9 o'clock. While Dr Nell gives a short Bible lesson, which the Bible woman then continues and then amplifies … I must say the people listen better to a native than an Englishwoman … Most of the patients are children for eye treatment & skin disease, about 80 patients dispatched before 10.30 then a few bad cases remained where Dr Nell had herself to operate on the eyes and the screams were terrible to the onlooker.[39]

This was not an uncommon scene. At the Hunter Education Commission hearings sixteen years earlier, in 1882, the evidence of Miss M. Rose Greenfield, daughter of missionaries but teacher trained, opined how eye affliction affected her Indian female learners. Working in the Punjab, she estimated 50 per cent of her students were suffering from defective eyesight, including ophthalmia. Her only solution was school texts with larger print. The need was so pressing that Greenfield would eventually leave teaching to establish a women's dispensary in Ludhiana, along with Edith Brown, that would later become India's first fully fledged Women's Medical College.[40] Eye infections and over-sensitivity to light were uncomfortable afflictions and difficult to treat. A generation later, government ophthalmic hospitals were making strong links between this affliction and the spread of gonorrhoea, which rapidly rose to account for an estimated 70 per cent all eye disease cases in 1919, compared to 50 per cent a generation earlier.[41]

As these diagnostic links were made, so too was the feminine medical carer space recognised in India. Missionary female agents projected some of the fiercest colonial attitudes towards Indian women of the era. Yet their spreading out of a field of action in India created a new feminine medical domain. This expansion was given impetus by running the cultural argument that intrusive female medical procedures required a gendered professional response. As a result, many more women could now participate in medical capacities away from the resident, but still dominant, medical patriarchies of the raj. There was also the capacity for Indian communities, far from being passive recipients of medical care, to develop their own forms of Christian modernity as a result of the interaction.[42] Furthermore, the realities of mission medical work also gave rise to a new Western vocational space in India that prompted zenana missionaries, such as Elizabeth Bielby, to return to England to pursue formal, secular medical training in order to be better able to minister to the female sick in India.[43]

Secular medical activism: new networks with England

By the late 1870s the female missionary medical agenda was also strong enough to prompt secular local bodies into action. These bodies began to worry that the missions, by virtue of their many hours of labour in the field, were gaining a stranglehold over Western philanthropy in India. An alternative professional view began to emerge at the hands of a much smaller number of European women. The dedication of most women missionaries could hardly be questioned, but the moral and ethical predication of their action certainly could. Concern over how missionaries viewed their Indian patients, as sites of moral suasion, was particularly strong in the bustling trading city of Bombay, which was well connected with the West. Remarkably, in this city, attempts to address ground-up missionary efforts with a secular and countervailing Western professional response directly engaged sluggish developments in female medicine in Britain. This was a different outcome from the responses to the polemic around teacher education, which instead remained largely raj-based.

In Britain, by the 1870s, there was still little direction in educating women as doctors. The first School of Medicine for Women was not established in London until 1874, followed by Edinburgh twelve years later in 1886. Three of the founders of the School of Medicine in London were also the first three women physicians to be registered in Britain. They were the feminists Elizabeth Blackwell, Elizabeth Garrett Anderson and Sophia Jex-Blake. Rather than receiving recognition from Westminster for their credentials as women physicians, they were forced to exploit legal loopholes to complete their training. Blackwell and Jex-Blake gained their qualifications to practise in Britain by undertaking examinations in the USA and in Germany, respectively, and then registering as foreign doctors in England.[44] It was not until the passage of the Russell Gurney Act in 1876 that all medical bodies in Britain were authorised to examine women for medical qualifications and to accept them for registration.[45]

There is no evidence that these three women had links with India, although the Quaker Blackwell took an active interest in America's anti-slavery campaigns and Jex-Blake wrote a chapter on women's medicine in the book *Women's Work and Women's Culture*, by anti-Contagious Diseases Act activist Josephine Butler, which was first published in 1869.[46] At a distance, in England, Jex-Blake also obtained a slanted view of the Indian zenana from her interviews with Indian male students studying in England and others travelling back from India, whose views she references heavily in her own book.[47] However, there was one very important link between Bombay and this generation of first female doctors in Britain. Edith Pechey, a feminist doctor and later suffragette, worked alongside Jex-Blake in Edinburgh to gain recognition of female doctors. Her medical qualification had similarly been achieved, out of necessity, in the Swiss city of Bern. At the suggestion of Elizabeth Garrett Anderson, Pechey was persuaded to take up a position in Bombay in 1883 as the senior medical officer of the 'Cama Hospital for Women and Children', founded by the first Parsi businessman to set up a trading house in London.[48] Pechey's work in Bombay involved the training of nurses, a very ambitious push for equal pay for female medical workers, and developing a wider interest among her peers in women's social reform in India.[49] Most significantly, Pechey's feminist activism, in favour of 'scientifically qualified' women, and against missionary medical care, was informed by the influential writings of Frances Hoggan: a female feminist physician who was based in Britain but who also made two visits to India.[50]

Pechey's work was given additional impetus by what was already happening in Bombay in response to earlier female missionary action. In the city, secular organisations had been spurred into action to counter the hold of the missions over the Western, female, social reform agenda. As a result, a powerful avenue for the exchange of women medics in India between England and the USA became possible. Connections between local white businessmen and wealthy Indian traders resulted in prosperous commercial partnerships; and these partnerships were reliant on close, cross-racial trading arrangements that also oriented these businessmen towards philanthropic work on the same basis. To this end, in Bombay, two male benefactors in particular, an American businessman, George Kittredge, and the education reformer and wealthy Parsi, Sorabji Bengallee, set up the Medical Women for India Fund in 1882.[51] Edith Pechey was to become closely involved in this organisation and her husband, Herbert Musgrave Phipson, wine merchant and naturalist, was its secretary.

From this base, Pechey's European imported feminism soon resonated with these hardy businessmen, and Kittredge found himself arguing that 'for success in India, women must be recognised as the equal of men in the medical care of their own sex'.[52] Kittredge and Bengallee hoped to educate clever Indian women at the London School for Medicine for Women, where Pechey had earlier delivered its inaugural address. They mistakenly believed medicine, as a non-racial enterprise, would soon see easy access by trainee Indian women to UK institutions, provided these women were given sufficient funds from benefactors in India first. This was despite the fact that Pechey's own diagnoses inclined towards new objectifications of Indian women: she ascribed rickets in children and scrofula (lymph node tuberculosis in children) to Hindu child marriage; consumption to Muslim purdah; and internal inflammation maladies to the long lying-in periods of Parsi women.[53]

Part of the emerging secular female medical cause in England came directly from India, at the behest of wealthy expatriate Europeans and Americans. In England, competition between evangelising female medical work (as promoted by pioneering medical missionary physician Fanny Butler and others) and secular medical training approaches was accentuated as a point of strong division, but without much by way of tangible outcomes that fed back to India.[54] At the metropole, medical activism of both kinds – secular and mission-inspired – was to prove mostly unsuccessful in securing creditable results in the importation of physician students who were Indian women. However, the division between these two rival brands of female medical carers was less apparent in India by the end of the century, even though Protestant missions, in particular, continued to dominate the medical mission landscape in India, as well as in China, while alignments with the national movement in India favoured those of a secular scientific foundation instead.[55]

In the late 1870s and the 1880s, the crossover and associated networks that drove change concerning female medical care were complex and interrelated between Britain and colonial India. In Britain, the barrier to females joining the medical profession as physicians was still too strong for women to be able to respond adequately, through their professional actions, to either the emerging missionary or the secular medical dynamic concerning women physicians coming out of India.

Meanwhile, in India, ICS mentalities continued to see one undifferentiated female medical care project: mission or secular. In England, the National Indian Association (NIA), founded by Mary Carpenter in 1870, hopefully looked to support the philanthropy project in Bombay of more nurses to 'adjust their pillow or alleviate their pain'. The NIA also pursued a broader plan to see a more equitable exchange of educated scholars between India and Great Britain, including female doctors.[56]

In a manner typical of many women's philanthropic committees concerning India at this time, the NIA's preoccupation remained the organising of other women in England, rather than what became its public objective: the raising of funds for the medical education of Indian women.[57] The NIA's biggest achievement was winning the patronage of Florence Nightingale, whose approach to India was to profess a broad concern for Indian women, without any of the Carpenter specificity concerning female education.[58] The NIA sent a female agent to India to judge the 'character' of those female Indian candidates most likely to succeed in their medical studies while in England. While working with like-minded women in the USA, this committee also optimistically constructed registers of female graduates who had completed their medical training in England or the USA, and who might be induced to work in India. Unfortunately the results were not encouraging. Little came of the work, as the few available candidates in Britain preferred a career 'at home', where salaries were much higher.[59] In the end, it was only the state-directed Dufferin Fund (discussed in the next chapter) that had much impact in the Britain-to-India trade in women physicians, with thirty-six mostly under-qualified women sent out to the raj by 1890.[60]

The female medical trajectory in India also exposed other deficiencies at the metropole. In 1873 the non-denominational Indian Female Normal School and Instructional Society, based in Calcutta, was sharp enough in its lobbying of Westminster to expose the almost impermeable professional barriers to educated Indian women coming to Britain. These barriers were even more robust than those in Calcutta. When satisfied that its Indian female candidates had converted, this society had pressed for their further 'scientific' medical education 'at home' in Britain. The society was prepared to pay £150 for 'passage, training and outfit' after its selected candidates had completed two years' hospital experience in India. However, racial and gender-based opposition in the UK prevented this organisation from ever enrolling any of its nominees in London.[61] Luminaries who were Indian converts, such as Pandita Ramabai, and who contributed to the female medical debate in India, could not qualify as doctors in England. In Ramabai's

Figure 5 Dr Frances Reid, a SPG Eurasian physician (in white clinical European dress), taking the pulse of an Indian patient with nurses looking on. © United Society and Bodleian Library, Oxford.

case, this was despite her travels to both Britain and the USA in the pursuit of Indian women's rights. Even in Scotland, by at least 1894, barriers to women doctors still meant the India mission lobby had to be content with concentrating on achieving a stock nursing education only for its candidates in Britain.[62] These barriers were also part of a broader restriction of Indian women being educated in Britain. By 1900 there were still only twenty-five Indian female students residing in England: thirteen were schoolgirls, nine were medical students and three were training as teachers.[63] It was not until 1906 that the Bengal government agreed to sponsor to England two female trainee teachers who were Indian in an effort to revitalise teaching at the Bethune College (as discussed in chapter eight).[64]

These well-meaning endeavours of women committees exposed an essential contradiction in the state approach to Indian medical affairs regarding women, particularly if they were to be given the opportunity to reach 'doctor' status. Feminist activism in Britain had yet to win the battle over women doctors and nurses and, even during the First World War, these professions remained class-based enterprises. In this context, it was relatively easy for the raj to cover over its own race objections to Indian women being educated as physicians in the UK by wrapping up such possibilities in red tape and criteria that were impossible for most of these Indian women to overcome. In sum, networks of women mission evangelists who engaged with Indian women, mostly outside the central mission compound in India, had produced a centre of female medical professionalism that had animated competing mission and secular 'scientific'-based philanthropy in India. However, in the process, what this dynamic exposed most was not Indian female medical need in India, that might again call out for 'remedy' from abroad, but instead a reluctant metropole, unwilling to support the work of Indian women who were physicians, even if these Indian women were in a position to temporarily relocate to Britain for an education based on Western medical procedures and protocols. Outside the tight control of the raj, male and military connections that had built earlier colonial medical endeavour in India gave way to strong female activism, at least in restricted enclaves of mission and hospital domains. Yet these India colonial domains provided a sufficient platform for international scrutiny as global communities of scientific medical knowledge developed, which demanded non-racial treatment and cure in India, particularly regarding Indian females.

Notes

1 From the 1860s onwards, colonial reporting on disease treatment and cure was some of the most thorough of all areas of governance. To begin with this reporting was only in the interests of protecting European communities, including soldiers. Mostly in statistical form, but also incorporating strong and fascinating narratives of British approaches to illness at the time, this data was broken down into race, caste and gender constituencies under various disease headings. By the twentieth century these reports became even more detailed, just as reporting on colonial schooling was becoming much more cursory. See, for example, Col. G. F. A. Harris (Inspector General, Civil Hospitals, Bengal), *Triennial Report on the Charitable Dispensaries Under the Government of Bengal for the Years 1908, 1909 and 1910* (Calcutta: Bengal Secretariat Book Department, 1911) (OIOC), V/24/748.
2 S. Sharma, *Famine, Philanthropy and the Colonial State* (New Delhi: Oxford University Press, 2001), pp. 28–78.
3 For a broad discussion of the colonial overlay in treating disease suffered by both genders in India for reasons of colonial power and Western accountability see D. Arnold, *Colonizing the Body: State Medicine and Epidemic Disease in Nineteenth-Century India* (Berkerley, CA: University of California Press, 1993), *passim*.
4 This assertion is based on the elevated numbers of patients recorded in government reports as being consulted each day by the medical carers, particularly in the Eurasian and Indian categories.
5 Gender categorisations were particularly strong in India concerning the European, Eurasian and Indian 'treatment' of Indian females.
6 G. Prakash, 'Science "Gone Native" in Colonial India', *Representations*, no. 40 (1992), 161.

7 M. U. Mashtaq, 'Public Health in British India: A Brief Account of the History of Medical Services and Disease Prevention in Colonial India', *Indian Journal of Community Medicine*, 34:1 (January, 2009), 7.
8 A. Eraly, *The Mughal World* (New Delhi: Penguin, 2007), p. 4.
9 G. MacKinnon, 'Diseases of Women' in W. Byam and R. G. Archibald (eds), *The Practice of Medicine in the Tropics*, vol. 3, Section xvii (1923), pp. 2471–98, also cited in Buettner, E., *Empire Families ...*, n. 30, p. 35.
10 For manifestations of this masculine medical collaboration see P. Bala, 'Introduction' in P. Bala (ed.), *Contesting Colonial Authority: Medicine and Indigenous Responses in Nineteenth and Twentieth-Century India* (Lanham, MA: Lexington Books, 2012), p. 2.
11 R. Hyam, *Empire and Sexuality ...*, p. 123. This ratio was a general average in the late nineteenth century where the number of British soldiers is divided by the number of known regiment-certified prostitutes.
12 R. Hyam, *Empire and Sexuality ...*, p. 123, 128. Captain Searight was an acquaintance of E. M. Forster. Between 1897 and 1917 Searight claimed his sexual partners' ages ranged from seven to twenty-eight, with those over nineteen only being British as Hyam analyses these figures. Hyam cites one other case study. Hyam's source regarding Searight is his journal. [K. Searight], 'Paidikion, I, An Autobiography, in which is set forth the secret diversions of a paiderast', unpublished mss [1917]. See also Hyam's other source T. Hammond, ' "Paidikion": paiderastic manuscript', *International Journal of Greek Love (NY)*, I (1966), pp. 28–37,
13 K. Ballhatchet, *Race, Sex, and Class under the Raj ...*, p. 162.
14 *Annual Report on the Military Lock Hospitals of the Madras Presidency for the Year 1889* (Madras; Government Printing, 1889), pp. 9–12 (OIOC).
15 S. Hodges, "Looting' the Lock Hospitals in Madras during the famine years of the 1870s' *Social History of Medicine*, 18:3 (2005), 379–98.
16 Bengal Public Department, September 21, 1842 no. 18 (OIOC) E/4/771.
17 Military Proceedings, March 1, 1843, Bengal Public Department, p. 662 (OIOC) E/4/773.
18 Major General W. N. Robertson (Surgeon General, Bengal), *Triennial Report on the Working of Hospitals and Dispensaries under the Government of Bengal for the Years, 1917, 1918 and 1919* (Calcutta: Secretariat Book Dept., 1920), pp. 5–14 (OIOC), V/24/749.
19 W. Ernst, 'Madness and Colonial Spaces – British India, c. 1800–1947', in L. Topp *et al.* (eds), *Madness Architecture and the Built Environment* (London: Routledge, 2007), p. 232.
20 D. Arnold, *Colonizing the Body: State Medicine and Epidemic Disease in Nineteenth-Century India* (London: University of California Press, 1993), pp. 11–60.
21 Bengal Public Department, April 1, 1843 p. 341 (OIOC) E/4/787.
22 CMS Annual Letter, Miss White, Bombay, January 21, 1863 (LB) CI3/0/80/256.
23 A. Johnston, *Missionary Writing and Empire, 1800–1860* (Cambridge: Cambridge University Press, 2003), pp. 56–7.
24 A. Burton, 'Contesting The Zenana: The Mission To Make "Lady Doctors For India," 1874–1885', *Journal Of British Studies*, 35:3 (1996), 369.
25 Lefroy to My Dear Min [his sister] January 7, 1880 (RHL) SPG Misc Series X1240.
26 R. R. Winter to Mr Tucker, April 3, 1889 (RHL) SPG E44, f. 495.
27 J. C. Muller, *Some Personal Reminiscences of Work in the Delhi Medical Mission, 1884–1910* (Suffolk: Richmond Clay, 1910), p. 3 (CBMA).
28 C. A. Swain, 'Medical Work', *Woman's Foreign Missionary Society of the Methodist Episcopal Church* (Boston, MA: Publications Office, 1906), p. 494; M. Nalini, 'Pioneer Woman Physician as Medical Missionary to the Women of the Orient, Clara A. Swain, MD (1834–1910)', *International Journal of Innovation, Management and Technology*, 1:2 (June, 2010), 148.
29 M. Nalini, 'Pioneer Woman Physician as Medical Missionary to the Women of the Orient ...', pp. 147–51.

30 Dr Elmslie's Report, 'Medical Mission', *Twenty-Third Annual Report of the Indian Female Normal and Instructional Society* (Birmingham: Josiah Allen, 1875), p. 102 (OIOC).

31 'Minutes of the Zenana Medical and Bible Mission, 1894–1904', Reel 49 (OIOC).

32 'The Twenty-Third Annual Report of the Indian Female Normal School and Instructional Society, April, 1875' (Birmingham: Josiah Allen, 1875) (OIOC). This organisation founded by Lady Kinnaird was nominally interdenominational but with a significant CMS membership that broke away from it in 1881.

33 'The Twenty-Second Annual Report of the Indian Female Normal School and Instructional Society' (London: Suter & Co., 1874), p. 56 (OIOC).

34 R. Seton, *Western Daughters in Eastern Lands ...*, pp. 149–50.

35 S. Guha, 'Dais to Doctors: The Medicalisation of Childbirth in Colonial India' in L. Lakshmi (ed.), *Understanding Women's Health Issues* (Delhi: Oscar, 1998), p. 2.

36 S. George, ' "Dirty Nurses" and "Men Who Play": Gender and Class in Transnational Migration' in M. Burawoy *et al.* (eds), *Global Ethnography* (Berkeley, CA: University of California Press, 2000), pp. 146–7.

37 J. Bold and T. Hinchcliffe, *Discovering London's Buildings* (London: Frances Lincoln, 2009), pp. 160–2.

38 'The Twenty-Third Annual Report of the Indian Female Normal School and Instructional Society, April, 1875' (Birmingham: Josiah Allen, 1875), p.102 (RHL).

39 Letters of Una Saunders, August 3, 1898 (OIOC) MSS Eur F 186/141.

40 Miss M. Rose Greenfield, Hunter Provincial Hearings, Punjab, pp. 226–32 (OIOC) V/26/860/12.

41 Surgeon General G. G. Gifford, 'Triennial Report Civil Hospitals and Dispensaries, Madras, 1919', p. 9 (OIOC) V/24/677.

42 For an account of tribal groups in Western India accepting Christianity and medicine on their own terms, and making use of missionaries for their own purposes, see D. Hardiman, *Missionaries and their Medicine* (Manchester: Manchester University Press, 2008).

43 D. Arnold, *Colonizing the Body ...*, p. 261.

44 E. M. Bell, *Storming the Citadel: The Rise of the Woman Doctor* (London: Constable, 1953).

45 J. Manton, *Elizabeth Garrett Anderson* (New York: E. P. Dutton, 1965), pp. 178, 230–3, 240–1, 250; P. Hollis, *Women in Public: Documents of the Victorian Women's Movement 1850–1900* (George Allen & Unwin, 1979), pp. 100–3 cited in R. Watts, *Women in Science: A Social and Cultural History* (New York: Routledge, 2007), p. 131.

46 S. Jex-Blake, 'Medicine as a Profession for Women' in J. Butler (ed.), *Woman's Work and Woman's Culture* (London: Macmillan, 1869), pp. 78–120.

47 S. Jex-Blake, *Medical Women: A Thesis and its History* (London: Hamilton & Adams, 1886), pp. 153, 208, 229, 234–5, 239, 240–4.

48 M. Ramanna, *Western Medicine and Public Health in Colonial Bombay* (Bangalore: Orient Longman Private Ltd., 2002), p. 185.

49 E. Lutzker, 'Edith Pechey-Phipson, MD: Untold Story', *Medical History*, 11:1 (1967) January), 41–5.

50 For a broader discussion of Hoogan's work see A. Witz, ' "Colonising Women": Female Medical Practice in Colonial India, 1880–1890' in L. Conrad and A. Hardy (eds), *Women and Modern Medicine* (London: Welcome Trust, 2001), p. 27.

51 M. Ramanna, *Western Medicine and Public Health ...*, p. 183.

52 G. Kittredge, *A Short History of the Medical Women for India Fund* (Bombay: Education Society's Press, 1889), p. 2.

53 M. Ramanna, *Western Medicine and Public Health ...*, p. 192.

54 A. Burton, 'Contesting The Zenana ...', pp. 378, 384.

55 R. Fitzgerald, 'Rescue and Redemption: The rise of female medical missions in colonial India during the late nineteenth and early twentieth centuries' in A. M. Rafferty *et al.*, *Nursing History and the Politics of Welfare* (Routledge: London, 1997), p. 67.

56 R. Temple, *Journal of the National India Association 1880* (London: King & Co., 1881), p. 89, 718–19, 723 (OIOC).

57 [R. Temple], *Journal of the National Indian Association, in Aid of Social Progress in India* (London: H. S. King & Co., 1882) (OIOC).

58 *Journal of the National Indian Association*, September 1883, no. 153, p. 509 (OIOC) L/PJ/6/105 no. 1492; L. McDonald and G. Vallée (eds), *Florence Nightingale on Social Change in India* (Ontario: Wilfrid Laurier University Press, 2007), p. 627.

59 *Journal of the National Association in Aid of Female Education in India* (London: Kegan Paul, 1883), pp. 509–10 (OIOC) L/PJ/6/105 no. 1492.

60 H. Dufferin, *A Record of Three Years' Work of the National Association for Supplying Female Medical Aid to the Women of India August 1885 to August 1888* (Calcutta: Thacker, Spink & Co., 1888), pp. 15, 31.

61 *Twenty Second Annual Report of the Indian Female Normal School and Instructional Society* (London: Suter & Co., 1874), p. 54 (OIOC).

62 Minutes of the Zenana, Medical and Bible Mission 1894–1904 nos. 36–7 (OIOC).

63 *Indian Magazine*, no. 349 (January, 1900), p. 71 cited in S. Lahiri, *Indians in Britain: Anglo-Indian Encounters, Race and Identity, 1880–1930* (London: Frank Cass, 2000), p. 10.

64 *Indian Magazine*, no. 349…, p. 11.

CHAPTER SIX

Feminine missionary medical professionalism and secular medical feminists, 1880–1927

British forms of female medical professionalism became consolidated in India towards the end of the nineteenth century, even though application in the field, by the raj, ignored the missionary versus secular medical carer dichotomy that was evident to most European participants on the subcontinent at that time. Significantly, the race and class divides in colonial India, so strongly enforced by this time for women teachers, were dissipated by a different kind of medical deployment concerning females. This deployment was at the hands of Indian, Eurasian and European women working both inside and outside these race and class divides and also with the broader Indian population in view. As would later happen in Britain, these women invented new plots and new narratives in India in which the quest for medical learning and productive work assumed a central role.[1]

Despite colonial India's engagement with the metropole concerning female medical care, the metropole remained unresponsive: officials at the India Office in London failed to see the medical field in India as providing opportunities that were at least comparable to the limited prospects that existed for women in Britain. In contrast to this approach, by the end of the nineteenth century, female societies based in Britain were forced to begin to examine precisely what was happening on the subcontinent, rather than merely to speculate about the deficits of Indian females from afar. This was because the professional space for female medics in colonial India was considered robust enough by some of these frustrated committees to begin speculating that even European women aspiring to be doctors could be attracted to the subcontinent from Britain to achieve advanced medical qualifications of the kind many were still being denied at the metropole.[2] In 1912, the influential 'National Association for Providing Female

Medical Aid to the Women of India', writing of women physicians in India, asserted that:

> Lady Doctors should now be granted entire control and independence of their hospitals and especially now women with higher qualifications in medicine can be safely trusted with the internal control of their hospitals.[3]

Male medical colleges

A parallel debate, internal to India, emerged during the 1880s through the aegis of male-dominated medical colleges, which ultimately offered more progressive possibilities for Indian female doctors. These debates were fought out in different ways in each major province. It was mostly women who cleverly manipulated these battles, in various ways, to win greater access for their gender to the medical profession than even their sisters in Britain had managed.

In Bombay, a substantial debate emerged when candidates who were Indian women were admitted to medical college-level training after the Lieutenant Governor of the province overrode his own council, which opposed the action. This rare move was not entirely driven by progressive thinking, but was, in fact, partly designed to avoid a potential lowering of medical standards in the province, which the supporters of women physicians had skilfully contrived as a means to force the hand of government. Their strategy was to propose that, unless Indian females were admitted to medical college, a three-year apothecary course would be created that was independent of Bombay University. The apothecary proposal deliberately offended the Western professional standards of the European male doctors who administered the Grant Medical College. To prevent the college's standards being sublimated in this way, these male doctors were persuaded to admit Indian women to their own education domain, as an unsatisfactory, but more palatable, alternative.[4]

The Madras Medical College proved more receptive to Indian women being trained as doctors; here the battle was more about basic physical, rather than intellectual, gender barriers. In this province the locally based Association in Aid of Female Education in India (AAFEI) exposed as obsolete the view that racially mixed classes of male and female medical students would compromise standards. The AAFEI further suggested that other objections regarding the need to build separated seats, screens and waiting rooms for patients of qualified women doctors in India were hardly reasons to prevent their training as doctors in the first place.[5]

In Bengal, however, the gender and racial barriers were not so easily broken down. Despite emotionally charged observations about the medical condition of many Indian females that could only be met by trained women physicians, the Calcutta Medical College refused point blank in 1882 to accept Indian women candidates to train as doctors, even though it was already accepting some expatriate European women candidates. In England, an outraged NIA, aligned to the AAFEI, took care to single out the obdurate Lieutenant Governor, Augustus Rivers-Thompson, for criticism. This criticism was informed by good local knowledge about the position of Indian women and claimed that his racial prejudice:

> encourages the evils viz zenana prejudices, increases barriers of caste & it suppresses the natural and reasonable aspirations of Indian ladies to enter a profession that would find in India as in all countries a wide sphere of action and beneficient service.[6]

This argument, and others like it, was constructed for domestic British consumption and carried wider significance. It was an argument that cleverly confined itself to the Indian context, conflating women's aspirations with the enduring colonial 'condition' of Indian women polemic. It was also an argument that was content to ignore the rigid patriarchal barriers still in place within Britain for women physician aspirants.

New knowledge

Separating out the raj medical field in this way was sustainable because the Western gifting of medical knowledge, especially concerning Indian females, was still defined by Europeans in cultural deficit terms. As a result, towards the end of the nineteenth century, the attitudes of women serving on key committees in India regarding local women medical professionals were sometimes more sympathetic than they were towards women professionals in the UK.[7] Sustaining such a dichotomous approach about gender and medicine in India, as compared with Britain, also went to the issue of Western constructions of colonial medicine itself.

It was difficult to argue against the utilitarian nature of mainstream medical treatment. A steep improvement in the status of medicine in Europe and the USA was attracting the best male minds to the profession. As part of this elevated status, rigorous scholarly academies were built in India, mostly by a small number of male doctors in the emerging medical colleges. These colleges were direct recipients of universal and mostly Western-predicated scientific knowledge transfer with other parts of the world, and, as a consequence, their scholar-informed style of education was too compelling to be side-tracked by other colonial agendas.

However, the raj did not understand or acknowledge the contribution of the subcontinent itself to modern medical knowledge and the complexity of this kind of information transfer. Medical knowledge of the ancient world had been preserved via the Arabic language when Latin texts had been lost to the West. In particular, the ancient Kushan empire of northwest India had codified medical information, partly derived from ancient Greece and Rome, that had since filtered to colonial India independently of Europeans.[8] Colonial India was also a laboratory for new, global research, including new sanitary knowledge that prevented large sections of the population, white and Indian, from succumbing to malaria, small pox and the plague. Other developments included onsite India-based epidemiological studies of diseases, the development of compulsory vaccination protocols, studies into the aphrodisiac properties of Indian cannabis, and the development of leprosy treatments that would be taken back to Europe.[9]

Away from the scholarly medical academies, raj education departments preferred instead to ponder over what they perceived as a cultural reluctance of Hindus, in particular, to handle dead bodies and human bones in its medical college anatomy classes. Perpetuation of this truism enabled these departments to sustain their narrative of the degenerate 'superstitions' of Indians, even while a rising generation of urbane trainee Indian doctors in the 1880s demonstrated no such proclivity.[10]

Strong racial overtones also remained in medical treatment itself. For example, as late as 1911, the Indian colonial agent Suri Sunder Das, inspector of the health and physique of children in school in the Punjab, objectified:

A European, much more than an Indian, shapes his environment; the latter studies means to submit to what he regards as inevitable.[11]

Das's 'shaping of his environment' argument won reportage rights in high-profile raj publications. It was a flagrant stereotype: diseases such as malaria, cholera and dysentery were, in fact, elevated by the colonial 'shaping' of the subcontinental landscape itself, where irrigation schemes and railway buildings isolated still, stagnant and festering pools of once fresh and flowing water.[12]

Midwives

Female medical care was also subjected to similar Western stereo-typing. As discussed earlier, this had been firmly built upon the foundation of mission conversion strategies directed towards broad sections of Indian communities because, in the previous two genera-tions, a masculine raj had been too slow to respond to even the needs of Western women. However, missionary medicine, especially for females, also projected a knowledge that was deeply flawed by its cul-tural judgements. Old missionary constructs about the 'degeneracy' of the Indian female had come sweeping back, with the 'malignant' maternal instincts of Indian women being portrayed as requiring the remedy of Western childbirth and midwifery techniques. The practices of traditional Indian *dais* (midwives) came under particular scrutiny in the missionary frame, and this mindset around degeneracy lasted until at least the First World War.

In traditional communities, dais were low-caste Hindus and poor Muslims. Western scholars supposed their low status was because of the 'unclean' act of cutting the umbilical cord.[13] This idea served raj politics well – for example, as late as 1909 a government research pro-ject at Cawnpore claimed to show that the high infant mortality rate for babies under one year of age was due to the 'unclean' methods of the dais, leading to many cases of tetanus. The Europeans blamed this 'neglect' on the superstitions of dais (which they claimed forbade the use by dais of modern antiseptics) rather than on the usual poverty and race of dais, which prevented their access to these, at first expensive, antiseptics – and which necessitated considerable cultural travelling on the part of dais to enter the white-tiled walled infirmaries of colo-nial medical institutions.[14] The European stereotype built on salacious stories from a generation earlier of supposed *dai* witchcraft practices, including forcing expectant mothers to stand astride cooking fires and infusing them with cardamom and ginger.[15] Miss Hewlett, in charge of the Maternity Hospital in Amritsar, saw her role as being to expunge, not modify, what she imagined to be traditional dai practices concern-ing birth control, which she supposed sometimes amounted to the:

> wilful murder of infants in the birth by breaking their backs, or twisting their necks. One old Dai confessed on her deathbed that she had herself destroyed hundreds of children.[16]

Even more moderate European views in the later colonial period clung to the belief that *ayahs* (household maids) and dais should be mistrusted, because they were suspected of using opium to put the children under their supervision to sleep more easily.[17]

Such accounts ignored the work of local village committees, which comprised majority Indian memberships. Such village committees were not interested in pursuing the raj education agenda, but they were closely involved in Western sanitation projects, including those concerning new childbirth techniques.[18] There were also Indian women, such as Anandibai Joshi, who studied in the USA and who argued, as early as the mid-1880s, that traditional Indian methods of childbirth coincidently chimed with Western sanitation protocols. Others in the same period, such as Miss R. A. Malabari, pointed to Western problems – for example, the deformities that the lacing of Western corsets might cause, and the contribution towards ill health created by poorly ventilated colonial classrooms.[19]

State compared to missionary summations of the medical deficiencies of Indian females did not align on the question of race, although they remained parallel in their respective judgements of superior Western practice. Crude comparisons on the 'practice' level also ignored the significant knowledge gaps in Western medical techniques and procedures at the time. In the West, operations were highly risky: it was an era in which even King Edward VII's appendectomy in 1902 was considered life threatening. In England and Wales, during the 1920s, maternal deaths in childbirth amounted to approximately 39,000 women.[20] It was not surprising, therefore, that the scene was little different in India, at least as far as Europeans knew it. Even in the civil hospitals for Europeans, located in the large Indian cities, only a tiny proportion of women presented for emergency caesarean operations, treatments for ectopic pregnancies and ovariotomies to remove dangerous tumours. Furthermore, in the most advanced medical institution in the country, the Sir Jamsetjee Jeejebhoy Hospital, affiliated to the Grant Medical College in Bombay, these operations still only numbered 238 out of a total 82,044 operations in 1908.[21]

State 'training' by gender

The different direction of colonial-inspired medical care for women, as compared to that for men, was also reinforced by the different way in which their respective formal training evolved in the second half of the nineteenth century. The medical training of women in colonial India lacked the structured academic approach made available to men. For example, the Lahore Medical College for men, established in 1860, closely followed its counterpart in Calcutta as one of the first institutional raj agencies for Western medical education in India. By 1872, a medical degree in this college required a pass in the Calcutta University entrance exam (written in English), followed by two and a half years of study that included: a hundred lectures in surgical anatomy, chemistry, anatomy and physiology; sixty lectures on Indian drugs; thirty lectures on botany and practical chemistry; as well as six-months' study of practical pharmacy during this time; and the dissection of a body by each student in each of three terms. This schedule imitated male medical training in England. However, the Lahore degree did not merely follow the dictums of the Calcutta University senate, nor the European bureaucrats who still dominated the medical departments in each province. Instead, it also embraced the study of some Indian medical practices and medicines, in order to better equip its graduating male Indian doctors, who were in very short supply.[22]

Admittedly, some infiltration by European women was permitted within these male medical education settings, although their subsequent employment required them first to serve in a mission hospital. St Stephen's Hospital in Delhi, founded by Priscilla Winter, was able to employ Dr Jenny Müller as its first full-time doctor in 1891.[23] Almost three decades later, in 1920, Dr Helen Franklin left the same institution to become Vice-Principal and Professor of Surgery at the Lady Hardinge Medical College (founded in 1916), also in Delhi.[24] By 1900, lead male doctors would occasionally invite European women doctors to assist in surgical procedures, if the patient was female.[25] Also by this time, in the NWP, the handful of caesarean operations performed were carried out solely by European women doctors as part of their 'experimental' training. These grim procedures were usually left too late, with a resulting survival rate of just 23 per cent of mothers and 8 per cent of their babies.[26] Furthermore, when the Universities Commission of 1902 recommended that all medical colleges split their degrees into separate medical and surgery degrees, significantly, all these colleges were obliged, unlike those in the West, to offer midwifery as a separate branch as part of the degree that led to candidates qualifying as physicians.[27]

However, the medical education of Indian women, taking place as it did away from the elite colleges for men, still carried forward earlier training models for women as 'native doctors'. This term was fluid and generic, and it related almost entirely to the earlier field of work of women in dispensaries and in the homes of sick females. In north India, as early as the 1850s, the Inspector General of Hospitals used the title of 'native doctor' to offer bright Indian females an education that was taught by amateur demonstrators and apothecaries. It was intended to make these women ready to meet the urgent basic needs of the communities they were already serving, particularly in Bombay.[28] However, this training was usually without reference to formal abstract knowledge or higher surgical skills. Furthermore, such basic preparation was not sufficient to get these women past impatient white college professors of medicine and chemistry, who were keen to be absolved from teaching Indian women in what they regarded as their already overcrowded male classes.[29]

Even in the 1890s, provincial authorities acknowledged that there was in India '[an] absence of any system of control of female practitioners & definition of their qualifications'.[30] In government medical colleges, such as the one at Lahore, there was only one woman graduate every five years.[31] At this time in Bombay there were three Parsi women with medical degrees, Misses Tankariavala, Pasikaka and Medhara. They were admitted to the rarefied ranks of government-covenanted medical employment, which brought better pay rates and some provision for a pension. The title given to these three exceptional women was 'woman assistant surgeon', rather than 'doctor', despite their holding medical degrees from Grant Medical College and impressive experience across several medical institutions in Poona, Ahmedabad and Bombay.[32] Other notable medical women included Kadambini Ganguli and Anandi Gopal Joshi, who later aligned themselves to the Indian Nationalist movement. They were the first two Indian women to graduate from the Calcutta Medical College in 1886.[33]

The colonial state provided a field of action for many Indian medically trained women, and although, still in control of their professional status, offered them much more inferior classifications to those of men, even by Western standards. Women medics were organised in three classes that were, significantly, available to all races. Class one was for assistant surgeons, certified practitioners and hospital assistants; class two was for compounders (chemists); and class three was for midwives. In the 1890s the pay of all three classes fell well short of that of their male counterparts: even after seven years' experience, the top rate for Indian women was Rs.115 per month – about a third of what was available to a Eurasian schoolmistress. Further down the scale, Indian women chemists were offered only Rs.20 per month, a barely subsistence rate.

By the 1890s training of midwives was placed under the regulation of the male civil surgeons in each province and the criteria for the initial selection of these midwives resembled the character filtering that had already been entrenched in teacher training for two generations. However, unlike most teacher training of any colonial standing, it was possible for these formally trained midwives to be Indian, and they had to be over the age of twenty for state recognition. The award of a midwife certificate required two years' supervised experience, attendance at twenty-four births and passing an oral examination in 'elementary anatomy of the pelvis, labour and obstetric emergencies'.[34]

Figure 6 Going home: SPG-trained midwife with mother and baby.
© United Society and Bodleian Library, Oxford.

Hospital work

An additional organisation was also influential, namely the Dufferin
Fund, nominally founded in 1885 by Lady Dufferin, the wife of the
serving Viceroy. This fund was organised by successive Vicereines and
did not technically end until 1957. The Dufferin Fund was a de facto,
state-sponsored, philanthropic organisation that was non-sectarian,
with a brief to finance the education of women doctors, midwives,
nurses and female dispensary staff. In its early years, it attracted
American as well as British donations.[35] However, the Dufferin Fund's
significance was not its money-raising capacities, but its collaboration
with the state in regulating and controlling the agency and activism of
female medics: agency already apparent in surrounding communities
of Indian women on a non-racial basis, mostly at the hands of zenana
medical missionaries and their networks.

Rather like Mary Carpenter and Florence Nightingale, Lady
Dufferin's work in India was given public presage by Queen Victoria,
who feared that the women of India 'were undoubtedly without that
medical aid which their European sisters are accustomed to consider

absolutely necessary'.[36] Although Dufferin's diaries reveal a different kind of woman from Carpenter and Nightingale – one keen to keep an Anglo-Irish distance and more typical of memsahibs of her era. Acting as hostess, with all the chintz and formality that went along with her husband's Viceroy duties, she was glad to offer superficial patronage to Indian princelings who funded women's hospitals in her name, and even to the schools they built where, she suggested, for 'a few pence' the girls having 'passed through it, all having learnt something'.[37] As for colonial-aligned women in India in the 1880s, according to Dufferin, their very femininity was at stake in the face of India's brutal social custom.

> No one will read [about their work] without a feeling of intense sympathy and admiration for ... each one of them; or without pride and pleasure in the fact that so much talent, perseverance, and determination should be found combined with so much gentleness, and with so many truly feminine qualities. One might, perhaps, have feared that women who had had to break through the hard and fast rules of caste and custom would have lost their more lovable characteristics in the struggle.[38]

While the state hierarchy of hospitals in India remained organised strictly on the basis of race, the Dufferin Fund was responsible for some effective medical outreach to Indian communities – an enterprise that involved many overworked female participants. From the mid-1880s, under the fund's auspices, a smattering of women's hospitals emerged across the subcontinent, away from the central city sites where hospitals for Europeans remained dominant. These outlying women's hospitals were severely understaffed institutions, run by Eurasian, Parsi or Indian women who went by yet another title: 'lady doctor'. Their duties combined a mixture of domestic management and professional responsibilities not countenanced by male doctors in the central hospitals. One lady doctor, Haimabati Sen, working in her women's hospital at Chinsurah (west Bengal) in 1895, described her daily regime in the following way:

> I would get up every day at four in the morning, prepare a breakfast for my husband and the children, and go downstairs with hot water and edibles for the patients. I would first help the patients wash ... I would give them a piece of batasa or candied sugar as their snack ... Where there were children staying with their mother I would make some hulua [sweet semolina] and give them small quantities of it. It would take me a little over an hour to attend to the patients and come back. I would go back home, have a wash, wake up the children, dress them, give them breakfast, arrange for my husband's meal, get dressed, have something to eat and then go back to the hospital. This was my daily routine.[39]

Feminist intervention

Tensions began to emerge in these women's hospitals in the early twentieth century, driven partly by Western feminist sensitivities. At least ten Indian males were admitted by the state as Indian civil surgeons to the Indian Medical Service between 1890 and 1900; and many more were given jobs by provincial governments to administer second and third-order hospitals for Indian women. This brought immediate unrest, as European women doctors, and particularly Eurasian women 'assistant surgeons', refused to submit to their new Indian male bosses.[40] By 1912, as the size and significance of women's hospitals grew, these antagonisms deepened as long-serving 'lady doctors' battled for control of their hospitals with the peripatetic male civil surgeons. It was the male surgeons who retained sole correspondence responsibilities with government, although, by this time, the women were able to exploit the de facto recognition Dufferin Fund membership gave them, with 573 women doctors being on the fund's books, most without qualifications as physicians.[41]

Other Dufferin women members took on the battle more directly, but ascribed the trouble to different causes. Kathleen Vaughan was a European doctor, with a medical degree from London University, based in the hill station of Mussourie. She voiced scepticism about the way the Dufferin Fund worked, seeing it, with good justification, as a force for the ongoing subordination of her Indian female colleagues by the colonial men who, in practice, ran the fund. However, Vaughan saw elite European women as the main culprits behind this oppression. In 1908, in the *British Medical Journal*, she observed of the Dufferin Fund's regionally dispersed 'local committees':

> The local committees, who are all independent of each other, far from securing unity of aim and effort, are subversive of all progress. They consist of various ladies chosen for their social qualifications as a rule, and the civil [male] surgeons. The ladies usually know nothing of hospital management, so that this task falls on the civil surgeon in addition to his already arduous duties. If he is interested in the work, he wishes in return for this drudgery to perform the major operations. The result is he cannot get well-qualified medical women to work under him and the whole scheme suffers.[42]

Such views had the potential to disrupt British sensibilities and decorum at the highest levels. On March 12, 1912, the Vicereine, Lady Hardinge, hosted the usual annual polite afternoon tea for Dufferin Fund members at Government House in Calcutta. By this time the fund had established 160 hospitals, wards and dispensaries, but it was also in deep crisis, with debt burdens that allowed its women doctors only poor pay and uncertain prospects.[43] As a result, at the 1912 annual meeting, the fight for recognition of women doctors came to a head at the hands of its most vocal women advocates. Vaughan and other feminist doctors argued forcefully, particularly in support of ascendant Indian women doctors, although these European women were wise enough to posit cultural reasons for their views rather than offering only a Western feminist line of argument. Essentially, they focused on the Indian female patient, rather than the fight for professional equality with males, arguing in astute cultural terms that operations should be carried out by senior, fully qualified women, because the patients' husbands would not allow males to oversee these procedures on their wives, or even to administer the anaesthetic.[44]

Missionary status

By the early twentieth century, the relatively broad colonial domain concerning female medicine, built earlier by women missionaries, was made more significant by the changing way that many missionaries were connecting ethically with the subcontinent. As Bellenoit argues, new 'fulfilment theology' of Protestant Christianity in India engaged more seriously with Indian religions to build a wider scholarly view of ethics and morals.[45] Students in missionary schools were also willing to engage positively with Indian religions on broader social issues.[46] Meanwhile, many Indian social service organisations were, by this time, critical of older forms of Indian charity, instead seeing their work, with a nationalist intent, as being based on modernity and national efficiency.[47]

Many more women and girls were educated in mission hospitals than in state institutions, and it was here that their status as autonomous professionals was more firmly built, in response to a rapidly evolving Indian social and political landscape. At Ludhiana in the Punjab, Martha and Kay Greenfield, Scottish missionaries, established the Christian Medical College and School in 1881; and after 1891 their work was aided by Dr Edith Mary Brown – a graduate of Girton College, Cambridge with a doctor's qualification from Brussels.[48] The work of these women effectively cut through state agendas to directly build a professional community with Indian women. Formalising what had already evolved as usual zenana missionary practice a generation earlier, the women leaders of this institution reinforced its strong connection with the Indian female medical community. They did this by emphasising the integration of medical education and health care services, offering well-regulated practical field experience, which was then reinforced by formal college teaching and examination.

Significantly, unlike trainee teachers, all students at this college and school were required to be over seventeen years of age. Edith Brown continued this college work until her death in 1956, aged ninety-two. By 1906 her institution, backed up by a strong medical staff of women doctors, already had sufficient profile to draw a student medical body from all parts of India. Success on this scale at Ludhiana, and other similar institutions elsewhere in India, attracted applications from women who aspired to be physicians from as far afield as the Deccan, Bengal, Telugu and the Malabar Coast. These applicants brought with them a mesmerising range of local languages and cultures for medical teachers like the Greenfields and Brown to contend with. In response, English was made the mission prerequisite common language for incoming women students, as the only tenable medium of instruction for the college.[49]

By 1911 Edith Brown's professional activism, based on connection to the local community, had produced a well-attended four-year course with a fifth-year hospital internship. Her course deliberately mirrored those available to men in the university medical colleges. As with activist teachers who were women in secondary girls' schools of this period (to be discussed in chapters seven and eight), Brown was eventually able to press the academic rigor of the courses she developed to win the right of her students to sit the final Lahore Medical College exam (for men), thus ensuring equal professional status in their future physician careers. In this sense, recognition of status was achieved by developing tuition of unquestioned quality. Such recognition was necessary to break into a male academy that was institutionally assured by the very longstanding tradition of paternalism in the military regarding medicine in India. The military tradition regarding medicine now stood dangerously aloof from emerging *swadeshi* (anti-British self-sufficiency) narratives of social service. As for the state, the trade-off for its official recognition of women's hospitals as college institutions of education was that it stipulated that these institutions needed to be of Christian foundation and willing also to offer courses for nurses, compounders and midwives as part of a replete community of Indian medical carers.[50]

Broadening the field: nursing and midwifery

It is tempting to measure female medical professional progress in colonial India only in terms of the number of graduating Indian, Eurasian or European women doctors. However, earlier mission conversion work, in particular, formed burgeoning female medical imperatives around different forms of community outreach. For all its plain, dull

and superficial Bible discourse, mission work had transcended racialised state policy concerning the education of some Indian women in
the 1860s and 1870s, and had partly moved the focus of female medical care to a colonial periphery: the secluded Indian household. While
almost 98 per cent of Indian girls receiving some form of colonial education were still at elementary level, by the early 1890s there were
eighty-seven medical schools for Indian women that provided some
form of vocational training, despite caste objections, at least supposed
by the West, to body washing and sanitation duties.[51] In addition,
leaders of secondary education for Indian females, such as the Parsi
Christian Mrs Francina Sorabji at the Victoria High School, Poona,
considered nursing and midwifery as offering far fewer racial restrictions than were in place for teaching. She saw the potential to provide
her students with new medical employment opportunities instead. To
this end, she suggested that her students might be employed 'teaching
midwifery and the use of simple household medicines' wherever civil
or military hospitals existed.[52] Francina Sorabji was an Indian who
had been brought up by European parents. (She was also the mother
of Cornelia, who will be discussed in chapter eight.) Her early missionary enculturation probably shaped her accommodative views,
together with a degree of pragmatism. However, the growth of medical schools for Indian women generally was also reflective of an emerging powerful, medical, ethnographic link that ultimately best engaged
Indo-Western scientific research on the subcontinent.

Another consideration encouraged some Indian females to take
up the role of a medical carer under the auspices of the British. By
the 1880s, colonial nursing, operating with greater cultural and
racial fluidity than teaching, was permitted by the state to reach
female recipients who were Indian with much more facility than the
limited possibilities for doing so within colonial classrooms. The
state could support this so long as the medical care of females was
of wholly Western origin and seen as part of the imperial mission.
The large population of eye-diseased, malaria and venereal-infected
Indian females on the edge of Western contact was also a visible
problem – more so than their uneducated condition. The poor health
of these women threatened the health of European men, and so
demanded Western intervention. This medical need was not part of
a feminised pedagogy in colonial classrooms, which the raj used to
project a racialised and normalised woman teacher who was a moral
guide. Instead, nursing and midwifery, and even the intervention
of female physicians, were concerned with the physical condition
of the Indian female body. State sanction of the medical remedying
of suffering Indian females was a visible international sign of the

seeming probity of the raj. It was also a means by which Europeans in India might be better protected and women of all races, particularly Indians, were needed to meet the scale of this problem, even within the limited spheres of colonial contact in India.

To this end, in 1899, the *British Medical Journal* reported that 324 women were undergoing medical training, mostly in the mission hospitals, with 121 women 'assistant surgeons', 191 hospital assistants and over 1,200 nurses, midwives and compounders already qualified to carry out these services for the public.[53] The expansion was greatly assisted by the Lady Reay Fund for Women in Bombay, as well as the Dufferin Fund.[54] Away from the direct gaze of the state, mission work also remained vibrant. Local medical outreach to purdah *nashíns* (elite women behind the screen) reached 4,009 in 1901 in the NWP alone.[55] Furthermore, in Bombay, this kind of nursing outreach resulted in almost half a million treatments of Indian females by 1910.[56]

The memsahib nurse

Elite colonial nursing remained directed, for the most part, by elite Western women and men who were strongly complicit in the racial organisation of their profession. Even after the First World War, the white race barrier in European hospitals in India still remained stronger even than in European schools in India. In these hospitals, *matrianis* (female untouchables) were considered useful enough to clean the latrines and take out bedpans. Local women religious (nuns) were occasionally successful in procuring admittance to nursing training in these hospitals for their most favoured mixed-race scholars. However, most other hopefuls were adversely vetted by the useful expedient of requiring a photograph in addition to the usual curriculum vitae. Vere, Lady Birdwood, a Eurasian (whose lineage was entirely European except for a Hindu grandmother) with only modest Railway schooling, recalled her own straitening recruitment experience as late as 1925:

> In 1925 I went to St Georges' Hospital and started my training ... by sheer accident I was lucky enough to get a job as a nursing sister on the North West Frontier Province which was not really intended for an Anglo-Indian [Eurasian] girl but because Matron was either short of staff or because a photograph showed me to be near white ... I was given this job.[57]

European nurses did have broader uses. They were relied upon to lobby, often successfully, dominant London-based drug companies in India, such as Burgoyne, Burbidges and Co., to reduce their prices on frequently used drugs for Indians.[58]

Lower down the hierarchy of hospitals, the racial bar was quickly dissipating by the turn of the twentieth century, although women medical educators were hardly any more sympathetic to their trainee nurses. Miss Jenny Müller was one such nursing educator. Her formal education had been at the Lawrence Military Asylum at Sanawar, and then at the Medical College in Calcutta. This education qualified her to train Indian nurses at the SPG's St Stephen's Hospital in Delhi.[59] She viewed these trainee Indian nurses in deeply impersonal terms. Rather than regarding them as young adult professionals about to achieve equal status with their European hospital-educated teachers, she conveyed an image of them as often immature and ill-disciplined children.

> Asked as to the punishment for nurses Miss Müller said that in many ways they had to be treated like children. The usual course was to fine them, but sometimes they shut them up & occasionally even corporal punishment was necessary. This however must never be done in temper, only by authority and never before patients.[60]

Müller was a passionate advocate for nurses in preference to women doctors. For her, what really mattered was keeping up a semblance of Western clinical and antiseptic decorum, even in the face of what she saw as the chronically dishevelled, yet indispensable, nursing agency of Indian women. Many memsahibs would have agreed. Some, such as the redoubtable Flora Annie Steel, inspectress of schools in the Punjab, even perceived differences between the dirt left behind in rented bungalows by neglectful European tenants and the more pernicious grime of their Indian servants.[61]

However, even at this level change was in prospect. In the generation after Müller and her ilk, leading women educators of nurses began to imagine a more expansive professional vista for their students; one that could embrace either married or unmarried life. In 1908 the SPG donated £1,000 to build a nurses' block at St Stephen's Hospital Delhi for unmarried Indian nurses.[62] Two years earlier the institution was reporting that some of its Indian nurses were 'as good as [the] English'. Furthermore, unlike in Europe, the institution also encouraged the marriage of nurses as part of their professional futures. Most particularly, the sanctity of marriage was seen as useful for those who wished to become district nurses visiting private houses without transgressing Indian 'customary' codes.[63]

Moving out to the *mofussil* offered highly variable personal stories of success and failure, particularly when working in dispensaries where resources were poor, and where private households had to double as examination rooms. When Miss Browne, 'a first class lady doctor', was installed at Partagarh (Bengal), patient numbers soared to almost twenty times the number of Indian females who were admitted to the nearby hospital. However, other women quickly lost their lives, such as Miss Milner at the Dufferin Dispensary at Aligarh (NWP), who contracted blood poisoning 'during the discharge of her duties' and Miss Pant at Fysabad (NWP) who soon succumbed to the plague.[64]

The leper asylum

One key disease, around which the female medical profession organised, when treating Indians, was leprosy. This was a biblical disease that attracted pan-Asian approaches from European missionaries.[65] Most leprosy 'hospitals', in the absence of any cure, acted as refuges rather than centres of medical care. These hospitals catered for only a tiny proportion of the estimated 120,000 cases in India at the peak of the disease in 1881. They also attracted polite, yet superficial, visits by titled and wealthy European women who vapidly wrote about their emotions upon returning to their parlours of European décor at night.[66]

Other women stayed longer. Zenana medical missionaries such as Rosalie Harvey at Nasik (northwest Maharashtra) provided lepers with shelter, 'a well built Asylum', after their eviction (she claimed) from the local temple that had been their traditional right to occupy. This institution would transform into a leprosy hospital in 1898, and Harvey carried out impressive work among this community for another fifty years.

> The chief haunts of the lepers of Nasik when I first became acquainted with them were on the verandahs or ôtas of the temples ... On Sunday's some beggars used to come to the Zenana Mission House to beg. The lepers got wind of this and came too. After a while we thought it unwise to let the lepers stream through the town every Sunday, and so we tried going to them, and in the courtyard of a heathen temple a little service used to be held, no one objecting ... Then came the famine of 1897, when we got permission to take uncooked food daily to the lepers. How they enjoyed that famine! It was a time of plenty for them. They got warm clothes as well as food ... At the end of 1897 the famine died out, and the old famine dole was stopped. The lepers had to go back to the old life, to the 'one day a meal, and two days none', and none at all without a weary tramp on weary feet.[67]

Harvey understood the politics of disease in India that could direct prognosis of a non-medical nature. Her commentary is detached and de-intellectualises, and perhaps even dehumanises, the human beings to whom she dedicated her life. Her Western medical methods were clinical, and probably intimidating to her mendicant Indian patients, as she 'treated' them dressed in her stiff and impeccably pressed late

Figure 7 Rosalie Harvey at Nasik in 1901 demonstrating a practical way to treat leprosy ulcers. Reproduced with permission of the Leprosy Mission International.

Victorian clothes. Yet there was a degree of intimacy in her role as a carer providing some relief from this terrible disease. Before effective treatments were developed in the 1930s, the sores were cleansed using mercury-based medication that was only a marginal improvement on the traditional Indian use of chaulmoogra tree oil. Nonetheless, mission communities built around discarded lepers, such as the CMS leper community at Puralia in westernmost Bengal, were seen as worthy enough for M. K. Gandhi to visit and praise as centres of 'loving service' even in 1920.[68]

Meeting new demand after the First World War

Professional medical experience, even of this kind, separated out European medical women in a sociological sense from those racial sisters who remained creatures of the club, the croquet wicket and the bungalow afternoon tea. The workloads for European women who were doctors and nurses increased dramatically after the First World

War. This was partly because the work of these medical women made the extent of subcontinental disease, much of it concerning females, visible to the West, and the state then had no choice but to 'treat' it. Miss Tatham, a European CMS nurse presiding over the crowded wards of her hospital among the tribal, agrarian Santals of Eastern India observed this phenomenon. Treatment of patients on a vast scale resulted in caste separateness, as she saw it, being covered over by a professional duty ethic of Hippocratic medical service. Tatham believed this was considered by her community of women Indian sponsors to be preferable to handing the work over to 'untrustworthy' men. Midwifery and gynaecological work by trained Indian women could also expand to meet local needs. Yet Tatham was sensitive to what such cultural medical crossovers could still mean for her young Indian nurses: caught as they were between these two worlds and faced with important and irrevocable life choices as a consequence.

> The whole idea of nursing as a vocation is new and strange ... so that conditions must be made to make life not too overwhelmingly difficult for the young girl who is brave enough to defy age-long customs and choose nursing instead of marriage.[69]

Furthermore, by the early twentieth century simple questions of building capacity again covered over longer-standing racial and gender barriers. After the First World War, increasing demand meant that Eurasian communities in intersection railway towns such as Ranaghat (north Bengal) were required to treat Indians, as well as their original Eurasian clientele. In Ranaghat, women Indian nurses and 'assistant surgeons' were sequestered for work in the local CMS Women's Hospital, where only four or five patients could be admitted a day out of twenty to thirty emergency applicants.[70] In addition, under-resourcing by the British of 'overflowing' state hospitals for women placed overwhelming pressure on the dispensaries and their nursing staff at the mission. These women worked from 7 a.m. to 5 p.m. in the blazing heat, treating over 1,000 patients a day, a number that rose to 1,400 in the monsoon season.[71]

These pressures resulted in more Indian nurses being admitted into the colonial domain of professional medicine as the raj scrambled, with little success, to meet new demand. Increased demand was also created by new medical breakthroughs. When new German treatments for *Kala Azar* (leishmaniasis, a debilitating ulcerating skin disease spread by sand flies) became available, most Indians could not afford the medication.[72] Yet, by 1922, the introduction of 'electrolytic chlorogen', a cheap, stable and highly efficient disinfectant, as well as new treatments for malaria and tuberculosis, produced overwhelming numbers of dispensary patients who were Indians. In 1922 over five and a half million patients were treated in the NWP, and almost two million in Burma alone. With the eyes of the world on them after the outrage by General Dyer at Amritsar in 1919, and the rise of the Khilafat movement (1918–22), it was scarcely possible for the raj to openly restrict its doctors and nurses from delivering available treatments to Indians.[73] This was an entirely different scenario to the restricted fare of colonial female teaching of females: a profession that was still, by this time, successfully excluding most Indian women.

The First World War also brought greater American engagement. By this time Christian Women's medical colleges had sprang up throughout India. One in particular, the India United Medical College (now the Christian Medical College) in Vellore, Madras, had a committee of management that was a mixture of women from all denominations from Britain, Sweden and Denmark. Typically, these women's medical colleges were supported by multiple missionary societies, and the one at Vellore had no fewer than fifteen contributing missions. Most significant among these were the American missions, who also had money, responding as they did to regular publicity about the Dufferin Fund in newspapers such as the *New York Times*.[74]

While Europe laboured under the heavy burden of debt that resulted from the war, American medical philanthropy was efficiently organised for work across Asia, including in India. In 1918, US$3 million was raised for this purpose, including US$2 million from the Rockefeller Trust, of which the Vellore Medical College's share was US$100,000. By raj funding standards this was an enormous donation that resulted in a 300-bed hospital for Indian women and children. Dr Ida Scudder, a third-generation medical missionary of the Protestant Reformed Church of America, was the founder of this institution, and she devoted her long life to fighting cholera, plague and leprosy until her death in 1960. With American money, she could afford to admit female patients of all castes and to treat them as outpatients in her extensive dispensary network. The new American money also allowed her to be more academically rigorous in the selection of trainee women physicians. In 1918 she accepted only seventeen candidates out of 164 applicants, who no longer needed to be only Eurasians or 'girls with not sufficient brains' for this, by now highly specialised, training.[75]

The enduring missionary medical hegemony

In Britain, a mostly secular women's medical education was galvanised by Western science. In Europe and in the USA, however,

there was a development that chimed with earlier missionary medical care approaches concerning India, and which complicated, in
socio-cultural terms, the transferral of scientific medical practice
concerning females to the subcontinent. Between 1880 and 1920,
in the context of rudimentary state welfare structures, women
in Europe and the USA had begun shaping state maternal and
child-welfare policy by claiming new roles for themselves by trans-
forming their emphasis on motherhood into public policy.[76] This
maternal activism, whether religiously based or not, had resonance
with the missionary approaches regarding female medical care of
Indian females that had developed in India in the mid to late nineteenth century.

In India, the missions remained in charge of much of the medical
education and medical employment possibilities for Indian women.
In 1927 the ninety-three mission hospitals for women represented
over half the total number of such institutions on the subcontinent.
Further, the 102 mission training schools for nurses compared to
just fifty-nine provided by government. By the Second World War,
90 per cent of Indian nurses came from the small Christian community and 80 per cent of all Indian nurses had been trained in mission
hospitals.[77]

Missionary female capacity, built for over two generations at least,
mostly through networks outside the mission wall, was responsible for
the dominance. This capacity transcended the strictures of raj race and
class constituencies, building new networks of medical care and with
it a new female professional space in India. The secular medical lobby
in India did not replace the missions, but was subsumed by them to
further broaden outreach to Indians for the rest of the colonial period.
Reluctantly, the state sanctioned the new terrain for female medical
care by females, as philanthropic networks and new feminised medical
approaches became anchored in the missionary mentality in India of
the late nineteenth century.

For these reasons, there was a strong distinction between the work
of female medics and that of women teachers. It is also probable that
many subaltern groupings of caste-sensitive Indian females were
more conflicted by the imported vocation of nursing than they were
by less attainable colonial-sponsored teaching. In Britain, feminist
advocates scarcely thought about this difference when advocating
both professions 'at home' and 'abroad'. Yet, as will be demonstrated
in chapter seven, teaching moved decisively in the opposite direction,
racialising the Indian and Eurasian female even more fiercely than
before.

Notes

1 C. Dyhouse, *Students: A Gendered Role* (New York: Routledge, 2006), p. 64.
2 Minutes of the Zenana, Medical and Bible Mission 1894–1904, nos. 36–7 (OIOC).
3 Special Meeting of the National Association for Providing Female Medical Aid to the Women of India, March 6, 1912 (OIOC) V/24/713.
4 *Journal of the National Association in Aid of Female Education in India* (London: Kegan Paul, 1883), pp. 509 (OIOC) L/PJ/6/105, no. 1492.
5 *Journal of the National Association in Aid of Female Education in India* (London: Kegan Paul, 1883), pp. 512 (OIOC) L/PJ/6/105, no. 1492.
6 *Journal of the National Association in Aid of Female Education in India* (London: Kegan Paul, 1883), p. 512 (OIOC) L/PJ/6/105 no. 1492.
7 See, for example, 'Minutes of the Zenana, Medical and Bible Mission, 1894–1904', Church Missionary Society Women, India, Reel 49 (OIOC).
8 For a translation of Vedic medical practice and diagnosis see: M. Saha, *History of Indian Medicine based on Vedic Literature* (Calcutta: Asiatic Society, 1999).
9 M. U. Mashtaq, 'Public Health in British India ...', pp. 6–13.
10 See the NIA's commentary on departmental attitudes along these lines: *Journal of the National Association in aid of Female Education in India*, no. 153, September 1883 (OIOC) L/PJ/6/105.
11 Suri Sundar Das, 'Health and Physique of Pupils in Public Schools' Appendix E, Punjab Education Report, 1911–12 (OIOC) V/24/938.
12 M. U. Mushtaq, 'Public Health in British India ...', p. 11.
13 S. Guha, 'Dais to Doctors ...', p. 7.
14 *Notes on the Annual Returns of the Dispensaries and Charitable Institutions of the NWP and Oudh ending 1910* (Allahabad: Government Press, 1911) (OIOC) V/24/713.
15 'Notes on the Annual Returns of the Dispensaries and Charitable Institutions of the NWP & Oudh ending December, 1910' (OIOC) V/12/713.
16 Countess Dufferin, *A Record of Three Years' Work of the National Association for Supplying Female Medical Aid to the Women of India, August 1885–August 1888* ..., p. 69.
17 K. Platt, *Home and Health in India and the Tropical Colonies* (London: Baillière, Tindal & Cox, 1923), pp. 18, 20–1 cited in E. Buettner, *Empire Families* ..., p. 38.
18 See, for example, 'Support of Schools from Municipal and Local Funds', W. Holroyd (DPI) to Government of the Punjab, February 7, 1877, no. 18 (OIOC) P/858; W. Holroyd, 'Report on Popular Education in the Punjab ... 1879/80' (OIOC) V/24/933, p. 11.
19 M. Ramanna, *Western Medicine* ..., pp. 198–201.
20 S. Rowbotham, *A New World for Women: Stella Browne, Socialist Feminist* (London: Pluto, 1977), p. 43.
21 'Report on the Civil Hospitals and Dispensaries Under the Government of Bombay 1908' (OIOC) V/12/700.
22 Scheme for Conferring Degrees, Government of the Punjab to the Registrar of the Punjab University College, March 8, 1872 (OIOC) P/136.
23 R. Fitzgerald, 'From Medicine Chest to Mission Hospitals: The Early History of the Delhi Medical Mission for Women and Children' in D. O'Connor (ed.), *Three Centuries of Mission: The United Society for the Propagation of the Gospel* (London: Bloomsbury, 2000), pp. 353, 355.
24 J. Cox, 'Independent English women in Delhi and Lahore, 1860–1947' in R. W. Davis and R. J. Helmstadter (eds), *Religion and Irreligion in Victorian Society: Essays in Honor of R. K. Webb* (New York: Routledge, 1991), pp. 170, 173, 177.
25 'Report on the Civil Hospitals and Dispensaries Under the Government of Bombay 1908' (OIOC) V/12/700.
26 'Notes on the Annual Returns of the Dispensaries and Charitable Institutions of the NWP & Oudh ending December, 1900' (OIOC) V/12/713.
27 *Quinquennial Education Report 1902–7...*, p. 162 (OIOC).
28 M. Ramanna, *Western Medicine* ..., p. 194.

29 C. Mackinnon, Inspector General of Hospitals, NWP to Government of the Punjab, August 12, 1859 (OIOC) P/203/61.
30 Government of the Punjab to the Government of India, April 5, 1895 (OIOC) P/4752.
31 Government of the Punjab to the Government of India, April 5, 1895 (OIOC) P/4752.
32 *Histories of Service*, Bombay, 1920, p. 467 (OIOC) V/24/306.
33 Countess Dufferin, *A Record of Three Years' Work of the National Association for Supplying Female Medical Aid to the Women of India, August 1885-August 1888* (Calcutta: Thacker, Spink & Co., 1888).
34 Government of the Punjab to the Government of India, April 5, 1895 (OIOC) P/4752.
35 G. Forbes, *Women in Colonial India: Essays on Politics, Medicine and Historiography* (Bangalore: Orient, 2005), p. 104.
36 H. G. Hamilton-Temple-Blackwood, *The National Association for Supplying Female Medical Aid to the Women of India* (Calcutta: Thacker, Spink & Co., 1886), p. 9 cited in D. S. Roberts, ' "Merely Birds of Passage": Lady Hariot Dufferin's Travel Writings and Medical Work in India', *Women's History Review*, 15:3 (2006), 451.
37 H. G. Hamilton-Temple-Blackwood [Lady Dufferin], *Our Viceregal Life in India* (London: John Murray, 1889), vol. ii, pp. 9–10, 14.
38 H. G. Dufferin, 'Preface' in E. F. Chapman (ed.), *Sketches of Some Distinguished Indian Women* (London: Allen & Co. 1891), pp. i–ii.
39 'The Memoirs of Dr Haimavati Sen' trans. Tapan Raychaudhuri, ed. G. Forbes and T. Raychaudhuri, unpublished mss., p. 220 cited in G. Forbes, 'Women's Work in Colonial India' in *Women in Modern India: The New Cambridge History of India*, vol 4:2 (Cambridge: Cambridge University Press, 1996), p. 157.
40 'Special Meeting March 6, 1912', *The National Association for Providing Female Medical Aid to the Women of India* (OIOC) V/24/713.
41 'The National Association for Providing Female Medical Aid to the Women of India' (1912) (OIOC) V/24/713.
42 K. Vaughan, *The British Medical Journal*, October 17, 1908, pp. 1219–20.
43 D. Arnold, *Colonizing the Body* ..., p. 267.
44 'Special Meeting' March 6, 1912 of the 'National Association for Providing Female Medical Aid to the Women of India' (OIOC) V/24/713.
45 H. Bellenoit, *Missionary Education* ..., pp. 28, 88, 134.
46 H. Bellenoit, *Missionary Education* ..., pp. 134–6.
47 C. A. Watt, 'Philanthropy and Civilizing Missions in India C. 1820–1960: States, NGOs and Development', in C. A. Watt and M. Mann (eds), *Civilizing Missions in Colonial India and Postcolonial South Asia* (London: Anthem, 2011), p. 280.
48 F. French, *Miss Brown's Hospital: The Story of the Ludhiana Medical College* (London: Hodder & Stoughton, 1954).
49 Punjab Education Report, 1906–7 ..., p. 33; 1908–9, p.15 (OIOC) V/24/936.
50 Punjab Education Report, 1911–12, p. 34 (OIOC) V/24/938.
51 J. S. Cotton, *Quinquennial Education Report, 1892–97* (London: HMSO, 1898) p. 288.
52 Journal of the National India Association in Aid of Social Progress and Female Education in India November, 1882 no. 143, p. 642 (OIOC) L/PJ/6/84.
53 *The British Medical Journal* (September 30, 1899), p. 888.
54 M. Ramanna, *Western Medicine* ..., p. 196.
55 Notes on the Annual Returns of the Dispensaries and Charitable Institutions of the NPW & Oudh, December, 1901 (OIOC) V/24/713.
56 'Report of the Civil Hospitals and Dispensaries Under the Government of Bombay, 1910' (OIOC) V/24/700.
57 'Selections from the edited transcript of interview with Vere Lady Birdwood, October, 1973' (OIOC) MSS Eur T 7.
58 'Notes on the Annual Returns of the Dispensaries and Charitable Institutions of the NWP & Oudh ending December, 1905' (OIOC) V/12/713.
59 R. W. Davis and R. J. Helmstadter, *Religion and Irreligion in Victorian Society* (London: Routledge, 1991), p. 173.

60 Minutes of the Ladies Association for the Promotion of Female Education Among the Heathen in the Missions of the SPG (Indian Subcommittee), February 2, 1906, CWW SPG (RHL).
61 F. A. Steel and G. Gardiner, *The Complete Indian Housekeeper and Cook* (Oxford: Oxford University Press [reprint] 2010), p. 188.
62 'SPG Committee of Women's Work: Indian Subcommittee', p. 80, CWW48 SPG (RHL).
63 'Committee of Women's Work 1906–7: Indian Subcommittee', p. 12, CWW 47 (OIOC).
64 'Notes on the Annual Returns of the Dispensaries and Charitable Institutions of the NWP & Oudh ending December, 1905' (OIOC) V/12/713.
65 S. Kakar, 'Leprosy in British India, 1860–1940', *Medical History*, 40 (1996), 217, 224.
66 *Report of the Leprosy Commission in India, 1890–1* (Calcutta, Government Printing: 1892), p. 219 (OIOC).
67 R. Harvey, 'Origin of Leper Work in Nasik' in J. Jackson (ed.), *Lepers: Thirty-One Years' Work Among Them* (London: Simpson & Co., n.d.), pp. 213–14.
68 Rev. G. B. Redman 'CMS Annual Reports, 1925–26', p. 132 (LB) XCMS/B/OMS/I1/G2/0.
69 Miss F. Hughes-Hallett, *CMS Annual Report 1926–27*, p. 293 (LB) XCMS/B/OMS/I1/G2/0.
70 CMS Annual Report, 1925–26, p. 129 (LB) XCMS/B/OMS/I1/G2/0.
71 CMS Annual Report, 1925–26, p. 129 (LB) XCMS/B/OMS/I1/G2/0.
72 CMS Annual Report, 1925–26, p. 129 (LB) XCMS/B/OMS/I1/G2/0.
73 'Annual Report of the Public Health Commissioner, Government of India, 1922', pp. 149–50 (OIOC) V/24/3659.
74 For example see *The New York Times*, May 3, 1896.
75 'Report by Miss Hughes and Miss Trollope on the Girls' Schools in India supported by the SPG', X564 SPG (RHL).
76 S. Koven and S. Michel, 'Womanly Duties: Maternalist Politics and the Origins of Welfare States in France, Germany, Great Britain, and the United States, 1880–1920', *The American Historical Review*, 95:4 (October, 1990), 1076–8.
77 R. Fitzgerald, 'Rescue and Redemption ...', pp. 65, 76.

CHAPTER SEVEN

Code school accomplishments and Froebel: race and pedagogy, 1883–1903

By the early 1880s, it was apparent, even from a Western perspective, that the teacher training of women involved a different professional approach to that of nursing. However, in the next two decades, teaching by women, unlike nursing, was to become even more constrained by official moral, class and race agendas. After the missionary experience of the 1870s and early 1880s, the Viceroy's government in Calcutta began revisiting Canning's 1860 Despatch, which deemed Eurasians to 'have a special claim on us'. By 1883, the state's mindset concerning Eurasians had moved away from the 1860 one of embarrassment, to a view that saw at least middle-class Eurasians as potential carriers of the banner of the newly accomplished woman. These Eurasian women were seen as a potential conduit to India for British feminine sensibility and genteelness, and as an antidote to the crusty misogyny of military and ICS raj personnel.

From the early 1880s onwards, official reportage began to mention women educators by name, albeit sporadically. Women such as Mary Carpenter were seen as individuals capable of enacting change, rather than as part of an anonymous aggregated mass of females merely projecting Western socialisation – feminine agents within a broader colonial mission. However, if the British were to stay in India, it would not be easy to build a new kind of society partly based on European, feminine, middle-class sensibilities. The missionary compound was not turning out as the state had imagined in terms of providing a refuge for the enculturation of educated women and girls. In the latter 1870s and the 1880s, women missionaries' preoccupation with outreach to Indian women and girls had led to what ICS deputy commissioners (who had chief carriage for the administration of raj education in each province) saw as uncomfortable racial revisions of state policy outside the mission wall. Even within the mission wall, grant-in-aid scholarships for teacher training looked too much like de facto salaries for students who were women, many of whom stayed on for five years or more with no real career opportunities.[1]

Potential costly teacher outreach to Indians at the expense of Europeans and Eurasians also raised a financial difficulty for the raj. Its response was to begin to rely on emerging educational commerce to solve the problem. The new strategy centred on a growing demand for teacher training from middle-class Eurasian parents for their daughters. As part of a reinvigorated racialised approach, the central government began to survey how to 'supplement existing effort' in Eurasian girls' schools and teacher training colleges in particular. This focus led to new concerted state action, with far-reaching implications for the education of women and girls. The end result was that, by the First World War, state attention was only focused on a coterie of accomplishment girls' schools and training colleges that were accessible to the very few. This was despite ongoing raj rhetoric about the education of Indian females being a key part of its revitalised imperial mission.

Favoured Eurasians

By 1880, it was not difficult to create stronger racial boundaries around females located at schooling sites. Governance efficacy brought to India over two generations earlier by Utilitarian approaches meant that bureaucratic fiat could easily be used to do some of the work. For example, Eurasian schoolgirl enrolments grew as state education efforts were 'centralised', away from the mofussil in the 1870s, and new, urban, English-medium schools emerged.[2] Furthermore, preferential Eurasian teacher grants in southern India had led to the founding of a modest, but significant, fifty Eurasian girls' schools by the early 1870s: enough for the state to deem them 'more deserving' than those schools serving 'indigenous' talent that included mission zenana work.[3]

Emphasis on an explicit argument around the spread of education among Indians was not new. The argument that Indian girls were less receptive to, and therefore less worthy of, government-funded education (as compared to Eurasians girls) had been proffered in government circles since at least the early 1860s. However, by the 1880s, official concern about losing control of the moral and Western agenda concerning the education of girls was more acute. Furthermore, the government continued to be careful to veil its position on this contentious issue, even in confidential reports. 'Learner' efficacy based on race was resonant of the eugenics polemic emerging in England at this time, led by Herbert Spencer, among others.[4] Although racialised, middle-class female recipients of teacher training in India offered a worthy vista for even the most parsimonious arch imperialists at Westminster. By this time, Britain could see a new schoolgirl in India that safely resembled those in the home country: schoolgirls that were almost invariably middle-class Europeans and Eurasians.

Class, as well as race, now also became a strong determinant concerning the education of women and girls in the 1880s. In part this development was due to a changing European demographic in colonial India in the later nineteenth century. Even within the European communities of India, there emerged class distinctions based on child schooling destinations: European families who could afford to send their children to England for their education were considered superior to those who could not.[5] Families also exerted constant vigilance against the possibility of their naturally receptive children picking up any of the traits of their Indian servants or, worse, beginning to speak what was pejoratively called *chi chi*: the turn of phrase and accent of Indians who could speak English.[6] At the other end of the class spectrum, poor whites in India numbered nearly half the European population by the end of the nineteenth century, becoming 'domiciled' in India after retirement and not returning to Britain.[7] Class determinants such as these also had racial consequences, with considerable intermingling and intermarriage between the poorer whites and Eurasians.[8]

Responding to these developments, the promotional language adopted by new Eurasian girls' schools began to closely reflect the middle-class and gender education signifiers of Europe. This was especially so as these schools turned to a more rigid form of the accomplishments curriculum, attempting to teach it, largely unrevised, along strictly English lines.

'The Code'

These arrangements were probably sufficient to deliver the desired outcome of allowing Eurasian girls to monopolise new state funding. However, in 1883, the raj went much further. It moved to legally formalise the distinction between female Eurasian scholars and their Indian sisters. The new legal device was the 'European Code' and it was conceived in the Viceroy's office, during Lord Lytton's tenure in 1879.[9] 'The Code' applied to males as well as females, and offered protected funding status for Eurasians across most fields of raj intervention on the subcontinent. For female Eurasian education, the Code was of particular utility for the state to justify its spending of the education rupee. This administrative separation had another purpose too: to prevent a repeat of the racial slippage already happening in the conduct of medical care for females under the missions.

The educational space that the Code created was as simple as it was exclusionary. It was directly applicable to a student 'of European descent, pure or mixed who retains European habits and modes of life'.[10] Schools other than those controlled by the missions, were also now in view as the chief beneficiaries of the new racial preference. Just as the most conservative Western education narratives regarding females had emanated from Bengal from the 1820s, it was this province that once again gave rise to the new conservative Code itself. In Bengal and other provinces, benefactions made by old Eurasian Catholic families were already favouring a cottage industry of education for girls, conducted by Catholic Eurasians, over which the state had little or no control.[11] There was too much risk for the raj in seeing something as important as its promotional rhetoric about the educated and moral female disaggregated on the altar of imported networks of educational sectarianism.[12] The Bengal Code was a powerful means to prevent this, and particularly to moderate the outreach vanguard of women missionaries that favoured Indian girls, because it was quickly applied by other states across all of north India. Madras and Bombay (the provinces with the highest and second highest European and Eurasian populations, respectively) followed suit soon after 1883, using grant-in-aid rules to achieve the same end.[13]

The administrative strength of the Code, as a new enforcer of official female education priorities, was signified by the reaction of the missions to it. The SPG missionaries who built on Mrs Winter's work in Delhi viewed it as an 'instrument of torture', because it rendered the schooling of Indian girls 'unsupportable' at this mission and others like it: they were now required to spend most of their limited state education funding on Eurasians only. An additional consequence was to make the SPG mission's 'education' outreach for Indian girls now fall entirely on its Industrial school (which made lace for the local markets) and a women's refuge (which rescued some of these Indian girls from prostitution).[14] Even William Hunter, after the very detailed provincial hearings of his Education Commission, argued in his 1883 report against such a 'Code' approach, instead urging access for all girls to colonial education, regardless of their race.[15]

There were some intriguing elements of the new imperative about Eurasian girls that was now to be conducted mostly via non-mission and private-venture schooling. The new legal regulations of the Code, in fact, turned inside out the gender relations that had emerged regarding nursing. This was because the Code was predominantly a masculine preserve. The powerful 'Conference for the Domiciled Community in India' (meaning Europeans and Eurasians) met annually and had direct responsibility for Code operation and regulation. Up until the First World War, the conference was wholly made up of men, and it expressly refused to allow a parallel conference of women to convene.[16] Furthermore, the chief inspectors of European and Eurasian schools were always male and usually directly imported from Britain. For example, as late as 1913, Geoffrey Maclear was selected for the post in Bengal. His appointment was based on his graduation from Oxford with a first-class degree in history, and his willingness, as a young man, to live in India. The suppositions made by the conference about what would serve as sufficient preparation for this complex role on the subcontinent are telling: visits for just ten weeks to Board schools in London in the company of their inspectors, and attendance for two terms at the London Day Training College (forerunner of the Institute of Education, London University).[17]

Maclear's 'training', and that of others like him, reflected the Code's intent. The Code was deeply predicated along British educational lines, and the Western cultural purity of its female learners was to be strictly enforced by the rubric of the accomplishments curriculum. This curriculum was relatively well shaped and formalised in India by this time, partly as a result of developments in the Lawrence military asylums as far back as the late 1850s.[18] Code schools also constructed a new English class consciousness, and, more particularly, a new middle-class hegemony, by charging relatively high fees. Such fees were needed for these schools to be sufficiently well resourced to appeal to middle-class Eurasian and European parents.

Middle-class girls

The most significant aspect of this new story of 'Code' education of girls in the last two decades of the nineteenth century was that India struggled to conform to the new European class enforcements – especially when race was used to direct Indian and Eurasian middle-class school enrolments. In short, more affluent middle-class girls who were Indian, and who wanted to follow the English accomplishments learning model, were excluded by their race, while most Eurasian girls were excluded because of their lack of financial means.

Significant groups of Indian women were already ready to take up the accomplishments mantle. Malavika Karlekar's work has demonstrated that the emerging Bengali *bhadralok* (middle-class) men and their *bhadramadhila* (gentle woman) spouses had been partly Westernised by their economic prosperity under the British. Their prosperity, and part acculturation under the raj, had led them to seek out an education for their daughters designed to make them better wives in a manner that mimicked the accomplishments canon. While not wishing their daughters' education to be so rigorous as to threaten culturally defined Indian femininity, these parents nonetheless modelled it on the Victorian prototype of the genteel middle-class woman.[19] By all official measures, these social motives should have qualified the daughters of affluent families for an accomplishments education, with all the Western moral and ethical baggage the raj had been claiming for its female scholar recipients since at least the late 1850s. However, the state's new racialised Code provided no place for these Indian girls, who struggled on mostly outside its ambit. Urbanised and articulate Indian middle-class communities felt rightly aggrieved by their exclusion from a very British-inspired educational trajectory, which they otherwise wished to embrace.

Conversely, only a small number of Eurasian women had the socio-cultural background and financial wherewithal to be able to participate in the Code's embedded middle-class educational aspirations. It had been the very poor state of many Eurasians, compared to some prosperous Indians, that had prompted the provision of the Code in the first place; and Canning's Despatch a generation earlier had been generated by similar concerns. However, ironically, these new middle-class restrictions limited the outcomes even the state imagined for Eurasian girls under the new Code regulations. And in provinces such as Bengal, 50 per cent of Eurasians were without any form of education at all.[20]

For these reasons, in the first fifteen years of its operation, the Code's educational transformation of Eurasian girls was significant only for a relatively small number of them. During this period (1883–98) the rise in Eurasian and European student participation in this form of schooling (boys as well as girls) rose from 18,780 to 29,176 pupils; with provinces in the north, such as the Punjab, recording a four-fold increase, and the NWP and Burma witnessing a doubling of enrolments. However, it is significant that this increase was almost entirely accounted for by an increase in enrolments in upper-middle-class Eurasian and European girls' schools.[21]

New schools

Schools for upper-middle-class Eurasians and Europeans could easily satisfy Code regulations, and their founders now felt entitled to provide a reinvigorated platform for accomplishments, and its associated teaching metier, in India. Most affluent Eurasian families still shunned the possibility of their sons becoming teachers – it was a last resort for those boys who could not even pursue a career in the railways.[22] Yet, for their daughters, becoming qualified to teach accomplishments, or using this qualification to become a more attractive marriage prospect (which might also bring social mobility), was a much more appealing option. As Miss Holland, headmistress of a hills girls', middle-class, accomplishments school at Mussourie suggested:

> Anglo-Indian [Eurasian] parents are, as a rule, far more willing to spend money on their daughters than on their sons. One reason for this is a feeling in the parents' minds that however well educated their sons are they can scarcely hope to rise to any position of importance; whereas, for a well educated and attractive girl there are many possibilities.[23]

Closely associated with these developments was the ascendancy of schools that were either privately owned or that were of larger private foundation. Private-venture schooling was already an empire-wide phenomenon. There was a longstanding British-led tradition (since the early nineteenth century) of very small schools for girls and boys being owned and operated by one or two self-employed teachers. For example, in the Sydney district of Australia, in the early nineteenth century, such schools for girls taught a 'suitable education' that was differentiated from that offered to boys, but that also went beyond the usual elementary subjects.[24] In Melbourne, Australia, over 700 self-styled 'ladies schools' were advertised in local newspapers between 1850 and 1875.[25] Earlier in the nineteenth century in India, poorly resourced private-venture day schools populated the plains of the subcontinent. And in Bengal alone, by 1903, there were 461 such institutions.[26] This tradition also included an ungainly collection of Railway schools, set out awkwardly along raj-directed ribbons of transportation between railway and trunk road. These schools imported European teachers, paid for through fees derived by means-testing parental incomes. The schools created new demand by providing children with free rail transportation to their school.[27]

There was other freelancing on offer as well. The daughters of officers found employment as teachers in the regiments based in India, as well as in Egypt and in the Levant. Their life was one of frequent travel – in two-year cycles – as in the case of Kate Georgina Frey. Frey spent much of her professional life in the 1880s on the noisy military ships sailing between Bombay and England, teaching in temporary composite classes the children of soldiers belonging to such battalions as the First King's Dragoons and the Second and Twenty-third Fusiliers.[28]

However, by the end of the nineteenth century, private-venture schools in India were encouraged by the Code to offer far more elite forms of education for Eurasian girls. This was a powerful evolution in a colonial domain that spent very little actual money on schooling for girls. It was also an evolution that attracted interlopers. Looking for a new parent market, some of the churches were able to inveigle themselves into this new elite form of education by establishing stand-alone, elite, private foundation institutions in the hills. Such schools included Auckland House in Simla and Caineville House in Mussourie (both in north India). Freelance female Eurasian teachers who taught girls were still able to muster some state funding, but it was the larger schools that became their most aggressive competitors once the Code was introduced.

This state-directed shifting in educational focus created strong tensions. Conscious of this takeover by the larger schools, one headmistress of a major new Code school justified her position on the following grounds:

> small venture schools for children are always being started, often by entirely incapable persons. Children coming from such schools to an efficient school have to spend much time learning what they should have been [already] taught.[29]

This was rather barren and self-serving reasoning. In fact, in the 1880s and 1890s, the new scene created by Code education engaged an intense rivalry between women that was not lessened by their shared Western social standing and this rivalry prevented the building of a new professional teaching community. Fierce competition arose between women teachers when parents played off one school against the other by switching the enrolment of their daughters during the long summer vacation. Additionally, American and European teachers often took advantage of the opportunity of paid passage to India, getting married once their probation period had expired, or, worse, opening a competing private-venture school.[30] Others were merely interested in offering a sectarian, but rarefied, educational haven to the daughters of like religious type missionaries serving on the plains and in India's rapidly growing cities.

In essence, there was really only one aspect upon which most of these middle-class women were agreed. Although they themselves were far from the bluestocking teachers that populated similar elite schools in other parts of the empire, they continued to see Indian teachers as being deeply inferior in their profession.

Doveton and Martinière

Within this flurry of market-driven competition between women professionals, two exemplar private foundations stood apart and require brief mention. These foundations were the Martinière schools in Lucknow and Calcutta, and the Doveton colleges in the cities of Madras and Calcutta. Both schools were relatively wealthy and longstanding, but had nonetheless long given preference to Eurasians over even European enrolments.

The Doveton girls' and boys' colleges were founded on the very large bequest of £50,000 from Captain John Doveton in 1853. These colleges were the direct result of the education activism of Doveton, along with fellow Eurasians John Ricketts and Louis Derozio, and were in response to the raj's antagonistic attitude towards Eurasians before 1850 as described in chapter two.[31] As abandoned Eurasian children, Doveton and his allies had been the recipients of what little charity education was available to them in India in the 1810s.

Doveton may have been inspired by an even older, but certainly more idiosyncratic, act of male philanthropy by General Claude Martinière. Martinière was a French opportunist, without children, who surrendered to the British after the battle of Pondicherry in 1760. He then pursued a career as the factotum of the Nawab of Oudh, collecting a tidy fortune in commissions for furnishing the Nawab's palaces, casting his cannon and grinding his indigo.[32] It is unclear what prompted Martinière to bequest his money to found schools in his name for Eurasian girls and boys, where even the boys were often taught by women. However, Martinière's legacy, and that of Doveton two generations later, offered up strong reference to educating Eurasian girls at post-elementary level by the time the Code was finally implemented in 1883.

A spatial West

With these uncertain and highly varied precursors, which so typically lay behind raj pro-activism in all fields, the preference given for Eurasian and European girls under the Code would reconfigure the official Western education approach towards females in India once again. The new approach would reorganise the relational class, gender and race elements of the colonial schooling enterprise for girls, this time with the middle-class Eurasian female learner as the prototype. And this while medical care for Indian women and girls, at the behest of the missions, was partly covering over the same race and class elements of British India.

A new physical and aesthetic boundary was also put in place for favoured female learners who were Eurasian. The new 'Code' schools actually built by the British were formal Western schoolhouse buildings. They bore little resemblance to the female learning spaces that the state had often appropriated from indigenous communities earlier in the century; nor were they mere mud-brick lean-tos with leaky thatched roofs at the back end of government secretariat compounds.

While there were some buildings, such as the Lawrence asylums, that already conformed to the new Western school building aesthetic, to date the forum for most schooling for girls had been in the Eastern architectural style, which many Westerners, in the late nineteenth century, viewed as compromised learning settings, made worse by the impoverishment of these settings at the hands of the funding parsimony of the raj.

In the 1880s, with new Western education buildings in focus, the Code stipulated that classrooms provided twelve square feet per student, were well ventilated and were furnished with Western accoutrements sufficiently commodious to attract the Eurasian and European middle-class parent market.[33] These Code classroom regulations were hardly remarkable to the raj apparatchiks who formulated them, and certainly not in terms of their pedagogic implications. However, they profoundly organised the new learning ambience nevertheless. Recent research has shown how classroom interior design, as part of any learning environment, constructs and shapes experiences and relationships. Elements of group identity formed through spatial organisation, choice of furnishings and fittings, access to resources, the use of colour, texture, materials and light – both natural and artificial – all work towards shaping teacher-learner relationships.[34] Most particularly, regarding India, Code classroom design, as a cultural language in itself, gave material expression to Western ideas about the work of students and teachers. These new physical classroom arrangements were more visible to parents than what was actually being taught within them. Western-acculturated teachers may not have been conscious of the impact of this new learning environment, particularly on their female learners. Yet, these classrooms taught Eurasian girls the cultural, as well as the class and race separateness, of their newly configured educational experience.

Student dress protocols also signified a largely uncompromising Western imposition. As noted earlier in this book, nearly all European professional teachers strictly adhered to European fashion dress codes until the 1930s. In addition, *bhadralok* Bengali women most closely associated with the raj began to 'reform' their dress into various dissonant combinations of sari and needlework blouse by the 1880s (see Frontispiece and figure 9).[35] In these new learning settings, where accomplishments were taught, students had enforced upon them uniform semblances of sari and blouse that displayed some form of Western needlework and smocking.

Of course, not all European teachers were able to cope with the racial domain in which the state now located their teaching. Tensions remained between Europeans and Eurasians, and not all Code school application in the field ran smoothly. Burma was a good case in point. Even as late as 1916, Doris Morris, headmistress of the Anglican St Mary's School, Mandalay, Burma, struggled with what she regarded as the 'very harsh voices' of her poor students who were Eurasian girls. Her professional rivals were both the European community and the nearby Catholic convent educators, who seemed able to tutor their female students well for government exams, keep on the right side of government inspectors, and even run teacher associate meetings that Morris was obliged to attend. Yet Morris's main struggle was not sectarian rivalry in recruiting students, but race warfare between the Europeans and Eurasians, in which her own stereotyping was complicit. Morris had to contend with composite classes and shabby dormitories of 100 girls each. She also had to mediate, as she saw it, between her 'spoilt' European and her 'slippery and fancy' Eurasian staff. Such concerns were enough to occupy her school day. Morris's race distinctions went further, seeing Eurasians as wholly unable to manage servants and 'English society so rotten snobbish ... [and] look on us as rather peculiar for teaching Eurasians at all'. Furthermore, in this part of the raj, perhaps uniquely, Morris felt that the influence of languid Europeans, rather than activist Indians, posed the greatest threat to the moral fibre of her students.[36]

Accomplishments

Most critical of all in terms of reconfiguring raj-directed education for girls, was the actual learning that took place in these new Code school spaces of learning. Although understanding its pedagogy, and precisely what knowledge both teacher and student privileged, is an awkward exercise for the researcher to undertake with only textual sources to hand. Teachers' qualifications, curriculum documents, and even the odd school textbook that survives, are poor indicators of how subjects were actually taught by teachers in sole charge of their classrooms; classrooms which themselves filtered the cultural capital of very different community settings across colonial India. Identifying how female students actually received this learning is an even more problematic academic exercise.

There are, however, discernable features in the manner the accomplishments canon made its way into the new Code girls' schools. What was happening at the metropole is important in better understanding these features because Code schools in India were now more direct channels of Western education than anything that had gone before them in India. As a result, they drew educational developments at the metropole into the colonial educational rubric in India, particularly for females. In mid-Victorian Britain, accomplishments, as a curriculum norm, had developed from its early nineteenth-century incarnation, responding to class-based, moral codes that were established by the 1850s. As part of these developments in England, new secondary schools for girls had begun to emerge, led by Frances Buss's North London Collegiate School and Dorothea Beale's Cheltenham Ladies' College. Emily Shirreff and Maria Grey had established the Girls' Public Day School Trust, which, by 1891, superintended thirty-six schools.[37] Additionally, in the late 1860s, the Taunton Commissioners, looking into what amounted to middle-class secondary education, gave secondary education for girls new standing in England as a movement by including this consideration in their inquiry.[38] Admittedly, some of these women educators at the metropole were also interested in pursuing a more academic curriculum for their girls. However, these broader institutional developments had curriculum ramifications for India, as the Code schools for girls hitched onto what was perceived to be a sharpened curriculum focus coming from England.

As a result, in India, reference to laundry or cooking classes of the kind found in the Lawrence asylums in the late 1850s was now missing, replaced by a new genteel sensitivity. The core business of accomplishments was accentuated, namely: drawing, needlework, music and modern languages. There was also the regulated academic fare of English, geography and history; although the latter included Western-rendered Indian as well as European history.

Except for history, all these subjects would have been recognisable in most middle-class girls' schools across the empire. Textbooks assisted the universality, even in England, because they were yet to find even a limited interpretative voice, beyond the usual repertoire of facts, as John MacKenzie has demonstrated.[39] However, what lay beneath accomplishments in India was how gender determined this ostensibly middle-class-directed curriculum. Most significantly, in India, the key divider between Code curriculums for girls compared to those for boys was the language of Urdu. Resonant of pre-British times in the north, the language remained the preserve of schooling for boys, readying them for careers in the civil service and in industry. As late as 1904, the Code commissioners were still prescribing Urdu only for males as a reluctant cultural concession to the East.[40] Furthermore, members of the Domiciled Community Education Conference, such as Sir Harcourt Butler, worried that female students 'looked over-worked' and that girls, unlike boys, should be saved 'from mental and physical pressure'.[41]

This perception of the frailty of females came, again, straight from Europe. Yet girls in the Code schools in India were given more licence in other subject areas compared to their sisters in England. For example, they were taught Euclid, Latin and a reasonably advanced form of algebra – subjects belonging mostly to boys' schooling in England.[42] On the other hand, in England, in the late nineteenth century, women were gaining access to the male preserve of science, largely though working with male relatives and as the field itself gathered prestige in European educational institutions.[43] However, in India, it would be another generation before colleges that taught women would achieve affiliation with Indian universities, thereby giving women access to this subject. By the late 1880s, Code girls' schools in India were also teaching dressmaking, the compounding of medicine, shorthand and typing, as well as calisthenics. These subjects completed a much broader curriculum compared to Code schools for boys, even though managing all these disciplinary imperatives must have been extremely difficult for women teachers, despite the usual part-time help.

There was good financial strategy behind the broader curriculum in India. It placed Code girls' schools in a much stronger financial position by commanding extra fees – in particular for offering music and modern European language classes. For this reason, Code girls' schools were always on a much surer financial footing than their male counterparts.[44] Furthermore, the lower rate of pay regulated by government for women teachers recruited in India, compared to their male counterparts, also helped Code girls' schools flourish, even though the average pay rate of Rs.60 per month, including board and lodging, was still almost three times that available to Indian women teachers in government employ who taught Indian girls.[45]

Constructing the racial teacher

The kind of woman teacher that the raj preferred for Code schools also determined the curriculum of their classrooms. Teacher 'competency' of women was measured in terms of accomplishment proficiency, feminine displays of deportment and, especially, in racial purity if these teachers were imported from England. These strict criteria were something the India Office felt it could enforce from London and went far beyond the usual recruitment practices that used patronage networks for male educators of the period in India. Women outside India wishing to teach in new Code schools were subject to direct vetting by the India Office before they were granted visas, thus creating a new academy of leaders who were woman teachers. Though well educated in Europe or the USA, these women still needed to be willing to teach in India. However, the new recruitment criteria also delayed the feminist agendas, from the same imported European source, from taking hold in most Code schools of the period.

Racial purity was, in fact, the object of chief discernment of the recruiting officers in England, who were directly answerable to the Secretary of State for India. This was a difficult line to hold, as candidates were scarce – there being only a few women who had attended 'ladies colleges' at Oxford or Cambridge, with even fewer going on to train as teachers.[46] In the face of such scarcity, the London Board of Education struggled to work within the racial boundaries the India Office insisted upon when considering Board nominees for women teachers who wanted to work on the subcontinent. Traces of Indian 'blood' in those whose families had lived in India were closely scrutinised by the India Office; and a strong measure of European anti-Semitism also precluded some candidates. For example, Miss Ada Haes, an Englishwomen with impressive teaching experience at the practising school for teachers in Bloemfontein in South Africa, was strongly recommended by the Board but was abruptly rejected by the India Office on the grounds that she was a 'bright alert person and has good manners; her appearance, however, is decidedly Jewish'.[47]

Such racism was fast becoming outdated in professional circles in England, and while the India Office could not hold its racial line regarding the appointment of Eurasian teachers who lived in India, racialised recruitment was still possible, particularly for the few it appointed to senior inspecting roles. Emma Florence Bailey, seeking the post of Inspectress of Girls' Schools in the Central Provinces, applied on the basis of being a 'lady of refinement and an excellent disciplinarian' but also with the commendation of being a 'pure European'.[48] Those long-serving women who had come out to India under Mary Carpenter's scheme in the late 1860s were also given preference for inspectorate positions, although at least their experience in India offered some justification for such appointments.[49]

There was also something missing in India regarding the essential accomplishments context that explains the state emphasis on race rather than curriculum. The deep racial divides between the teaching of Eurasian and European girls, away from the vast Indian female population, created obvious educational schisms as far as race was concerned. These schisms cut off broader possibilities for accomplishments to reproduce a dominant culture according to class and gender among the Indian population that was the case in mostly white colonial domains. Yet, paradoxically, there was one strange parallel. Accomplishments for educated women was for the private, rather than the public, domain and this seemed to confirm, at a superficial level, traditional educational trajectories in the Indian household that also stressed a similar domestic separateness based on gender; a divide for Indian women that would inform their activism during the coming national struggles in a way different from Indian men.

Perhaps as part of the racialised, subcontinental opportunities for the accomplished Eurasian woman, fiascos abounded at the turn of the century in Code girls' schools: particularly when there was a staff of just two women of European, versus Eurasian, racial designation. Disputes were mostly about professional jealousy and flimsy affectations of Western teacher propriety. However, the proceedings of government at the turn of the twentieth century are full of arguments over pay rates, accommodation status, the sudden permanent departures of head European women teachers with school funds in hand, as well as cavil in front of students over the division of duties. These disputes were often between European teachers and their mixed-race subordinates; with the latter quite possibly investing more of themselves in the girls that they taught, lacking, as they did, the professional recognition the raj continued to assign to European-only heritage and Europe-based training.[50]

Furthermore, in a sprawling India, there were some attempts by European women to teach accomplishments to well-heeled Indian girls, despite the official racial bar. Some of the *vakils* (agents) of the princely states were tempted by this type of education as an entrée for resident elite Indian girls in these states to the European social scene in India, and even abroad. The vakils could attract European teachers by offering good salaries, although this alone was not always enough. Florence Wyld, who founded the Mahbubia Girls' School for Indian girls in the princely state of Hyderabad, arrived in India with only an accomplishments mindset from Europe in view. In her nineties, in 1972, she reflected on her early work on the subcontinent:

> I knew little, except Purdah for upper classes but assumed [teaching] would be like a school in England except for Indian girls. I was told to engage three other teachers ... I decided my three should specialise in Mathematics, Kindergarten and Music & that we could share in any general subjects left over. [However] English music was little known and not wanted ... I took a good stock of books, exercise books & stationary, pencils & so on, cards for testing eye sight, such games as might be useful, Kindergarten needs, all my medical books & the usual reference books. Luckily I did.[51]

As far as smaller elite Eurasian Code schools were concerned, there were never very many of them. In north India, for example, in 1904 there were eleven boys' schools with a staff of ninety-two, eleven of whom were women teachers. There were also eighteen Code girls' schools in this part of India with a total staff of 210, nearly all of whom were women, with only about half of these teachers having received a secondary education. The student:teacher ratio was a generous ten to one.[52]

This category of education was transformed when larger diocesan and religious orders appropriated some of these earlier Code schools to make them into larger, strongly promoted enterprises. These larger institutions viewed themselves as unashamedly separate from the missions. They also had the financial wherewithal to boast common rooms of at least four or five European-educated teachers. Yet the common rooms rarely saw themselves as part of a broader professional community of women in India, as perhaps best shown by how little they agreed on core matters such as curriculum renovation. For example, as late as 1904, the headmistress of the Anglican Clewer Sisters Diocesan School, Darjeeling saw the Code curriculum as too simple for secondary-level girls, arguing for the Cambridge exams instead, with the more academically demanding study of botany and chemistry. Meanwhile, Miss Knowles, headmistress of the American Methodist Queen's Hill School, also in Darjeeling, argued an opposite case that the Code curriculum was too difficult, particularly for primary children.[53]

Kindergarten and the Kurseong Female Teacher Training College

The state was not especially troubled by the lack of professional agreement between women who were European Code teachers and who were often proximate in the comfortable hill stations of north and south India. However, these conflicts did bring new educational outcomes regarding the learning of primary schoolgirls in particular.

In 1904, at the remote hill station of Kurseong in north Bengal, a key teacher training college for women was established. This development was to turn out to be the most significant event in disseminating very junior-level teaching in colonial schools across India.[54] The college's location epitomised the separateness by which the British viewed their most precious education endeavour by this time – Code education – and the establishment of the teaching college, separate from the adjacent Dow Hill School for Girls, was based on equally restrictive calculations.

In 1895 the state had moved to provide a ready student market for the Kurseong College and other institutions like it in India, and to reinforce the racial barrier around its rarefied educational endeavours

Figure 8 Dow Hill Girls' School, Kurseong.

for women. Regulations were enacted that made school funding dependent on school inspections and on the qualifications of female staff, including their certification as qualified teachers. Teachers already in Code schools were automatically certified, but the state made certification of a new generation of Code schoolteachers dependent on their qualification in one of the Code teacher training institutions in India.[55]

The alignment of the Froebel kindergarten movement to India was another, more significant, development, the details of which are important for the female education story in India. As with most educational ideas, the provenance of Froebel teaching in India is difficult to identify, although its rudiments were not completely new to the subcontinent. Even in the Lawrence asylums in the 1850s, it is likely that very young 'orphans' were occupied with kindergarten-like games. The use of sandboards in Bell's influential monitorial school in Madras, three generations earlier, could also be said to have been unconsciously accommodative of very early childhood pedagogy that chimed with developments in Europe. Friedrich Froebel (1782–1852) himself, as a German educational theorist, had already embraced the East, being influenced by Taoist and Buddhist teachings. A derivative of earlier learning theorisation, Froebel's pedagogy centred on 'gifts', 'object lessons' and 'occupations' for the very young child. His six original, fix-formed 'gifts' were simple toys, mostly built from wood, specifically designed to enable children to learn how to create and shape their environment. Froebel's 'objects' drew upon Swiss theorist Johann Pestalozzi's idea of observing and organising commonplace objects and plants. Furthermore, Froebel's 'occupations' involved children shaping clay, sand, beads and string in a garden setting, taught by the teacher who, as a woman, was an extension of the 'loving' mother.[56]

One key example of the deployment of this movement in India was the work of Pandita Ramabai (1858–1922) (discussed further in chapter eight), who was one of the first champions of Froebel in India.[57] Ramabai was one of the very few Indian women to take up an educational appointment in Britain in the nineteenth century, where she worked as a professor of Sanscrit at the Ladies College in Cheltenham (1884–6). (This lack of opportunity in Britain contrasted with the opportunities for Indian men, whom the NIA estimated to number 160 at British universities in 1885, climbing to over 700 in 1910.[58]) However, it was during time Ramabai spent in American kindergarten Froebel schools in Philadelphia in the USA that she first saw Froebel's applicability to the female educational scene in India. For her, Froebel's approach was not primarily about pedagogy. Instead it could be taken further to be socially transformative for the oppressed mother who had little prospect of secondary or college education, and used as a clever means of self-actualising Indian women suffering under traditional patriarchal oppression. Ramabai saw that placing the natural child-mother loving relationship at the centre of the learning process was transformative for the mother, just as much for the child, in assigning her a new role as the intellectual and creative custodian of her child learner. Upon her return to India in 1887, Ramabai set about printing a series of Froebel primers in Marathi distinctly for this purpose.[59] Froebel also made headway in India as an education brand via the Froebel Institute in England, led for many years by Elizabeth Adelaide Manning (1828–1905), who was Mary Carpenter's successor as secretary of the National India Association.[60]

Details about kindergarten teaching are important, because in India, at Dow Hill, Kurseong, Froebel would turn out by the early twentieth century to be a point of delineation between old and new-guard European women teachers. Kindergarten was also one level of schooling where young women teachers, once trained, eventually engaged with Indian girls without too much opposition from government, despite its race agendas. Most schooling for Indian girls languished at lower elementary level as ongoing English-language barriers, the urbanisation of raj schools and hidden race exclusions, most notably the Code, excluded most Indian girls from secondary schooling. Yet Froebel had the capacity to engage Indian schoolgirls in expansive ways, and its teaching by a few very strong women could make a difference.

Llian Brock, Elinor Green and the Welland school

New pedagogy superimposed on older raj race and class agendas soon provoked conflicts between elite schoolteachers themselves, including between Llian Brock and Elinor Green, whose professional disagreements about kindergarten, replicated elsewhere in the raj, will be detailed below. Within the problematic Eurasian and European race domain of the Code schools, pedagogy itself became the issue in contention. Froebel, as mostly a European-inspired and self-contained pedagogy, was seemingly incapable of being adulterated by subcontinental educational 'laxity'. However it also represented recognisable professional teacher innovation for newly trained women teachers.

This view about laxity, and about European teacher innovation, was especially important to the Bengal government, which sought to add additional controls. At the time of the establishment of Code schools in the hills in the early 1880s, a key condition of the Bengal government was that graduates of hill station Code schools in Bengal, who wished to train as primary-level teachers, would be required to travel to Calcutta to train at the Welland Memorial School. At this school for Eurasians, Froebel had already been instituted as the most convenient pedagogy brand by which to train primary school women teachers. This was because, like most colonial girls' schools in India, it contained only primary-level pupils. The endeavour was also urged on by genuine state-inspired philanthropy. Canning's concern in 1860 about European racial frailty had, by the early twentieth century, developed into new official concerns about the feeble physiques of Eurasians in large cities such as Calcutta, and about their dangerous poverty levels. Furthermore, schools for Eurasians might serve as cultural separators where their habits 'practically native, their ordinary method of communication Hindustani or Bengali' could be cleansed in a world in which they were increasingly cut off from both Indian and European communities alike.[61]

By 1904, Welland had supplied Eurasian teachers trained in kindergarten techniques to mostly mission schools in Bengal, Burma and the NWP. Its teacher trainer curriculum, nominally based on Froebel, now placed Welland in the sights of a new class of professional women coming to India after a much more precise training in Froebel in Europe. One of these women was Miss Llian Brock, recruited in 1904 from England to head the Welland school. Brock had just such European training in mind, rather than any state racial tidying, when she arrived in Calcutta to take up her post. Upon her arrival at the Welland school, Brock tactfully critiqued a curriculum that had already regressed into melding early childhood work with the usual approach of supplying local markets with decorative mat plaiting, as well as object lessons that were referenced only to bottled specimens and not to living animals or growing plants.[62] Brock was an intelligent woman whose professional approach included a strong intuition about how to win consensus among her fellow women teachers. She also knew Welland's previous pedagogic compromises were partly driven by a lack of state funding and by the poverty of its Eurasian students. Yet, for Brock, Welland's chief danger was of polluting Froebel's broader application in India by training more affluent Eurasians as women teachers from Dow Hill, Kurseong and other elite Code girls' schools, whose racialised educational agenda was something quite different.

Brock's professional standards, and the reasons for them, were sufficient to be noticed by the undersecretary for education at the time, William Bell. Brock had a first-class degree from the University of London and her last two teaching appointments in England had been at the Maria Gray Training College (preparing secondary school teachers) and then conducting Board school evening classes for kindergarten teachers. This last post was where her interests really lay, with glowing testimonials referring to her refining of Froebel in the light of new educational ideas and to her capacity to adapt her approaches to the social needs of young children.[63] However, once in India, Brock's tactful criticisms of Welland soon put her out of a job, as the institution itself was wound up as a result (although Brock would be later appointed to the more influential post of Inspectress of Schools in Bengal: a post she held for many years).

Brock's immediate, seemingly cavalier, intervention was not viewed very sympathetically by those women who had already staked a claim on the status quo. Most particularly, her actions brought her into conflict with the more mercurial Elinor Green, who had been headmistress of the Dow Hill Girls' School, before taking on the nearby Kurseong Female Teacher Training College.[64] As a result of Brock's actions, this college now had to conduct the kindergarten teacher training classes in place of the Welland school in Calcutta.

Green was very much old school, and without a sense that pedagogy refinement was as important as technical proficiency in accomplishments. Dow Hill Girls' School was Green's first appointment, and she had gained rare access, despite a lack of professional qualifications, to the Provincial Education Service with its favourable pay rates and pension arrangements, most probably as a result of being a European with connections in India.[65] This official standing offered Green a rare professional locus in India. Further, her Dow Hill school had originally been established by the British to educate the children of middle and lower-class Europeans and Eurasians, whose parents could not afford to send them to the more elite Hill station schools or to Europe. For Green, accomplishments was the social remediation her girls needed for good marriages, and not Froebel, which, to her, was a professional trajectory into an unwanted career in teaching.

Green was promoted by the Viceroy to head the adjacent teacher training College for women at Kurseong. However, her social views, regarding the true purpose of elite education for girls in India by this time, soon brought her into conflict with a new cohort of imported women teachers, who formed her new staff in the Kurseong teacher training college. These incoming teachers brought with them, like Brock, a new pedagogic outlook. At one level, Green looked down on these new women teachers whom she was forced to administer, and her martinet approach sometimes induced swift resignations among her subordinates, who complained that their standing as teachers was not always respected.[66] Green's criticism of her new colleagues in the company of male administrators was also a useful ploy to secure her own job.[67] But mostly, she was sceptical of the idea that any new pedagogy could transform learning. Feeling aggrieved at being lumbered with the responsibilities of kindergarten teacher training that had formerly been located at the Welland school, she complained:

> [The] kinder proposal puzzles me. Is there or will there be any demand for Kinder teachers? I mean those who teach 3 to 6 year olds? ... seems to me children are so old when they come to school they should at once get seriously to work.[68]

Green's complaints were not enough to intimidate the likes of Miss Brock, newly empowered as inspectress of Bengal. Nor did these complaints discourage the new teachers from England whom Brock now installed at Green's Kurseong training college to teach Froebel. Froebel soon became ensconced at Kurseong, and it was Brock's surveillance at a distance by examination and inspection that enforced the new and exact teaching kindergarten science, as Brock saw it.

In the end, the teacher training course at Kurseong turned out to be a relatively sophisticated amalgam of Green's philosophy of accomplishments and Brock's insistence on well-taught Froebel. The compromise certainly had its merits. The new teacher training course for women at Kurseong was placed under the supervision of Miss Gwladys Heuer, who had been directly appointed to the post by the Secretary of State in London.[69] In the first year of the two-year certificate, much time was given over to the study of child psychology and child physiology (the latter not usually taught in such courses today) as well as the history of educational thought. In the second year, for those students wishing to become kindergarten teachers, and with the added attraction of the patronage offered by Brock in Calcutta, a well-differentiated course of studies was embarked upon. Not surprisingly, Froebel's gifts lay at the centre of this second year of study: including the theory and practice of teaching kindergarten, the place of the child in schooling for girls and the practical aspects of managing very young school children.[70]

As it turned out, negotiating this kind of curriculum arrangement, along with middle-class sensibility and deportment, at the hands of Froebel experts from Europe, offered new teacher training vitality in India, albeit mostly only in Code schools. As a result of similar transitions, usually through the teaching of new professional women from Europe, teacher training in Froebel in India was to become sophisticated enough for teacher training colleges, such as the Cathedral High School for Girls in Bombay, to win rare recognition in England. This recognition took the form of the Home Office in London declaring its willingness to employ women graduates, proficient in Froebel and trained in India, to teach in England – provided they were European.[71] (Until the First World War, attempts by inspectresses across India to win similar concession for Eurasian women fell on deaf ears.) Access to England was only permitted in rare cases for Indian women doctors, but not those aspiring to the 'scholastic professions' that included teaching.[72] Yet, in India, Kurseong and other similar colleges for women began to produce women teacher graduates for whom their professional status lay ahead of that of their race. At least some of these women graduates would eventually find poorly paid, but professionally satisfying, careers in the kindergarten schools for Indians that emerged in late colonial India.

Isabel Brander: new model teacher

The possibility of crossing the fierce racial boundary in this way in Code schools for European and Eurasian females brought into view the business of actually teaching Froebel to Indian girls. Women agents were part of the new racial crossover, counter to the state preference, just as their sisters had begun with mission zenana teaching and mission medical care fifteen years earlier. The woman who devoted more time than any other to this pursuit in India was, in fact, a European. Her name was Isabel Brander.

In many ways Brander's professional pedigree placed her strongly within the ambit of the Code mentality of race-restricted education for women and girls. Brander's approach, typical of nearly all European women in colonial India, even by 1900, was maternal.[73] She was also sure-footed in seeing Western education as the principal means of social remediation for the Indian female. As Miss Bain, a graduate of Queen's College, London, she was appointed headmistress of the Madras Normal School in 1870 after the province had excluded Mary Carpenter. She reluctantly accepted the necessity of resigning this appointment when she married in 1875. On the death of her husband five years later, she returned to India, as Mrs Brander, this time as Madras Inspectress of Schools, and finally able to accept some patronage from Carpenter's National India Association.[74]

Despite Brander's professional pedigree, there was a strong strand of intellectualism and even a limited feminism in her approach. Her Scottish father was an electrical scientist. Her friends in London included teacher, artist and social worker Octavia Hill (1838–1912) and she travelled to the USA with Sophie Jex-Blake to study normal schools there, principally in Salem, Massachusetts. Brander's testimonials attested to her experience of the 'systems of tuition' in England, France and the USA.[75]

It was this latter side of Brander's professional outlook that seems to have taken hold on her arrival in Madras in 1870. Her immediate interest was in learning the local Tamil patois, while also ejecting time-serving Eurasian students from her normal school, and sending unsuitable teachers packing back to Bangalore.[76] Her normal school in Madras city emerged still mostly as one for Europeans, Eurasians and Christian converts 'of good character and respectable social standing'. However, it contained more of a racial mix than most other institutions of its kind and the attached model (practising) school for her women student teachers to learn their craft consisted of eighty girls, two thirds of whom only spoke Tamil or Telegu.[77]

Brander's sense of what an effective European teacher professional might do in India saw her step more emphatically over the state race divide concerning the education of women and girls when she became Inspectress of Schools in Madras in 1880. This appointment was significant enough to make it into the London newspapers.[78] Meanwhile, her interest in Froebel brought her more directly into contact with Indian girls, where Code boundaries could not apply.[79]

There was a price to be paid for all of this. Being inspectress of all British Madras, with just one assistant, Miss Carr, meant a purview of 367,010 square kilometres – almost three times the size of England. This was manageable if the inspectress chose, as most of those in other provinces did, to concentrate only on central and mission schools for girls. However, Brander's interest in neglected village schooling for Indian girls meant she had an impossible workload, by 1892, of visiting 152 schools with 8,569 students in a circuit tour of just 138 days.[80] Her unsympathetic superiors viewed this workload as being of her own making. As a woman, her pay was just two-thirds of her comfortably ensconced city-based male counterparts. Yet Brander soon embraced her onerous work, which now required her to travel eight months in any given year: still very much a European abroad, but ready to take on the Madras *kurinji* (mountains) and *marudham* (fertile plains) in pursuit of her profession.[81] The following is one of her accounts of her enforced travel arrangements.

> It is necessary to take a bath, a cot, crockery, cooking apparatus, and a chair. My luggage also includes a big box for official stationary, and another of toys, pictures, and other presents for children ... My staff consists of two assistants, three clerks and two *poens* [messengers] ... we form a company of eleven or twelve persons. Our travelling is done in ... trains, steamers, boats, palanquins, and country-carts drawn by bullocks at the rate of two miles an hour when the roads are good. At the beginning of the year I journeyed for nearly 500 miles in country-carts, travelling each night, inspecting schools each day ... Very kind hospitality is offered to me by officials and missionaries, but rarely am I able to avail myself of it and in many places there are no Europeans. The *dak*-bungalows (rest houses) are fairly comfortable, but some are very primitive ... Occasionally ... Rajahs place a large house, servants, carriages and horses at my disposal, the transitions from a ruined bungalow to a palace, and back again, are often very sudden and rather amusing.[82]

Brander's good humour and even stoicism were mostly borne out of her desire to reach Indian girls. However, there was, of course, the key question of Froebelian pedagogy that lay at the centre of Brander's professional identity. At first, her teaching involved the rather crude technique of using European-referenced pictures of the *Illustrated London News* and she was quizzical as to the reason for her unresponsive students. 'I often find it most difficult to enable Hindu girls to *realize* [her italics] what they learn'.[83] Yet, as Brander's interest and experience of teaching Froebel in India deepened, she began pursuing a refined methodology. She added new Froebelian occupations that involved Indian 'form, colour and other striking qualities of the materials used'. The use of Indian music to help young Indian children to reason and create remained beyond her grasp, but she compensated by using what amounted to Anglicised vernacular stories and 'action songs' that were designed to achieve the same end.[84]

In 1892 Brander knew well the unequal educational opportunity for Indian girls that the raj had amplified along race lines in the previous four decades. She also knew that she could only interact with very few of these girls. Yet she genuinely invested herself emotionally, albeit

Figure 9 A bilingual nature study class: sunflowers for little girls.

somewhat maternally, in their schooling environment and in their learning.

> An Indian girls' school is almost always a pretty sight. The buildings vary from substantial many storied brick buildings, furnished with chairs, tables, benches, blackboards, down to a leaf and mud shed where the children sit on the ground. The former schools are supplied with good maps, and the children use printed books and English slates; but in the latter, *cadjan* [palm leaf] books and *takhtis* [wooden boards] ... are often used. The pupils are almost invariably graceful, pretty, little women, in bright picturesque raiment, and are exceedingly docile, intelligent, and eager to please. They are very earnest about their lessons, and as one goes round a class, marking their sums right or wrong ... their bright black eyes search one's face to see if they have succeeded.[85]

Of course the Froebelian approach demanded something quite different of its practitioners in India. If colonial teachers were to directly engage poor Indian children, or even wealthy Indian girls, it was an Eastern, not Western, epistemology and experiential learning domain that mattered. Brander's hard work in the field brought her to this realisation early. In response, in 1899, she published her *Kindergarten Teaching in India*, an elegantly presented teaching guide that summed up what worked best for her when teaching in India.

> As close a connection as possible has been established between the stories, object lessons, occupations and songs [of India] and even between these and reading, writing and arithmetic, as such concentration is believed to have high educational value.[86]

Brander was also experienced enough by this time to know that selling her teaching approach in India to intrusive deputy commissioners required more than a little sensitivity. In her text she made careful reference to circulars issued by the Board schools in England about object lessons deemed suitable for teaching at the metropole. However, her difficulty was that, for India, the 'rajah', the 'rani', the date palm and the lotus were the motifs by which Indian children learnt Froebel. Moral stories built upon these objects could not be Moses and the Exodus. Instead, it was Shiva's five fingers stroking the 'foolish, greedy but repentant' monkey's back, delivering the monkey's family from the ravages of the Arabian sea.[87]

Code schooling for girls, with its racial exclusiveness and its new Western learning spaces, remained the preference of government. However, the work of Brander and the Froebelian Association, in deploying Froebelian pedagogy in India in a manner that could not be challenged, eventually succeeded in shifting part of the cultural and racial frame of raj schooling for very young Indian girls. The Bengal government began legislating kindergarten schooling in favour of Indian children in 1903.[88] Such was Brander's standing on this issue that the Madras government began identifying the 'best' schools for Indian girls as those that taught Froebel rather than mere rote. The influential Bengal DPI Alexander Pedler rightly identified the distinctiveness of her work as 'entirely discard[ing] the uses of the European forms of Froebel's gifts'.[89] The Bengal education conference in 1896 had earlier reluctantly offered a similar view. Yet this praise came with the backhander of approving the cheapness of Brander's Indian Froebel's 'gifts' and with the insistence – un-Frobelian – that gender differences in the 'play' of these little Indian children were to be maintained at all times.[90]

At the end of her time in India in 1903, Brander emigrated to the USA to share her expertise in a country where Froebel had been strongly embedded by German immigrants two generations earlier. In India there was no such recognition of her contribution. This distinguished woman was left to fight it out with an unsympathetic Viceroy, Lord Curzon, who directly criticised her Indianised pedagogy, for a very modest pension after almost thirty years of educational service to education on the subcontinent.[91]

Struggling to rise above such small-mindedness occupied much of the correspondence between government and Brander, and others like her, in this late nineteenth-century period. Brander's departure from India was made particularly sad by the fact that, despite her long career, remarked upon abroad both in Europe and in the USA, Froebel teaching in India was still no match for the racial barriers that surrounded Code schools. The National Froebel Union was founded in the UK in 1887 to oversee, among other duties, the standards of the Froebel Teacher's certificate throughout the empire. However, in India, as another brand of imported professionalism, even this certificate was used by the state to racially exclude many others. In 1904 the new appointment of a kindergarten teacher at the Dow Hill School for Girls at Kurseong could only be a Miss Davies, as, in London, the Secretary of State for India decreed:

> [She] was trained at the North Hackney Training College, London and gained both the elementary and higher certificates awarded by the National Froebel Union of Great Britain and Ireland ... The reason why a native of India cannot conveniently be appointed is obvious in this case. In the first place no native of India is qualified in the manner indicated, and in the second place the post is attached to a training college for European and Eurasian girls [only].[92]

In the last two decades of the nineteenth century the Western professionalism of many women teachers saw the adoption of accomplishments in girls' schools in India as part of the broader racial imperatives of a now self-confident British raj. The knowledge transferred to India regarding the teaching of Froebel also distinguished, within this very limited sphere of influence, long-serving European, women teachers from their generally younger, but European professionally trained, colleagues. Both groups of women came to share teaching in Code schools that was intended by the state only for Eurasian and European schoolgirls. However, this teaching still highlighted important differences in professional approach. For Elizabeth Brander and others, who decided to step outside this state-imposed racial boundary regarding teaching, new professional opportunities emerged, as they had done for women who had earlier decided to do the same regarding medicine. As with innovation in tropical medicine, the learning of Froebel by Indian girls demanded new pedagogy and cultural adaption by women teachers in India. The intellectualising required, based on first-hand experience as to what was productive teaching for Indian girls, would establish new networks of knowledge from the Indian colonial domain: networks that transferred this knowledge back to Europe, the USA and even Japan for the learning of, and appropriation by, interested educators in each of those countries.

Notes

1 DPI to Government, March 31, 1875 no. 56 Punjab Government Proceedings (OIOC) P/139.
2 The best accounts of the institution of the English Middle School exams in Indian schools in the 1870s are to be found in the respective preambles of the provincial hearing reports of the Hunter Commission published in 1883. W. W. Hunter, *Report of the Indian Education Commission* (Calcutta: Government Printing, 1883).
3 'Resolution', Government of India Proceedings, March 1874 (OIOC) P/520.
4 J. Offer, *Herbert Spencer and Social Theory* (New York: Palgrave Macmillan, 2010).
5 E. Buettner, *Empire Families: Britons and Late Imperial Britain* (Oxford: Oxford University Press, 2004) pp. 81–2. See also A. L. Stoler, *Race and the Education of Desire: Foucault's History of Sexuality and the Colonial Order of things* (Durham, NC: Duke University Press, 1995).
6 E. Buettner, *Empire Families ...*, pp. 41–2.
7 D. Arnold, 'European Orphans and Vagrants in India in the Nineteenth Century', *Journal of Imperial and Commonwealth History*, 7:2 (1979), 104–7; D. Arnold, 'White Colonisation and Labour in Nineteenth-Century India', *Journal of Imperial and Commonwealth History*, 12:2 (1983), 133–58.
8 L. G. Bear, 'Miscegenations of Modernity: Constructing European Respectability and Race in the Indian Railway Colony, 1857–1931', *Women's History Review*, 3:4 (1994).
9 'Education of Europeans' in J. S. Cotton, *Progress of Education ... Third Quinquennial Report 1892–97* (London: HMSO, 1898) (OIOC) V/24/4429.
10 'Draft Code of Regulations for European Schools as Finally Accepted by the Government of India, October 1884' (OIOC) P/2257.
11 R. Nathan, *Progress of Education in India 1897–98* (Calcutta: Government Printing, 1904).
12 Committee upon the Financial Condition of Hills Schools For Europeans in Northern India' (Calcutta: Government Printing, 1905), vol. II, Appendix III (OIOC).
13 J. S. Cotton, *Third Quinquennial Education Report 1892–97...*, p. 329.
14 Report of Rev. J. Williams, March 31, 1889 E44 f. 433, SPG (RHL).
15 W. W. Hunter 'Education Commission Report' Home Department (Education) (Calcutta, 1883)' in M. A. Chishti (ed.), *Committees and Commissions in Pre-Independence India, 1836–47* (New Delhi: Mittal Publications, 2001), vol. 2, pp. 37–40.
16 Report on the Conference of the Domiciled Community, January 8, 1913 (OIOC) P/9193.
17 India Education Proceedings March 6, 1912 no. 2052 (OIOC) P/9193.
18 'Annual Report, Lawrence Military Asylum, 1887–8', Punjab Education Proceedings, 1888 (OIOC) P/3154.
19 M. Karlekar, 'Kadambini and the Bhadralok: Early Debates over Women's Education in Bengal', *Economic and Political Weekly*, 21:17 (April, 1986), 3.
20 A. D'Souza, *Anglo-Indian Education: A Study of its Origins and Growth in Bengal up to 1960* (Delhi: Oxford University Press, 1976), p. 127.
21 J. S. Cotton, *Third Quinquennial Education Report 1892–97...*, p. 316.
22 'Committee Upon the Financial Condition of the Hill Schools For Europeans in Northern India', p. 24 (OIOC) V/26/861/1.
23 Miss Holland, MA, Principal and Proprietress, Hampton Court School, Mussourie, 'Committee upon the Financial Condition of Hill Schools for Europeans in Northern India', vol. ii, p. 46 (OIOC) V/26/861/2.

24 C. Mooney, 'Securing a Private Classical Education In and Around Sydney: 1830–50', *History of Education Review*, 25:1 (1996), 38–9.

25 M. Theobald, ' "Mere Accomplishments?" Melbourne's Early Ladies Schools Reconsidered" in A. Prentice and M. Theobald (eds), *Women Who Taught* (Toronto: University of Toronto Press, 1991), p. 73.

26 J. S Cotton, *Third Quinquennial Education Report 1892–97...*, p. 342.

27 H. Wood, Secretary to the Agent of the East Indian Railway and Superintendent of the East Indian Railway Schools, 'Committee upon the Financial Condition of Hill Schools for Europeans in Northern India', vol. ii, p. 11 (OIOC) V/26/861/2.

28 Diary of Kate Georgina Frey (née Stewart) Army Schoolmistress in India and Egypt (OIOC) MSS Eur Photo 143.

29 Miss Holland, Principal and Proprietress, Hampton Court School, Mussourie 'Committee upon the Financial Condition of Hill Schools for Europeans in Northern India', vol. ii, p. 46 (OIOC) V/26/861/2.

30 Miss Birrell, Proprietress, Ayrcliff High School, Simla, 'Committee upon the Financial Condition of Hill Schools for Europeans in Northern India', vol. ii, p. 51 (OIOC) V/26/861/2.

31 R. Nathan, 'Progress of Education in India 1897–98', p. 327 (OIOC) V/24/4430.

32 'Report on the Existing Schools for Europeans and Eurasians Throughout India [1872]', p. 15 (OIOC) V/27/861/1.

33 'Draft Code of Regulations for European Schools as Finally Accepted by the Government of India, October 1884' (OIOC) P/2257.

34 D. Whitehouse and K. Frith, 'Designing Learning Spaces That Work: A Case For The Importance of History', *History of Education Review*, 38:2 (2009), 94–108.

35 G. Murshid, *Reluctant Debutante: Response of Bengali Women to Modernization, 1849–1905* (Rajshahi: Sahitya Samsad, 1983), p. 248.

36 Doris Sarah Morris Papers (OIOC) MSS Eur C 399/1–3.

37 J. Kamm, *Indicative Past: A Hundred Years of the Girls' Public Day School Trust* (London: George Allen & Unwin, 1971).

38 M. Theobald, ' "Mere Accomplishments?" Melbourne's Early Ladies Schools Reconsidered' in A. Prentice and M. Theobald (eds), *Women Who Taught* (Toronto: University of Toronto Press, 1991), p. 71.

39 J. M. MacKenzie, *Propaganda and Empire: The Manipulation of British Public Opinion, 1880–1960* (Manchester: Manchester University Press, 1984), pp. 174–9.

40 'Committee Upon the Financial Condition of the Hill Schools For Europeans in Northern India' (OIOC) V/26/861/1.

41 'Report of the Conference on the Education of the Domiciled Community in India [Simla]' (Calcutta: Government Printing, 1912) p. 37 (OIOC).

42 M. Theobald, ' "Mere Accomplishments?" Melbourne's Early Ladies Schools Reconsidered ...', p. 74.

43 R. Watts, *Women in Science ...*, pp. 194–7.

44 W. C. Madge, Oral Evidence, 'Committee Upon the Financial Condition of the Hill Schools For Europeans in Northern India', p. 1 (OIOC) V/26/861/2.

45 'Committee Upon the Financial Condition of the Hill Schools for Europeans in Northern India', p. 24 (OIOC) V/26/861/1.

46 Robert Morant to the Secretary of State [for India], July 6, 1904 *Home Office Proceedings* July–December, 1904 (OIOC) P/6808.

47 Robert Morant to the Secretary of State [for India], July 6, 1904 *Home Office Proceedings* July–December, 1904 (OIOC) P/6808.

48 'Application of Miss E. F. Bailey' *Home Office Proceedings* July–December, 1904 (OIOC) P/6808.

49 Provincial editions of *Histories of Service* (OIOC).

50 See, for example, Education Proceedings (Home) July–December, 1901 (OIOC) P/6111.

51 'Memoirs of Miss F. M. Wyld' (OIOC) MSS Eur B 320, f. 10.

52 'Committee Upon the Financial Condition of the Hill Schools for Europeans in Northern India', p. 24 (OIOC) V/26/861/1.

53 'Committee upon the Financial Condition of Hill Schools for Europeans in Northern India [1904]' vol. ii, pp. 18, 22 (OIOC) V/26/861/2.

54 A. D'Souza, *Anglo-Indian Education* ..., p. 135.

55 'European Education' in J. S. Cotton, *Third Quinquennial Education Report, 1892–97...*, p. 311.

56 M. Shapiro, *Childs Garden: The Kindergarten Movement from Froebel to Dewey* (University Park, PA: Penn State University Press, 1983).

57 An organisation devoted to the renovation of Hinduism as it related to child marriage and widows.

58 A. Burton, *At the Heart of Empire: Indians and the Colonial Encounter in late Victorian Britain* (Berkeley, CA: University of California Press, 1998), p. 26.

59 See an extract of Ramabai's thoughts in the Chicago Newspaper (unsourced) quoted in E. F. Chapman, *Sketches of Some Distinguished Indian Women* (London: Allen & Co., 1891), pp. 39–40.

60 A. B. Murphy and D. Raftery (eds), *Emily Davies: Collected Letters, 1861–1875* (Virginia: University of Virginia Press, 2004), p. 503.

61 Inspector of European Schools to the Government of Bengal, June 21, 1906 (OIOC) P/7591.

62 'Miss Brock's Report in Which the Welland Memorial Kindergarten is Dealt With' 'Annexure C' incl. in Pedler to the Government of Bengal, July 12, 1904 (OIOC) P/6808.

63 William Bell to the Government of India, December 24, 1903 (OIOC) P/6807.

64 Details of the abrupt manner of Green when dealing with staff disputes over accommodation, teaching workload and pay rates can be found in Education Proceedings (Home), July–December, 1901 (OIOC) P/6111.

65 History of Service, Bengal (1900), p. 1006 (OIOC) V/12/132.

66 'Additions' Education Proceedings (Home) (OIOC) P/6111.

67 'Additions' Education Proceedings (Home) (OIOC) P/6111.

68 Report of Acting Principal of the Dow Hill Training College ...' 'Annexure B' incl. in Pedler to Government of Bengal, July 12, 1904 (OIOC) P/6808.

69 Appointment of Miss Gwladys Alvina Heuer as Mistress of Method, Dow Hill Training School, Kurseong (OIOC) IOR/L/PJ/6/734.

70 Pedler to the Government of Bengal, July 12, 1904 (OIOC) P/6808.

71 'Recognition of Certain Schools in India for the Purposes of Registration of Teachers in England' Home Department Proceedings (July–December, 1904) (OIOC) P/6808.

72 Government of India to all Provinces, November 29, 1911 (OIOC) P/8611.

73 I am using the word 'maternal' rather than 'paternal' here in view of the research of S. Koven and S. Michel, 'Womanly Duties ...', *passim*. This research identifies a new sphere of action by women in Europe and in the USA between 1880 and 1920 that transformed their emphasis on motherhood into public policy. I suggest that by using this term this mentality extended to the activism of European women such as Brander in India. The term 'maternal' is more applicable than the usual postcolonial nomenclature of 'paternal' when viewing European 'redemptive' activism in colonial settings.

74 Secretary of State to Government of Madras, May 12, 1870 (OIOC) P/439/15.

75 *Woman's Herald*, vol. v, no. 176, March 12, 1892 (OIOC).

76 DPI to Government of Madras, December 1, 1870 (OIOC) P/439/15.

77 *Journal of the National Indian Association*, no. 46, May 1874, p. 244 (OIOC).

78 *The Times*, April 1880 (BL). See also *The Woman's Herald*, March 12, 1892 (OIOC).

79 *History of Service* (Madras), July, 1899 (OIOC) V/12/264.

80 *Report on Public Instruction in the Madras Presidency 1893–94* (Madras: Government Printing, 1894), p. 26 (OIOC) V/24/843.

81 DPI to Government of Madras, June 20, 1892 (OIOC) P/4109.

82 *Woman's Herald*, vol. v, no. 176, March 12, 1892 (OIOC).

83 *Journal of the National Indian Association*, no. 29, May 1873, pp. 332–3 (OIOC).

84 Mr Cotton, 'Madras Quinquennial Education Report' incl. in Bengal DPI to Government of Bengal, October 17, 1900 (OIOC) P/6111.

85 *Woman's Herald*, vol. v, no. 176, March 12, 1892 (OIOC).

86 E. Brander, *Kindergarten Teaching in India: Stories, Object Lesson Occupations, Songs and Games* (London: Macmillan & Co., 1899), pp. v.

87 E. Brander, *Kindergarten Teaching in India ...*, pp. 10–14.

88 P. Gottschalk, 'Promoting Scientism: Institutions for Gathering and Disseminating Knowledge in British Bihar', in I. Sengupta and D. Ali (eds), *Knowledge Production, Pedagogy and Institutions in Colonial India* (London: Palgrave Macmillan, 2011), pp. 188–9.

89 A. Pedler to Government of Bengal, October 17, 1900 (OIOC) P/6111.

90 Government of India to Government of Bengal, April 3, 1900 (OIOC) P/6111.

91 Government of Madras to Government of India, July 12, 1901 (OIOC) P/6111.

92 Secretary of State to the Government of India, June 17, 1904 (OIOC) P/7591.

CHAPTER EIGHT

'Better mothers': feminine and feminist educators and thresholds of Indian female interaction, 1870–1932

Hidden away in the India Office Library is an account of one of the most extraordinary conversations of the twentieth century. The conversation was between Sir Philip Hartog and Mohandas 'Mahatma' Gandhi. It occurred in 1931, in London, at the time of Gandhi's attendance at the second Round Table Conference to 'decide' India's future. Gandhi, as a leader of the Indian National Congress, was already deeply frustrated by disingenuous British proposals for how best to navigate towards a self-governing India. In contrast, Hartog was the last man to write a major government report on colonial education on the subcontinent. This was an auxiliary report to the much-criticised, earlier, all-European-member 1928 Simon Commission, which had also been set up to determine India's 'future' without Indian representation.

Part of the conversation between Hartog and Gandhi concerned female education in India. Hartog's assessment of this 'question' measured British 'achievement' in terms of Western literacy testing: usually the ability of Indian girls to read a prescribed passage from a Western text. This was shaky ground, even by the standards of the time. In response, Gandhi had at his disposal a bewildering array of possible criticisms about a clearly failed education system, yet he posed a simple question: would Hartog's colonial education make Indian girls better mothers?[1]

This chapter examines the emerging receptiveness of leading European females to the increasingly recognisable, to them, veracity of Indian cultural and intellectual educational spaces. This receptiveness was not a recovery of orientalist interactions of the early nineteenth century. Nor did interacting Indian women, in this latter period, engage in any significant numbers with this limited Western accommodation. However, the interaction between Western and Indian women is important, despite at the same time being complex and dispersed

[233]

across the subcontinent. There were also liminal, or Indian threshold responses, to Western femininity values at the turn of the twentieth century that seemed to renegotiate at least some of the colonial influence from abroad.

Gandhi's question, unwittingly perhaps, touched on the broad socio-cultural issues that sociologists such as Pierre Bourdieu and sociolinguistics such as Basil Bernstein later considered as the accompanying constructions of any educational setting: that students themselves are shaped by and shape educational settings. Eastern socio-cultural paradigms, if they had existed, might have been even more incisive.

Gandhi often assimilated strong gender issues in his own writings that were unrecognisable to most Westerners at the time: particularly *dharma* (an individual's proper conduct) of female *seva* (selfless service), being female qualities of nursing and compassion.[2] He had already implemented these values at the Phoenix Settlement, and later at his Tolstoy Farm, both in South Africa, founded in 1904 and in 1910, respectively.[3] Gandhi's response to Hartog in 1931 was probably also aimed at undermining British pretensions to a superior brand of masculinity that had built empire.[4] Gandhi's question was not one of decrying the influence of Western women per se in the education settings they occupied on the subcontinent. Even the National movement did not exclude these Western women. British-born Theosophist and socialist Annie Besant, who in some senses was a special case, was elected president of the India National Congress in 1917, and her like-minded younger countrywoman, Margaret Cousins, served as president of the All India Women's Conference in 1936.[5] Yet there were other complexities to Gandhi's approach that cut across the usual contours of colonial thought regarding the education of females. If teachers were virtuous, Gandhi supported co-education, but he also could characterise himself as projecting 'a mother's love' when supervising boys and girls as they were living, sleeping and even bathing together at close quarters in his ashram.[6]

There was also the thought of a very small number of women who were part of the raj about what an educated female might aspire to when she had endured its fierce race and Western class strictures. As early as 1904, Besant rejected Western brands of female professionalism in India. The rejection was not on the grounds of any imported feminist ideology, which might be equally rejected by Indian nationalists as a mere Western fetish not applicable to the Indian female. It was because such professionalism – more so for women teachers than for nurses or women physicians – remained affected by deeply rooted raj mentalities about the moral, elite and racialised, educated female. On this theme Besant asserted:

> India needs nobly trained wives and mothers, wise and tender rulers of the household ... skilled nurses of the sick, rather than girl-graduates, educated for the learned professions.[7]

A generation later, in 1930, the eminent poet and writer, Sarojini Naidu, second woman president of the Indian National Congress, also saw India as different to the West on the questions of femininity and feminism. Like others in her generation, she viewed favourably what she saw in India as a lack of economic competition between men and women.[8] Yet she also declared that she 'was not a feminist' at the All India Women's Conference (AIWC) in 1930. She justified her view because the phrase 'feminist' did not characterise the social context of Indian women, who she considered were psychologically and spiritually different from men. For Naidu, a feminist was one who admitted 'her inferiority and there is no need for such a thing in India as women have always been by the side of men both in councils and the fields of battle'.[9]

Unlike what was happening in Europe, these views, and others like them, helped to prevent the consolidation of a Western female teacher community in India, although it was not entirely the case for the female medical profession. These views also demonstrate the increasingly difficult position occupied by European women educators. Meanwhile, the failing colonial state and female professional networks coming from new centres in England (such as Newnham and Girton Colleges in Cambridge) offered little direction as to how best to interact with the Indian female that the Nationalist movement now projected.

The Maharani of Baroda was well known in colonial circles by the 1930s for her active interest in the education of Indian females, to better their social and political position, particularly for teachers. In 1910 she had proposed sending a Hindu and a Muslim female scholar from each princely state to Europe to train as teachers.[10] However, even from her elite standpoint looking at education practice in Britain, Europe, the USA and Japan, she still saw navigating Indian 'feminine individuality' as something distinct in her own country. While keen to understand how Western women were breaking male dominance, particularly in the field of education, for the Maharani the justifiable and different 'deep-rooted' cultural roles for Indians of both sexes meant Indian female activism would follow a course that was 'evolution not revolution'.[11]

Western women projected radically different perspectives concerning the applicability of Western feminism to colonial India from the end of the nineteenth century onwards. These different views were encouraged because the thin veneer of raj interaction with Indian women up to that time offered few tangible outcomes that might be considered to judge this issue. These perspectives ranged from ideas about India's ethnicity preventing Western feminist activism, through to a view that Indian women could participate and influence much broader global female engagement. For example, there were those European women who railed against what they saw as misapplied feminism. Mary Billington and Eliza Lynn Linton researched Indian women in their local contexts. In 1895 they saw a universal sisterhood stamp as being naively applied to India's different cultural settings. In Linton's words:

> New women ... swarm over India, knocking at the door of the Zenana, and doing their best to disturb the ancient serenity and seclusion of the Hindu home ... They do not stop to remember both the ethnic and ethical differences between the East and the West, nor can they believe in happiness where those differences exist.[12]

Almost two generations later, in the 1930s, the journal, *Stri Dharma* (Destiny of Women), mouthpiece for Margaret Cousins' Women's Indian Association (WIA), was still attempting to create a community of women activists involved in both international and indigenous feminist and Indian nationalist movements. The original conception of the journal was neither completely Indian nor completely Western but it emerged, for a time, as an international feminist news medium that targeted Indian, Eurasian and British women readers alike.[13]

Problems eventually emerged even in this rarefied writing environment. The journal did not become a focus for international feminist cooperation, as originally intended, where Indian and Western feminists might come together deploying an internationalist feminist model. Instead, the journal's ultimate failure illustrated that these women actually belonged to little more than an imagined community, as growing nationalist consciousness in India offered reconfigured opportunities for Indian women, separate from their Western sisters.[14] It is significant here to note the manner in which the Maharani Gaekwad of Baroda publically defined her well-publicised support of education for Indian females, at Margaret Cousins' first All India Women's Conference at Poona in 1927. The Maharani did this in terms of an education that understood the special social position of Indian females and that was compatible with their feminine Indian 'nature'.[15] Rather than the appropriation of Western feminism, this was an approach that was part of a broader phenomenon among some Indian traditional elites in the colonial period. It was where a self-sense of 'other' in cooperating with the British developed, which then compelled these elites to negotiate with Western modernity while maintaining their claims to be upholding strong Indian cultural lineage.[16]

There were also strong disciplinary elements to the way feminine and feminist articulations were projected by colonial women. These articulations drew on the different forms of knowledge, and the ideologies associated with them, that had been built in the nineteenth century by the colonial state: female medical care compared to female teaching. As shown in chapter six, there was at least some articulation of feminist viewpoints by some European women doctors by the 1910s. These women resented the interference of less-qualified male administrators in their hospitals, and also the men that drove the workings of the Dufferin medical fund. Admittedly, some of this Western feminist articulation was driven by racial prejudice when these women were obliged to submit to male administrators who were Indian or Eurasian. However, the largely undisputed universal understanding of medical care provided a solid backdrop for the articulation of at least some Western feminist critique in India on this topic.

School teaching by women was different. The thinly ranged professional body of Western women was disempowered by its dispersal across the subcontinent. The disaggregation was exacerbated by the now entrenched racialised moral codes of colonial schooling for females that were also sensitised, in different ways, by what the British euphemistically called 'local conditions'. This phenomenon will be further examined later in this chapter. Leading women teachers sometimes came together at times of important inquiries or conferences, but their language rarely evoked a recognisable Western feminist ideology that tested new political ground for their colleagues and their students to follow.

So why was India so different in comparison to other parts of the empire, regarding how Western feminism and Western femininity canon were received? Joyce Goodman and Rebecca Rogers rightly point to the work of women engaging with internationalised practices and ideas regarding education that included Europe as well as colonial domains.[17] At a superficial international level, colonial India participated in this process, as a recipient and as a donor, through the labyrinthine international networks that engaged the subcontinent concerning education and medical care. It was true that Indian women also used colonial legal and constitutional processes, partly through a Hindu *bhaginivarg* (sisterhood), to redress oppression in mostly Indian household spaces concerning property rights, abusive husbands and the custody of children.[18]

However, the application of Western feminist discourses in particular, even by Western women working in the raj, was still ambivalent when compared to the 'white' British dominions. In part, this ambivalence can be explained by the distinctive Indian fare that power-fully drove the process from 'beneath', and by how the national move-ment articulated this perspective in the 1910s and 1920s. Further to this argument, Suruchi Thapar-Björkert identifies an Indian women's movement as recognising priorities that were not always the same as those of men. However, this movement hesitated to use the word 'fem-inist', because it conveyed unpatriotic connotations in placing Indian women's demands before the nation and the concept also appeared antithetical to men.[19] In addition, Western and Eastern conceptions of femininity in the context of the national struggle offered more cross-over than those conceptions concerning feminism. This was mostly because of the refusal of nationalists to make the women's question an issue of political negotiation with the colonial state.[20]

Within this distinctly Indian frame of colonial gender interaction, this chapter examines some of the complexity by looking at examples of colonial women teachers and learners in the last quarter of the nine-teenth century, and by exploring how the professional realities of India set up ongoing conflicts within their fragmented and dispersed commu-nities. The time periods concerned are overlapping; the issues raised did not impact upon all of these females at the same time, and they are therefore difficult to systematise in a broader frame. The chapter then goes on to examine emerging Indian responses to the colonial female education project in the late nineteenth century, and the contrasting official view that was based on statistics and weighty commissions of inquiry. Finally, this chapter considers how colonial women educators, in their relatively isolated local domains, began to imperfectly realign at least some of their, mostly unrelenting Western, educational activ-ism in terms of a nationalist Indian female liminality.

Self-actualising at the local level, 1870–5

It was hardly surprising, when European women found their institu-tional 'place' in India, away from the social and cultural context of Britain, that their professional perspectives became quickly realigned. This realignment took many of them away from the Western pro-fessional narratives, feminist or not, that had, before their arrival, grouped them together as women travelling to India. In this sense, Mary Carpenter's work in the 1870s (discussed in chapter three) needs to be examined in terms of the self-actualisation of her intended prox-ies, who were European women, once they began responding to local situations upon their arrival in India. Notably, Carpenter's most qual-ified agents, Miss Stuart Richmond and a Miss Martin, caused the Carpenter experiment most trouble in this regard. Richmond, already a London-certified teacher, refused to recognise Carpenter's authority once she was installed as mistress of a high-caste girls' school under the benefaction of the Bombay shipping merchant Gokuldas Morarji. Carpenter's imperative to suddenly turn this girls' school into a normal (teacher training) school, without first adequately educating its very young girls, rightly offended Richmond's professional sensibilities.[21] Carpenter's other key agent, Martin, possibly for similar reasons, refused to take up her position as principal of the Poona Teacher Training College, preferring instead a more comfortable living as headmistress of the Alexandra School in Bombay.[22]

These conflicts forced a change in tack in the way Carpenter chose to apply her experiment in India, particularly after the scandal at Nagpur dried up government funding. After attempting to have Richmond and Martin shipped back to England, she was forced to rely instead on the patronage of two princely Indian women in Maharastra, the Ranis of Sangli and Nath. The Ranis' caste sensibilities left Carpenter with no choice but to limit her endeavours to upper-caste girls in south west India. Backup help from the wives of missionaries, such as Mrs Mitchell, at Poona, also required partial compliance by Carpenter to their particular missionary agenda.[23]

The most common British background of European women teachers in India who were not missionaries, was Unitarianism or Quaker heritage. In the later colonial period, many European women with these backgrounds worked in India's ashrams. Watts' research shows that, for Unitarians, at least in England, their networks, including Mary Carpenter, Harriet Martineau and English novelist Elizabeth Gaskell, were well developed.[24] As early as the 1850s these religions were already elevating European women to roles of independent leadership and, while Unitarians were anxious to work within 'respectable' female circles, which made them appear conservative in practice, they strongly believed in female intellectual capacity.[25]

The local accommodations of Annette Ackroyd, 1873–6

The Unitarian networks in India worked their way through in other local forums too, although with less success. Another woman with a Unitarian background was Annette Ackroyd (mother of William Beveridge, founder of the British welfare state). In 1873 she was the first headmistress of the Bangiya Mahila Vidyalaya (BMV) (school for Hindu women), a boarding school at Entally, Calcutta. Her repositioning, once in India, was even more important than that of Richmond and Martin, who had helped skew Mary Carpenter's normal school experiment in its strongest remaining locations in Maharashtra. Ackroyd was a complex character, and the establishment of her secular school turned out to be highly significant, although for reasons that were little to do with her contribution to the education of females.

Before Ackroyd's arrival in India, Keshub Sen had set up the Native Ladies' Normal School in Calcutta in 1871 in sympathy with Carpenter's lobby, whose creation he had influenced. However, Sen's opposition to higher education for girls, particularly their learning of mathematics and the sciences, led to a break with the radicals of the Brahmo Samaj. These radicals went on to establish the BMV secondary school, which Annette Ackroyd was then recruited to run.[26] The school was well positioned to do something distinctive for Indian women and all might have been well if it had not been for the rather contemptuous attitudes Ackroyd developed towards the subcontinent once she had settled there.

Vron Ware rightly identifies Ackroyd's initial hostility towards British paternal and racist attitudes regarding Indians and their culture.[27] Ackroyd was also determined enough to remain outside the close and supportive networks missionaries provided for many European expatriate women of her generation.[28] However, to Ackroyd, once she had lived there for some time, India was to become a land of 'stone idols ... and where at every point the fact of sex is present to the mind'.[29] Ackroyd indulged in gossip with her possible suitors and her many diary entries suggest little common purpose with even an imagined European women's teaching community in India. Some of her views also demonstrated knowledge of past Indian intellectuals, although she remained sceptical of the hagiography that had since been built around their educational contribution.

> [Ram]mohan Roy they tell me took bribes & had a Mahommadan mistress ... of course you will not find any notice of this in Miss Carpenter's [book] *Last Days*.[30]

Like many of her generation in India, Ackroyd's attentions were soon distracted elsewhere. She was well pampered, with a domestic staff of twenty-one servants, but felt bereft because some of her European sisters commanded households of 110.[31] This was high living; diversion for Ackroyd was not the scholarship of the classroom but rather the indulgence of the club, *dansants* and the tennis court. Even with these comforts, she came to consider living in the Calcutta of the 1870s as little more than 'semi-suicide'.[32]

Local engagement with Indian schooling did, however, compel Ackroyd to think anew of Indian social issues. Offended by the racism practised by British women when forced to mix socially with Indians,

Ackroyd's interest in the broader British social scene in India encouraged her to reflect on deeper educational and cultural issues.[33] In later life she worked on translating Indian medieval texts into English. Unlike European female adolescents within English middle-class society, Ackroyd saw India as having no girls who could play and be irresponsible, but only children and married women.[34]

The curriculum in her school was designed to provide her Indian women and girl students with an education that was the same as that for Indian boys, with the idea of equipping them additionally with English etiquette and table manners.[35] The school's biggest problem was that it attempted to cut across Indian caste lines, superimposing a Western notion of middle-class respectability instead. It also had an enrolment that included young women in their early twenties as well as much younger girls. Working to break down caste and the purdah confinement of women to homes in India, Ackroyd claimed her school would teach 'respectability', meaning British middle-class respectability, which she saw as based not on caste, or Indian wealth, or traditional Indian education. Scholarships were offered, but most students paid the very high fee of £20 per annum.[36]

Ackroyd also needed to accommodate the religious requirements and cultural sensitivities of her students, enforced by her school committee, when living away from their homes. She imagined that this was a necessary accommodation of the strict caste requirements in their homes: caste awareness that the British in India more rigidly and artificially categorised from the 1870s onwards.[37] However, the school curriculum, as described by Ackroyd, was just as reflective of a Western accomplishment agenda, with little cultural compromise when attempting to enforce her brand of Western feminine respectability.

In the early morning they [the students] ... sit in sunny corners to say their lessons aloud, and also dry their long black hair. The hair receives much attention in a Hindu's toilet ... At first it is a trial to women who habitually lounge as though they have no back-bones, to have to sit straight and upright. It is a great innovation for Bengali women to use tables and spoons and forks. This last is considered such a great change that no girl is allowed to use a spoon or fork without the written permission of her guardian ... Our girls learn English history, some natural science, and the elements of the laws of health, besides the grammar of their own and our language ... All our girls are taught to darn socks; some darned without fault at the first trial ... Hindu women have clever but ignorant fingers, and, unlike Mahomedan women, do not learn to embroider ... At first there was a great shyness about walking, probably because genuine Bengali dress is quite unfitted for exercise, but soon no opposition was made to the rule of a daily fixed walk in the garden.[38]

While genuinely fond of her 'affectionate' Hindu female students, Ackroyd remained distrustful of most of her Indian staff and kept largely separate from them. However, she was happy to abandon her female Indian students after just one year in the job. She married in 1875 a senior European official, Henry Beveridge, a judge in the ICS, who offered her social and material advancement.[39] This was a pattern similar to many of her generation.[40] While Ackroyd had engaged with India, so, too, had she let go her earlier Unitarian-influenced philanthropy. Her focus became her young family, and she spent much of her time agonising about her separation from them and her visits to their boarding schools in England.[41] Years later, with limited feminist sensibilities, she would go on to oppose women's suffrage in England.[42]

Bethune, 1878–1920

The future of Ackroyd's school had more significance in bringing Indian girls to college education than did Ackroyd's own local experience. This significance warrants deeper discussion in terms of the evolution of the Bethune school located nearby. Ackroyd's problems were mostly concerned with her interventionist school committee and related to Indian religious matters regarding the Indian women and girls in the school. The committee was made up of Brahmo Samaj, intellectuals who were Indian males, as well as the wife of Principal of the Bethune School, Mrs J. B. Phear. This committee was wary of Ackroyd's cultural attitudes to Indian women and, caught up in the politics of the school, her criticism of Keshub Sen's apparent opportunistic betrothal of his young daughter to a 'boy rajah', despite the Brahmo Samaj's stance against child marriage.[43] However, these problems also made Ackroyd partly dependent on Phear on educational matters, and Phear attempted some mediation with the Brahmo Samaj members of Ackroyd's school committee. Conversely, Phear worked hard to assimilate Ackroyd to her work with older Indian girls, but without success. Nonetheless, institutional linkage between Ackroyd's school and the Bethune school, after Ackroyd's departure, eventually meant that Ackroyd's BMV school would become one of the most important colleges for Indian women in late colonial India.

The relatively longstanding Bethune school itself was already the most significant female education institution in Calcutta. The Bethune school was established in 1849 by John Drinkwater Bethune, President of the Governor General's Council of Education. As a secular Hindu school that taught in Bengali, it stood out from the CMS mission girls' school approach that was dominant in Bengal at the time. The distinctiveness was partly because Bethune and others were influenced by the earlier educational thought and limited work in Bengal that pre-dated even Mary Ann Cooke's CMS schools of the 1820s: CMS schools that had strongly influenced later raj policymaking regarding education for females across India in the first half of the nineteenth century. Given his official position in Bengal, Bethune's school also represented state recognition of female education at a time when the Company itself rejected applications for grants-in-aid by Indians to build schools for Indian girls, even when these applications were made by wealthy Indian merchants and *zamindars* (landlords) closely connected to raj commerce.[44]

The different education approach that informed Bethune's female schooling stemmed from David Hare's School Society, and some Baptists, in Calcutta. This approach supported low-caste Indian girls, taught in Bengali, having the same education as boys.[45] With bona fides such as these, a generation later, in the middle of the nineteenth century, high-caste Brahmins and wealthy Indian merchants also began sending their daughters to the Bethune school.[46]

Significantly, these middle-class Indian parents began seeking out a college education for their daughters that was not in the hands of the missions. Responding to the demand, a new generation of Indian women were able to superintend and develop the Bethune legacy well into the twentieth century. After Akroyd's departure, the leaders of the Bethune school began encouraging the daughters of eminent Indian educationalists to attend her BMV school. These students included luminaries such as the daughters of Brahmo Samaj social reformer Durga Mohan Das: Abala Bose (who would later be heavily influential in widows' education and the Brahmo Samaj Girls' High School in Calcutta), and Sarala (who began the Gokhale Memorial Girls' school in 1920, also in Calcutta).[47] With a clientele such as this, by 1878 the BMV school was in a position to merge with the Bethune school to become its college.[48] Run by the 'unaffected' Miss Bose, the school and college attracted many Indian visitors during the coming decades, with at least one recording her impressions in her diary. Bethune's grey stone walls and cement floor offered an austere existence, where most teachers were former students and where, as a concession to different parental backgrounds, the Hindu girls were permitted to dress in either saris or Western frocks.[49]

The Bethune school and college evolved in the context of Brahmo Samaj politics in Bengal, which had already given rise to other schools that Indian girls could attend. However, even its high-calibre enrolment, its long tradition that was attractive to a Hindu intelligentsia, and its boarding house for forty-five girls, were not sufficient to assure Bethune a secure future. Soon after the First World War, its headmistress, a Mrs S. Sindha, worried that the college's teaching, mostly by lecture, encouraged only superficial learning, rather than digging more deeply, particularly into the sciences.[50] There were other fears in the 1920s that its female students lacked sufficient fluency in English as a world language, and a prescient concern about how to ready its girls for the potential communal ramifications of an independent India.[51] However, by 1929, a careful legacy of Indian inter-generational trust that engaged with Indian as well as European scholarship meant that the profile of the Indian parents of Bethune College's female students was not just city-based or engaged with raj commerce or employment. By this time, even Hartog was forced to concede that, of the 486 girls in its secondary school and college, 50 per cent came from the mofussil and 75 per cent were 'orthodox' Hindus.[52]

Outside the raj, 1885–1910

Not all female education initiatives were influenced by initial European intervention such as that of Bethune, Carpenter or even Ackroyd. There were leading Indian intellectuals, most notably Rabindranath Tagore, who appropriated Western epistemologies in his prescriptions for learning, even though he rejected flimsy raj pretensions to be gradually educating the subcontinent.[53]

Several vibrant female schooling movements led by Indians also more seriously undercut the modest efforts of the British. The most remarkable and quickly successful, from 1885 onwards, was the Arya Samaj in north India. This organisation was founded by the Gujarati ascetic Swami Dayananda Saraswati. Like the Brahmo Samaj, its creed focused on Hindu renovation by opposing the caste system and child marriage and advocating a return to the ancient teaching of the *Vedas* (sacred Sanscrit texts) as a means to reform the Hindu polity.[54] A new curriculum was developed under the leadership of Lala Devraj at the Kanya Mahavidyalaya school at Jalandhar, in the Punjab. The curriculum controversially introduced the music and dance of courtesans and low-caste *nautch* (dancing) girls, which extolled a culturally based education that also involved close teacher collaboration with student families. Internal division in Arya Samaj ranks was caused when Devraj felt compelled to teach his schools English, but only so that they could 'function in modern life', travel the world and spread the Arya Samaj message.[55]

The Arya Samaj also outflanked Europeans, especially regarding female schooling. Missionary women, in particular, wrongly took the Arya Samaj's message as aligned to their efforts, only to be later repulsed by the strong anti-British, pro-nationalist stance of its Vedic schools and college.[56] Just how antagonistic the Arya Samaj's early message was to Western female education aspirations in India can be found tucked away in the archives of the Cambridge Brotherhood mission in Delhi. In this depository lies a rare copy of the first issue of the Arya Samaj's journal, the *Arya Patrika*. Its logic was counterintuitive to anything the British prescribed for Indian schoolgirls. Rather than cramming girls into urban-based schools and subjecting them to Western medicines that 'aggravate evil', the journal prescribed that they should be educated benefitting from the 'change of air' in their 'native' towns to rebuild their 'shattered constitutions'. Furthermore, the agency of the Indian schoolgirl was to be empowered. Testimonials by female students were proffered, such as that of Bhagwan Devi, in the fifth grade of the Arya Samaj's Ferozpore school, who extolled the advantages of her education. The moral character of females was better projected from Indian Vedic principles because the more modern Koran and the Bible were 'littered with miracles and minor heroes' that were against the truths of science that came first from the East. Such falsely based metaphysics, the Arya Samaj claimed, was responsible for Europe's regrettable drift into atheism.[57]

This clever contradiction of the usual colonial educational mentality for female education at the end of the nineteenth century brought the Indian schoolgirl to the edge of the Indian nationalist agenda. In less abrasive terms, girls' schools were set up in the name of Sen's Brahmo Samaj in Bengal, possibly numbering as many as 2,238 by 1890.[58] There was also G. K. Gokhale's Servants of India Society in Poona, the Theosophical Society's national network and, later, Muslim girls' schools supported by the work of Amina Tyabji and Begum Abdullah at Aligarh.[59] These schools all fed in different ways into a vision of female education that was Indian predicated and was not only about Western imposition. Only Hartog and his fellow administrators in 1929 had a different view. They still officially conflated the 'volunteer efforts' of these Indian-led organisations as part of just one modernising education project under the control of the British.[60]

Fragmenting Western feminism, 1910–29

In fact, nationalist spiritual awakening of this kind aligned to little that Western feminism had to offer. By the end of the 1920s the mediation of some Indian women could also play into apologist British hands. For example, in 1928, Dr Muthulakshmi Reddy compiled a survey of Indian secondary girls' schools as part of Hartog's education information gathering of that year. These schools were rarities, with only two or three in each province. Even though Reddy had worked in Madras against child prostitution and brothels, and viewed herself in terms of strict equality to men, her agenda of social uplift for Indian women cut across the feminist critique. Reddy acknowledged accomplishments curriculums at schools such as the Balika Vidyalaya Girls' High School at Cawnpore, and others such as the Sakhawat Memorial Girls' School in Bengal, as empowering widows and decrying purdah.

However, the female pathway to university was mostly covered over by Reddy's stronger philanthropic agenda. Only brief mention was made by her of these schools in terms of preparing bright girls for college, university and professional careers. Furthermore, schools such as the Theosophical School and College at Benares, and the Montessori school in Allahabad, were noteworthy to the official colonial mind only in terms of saving girls from child marriage. Even the Bethune school was problematised by Hartog's deliberations when writing his report in the late 1920s. He described its crammed conditions as offering new threats to student hygiene, rather than as being indicative of a strong demand by Indian women for university education of the kind now available to some Indian men.[61]

The national movement's social service agenda for Indian females was convenient to a raj that remained unwilling to spend money on girls' secondary education in a similar manner to that beginning to occur in Britain and other parts of the empire. The emergence of the social service agenda among the very few females in India in a position to influence state policymaking also meant that the chief custodians of Western feminism were those who mostly only visited India. In the mid-1890s, Josephine Butler sponsored Elizabeth Andrew and Kate Bushnell's travel to India to expose to the British public the consequences of lock hospitals for women of the Contagious Diseases Acts there.[62] In 1910, Agnes de Selincourt, promoter of the Missionary Settlement for University Women in Bombay, worked through UK women's university networks to give leading women missionaries more say in the decision making of missionary societies throughout the empire.[63] There were also the travel diaries of European feminists, some of which were published in Europe. Most notable in this category were those of Fabian socialists Sidney and Beatrice Webb who, significantly, did not mention female education specifically, but nation building through 'new Hinduism' instead, in their account of their one-hour meeting with Annie Besant at Benares and a visit to her Theosophy Hindu Central College for boys in 1912.[64]

In this frame there were also British women who came to India to teach. They originally self-identified with the feminist landscape 'at home' in England, but lost this Western politicisation once they were established in India. As with Carpenter's European women agents, the motivation for their journeying to the raj was quickly swamped by the keener imperatives that they met in India.

The best example of such women is Miss F. M. Wyld, a graduate of St Hugh's College Oxford and an 'active suffragette' while employed at St Paul's School in London. She was attracted to India by the fabulously rich Nizam of Hyderabad to become the second headmistress of the 'high-caste' Mahbubia school in his princely state. Wyld openly admitted that she needed the higher salary on offer in India because, in 1909, the live-out annual salary of £80 available to her in England was not enough to allow her to live a life independent of her father. Yet, in Hyderabad, she found herself working with the purdah Khujista Sultana Begum, a former member of the Mughal former royal family of Delhi. The Begum was a strong supporter of Western education for elite girls in India, and Wyld was able to draw on this patronage for ten years before taking up another position in South Africa. However, in this arduous work there was little scope for communication with other European women in India, even if there had been a feminist conversation on offer.[65]

There were other examples too. Given the rather barren context of activism in India in support of Indian schooling for girls, Besant was forced to look abroad, recruiting Leonora G'meiner from Australia, who came to Delhi in 1904 as the first headmistress of the Indraprastha Hindu Girls' Secondary School in Delhi. Under G'meiner's influence, and against the Western class strictures of accomplishments, the school was, in 1924, the first in Delhi to provide its girls with science classes with their own laboratory and to provide non-formal education for local married women.[66]

Generally, even in the 1930s, feminist writers and activists rarely held colonial teaching positions in India. The 5,000 Indian and European lives covered in the 1937–8 Indian *Who's Who* reveal very few exceptions, the two most notable being: Mrs Keron Bose, who was a delegate of the National Council of Women in India to the Stockholm conference of 1933; and Kamala Bose, who also worked in education circles in India and who attended the World Conference on Education in Locarno in 1927.[67]

Connections by Indian women back to radical feminists in England were even more unlikely. Relationships between feminist women in Europe based on 'affectionate celibacy' – whether sexually consummated or not – were an alien landscape for Indian intellectuals of the early twentieth century. The works of radical feminists on female sexuality, such as Marie Stopes' women's sex manual *Married Love* (1918), or even Josephine Butler's views of the sexual oppression of women a generation earlier, were usually seen as just as culturally taboo.[68]

In the same period, and responding to the different Indian female domain, English feminist Eleanor Rathbone argued that it was European, rather than Indian, women who were best placed to represent the political rights of Indian women.[69] Furthermore, those relatively few Indians living in India who did take up a discernable Western feminist cause were often oriented to do this through earlier enculturation as Christian converts. Such was the case for Krupabai Satthianadhan (1862–94), who was the first Indian women to study medicine at Madras University. A Christian convert, and a strong advocate of education for Indian women, her writing advocated an intellectual and independent life for Indian women away from the driving ambitions of marriage, home life, 'dressing' and 'looking pretty'.[70] In 1879, Samuel Vedanayagam Pillai, partly Western educated and a Christian convert in Madras, published *Prathapa Mudaliar Charithram* (Life of Prathapa Mudaliar). This was the first novel, published in Tamil, where the heroine was of equal standing and intelligence to the hero in a traditional Indian setting.[71] Furthermore, in India, European and Eurasian schoolmistresses generally did not take up official positions outside their schools to promote a discernable female 'cause', in the way that Dorothea Beale and Frances Buss did in England as members of the Kensington Ladies Discussion Society, or as Emmeline Pankhurst did as a member of the Manchester School Board.[72]

Christian complicity, 1880–1910

By the turn of the century, while there was little chance of an applied Western feminism within Indian secondary schools for girls, Indian women who had converted to Christianity proved more influential in directing female futures. Converts who were Indian women could be complicit in reinforcing colonial race and class constituencies through their own subservience. In 1900, Eva Dutta (sister of Surendra Dutta, professor of Medicine at Edinburgh University and later president of the Indian Young Men's Christian Association – YMCA) was eager for employment as a teacher at her alma mater, the Alexandra School in Lahore, to escape the privations of a mission middle school in Gujarat (western India). Dutta cheerfully described the purdah parties of the students at the Alexandra school, the peccadillos of its Eurasian staff and the European women who 'much change in their friendship networks as institutional arrangements in proximate female schools change'. Yet these cultural, racial and social arrangements – from all of which she saw herself as separate as an Indian – did not seem to destroy her faith in the school itself, even when she was repeatedly refused a staff appointment there on the grounds of her race.[73]

Other Indian women who were Christians had a different outlook and were able to achieve greater professional success in the raj in the later nineteenth century. Like Gandhi and Rabindranath Tagore in the early twentieth century, some of these Indian women sought to build what they saw as a universal, largely gender-neutral, classroom, independent of the constraints of empire. Manorama Bose was one example. Her father was a medical officer at Lahore who had converted to Christianity under the influence of the American mission at Ludhiana. His financial means meant that he could send his daughter to London to train as a teacher – a very rare circumstance at the time.

Manorama Bose's intellect and her forceful personality allowed her to return to Lahore to tap into the city's mostly male intelligentsia: animated at this time by John Lockwood's (father of Rudyard) 'Magic Lantern Lectures' on topics ranging from science to history.[74] Not only was Bose able to enter this male preserve in this way – both European and Indian – she eventually became headmistress of Victoria School in Lahore (in the Punjab) with its exquisite, and still extant, Sikh *haveli* (private mansion).[75] After the 1880s, the Punjab was reliant on the benefaction of ancient Indian families to fund key educational institutions such as the Punjab University, which honoured these families by conferring local language degrees as an alternative to English.[76] Taking advantage of this context of Indian patronage, Manorama Bose and her allies were able to separate out a secondary female school learning space, this time away from the strictures of the European Code.[77]

The macro colonial view and the Parsis, 1882–1917

At the same time, an entirely different reality was created at the centre, where British administrative surveillance was focused. This surveillance was based on statistics gathering and cultural stereotypes, with little connection to local Indian needs. In the 1880s, well before those developments in the early twentieth century mentioned earlier in this chapter, influential administrators such as Sir Alfred Croft, DPI for Bengal, saw little potential in teacher training for Indian women. For him, Indian women teachers were usually married, widows or 'un-trustworthy' non-converts, none of whom seemed likely, when it came down to it, to fit the bill regarding the new model accomplishments *maitresse*.[78]

The chair of the 1882 Hunter Education Commission, Sir William Hunter, also began to reveal Western quantifiable failure. Rather than using grossly inflated departmental figures for each province regarding female education, Hunter relied on the more modest estimates of dependable provincial commentators. For example, Bombay was considered the most advanced presidency in the raj on the question of education for Indian females by this time. Concentrating on this Indian Presidency, Hunter drew on the statistics of the eminent Parsi educator and intellectual Dadabhai Naoroji. Naoroji estimated that the number of Indian girls under some form of government or mission instruction in Bombay was only 75,443, but with less than 1 per cent of these girls in so-called high schools. So poor was the official data on unfunded indigenous girls' schools that Naoroji was forced to guess at 24,557 to make up a total enrolment of 100,000 girls, or one in fourteen of school-age primary girls.[79]

It was in the North Western Provinces where Henry Reid's *halka-bandi* village schooling experiments had included Indian girls in the 1850s. However, thirty years later, in this province, the cupboard was essentially bare. Here Mrs Etherington, inspectress of government schools for the NWP, had been dismissed in 1878 to save money as the province retreated from its earlier promising work. With a good institutional memory of Reid's former schooling experiments, she understood the convenience of the raj mantra that Indian females now 'did not seek education'. She argued with some force that a demand for education first required an understanding of its utility and the example of others. For her the time had arrived, in 1882, for the government to simply invest more money and stop hiding behind bureaucratic obfuscation.[80] Her powerful arguments impressed Hunter. Yet the following exchange gives a flavour of the language of failure that he confronted.

> **Hunter**: Then ... the true obstacle to the extension of female education ... is simply and solely due to the fact that Government gives no help whatever to it, and has withdrawn even the little aid which it once gave?
> **Etherington**: The sole obstacle is want of funds.
> **Hunter**: Is ... there now not a single Government Normal school for female teachers in the North-Western Provinces ...?
> **Etherington**: There is not a single one.[81]

In some senses the NWP was a distinct case, because it was embroiled by this time in a fierce communal debate over whether Urdu, as the medium of instruction, ought to be written in the Persian form (acceptable to Muslims) or in the *Devanagari* (Hindu/Sanskrit alphabet and script, more palatable to Hindus).[82] The NWP also lacked a significant colonial presidency city and a large Eurasian population, both of which were usually prerequisites for even modest government efforts concerning the education of females. However, Etherington's evidence was typical of many other women educators who were keen to expose deliberate government regulatory barriers, and to act as iconoclasts regarding the monotonous raj female education mantra of the late nineteenth century.

At the time of the Hunter Commission, the most revealing evidence in terms of British intransigence in actually implementing education initiatives for Indian females also came from Bombay. Unlike the NWP, this province had managed to keep some of its earlier culturally sympathetic enterprises that concerned colonial female education, which had begun as early as the 1810s. However, intersecting across the local Bombay scene was another critical local factor. This factor was the strong influence of the Parsi community – immigrants from Persia in the eighth century and later generally Anglophile traders with Europe, China and South East Asia – who were traditional supporters of academic female education.

A Parsi Girls' School Association emerged in July 1857 as the Great Revolt raged mostly in the north. The Association owed its formation to earlier societal work where students and ex-students of the Elphinstone College established and taught pro bono each morning in experimental schools for girls. By the time the Parsi Girl's School Association gave its evidence to the Hunter Commission, this eleemosynary instruction had been replaced by that carried out by paid teachers, supported by local Parsi merchants, modest school fees and donations from a strongly supportive Parsi community. These well-run schools were mostly independent of the British, but their identity mimicked much of their colonial-sponsored, school counterparts. They employed their own inspectress and seventeen Parsi female teachers, who were identified as 'respectable'. The schools taught a stronger academic fare than in most girls' schools in India. However, the usual accomplishments with sufficient Western sophistication were also imparted, including 'Berlin wool and net work, embroidery, plain sewing and knitting': an impeccable curriculum by any official colonial standards.[83]

However, these Parsi female schools had one serious flaw. Female ethics and morality were taught from Zoroastrian principles that embraced Islam, Christianity and Judaism. For the British, the canon of the professional teacher who was female and a moral guide was not negotiable, even when such ethics and morality was drawn from a conflation of faith traditions that went beyond simpler Christian ecumenism.[84] Without official support, the Parsi education community remained a detached enterprise, at least from British governance considerations. Yet the power of strong Parsi, community-based education was later reflected in the enrolments of girls in Maharashtra. In 1919 school enrolments of girls as a percentage of the female school-age population stood at: Parsis 14.6 per cent; Europeans and Eurasians 23 per cent; Indian converts 8.3 per cent; Muslim girls a mere 1.1 per cent; and Hindu girls just 0.9 per cent.[85]

Little was to change in the rigid macro view of the colonial state in the following generation. In 1916, Austen Chamberlain, Secretary of State for India, once again set up an inquiry into the education of Indian females. Nearly all the responses by European women in India to this inquiry merely repeated complaints about lack of money and the need for cultural accommodation with India that had been heard at Hunter thirty years earlier.[86] The struggle for at least some professional colonial women in India to find an official professional language in India, whether feminist derived or not, was to continue.

The thirteen-volume Calcutta University Commission of 1917 serves as another case in point of how little could really change regarding the British official mindset, even after the First World War. The Commission supported the same Western academic standards for women as for men at university level, but an important caveat remained. For women teachers and women doctors, special emphasis ought to be placed on feminine subjects that 'need not be so important to men'.[87]

Homely modesty and Montessori in the early twentieth century

It is tempting to see European women educators and medical carers, when resisting raj reportage and procedure, as displaying a femininity, or even a feminism, better able to connect with what these women found in the local school and in the local hospital. However, when looking to their own personal bodies and professional identity, their separate European mentalities continued to project rigid, yet contradictory, European signifiers as to their professional and class status in India.

As in England, college-educated women who sought out prized government jobs as inspectresses or headmistresses of Code schools took the moniker 'Miss', were unmarried, and remained so as a sign of their professionalism and their vocation. This designation also signified their aspiration to the middle-class. A less 'refined' teacher with a non-ecclesiastical, working-class background was usually given the title 'Mrs', whether married or not. Such teachers were employed in very lowly positions, such as minor junior schools for poor children or as non-commissioned officers in army schools, where they were encouraged to marry and to stay on after their marriage.

Furthermore, with the possible exception of Elizabeth Brander, those in elite government employment also took the Indian schoolgirl back into the Indian household, rather than attempting to teach her about new social freedoms and human rights even in the Indian context. In the Punjab, in 1906, Inspectress Miss Fanny Ann Francis urged the teaching of domestic weaving and industrial craft to low-caste Indian girls, even if they had converted.[88] While inspectresses in Bengal also saw only household futures for Indian girls. They crafted new schooling subjects accordingly:

> I was particularly struck with the gap existing at the present between the education of the schoolgirl today and the young housemother of tomorrow ... We must build the bridge by which the young mother can pass from one to the other with benefit to her own self and all dependent upon her care, for comfort and for wise rearing, and that bridge is Homecraft.[89]

Homecraft in this sense might be seen as a similar conception to the Arya Samaj's *pati seva* (service to the husband), or consistent with Radharani Lahiri's (Convenor of the Brahmo Samaj's Women's Association) view in 1875 that whatever an Indian woman or girl may learn she could not claim any reputation unless she was proficient in housework.[90] Yet this similarity was only a convenient and superficial agreement with nationalist sentiments and Gandhi's later 'better mothers' call. In reality, the raj had very few jobs in the professions to offer a rising generation of Indian girls, even if they wanted them.

Another intervention, a generation later after the First World War, was that of the Italian physician Maria Montessori. The reception of her method in India reflected a complex education scene that had developed as a result of the advocacy of female education and the manner in which this advocacy related to the rising national movement. The Montessori method emphasised freedom of child action and education that was adapted to their natural social, physical and psychological development.[91] However, unlike most other colonial attempts at education, Indian leaders were divided as to the applicability of this new approach to the subcontinent.

Gandhi was dismissive of the method as having 'a great deal of tinsel about it' and, in the 1930s, his opposition hardened given that the Montessori method was relatively expensive, foreign and not a purely home-grown national system of education.[92] Other nationalists, however, supported it, even though Froebel's kindergarten movement in India was more circumspect.[93] Rabindranath Tagore saw the method as closely aligned to his philosophy of spiritual learning, even though his emphasis was the aesthetic and cultural development of the child, rather than Montessori's focus on intellectual development.[94] Parsi communities in Bombay set up a Montessori school in 1925. The Theosophists were Montessori's strongest advocates, seeing this education method as strongly chiming with ancient Hindu traditions of sensory motor development in the learning of the child.[95]

'Outward-bound' configurations, 1910–22

Greater changes were afoot well beyond this, by now overly visited but conceptually intractable, colonial teaching space. The end of the First World War brought changes in world outlook for the one million Indians who had served, including 130,000 on the Western Front. Just before the war, official education policy was still identifying the barriers to the education of females as being India's need for 'social development', while also advocating a different, non-academic, education for girls compared to boys that focused on hygiene awareness and 'practical' education ready for their future 'social life'.[96] However, the Indianisation of educational administration in 1919, as part of the Montague-Chelmsford reforms that partly decentralised British governance in favour of some elected Indians, took the raj largely out of the women's education story.[97]

By the 1920s, there were other new realities to be faced too. Racial slippage began to occur across the European Code barrier. In the five years between 1921 and 1926, limited India provincial self-government in education matters resulted in a 111.9 per cent increase in Indian girls studying in European/Eurasian schools, while the number of Europeans and Eurasians studying in Indian schools increased by 62.9 per cent.[98] These increases came off a low base, but rapid change in schooling demographics of this kind also changed the educational landscape for a Western teaching profession. Additionally, international linkages other than with Britain, particularly with the USA and Japan, also began to import new cross-institutional, global movements concerning schoolgirls.

For example, many European women educators in India noted approvingly the Girl Guide movement that cut across the race boundaries still endemic in girls' schools in particular. Founded in 1911, the guiding movement had over fifty companies in India by 1915 and an All India Girl Guides Association was formed in 1916. Louise Ouwerkerk, teaching in southern India, noted how Indian Boy Scouts adapted the Baden-Powell credo by using their turbans to build tents over rickety wooden frames: six turbans per eight-boy tent.[99] To Ouwerkerk, the Girl Guides offered even greater Western articulation to social service and provided better training of Indian girls in domestic duties – although she was concerned that the organisation was not overtly Christian enough.[100]

In Britain, too, by the First World War there was a rapid redefining of femininity in terms of women's physical empowerment. Vigorous physical exercise by females had earlier been viewed, mostly by males, as a threat to the gender and respectability of their sisters and daughters. In the 1920s it became viewed as an activity that actually liberated the female body.[101] In India, female physical exercise could even produce colonially acceptable non-racial mothers by this time. That is, advocates hoped that these new forms of physical exercise, when taken up by Indian girls, would also lead them to relinquish at least some of their cultural practices in favour of a new pan-empire, cross-racial mentality that understood the superiority of the British. Games for girls, including calisthenics in modest dress, were seen by Ouwerkerk as a 'real levelling force where the Hindu Muslim question is overcome'.[102]

Girl Guiding in India offered other seeming Western entrees into Indian society, although Indian receptivity to these movements was more complex than the British supposed. For example, Carey Watt's *Serving the Nation* illustrates how Indian notions of social service in north India actually had much more to them, in a cultural and philosophical sense, than mere imitation of Western innovation. His work shows that, between the 1890s and 1920, almost every Indian society of self-help and every social uplift organisation had a social service *sabha* (society) attached to it. This social orienting in north India also influenced the action of Indian Girl Guide troops.[103]

Furthermore, a generation earlier, a more profound cross-institutional engagement occurred with the Young Women's Christian Association (YWCA) in India. The entry of this organisation into India was facilitated by the earlier failure of other European women, who had merely promoted unnegotiated educational fare. In the 1890s, a broadly based network of women graduates in Britain hoped to transplant a wholly British-specified women's college directly to Bombay. To this end, Agnes de Selincourt of the Missionary Settlement for University Women in Bombay (referred to earlier in this chapter) delegated Marion and Ellen Storres to India to begin the arrangements. Despite the backing of powerful patrons in Oxford and Cambridge, who envisaged a direct extension of the opportunities of British university education to the women of India, these sisters were ultimately blocked in their efforts in India by what they saw as a monopoly of Parsis and Catholics in Bombay and Poona. There was also opposition from Miss Bose, then principal of Bethune College in Calcutta.[104]

Despite having Christianity at their back, and the promise of good funding from the Missionary Settlement's British patronage networks of women graduates throughout Britain, it was clear that there was little room for the mere transplantation of Oxbridge to India, at least for women. In the end, the Missionary Settlement had to limit itself to building a hostel for women instead. Later in the year, this hostel was affiliated to the rapidly expanding international organisation for women and girls, the YWCA, whose first Indian branch had been set up in Bombay in 1875. By 1910, the YWCA saw itself as providing residential accommodation for those women attending non-residential schools and colleges throughout India. Its dormitories were still racially segregated and there was considerable Christian moral training to be endured; however, at least Indian girls could attend more secondary schools without fearing moral danger, particularly as Code school barriers began to melt away.[105]

New widow scholars, 1889–1920

Other forms of female activism regarding Indian women changed the Western and Indian conceptions of Indian 'widowhood'. Ethnographic studies of young Hindu widows were illustrative and evocative, but also demonstrative of the compromises that even 'reform' might bring. In Bombay, in 1911, the story was of at least one widow with a shaved head for every family after famine, where a father dare not even accept sandalwood paste and arranged flowers for the worship of idols from his widowed daughter who was traditionally isolated because of her widowhood.[106] High-caste widows fared worse in some of the households where there were abusive fathers-in-law. However, the self-limiting prescription from those women seeking reform regarding these Indian widows' education was for only nursing, and not a college education.[107]

In 1889, Pandita Ramabai had already set up her *Sharada Sadan* (home for learning), a secular residential school for high-caste widows in Bombay that moved to Poona in the following year. A generation later, another significant widows' enterprise, founded in 1912, was the Brahmin Widows' Hostel in Madras, which offered other socially transformative possibilities. Within this hostel there were different limitations and freedoms to those that existed outside it. Most notably, these young widows were not bound by the traditional restrictions of purdah and could therefore walk to school. Their school, known locally as the 'Icehouse', was near fishing communities on the coast and the local crematorium. It was shunned by the local Telugu people, who believed it to be haunted and responsible for the encroachment of the sea. However, by 1920, the hostel was successful in encouraging its orthodox Hindu students to stay at school until the eighth grade and then to train as elementary schoolteachers. The founder of the hostel was Sister R. S. Subbalakshmi, a member of Cousins' Women's Indian Association. She believed that the effect of the work of her hostel was profound enough to raise the average early marriage age to sixteen in the surrounding community a decade later.[108]

The most significant female education enterprise to come out of efforts to renovate Hindu widowhood was when Dhondo Keshav Karve, a mathematics graduate of Elphinstone College who was strongly influenced by Pandita Ramabai, established an ashram for widows near Poona. Karve's initiative was viewed by Indian nationalists as a 'Hindu alternative' to Pandita Ramabai's Sharada Sadan, which was alleged to have engaged in Christian proselytisation and which was boycotted as a result in the mid-1890s. In 1914, Karve's ashram in Bombay developed into a school and then a college of thirty widows. As a concession to what might reasonably be on offer to these girls upon graduation, it melded academic subjects with nursing and a smattering of accomplishments. To this end, the curriculum combined English, a local language, history, physiology, psychology and hygiene, along with domestic economy. The institution was to become the SNDT Women's University that today has an enrolment of some 70,000 students.[109]

New citizenship, 1923–32

As talk of an emerging sense of Indian independence began to permeate European-led education communities in the later 1920s, senior schoolgirl educators found a sharper edge to their teaching that concerned politics and citizenship as a hallmark of modernity. This teaching was not always productive for Indian women. The dynamic created by the discussion of India citizenship could assert artificial Western-predicated ethnic spaces, while also identifying supposedly inadequate or deficient Indian citizens who included women.[110] There was also an ongoing debate in Britain by this time as to whether citizenship throughout its empire was an extension of a one nation state or whether it was defined differently within a collection of separate and distinct communities.[111] Colonial women teachers in the first three decades of the twentieth century also imported Western forms of citizenship that were mostly about conventional politico-state formation processes, in which educated Indian women might also supposedly participate.

There are good examples of the views colonial women educators took in the 1920s and 1930s as to how their Indian female students should learn such Westernised citizenship values. Louise Ouwerkerk viewed her female students as wilfully unable to think for themselves or to learn anything that was not taught by rote. For her, it was not gender that was the burning issue, but politics. More generally, Ouwerkerk viewed the subcontinent as 'simply not fit for home

rule', although she also saw Western universities in India as 'nurs-
eries of Western Imperialism and exploitation'. She was a supporter
of British Prime Minister Ramsay MacDonald and taught his brand
of pacifist internationalism that included greater self-government
for India.[112] Her approach was to teach political science after hours,
away from the scrutiny of her colleagues, working at ways of 'applying Western methods' in culturally sensitive terms to teach notions
of Indian citizenship to her college girls.[113] This pathway took
Ouwerkerk into contentious political ground, because technically
Indians could not be citizens while still under British rule, particularly not the brand of citizenship the national movement had been
proffering since the 1910s.[114]

Also in the early decades of the twentieth century, in the city of
Madras, the senior European staff of the Women's College were led
by Miss Eleanor McDougall (a graduate from Edinburgh University
in English Literature and History). For over twenty-three years, she
developed a college degree course, including teacher training after
a solid secondary education.[115] This institution was an imaginative
inter-denominational venture involving missions from Scotland,
England, North America and Canada that recruited and funded
women teachers mostly with tertiary qualifications from Britain, the
USA and within India itself. By 1932, the failing imperial mission
was in view and missionaries such as C. F. Andrews, and American
journalists, were sympathetically interpreting, for American audiences, the significance of Gandhi's recent Salt March.[116] Responding
to this publicity, the American sponsors of the college questioned
McDougall's wish to teach academic subjects using British topics
only. Mindful of the developing national movement, one American
patron cautioned:

> I write this in no imperial sense, and I am quite sure that Miss McDougall
> has no such thought in her mind. It does appear vital, however, to the
> best development of India, that there should be as close an understanding
> as possible between those to whom the destinies of that country have
> been entrusted and the people of the country itself. I think it would seem
> to the people in the Philippines [if] a suggestion in a similar sense were
> made from the American side.[117]

McDougall's institution was unusual in that Indian girls were initially given preference, with modest residential arrangements designed
to deter wealthier Europeans. There was also a personal female citizenship to be played out at this college. Students were compelled to
change meal tables weekly, to share student companions, and a student committee was established and chaired by a senior student to

ensure that there was mingling between girls of different communities and languages. The working day began at 6 a.m., with a *neend* (slumber) at midday. Again as a means to connect with the surrounding community, Friday was 'social work day', where the girls went into the surrounding poor districts to distribute gifts: a form of social progress through individual growth that Gandhi might have been willing to recognise.[118]

McDougall was a popular and capable teacher who eventually found herself on the Madras University Senate. Her strategy was to employ younger European teachers who were flexible in adapting to India, even if they had not yet attained the academic qualifications of other applicants. One junior teacher saw McDougall as being homely in appearance despite her academic reputation, her 'gait halting' and with a blend of sadness, humour and tenderness in her smile.[119] She was also sufficiently confident to allow her diverse staff to speak freely on academic matters. As Margaret Hunt, a professor in the college at the age of twenty-four because of her European MA, recalled in the early 1930s:

> I cannot remember talking politics at our senior table but [I] had more conversations with my younger Indian colleagues and have shared their devotion to Gandhi and their concern about his imprisonment.[120]

Global feminine spaces, 1900–32

Within India, and by the early twentieth century, important Indian feminists such as Sarala Devi Chaudhurani and Rokeya Sakhawat Hossain, who were strongly involved in the Bengal Indian national movement, were advocating a non-British education for Indian women and girls.[121] However, other more affluent Indian women, through their travels abroad, began to see their own cultural space in world view. Atiya Fyzee, an Indian Muslim from Bombay who travelled to Edwardian Britain, left behind a lively travel diary published in Urdu of the cultural travelling required of her, as a woman, during this journey.[122] Parsi families in Maharashtra also produced powerful women advocates of female education, whose activism was still mostly internal to empire and borne partly out of relatively long family commercial collaborations with raj trade and commerce. These women were vested with the self-confidence to reach out to international Western education communities, partly because their forebears had learnt in commerce to understand a global scene that went beyond India. Furthermore, their activism often cut across the usual East/West binaries that defined women engaged in some way with the raj and as a result, by the 1920s, this orientation established more nuanced philosophies regarding female education.

Most notably in this category was Cornelia Sorabji (1866–1954), fifth daughter in a Parsi Christian family at Poona. The first woman graduate of Bombay University, she used her degree to eventually gain admittance, on scholarship, to Somerville College, Oxford to read law. This came after she had spent time teaching English literature at Gujarat College at Ahmedabad. While in England, she met luminaries such as Gladstone, Asquith, Balfour and Nightingale and she was presented to Queen Victoria. Sorabji showed little sympathy for the Indian Nationalist movement and was one of Gandhi's sternest critics. However, she returned to India to work for twenty years melding legal and education work with Indian *purdahnasheen* (behind the curtain) women with her brand of social service work, infant welfare and district nursing.[123] For Sorabji, the Indian girl was best taught in single-sex schools and, despite her own conversion and Parsi heritage, she advocated only Hindu Vedic ethics as their religious fare.[124]

In the early 1930s, Cornelia's Sorabji's Sister, Susie Sorabji (1868–1931), was also able to build networks out to international organisations and benefactors, even though many of these networks really failed to engage fully with the issues that faced the education of Indian women and girls in India. These committees ranged from the National Missionary Association, the Women's Temperance Movement and even the Indian chapter of the Canadian Daughters of the Empire.[125] Her membership of these organisations reflected her deeply held Christian beliefs, and explained her later alliance with the CMS in Bombay. Loyal to the empire, Susie Sorabji was wise enough to build an international profile for what she regarded as her non-racially predicated education work in India. Like her sister, she achieved the building of this profile through international charity networks and she travelled to the USA three times to raise funds for her girls' high school, St Helena's at Poona. Susie Sorabji was able to establish networks of benefactor friends in both the USA and in Canada, and her visits also included direct personal representations to President Teddy Roosevelt in 1906 and John D. Rockefeller – the latter enamoured by her 'Indianess'.[126]

The Sorabjis were an exceptional case. More typically, other influential women, without such a relatively privileged background, followed the course of Ramabai Ranade, who belonged to the previous generation. Ranade's early voice concerning the ethics of Indian women's issues was partly positioned by her academic and social-reformer husband, Mahadev, whom she married at just eleven years of age and whose teaching helped her to escape illiteracy as she became proficient in both Marathi and in English.[127] In 1908, Ranade founded the Poona branch of the *Seva Sadan* (Home of Service) that developed into what Margaret Cousins later viewed as 'the finest education institution in India for married women' with a daily attendance of 900 by the early 1920s.[128] Closely supervising the *Seva Sedan*, Ranade worked on social service initiatives to help widows and women in jail, while advocating Indian women's social awakening through compulsory elementary education for girls and legal rights equal to men.

There was also Pandita Ramabai (1858–1922), referred to in the preceding chapter, and founder of the *Arya Mahila Samaj* (Noble Women's Society) in Maharashtra. Her work was perhaps the most influential in inspiring similar ventures in this part of India, even more so than that of Ramabai Ranade. Although more sympathetic to the national movement in India than the Sorabjis, Pandita Ramabai's agenda was in many ways a precursor to their work. A key influence was her Christian conversion and employment at Dorothea Beale's Cheltenham College in England in 1883.[129] She shared, along with Josephine Butler and other like Western women, a perspective of Christian teachings that saw these teachings as social doctrine and the embodiment of social equality.[130] As a result, and through the Arya Mahila Samaj, Ramabai built networks of Indian women, who were mostly the wives of Indian officials, to offer urgent women's relief work in times of famine or plague.

These actions were not merely about the placement of 'charitable works'. They also had important political, socio-cultural and educational implications for Indian women. Unlike the Sorabjis, both Ramabai Ranades and Pandita Ramabai's intimacy and affinity with India's poor gave them greater access to an evolving and broader tapestry of Indian social service and philanthropic organisations. These organisations could be critical of India and Indians, as well as of the seemingly perennial inaction of the colonial state. However, their prescriptions for action and modernity to alleviate suffering could also cause educated Indians to internalise a belief in a superior Europe and to relegate a less developed Asia and Africa.[131]

Margaret Cousins, 1927–32

Margaret Cousins (1878–1954), operating as part of the next generation of activist women in India, also presents a complex colonial predication in her prescription for the betterment of Indian women. Writing in 1922, Cousins' thoughts on the education of women and girls followed on from the agenda of Gopal Krishna Gokhale and others who had failed to convince the British to introduce compulsory elementary education in India in 1911.

At one level, Cousins lauded the Women's Charter of Freedom of Opportunity that had been passed by the first Women's India Association in 1917, that she had convened with Dorothy Graham Jinarajadassa. Cousins saw the charter as being ahead of the West in seeing gender as no barrier to any woman 'entering any position or profession for which she shows herself capable'.[132] However, her deconstruction of the ideal was qualified by what she saw as the Indian female condition. Furthermore, strong concessions to nationalist sentiment regarding women took her away from arguing a purely feminist case. For Cousins, the want of female education denied the Indian nation of being able to better deploy the 'natural' feminine attributes of 'imagination and sensitive emotion' that were embodied in its child bearers. The view chimed with the nationalist spiritual image of the Indian woman as 'goddess' or 'mother' and that erased her sexuality in the world outside the home.[133] However, Cousins also used a simpler rationale that only really employed a European perspective. She saw the need of Indian women to escape from the zenana, given its 'lack of fresh air and sunlight' and the need for physical exercise as the best means of invigorating the female intellect. If not a eugenics predication, this view strongly borrowed from the calisthenics movement abroad, as well as concerns now often voiced about Indian, especially Hindu, racial weakness and decline.[134]

There was nothing particularly unusual in appropriating Western thought and applying it to India's educational future in this way. In fact, in the early twentieth century, India, along with Japan, was a fulcrum for thought on adolescent health and fitness. For nationalists such as Gokhale, and Punjab education reformer Lajpat Rai, British education was a means to address the problems of colonial oppression. Rai, like many of his nationalist contemporaries, was influenced by Social Darwinism to address what they feared was Hindu racial degeneration,[135] even though, from the British point of view, controversies over eugenic thought were much more active in other parts of its empire, particularly in African colonies such as Kenya.[136] Women graduates of Bethune College were no different in appropriating the ideas of the West with relative ease. For example, Shrimati Abala Bose (née Das as referred to earlier in this chapter), saw women as foremost 'with a mind' the equal of men. She was one of the chief introducers of Montessori from Europe into India, although she also presided over a patriotic nationalist household, including Gandhi's, non-cooperation homespun garments, Dacca saris and Indian art.[137]

New feminism?

The negotiation of feminism in colonial educational circles was much more problematic, largely because feminist international narratives, imposed from outside, could not easily accommodate the strong traditional cultural domains of the subcontinent, tended to as they were by different cultural groupings of influential Indian men and women. These cultural domains and constituencies mostly did not acknowledge Western feminist narratives as 'progress' or as a modernity worthy of signing up to, even as Indian nationalism entered its most radical stage after 1927.

Cousins' feminism, in fact, objectified Indian women through simplistic constructions that filtered what she categorised as regional cultural settings, holding them back from joining a world sisterhood. Those women who had escaped this oppression were, as she saw it, of particular interest. They included Sarojini Naidu, a follower of Gokhale, who impressed Cousins because she was 'concerned with the feminist problems of the East'. Significantly, this was Cousin's view and not that of Naidu herself. Cousins' evidence as to Naidu's 'feminism' was that she had led deputations to the Viceroy on behalf of indentured Indian women in Fiji and supported the franchise for Indian women on the subcontinent.[138] However, even here, Cousins saw Naidu's ideas for a different role for women as stemming more from the ideas of English writer and art critic, John Ruskin, of women being the 'inspirer and guide', rather than the 'dominator or leader' of men who led Indian politics.[139] Naidu, knowledgeable of India's past and calling for the restoration of women's 'ancient rights', would have disagreed with Cousins' assessment of her, principally because Naidu continued to see India as different from the West regarding women. In this light, Geraldine Forbes labels Naidu's ideology as really 'social feminism', even though her work, like that of many women intellectuals of her generation, rarely touched upon Indian women working in low-class workplaces.[140]

The complex response of women educators, self-actualising in local schooling situations, but mostly equivocal about where Western paradigms of learning might fit within this shifting scene, was, in fact, the backdrop to the Hartog/Gandhi conversation of 1931. Gandhi's 'better mothers' invocation was not a response to an imagined imposition of Western feminism in India that could find root in raj schooling in the future. Instead, his *Nai Talim* (basic education for all) had other priorities. In opposition to the British, Gandhi's education model was more about re-building the sociology and micro-economy of self-reliant Indian village communities, damaged as they were by urban-based hegemonies created by an over-blown, exploitative colonial state, and even other hegemonic deities in the pre-British period.[141] The priority for Gandhi, rather than a gender narrative, was for a different kind of 'new' education for broader Indian social rehabilitation and amelioration. To this end, his Wardha scheme approach centred on the production of handicrafts and small-scale industries. The scheme focused on small cooperative communities, where the teacher was also learner, and citizenship was defined by community industriousness and munificence.[142]

At a first glance, for Indian women, this scheme might seem to offer space for another kind of feminisation to direct the future learning of Indian females. However, as Kumar characterises it, Gandhi's programme had a different sociology about it, which aimed to break from pre-colonial, indigenous education that had inappropriately entrenched upper-caste male cultural and material interests mostly through the promotion of their learning of literary knowledge and accountancy.[143] Gandhi's priority was addressing what he saw as India's internal cultural and religious deficits, as well as the more urgent pressures of protest against the British. While other nationalist leaders had a broader agenda in view regarding the future of Indian women, Gandhi ultimately saw them as playing a national, if separate, role to men in *satyagraha* (insistence on truth), although there were still very real limits for him regarding the public role of these women.[144] Nationalists generally in the 1920s and early 1930s may have elevated Indian women, by straining against the household domain in different ways to those that might be imagined by feminists in the West, particularly concerning the need to protect the Indian domestic 'spiritual' base.[145] However, it was just as clear by 1931 that there was now little room for more Western 'remedy' wrapped up in literacy testing, moral feminine teachers or a belated intervention in these forums of Western feminist modernity.

As the colonial state began to fail, the networks of female interaction built some superficial accommodation across the colonial divide. However, what was made more apparent to both sides of the nationalist debate by this limited interaction, by the early 1930s, was the actual irreconcilable cultural differences that lay behind the ethical, pedagogic and sociological foundations of colonial education for Indian women and girls in India. Most colonial-predicated teaching by women remained localised, and these women were mostly not cognizant of these emerging irreconcilable cultural differences as they related to their professional work. In the first decades of the twentieth century, the political struggle for greater Indian self-government and, later, for outright Indian independence, accentuated separate Indian feminine thresholds that remained mostly unnegotiated by the colonial state, and that only some European teachers now attempted to accommodate. Emerging global narratives in the twentieth century concerning world citizenship, social service, eugenics and international youth movements for girls provided the means for some of this accommodation. However, by the early 1930s, Indian cultural receptivity, as part of the broader nationalist response to global movements including Western feminism, was highly nuanced and often antagonistic. This nationalist response disaggregated what the colonial state, including Sir Philip Hartog, still imagined was one female education message comprehended only through Western schooling.

More distant from the sphere of influence of the colonial state, there was at least one other network of Western women that was mostly not drawn into the colonial/nationalist impasse. This network, described in the next chapter, would endure beyond Partition and was organised by Loreto women religious (nuns).

Notes

1 'Interview with Mr Gandhi December 2, 1931'. Correspondence Between Sir Philip Hartog and M. K. Gandhi (OIOC) MSS Eur D551, f. 30.
2 J. M. Brown, *Gandhi: Prisoner of Hope* (London: Yale University Press, 1989), pp. 208–13.
3 T. S. Avinashilingam, *Gandhiji's Experiments in Education* (New Delhi: Government of India, 1969), pp. 1–23.
4 For a deeper discussion of colonial constructions of masculinity in British India see M. Sinha, *Colonial Masculinity* ..., *passim*.
5 See also A. Basu and B. Ray, *Women's Struggle. A History of the All India Women's Conference, 1927–2002* (New Delhi: Manohar, 1990).
6 T. S. Avinashilingam, *Gandhiji's Experiments in Education* ..., p. 21. For Hindu beliefs regarding the 'right hand' worship of God as 'Mother', favouring spirituality over material prosperity see S. Kakar, *The Inner World: A Psycho-analytic Study of Childhood and Society in India* (New Delhi: Oxford University Press, 1978).
7 A. Besant, 'Annie Besant on the type of education for Indian Girls, 1904' in S. Bhattacharya *et al.* (eds), *The Development of Women's Education ... Documents ...*, p. 316.
8 G. Forbes, *Women in Modern India* (The New Cambridge History of India), vol. 4:2 (Cambridge: Cambridge University Press, 1996), p. 158.
9 All Indian Women's Conference, Fourth Session, Bombay, 1930, p. 21 cited in G. Forbes, *Women in Modern India* ..., p. 158.
10 Maharani of Baroda 'Preface' in Maharani of Baroda and S. M. Mitra, *The Position of Women in Indian Life* (New York: Longmans and Green, 1912), pp. xiii–xiv.
11 Maharani of Baroda 'Preface'..., pp. xvi–xvii.
12 E. Linton, 'A Word in Season', *Literary Digest*, October 5, (1895) (OIOC).
13 M. W. Tusan, 'Writing Stri Dharma: International Feminism, National Politics, and Women's Press Advocacy in Late Colonial India', *Women's History Review*, 12:4 (2003).
14 M. W. Tusan, 'Writing Stri Dharma: International Feminism, National Politics, and Women's Press Advocacy in Late Colonial India ...', pp. 623–49.
15 G. Forbes, *Women in Modern India* ..., p. 79.

16 S. H. Rudolph, L. I. Rudolph with Mohan Singh Kanota, *Reversing the Gaze: Amar Singh's Diary, a Colonial Subject's Narrative of Imperial India* (New Delhi, Oxford University Press, 2011).
17 J. Goodman and R. Rogers 'Crossing Borders in Girls' Secondary Education' in J. C. Albisetti, J. Goodman and R. Rogers (eds), *Girls' Secondary Education in the Western World* (New York: Palgrave Macmillan, 2010), pp. 191–202.
18 P. Anagol, *The Emergence of Feminism ...*, pp. 1–18.
19 S. Thapar-Björkert, *Women in the Indian National Movement* (London: SAGE, 2006), p. 45.
20 P. Chatterjee, *The Nation and its Fragments ...*, p. 132.
21 N. Sargant, 'India My Appointed Place' [unpublished biography of Mary Carpenter]', pp. 86–94, 103–8 (OIOC) Photo Eur. 280.
22 N Sargant, *Mary Carpenter in India ...*, pp. 91–2.
23 Government of Madras Resolution, October 29, 1869 no. 311, p. 112 (OIOC) P/434/32.
24 R. Watts, *Gender, Power and the Unitarians ...*, pp. 207–8.
25 R. Watts, *Gender, Power and the Unitarians ...*, pp. 212–13; H. Martineau, 'Suggestions Towards the Future Government of India, 1858' in P. Tuson (ed.), *The Queen's Daughters* (Reading, UK: Ithaca, 2007), pp. 42–51.
26 A. Basu, 'A Century and a Half's Journey: Women's Education in India, 1850s to 2000' in B. Ray (ed.), *Women of India: Colonial and Post-Colonial Periods* (New Delhi: Bhuvan Chandel, 2005), p. 193.
27 V. Ware, *Beyond the Pale ...*, p. 122.
28 For her son's view on Ackroyd's isolation in India see W. H. Beveridge, *India Called Them ...*, p. 128.
29 W. H. Beveridge, *India Called Them* (London: George Allen & Unwin, 1948), p. 248.
30 Ackroyd to Beveridge, June 9, 1873, W. H. Beveridge, *India Called Them ...*, p. 99.
31 W. H. Beveridge, *India Called Them ...*, p. 195.
32 W. H. Beveridge, *India Called Them ...*, p. 128.
33 Annette Ackroyd Diary entries: December 18, 27, 1872; March 27, July 1, August 14, September 12, October 3, 1873; February 17, April 8, 11, 17, June 23, July 6, November 5, 1874, W. H. Beveridge, *India Called Them ...*, January 9, 16, February 25, 1875, Diaries of Annette Beveridge (OIOC) MSS Eur.c.176/48; Annette Ackroyd to Henry Beveridge March 23, 30, March 26, 30, April 2, 3, 1875, Letters of Annette Ackroyd to Henry Beveridge (OIOC) MSS Eur.c.176/3.
34 W. H. Beveridge, *India Called Them ...*, pp. 128–9.
35 M. Karlekar, *Visual Histories: Photography in the Popular Imagination* (New Delhi, Oxford University Press, 2013), p. 99.
36 A. Ackroyd, "The Hindu Mahila Bidyalaya, 1876', a paper read to former pupils and friends in the College for Men and Women, 29, Queen's Square, WC, January 15, 1876' in P. Tuson (ed.), *The Queen's Daughters ...*, pp. 110–11.
37 J. Marriott, *The Other Empire ...*, pp. 207–9.
38 A. Ackroyd, 'The Hindu Mahila Bidyalaya ...', pp.112–15.
39 Letters of Annette Ackroyd to Henry Beveridge, March 26, 1875 to April 3, 1875 (OIOC) MSS Eur C176/3.
40 A. de Courcy, The Fishing Fleet ..., pp. 230–40.
41 E. Buettner, *Empire Families ...*, pp. 116–17.
42 W. H. Beveridge, *India Called Them ...*, pp. 66, 89, 90.
43 W. H. Beveridge, *India Called Them ...*, p. 89.
44 Bethune to Governor General, March 29, 1850 in J. A. Richey, *Selections from the Records ...*, vol. ii, p. 52.
45 P. C. Mitra, *A Biographical Sketch of David Hare ...*, passim.
46 'Report of the Director of Public Instruction (Bengal) 1862–63', pp. 57–59 (OIOC), V/24/966.
47 M. E. Cousins, *The Awakening of Asian Womanhood* (Madras: Ganesh & Co., 1922), pp. 127–38.
48 A. Basu, 'A Century and a Half's Journey ...', p. 189.
49 Monarama Bose Diaries, August 7, 1879 (OIOC) MSS Eur F178/71.

50 Annual Report, Bethune College, 1917, in Bengal Education Report, 1917 (OIOC) V/24/4455.
51 Annual Reports, Bethune College, 1920 and 1921, in Bengal Education Reports, 1920 and 1921 (OIOC) V/24/4455.
52 'Notes and Memoranda on the Growth of Women's Education in India, August, 1928-January, 1929' Hartog Collection (OIOC) MSS Eur E221/51.
53 J. J. Cornelius, *Rabindranath Tagore: India's Schoolmaster, a Study of Tagore's Experiment in the Indianization of Education in the Light of India's History* (New York: Columbia University, 1928).
54 K. C. Yadav, *Arya Samaj and the Freedom Movement* (New Delhi: Manohar, 1988).
55 M. Kishwar, '*Arya Samaj* and Women's Education: Kanya Mahavidyalaya, Jalandhar', *Economic and Political Weekly*, 21:17 (1986), 1–17.
56 Reports of Rev. J. Williams, March 31, September 30, 1889 and January 10, 1890 E44, ff. 433, 409, 444 (RHL).
57 *The Arya Patrika* (Lahore) November 21, 1885, pp. 2 and 5; April 24, 1888, p. 3; July 12, 1887, p. 4, Cambridge Brotherhood Mission (CBM). Vedic refers to the ancient Hindu Sanscrit texts, the Vedas.
58 P. Chatterjee, 'The Nationalist Resolution of the Women's Question' in K. Sangari and S. Vaid (eds), *Recasting Women: Essays in Indian Colonial History* (New Brunswick, NJ: Rutgers University Press, 1990), p. 245.
59 P. Chatterjee, 'The Nationalist Resolution of the Women's Question' ... p. 245; P. Mohapatra and B. Mohanty, *Elite Women of India* (New Delhi, APH, 2002), p. 62.
60 Mary R. Dobson 'National Young Women's Christian Association of India, Burmah and Ceylon' [1910] (OIOC) MSS F186/324 (ii), p. 9; 'Notes and Memoranda on the Growth of Women's Education in India, August, 1928–January, 1929', Hartog Collection (OIOC) MSS Eur E221/51, f. 7.
61 'Notes and Memoranda on the Growth of Women's Education in India, August, 1928–January, 1929', Hartog Collection (OIOC) MSS Eur E221/51.
62 E. Andrew and K. Bushnell, 'Cantonment Life in India' (February, 1898) in P. Tuson, *The Queen's Daughters* (Berkshire: Ithaca Press, 2007), pp. 176–97.
63 'Committee of the World Missionary Conference, Edinburgh, 1910', Women's Colleges in Madras (OIOC) MSS Eur F220.
64 N. G. Jayal, *Indian Diary: Sidney and Beatrice Webb* (Delhi: Oxford University Press, 1987), p. 20.
65 'Memoirs of Miss F. M. Wyld' (OIOC) MSS Eur B320.
66 M. Bhargava and K. Dutta, *Women, Education and Politics: The Women's Movement and Delhi's Indraprastha College* (New Delhi: Oxford University Press, 2005), *passim.*
67 *The Indian Who's Who of 1937–8* (Bombay: Yeshanand & Co., 1939), *passim.*
68 M. Pugh, *The Pankhursts* (London: Allen Lane, 2001) p. 93; M. Stopes, *Married Love* (London: G. P. Putnam's Sons, 1918).
69 M. Sinha, *Specters of Mother India: The Global Restructuring of an Empire* (Durham, NC: Duke University Press, 2006), pp. 215–17, 221–2.
70 S. Mund, 'Krupabai Sattianadhan: The Portrait of an Indian Lady' in *The Ravenshaw Journal of English Studies* 6:1 (1996), 1–16.
71 L. M. Surhone, M. T. Tennoe, S. F. Henssonow (eds) [S. V. Pillai], *Prathapa Mudaliar Charithram* [originally published in 1879] (Saarbrücken, Germany: Betascript, 2010).
72 R. Hattersley, *The Edwardians* (London: Abacus, 2004) p. 201; A. N. Wilson, *The Victorians* (London: Arrow Books, 2002), p. 313.
73 Diary of E. M. Datta (OIOC) MSS Eur F 178/78.
74 G. Prakash, 'Science "Gone Native" in Colonial India ...', pp. 153–78.
75 This was the haveli of Naunihal Singh, son of the Punjab's pre-British ruler Ranjit Singh.
76 T. Allender, 'Bad Language in the Raj: The 'Frightful Encumberance' of Gottleib Leitner, 1865–1888' *Paedagogica Historica*, 43:3 (2007), 383–403.
77 Diary of Monorama Bose (OIOC) MSS Eur F178/71.
78 A. Croft, 'Review of Education in India in 1886 with special reference to the report of the Education Commission', pp. 74–9 (OIOC) V/24/442.

79 A note on "Female Education" submitted by Dadabhai Naoroji to the Indian Education Commission, 1882 in S. Bhattacharya *et al.*, *The Development of Women's Education ... Documents ...*, pp. 88–90.
80 W. Hunter, 'NWP Provincial Hearings ...' (OIOC) pp. 189–93.
81 W. Hunter, 'NWP Provincial Hearings ...' p. 193.
82 P. R. Brass, *Language, Religion and Politics in North India* (Lincoln, NE: iUniverse, 2005), 129–31, 134, 156–58.
83 Managing Committee of the Parsi Girls' School Association, 'Memorials relating to the Bombay Education Commission', Hunter Provincial Hearings, Bombay, vol. ii, p. 22 (OIOC) V/26/860/6.
84 Managing Committee of the Parsi Girls' School Association, 'Memorials relating to the Bombay Education Commission', Hunter Provincial Hearings, Bombay, vol. ii, pp. 22–4 (OIOC) V/26/860/6.
85 J. A. Richey, 'Eighth Quinquennial Education Report, 1917–1922', vol. 1, p. 126 (OIOC) V/24/4432.
86 Department of Education Proceedings [India], October, 1917 (OIOC) P/10167.
87 [M. Sadler] *Calcutta University Commission* (Calcutta: Government Printing, 1919), vol. ii, pp. 19, 28, 34.
88 *Punjab Education Report, 1906 ...*, p. 43 (OIOC) V/24/938.
89 *Bengal Education Report, 1904 ...*, p. 25 (OIOC) V/24/986.
90 P. Chatterjee, *The Nation and its Fragments ...*, p. 129.
91 A. S. Lillard, *Montessori: The Science Behind the Genius* (New York: Oxford University Press, 2005).
92 C. A. Wilson, 'Montessori in India: A Study of the Application of Her Method in a Developing Country'. PhD thesis, 1987, University of Sydney, pp. 129, 169.
93 C. A. Wilson, *Montessori in India ...*, p. 140.
94 C. A. Wilson, *Montessori in India ...*, pp. 160–1.
95 C. A. Wilson, *Montessori in India ...*, pp. 150–1.
96 *Indian Education Policy, 1913 being a resolution issued by the Governor General in Council on the 21st February, 1913* (Calcutta, Government Printing, 1914), pp. 15–16.
97 This was because female, as with male education, was mostly administered at the provincial level where most 'decentralisation' in favour of Indians took place under the 1919 Montague-Chelmsford reforms.
98 'Memorandum on the Progress of Education in British India, 1916–26' pp. 45, 70 (OIOC) V/27/860/11.
99 Ouwerkerk Collection, November 10, 1929 (OIOC) MSS Eur F232/60.
100 Ouwerkerk Collection, August 3,1929 (OIOC) MSS Eur F232/60.
101 I. Zweiniger-Bargielowska, *Managing the Body: Beauty, Health and Fitness in Britain, 1880–1939* (Oxford, Oxford University Press, 2010), pp. 106–9.
102 Ouwerkerk Collection, August 3, November 17, 1929 (OIOC) MSS Eur F232/60. See also H. Marland, *Health and Girlhood in Britain, 1874–1920* (Basingstoke, UK: Macmillan Palgrave, 2013), esp. chs 4 and 5.
103 C. A. Watt, *Serving the Nation: Cultures of Service, Association, and Citizenship* (Oxford: Oxford University Press, 2005), pp. 76–103.
104 Marion Storrs to De Selincourt, January 10, 1896; 'Report of Ellen Storrs', May 6, 1896, 'Missionary Settlement for University Women in Bombay', MSS Eur F186, vol. 140.
105 Mary R Dobson 'National Young Women's Christian Association of India, Burmah and Ceylon [1910]', p. 20 (OIOC) MSS F186/324 (ii).
106 'Nine essays by girls of Poona Widows and Orphans' Home', Papers of Sir Herbert Hope Risley, 1851–1911 (OIOC) MSS Eur D356.
107 'Nine essays by girls of Poona Widows and Orphans' Home', Papers of Sir Risley Herbert Hope (OIOC) MSS Eur D356.
108 Rabindranath Tagore Papers (OIOC) MSS Eur B183.
109 Bombay Quinquennial Education Report, 1919 (OIOC) V/24/880, p. 98; I. Gandhi, *Shreemati Nathibai Damodar Thackersey Women's University* (Bombay: Golden Jubilee, 1966).

110 A. Roy, *Mapping Citizenship in India* (New Delhi: Oxford University Press, 2011), p. 11.
111 D. Gorman, *Imperial Citizenship: Empire and the Question of Belonging* (Manchester: Manchester University Press, 2006).
112 A. Morgan, *J. Ramsay MacDonald* (Manchester University Press, 1987), chs 5 and 6.
113 Louise Ouwerkerk (1904–39), Travencore 1929–39 Ouwerkerk Collection (OIOC) MSS Eur F232 vol. 60, entries for June 28, July 7, 14, 19, August 3, September 27, October 4, 11, November 10, 1929.
114 Ouwerkerk Collection, June 28, 1929 (OIOC) MSS Eur F232/60.
115 'Minutes Regarding Appointment of Women's Sub-Committee, July 4, 1912', Continuation Committee of the World Missionary Conference, Edinburgh, 1910 (OIOC) MSS Eur F220, 'Principal's Journal, no. 14, 1923: The Christian College For Women, Madras' (OIOC) MSS F220/138.
116 C. Chatfield, *The Americanization of Gandhi: Images of the Mahatma* (New York: Garland, 1976), pp. 215–97.
117 Dr Barton to Mr Oldham August 15, 1916 (OIOC) MSS Eur F220/9.
118 Papers of Margaret Hunt (OIOC) MSS Eur F241 p. 47; R. S. Mann, *Culture and the Integration of Indian Tribes* (New Delhi: M. D. Publications, 1993), p. 59.
119 Papers of Margaret Hunt, p. 32 (OIOC) MSS Eur F241.
120 Papers of Margaret Hunt, p. 65 (OIOC) MSS Eur F241.
121 B. Ray, *Early Feminists of Colonial India* (New Delhi: Oxford University Press, 2002).
122 S. Lambert-Hurley and S. Sharma (eds), *Atiya's Journeys: A Muslim Woman from Colonial Bombay to Edwardian Britain* (New Delhi: Oxford, 2010).
123 C. Sorabji, *India Calling: The Memories of Cornelia Sorabji, India's First Woman Barrister* (London: Nisbet, 1934).
124 C. Sorabji to DPI, July 7, 1916, no. 10002, Education Proceedings, Bengal (OIOC) P/10110.
125 H. Rappaport, *Encyclopaedia of Women Social Reformers* (California: ABC, 2001), p. 662.
126 'Susie Sorabji by Mary Sorabji' *Sorabji Collection* (OIOC) MSS Eur F165/209, ff. 1–39; *The Sun*, January 3, 1906, p. 6.
127 M. E. Cousins, *The Awakening of Asian Womanhood* ..., p. 110.
128 M. E. Cousins, *The Awakening of Asian Womanhood* ..., p. 107.
129 M. Kosambi, *Pandita Ramabai Through Her Own Words: Selected Works* (New Delhi: Oxford University Press, 2000), p. 9.
130 P. Anagol, *The Emergence of Feminism in India* ..., p. 29.
131 C. A. Watt, 'Philanthropy and Civilizing Missions in India c. 1820–1960...', p. 281. For Indian Christian converts, such as Pandita Ramabai, 'modernity' from the West could be even more insidious. In this light Meera Kosambi questions Ramabai's constructions of oppressed Indian women, seeing her rationale for this philanthropy as lodged within a 'Western Orientalist Christian discourse', M. Kosambi, *Pandita Ramabai Through Her Own Words* ..., p. 24.
132 M. E. Cousins, *The Awakening of Asian Womanhood* ..., p. 102.
133 P. Chatterjee, *The Nation and its Fragments* ..., p. 131.
134 M. E. Cousins, *The Awakening of Asian Womanhood* ..., pp. 9, 22, 52, 102.
135 C. A. Watt, 'Philanthropy and Civilizing Missions in India ...', pp. 281–2.
136 C. Campbell, *Race and Empire: Eugenics Thought in Colonial Kenya* (Manchester: Manchester University Press, 2007).
137 M. E. Cousins, *The Awakening of Asian Womanhood* ..., pp. 127–35. 'Homespun' garments were symbolic in resisting the British by discouraging an Indian market for the manufactured goods of Britain, made from Indian raw materials bought at exploitative prices, that were then sold back by these manufacturers to wealthier Indians at great British profit.
138 M. E. Cousins, *The Awakening of Asian Womanhood* ..., pp. 116–26.
139 M. E. Cousins, *The Awakening of Asian Womanhood* ..., p. 121.
140 G. Forbes, *Women in Modern India* ..., p. 158.

141 M. K. Gandhi, *Basic Education* (Ahmedabad: Navajivan, 1951).
142 K. S. Bharathi, *The Thoughts of Gandhi and Vinoba: A Comparative Study* (New Delhi: Ashok Kumar Mittal, 1995), pp. 135–36; R. A. Huttenback, *Gandhi in South Africa* (London: Cornell University Press, 1971), pp. 281–2.
143 K. Kumar, *Political Agenda of Education* ..., pp. 47–69, 167–80.
144 G. Forbes, *The New Cambridge History of India: Women in Modern India* (Cambridge, Cambridge University Press, 1996), pp. 100–1, 124–6. For a more expansive explanation of this gender differentiation see C. Watt, *Serving the Nation* ..., pp. 98–103.
145 P. Chatterjee, *The Nation and its Fragments* ..., pp. 119–22.

CHAPTER NINE

Loreto and the paradigm of piety, 1890–1932

By the First World War an enormous gulf was clearly apparent between colonial state education for Indian women and girls, and that offered by other stakeholders who were more closely aligned to either a hardening national movement or to other, non-British, agendas. In one sense, this gulf exemplified the irreconcilable differences that existed between the colonial state and the Indian populous. For at least the previous seventy years, as part of India's imperial renovation, official rhetoric regarding female education had been an important selling point for the British. Yet it was apparent to all that little of any importance would happen in this regard under the raj. After 1919, central government records dry up. The British lost interest in their education project and 'Indianised' education administration, as part of a limited decentralisation, was set in train by the Morley-Minto reforms of 1909.[1]

However, several important female schooling enterprises of private foundation endured, even after Partition. In particular, some Roman Catholic orders of teaching sisters proved remarkably durable: the most distinctive of these being the Institute of the Blessed Virgin Mary (IBVM), otherwise know as Loreto. Loreto was one of two main institutions that produced activist Indian women in the early twentieth century in Bengal, the second being Bethune. The background and connective networks of these two institutions represented parallel universes regarding the schooling of girls. This final chapter focuses on Loreto's agency in India and presents it as being different from other state and private education enterprises for women and girls. In fact, of all the large ventures concerned with the Western education of females in India in the early twentieth century, Loreto turned out to be least aligned to empire.

The Jesuits provide a significant underlay to Loreto's actions in India. They were part of a deeper information order of East-West male networks that sublimated the British and later allowed Indian nationalists to exploit the raj.[2] Their longstanding presence in India meant that they were more indigenised than most Western religious orders and could draw upon many links with Indian intellectuals and educators.[3] From the seventeenth century onwards, these interactions had been so powerful that the Vatican had, at times, felt compelled to require the Jesuits to moderate their behaviour, in the interests of keeping good relations with Portugal, and with the British who followed.[4] By the later nineteenth century, the Jesuit information order was less abrasive, but nonetheless sometimes provided alternative educational pathways for Loreto to occupy as well, compared to those offered by the British colonial power, and they continued on even in post-independence India.

Another factor contributing to Loreto's durability in India was its separateness from the administrative and classifying hand of the state. This separateness allowed Loreto to build multifaceted enterprises on its own terms, with cross-subsidy, and with greater spontaneity concerning 'local conditions'. As such, these enterprises turned out to be much more self-sustaining than isolated government schools did, or even than some missions that focused on plying the lonely mofussil, with conversion as their primary objective.

Loreto's own networks reach well back in time to countries in Europe, where Mary Ward established the Roman Catholic female order. Ward was an exiled English woman who, in 1609, founded a community at St Omer, France for the purpose of educating girls and young women. She had a revolutionary vision for her community: it was to be non-cloistered, pontifical and modelled on the Jesuits.[5] Loreto's founding educational precepts were simple, yet exceptional for the time. Ward believed that girls, as well as boys, should be educated, and that their education should involve acts of charity to surrounding communities and regular contributions to the education of others.[6] Simple enough in its articulation, the actual application of this principle offered a degree of sympathetic connection to local aspirations met by the order around the globe in the age of empires. As for colonial India, this Loreto philosophy, and the mostly Roman Catholic ecclesiastical networks it worked within, were accommodating enough to Indians to be seen by them as standing outside the agenda of the British, as the national movement grew in the early twentieth century.

Ward's labours are best viewed in terms of the Catholic religiosity of her day. She also hoped to avoid control by men: namely the bishops. In essence, piety drove her vision. Two centuries later, Loreto efforts followed in the footprints of a Protestant *Pax Britannica* in India and involved, in part, elite forms of education for women and girls. This made the efforts of these women religious appear to be, at first glance, at the sharp end of the imperial project. Yet, as new scholarship of 'non-Western missions' demonstrates, networks of Irish Roman Catholic revivalism transmitted a countervailing ethic, as its Irish proponents saw it, of an empire of the 'spirit' that contrasted with the British empire, which was merely one of the 'flesh'.[7] It was also the appointment of Roman Catholic bishops in India that saw the rise of teaching orders, such as Loreto and the Christian Brothers (for boys), who were active in the carriage of Western knowledge and praxis, often independently of British empire power structures.[8]

Loreto in India

The landscape of colonial India was dotted with Catholic women religious (nun) orders that were separate from the missions. Some of the most important of these were: the French Sisters of Jesus and Mary at Agra, the Irish Presentation Sisters at Madras, and the Good Shepherd Sisters at Bangalore. The Loreto order was established in Calcutta in 1842, before spreading west, and then eventually south. Eleven young women religious set out from Ireland (where the order had relocated after its Vatican suppression in 1639), waving goodbye to their loved ones from a cold, windswept Rathfarnham in the knowledge that they would never return. The sudden transplantation of these women educators – most of whom had long careers ahead of them in India – answered a clarion call of sorts from English and Belgium Jesuits in Bengal, who were concerned about the lack of education available to Catholic girls.

Most of the Catholic girls in Bengal, in the India that Loreto now surveyed, happened to be classified as Eurasian, because they were the legacy of pre-British, French and Portuguese settlements there.[9] By the 1880s, like most government middle-class girl's schools, Loreto's student base was supposed to be Eurasian. This racial-religious affiliation was accentuated in the early 1890s, with the receipt of a bequest from two financially successful Eurasian women, the Misses Bruce. Their bequest carried the proviso that it be used to help educate poor Eurasian girls in Calcutta, thus serving to provide a kind of social mobility, but only for this racial 'type'. However, Loreto outreach was never to be so restricted or racially predicated, even though its three branch schools were situated adjacent to the main Calcutta train station and its Eurasian communities. The Calcutta of the 1840s was a vast sprawling city that belied the neat inner-city Victorian vistas portrayed by contemporary colonial lithographs. To manage this urban enormity, Loreto was eventually forced to divide the vast, Indian urban field that lay before it: itself taking one side of the Hooghly river, while another Catholic order, the charitable Daughters of the Cross (based in Belgium), took the other.

Patriarchal Roman Catholic governance in India

In Europe, the Jesuits, as a male teaching order, were the natural allies of Loreto, and this alliance continued in India. In Calcutta, St Xavier's school, founded by the Belgium Jesuits in 1860, lies about a kilometre from the main Loreto convent. In colonial times the Jesuits provided priests, who would administer the sacraments to Loreto, including the Eucharist and confession. However, it was a different order of teaching brothers, the Irish Christian Brothers, located near to the Loreto compound, that had closest jurisdiction over Loreto's affairs. This latter relationship was not always a congenial one. Left to their own devices, the Christian Brothers could be both antagonistic and capricious in their dealings with 'their' meddlesome sisters. Disparaging notes exist within Christian Brother records, such as, for example, 'many nuns are disastrously stupid', written in correspondence addressed to the Catholic Archbishop of Dublin.[10]

European church heritage threw up a complex web of ecclesiastical patriarchies in India, based on conflicting pontifical and diocesan territorialities. Loreto was ensnared in these, and some senior women religious of the order were active in attempting to loosen their grip, even making personal visits to the Vatican in the early twentieth century, although it is beyond the scope of this chapter to fully document these struggles.

However, the conflicting boundaries of Roman Church versus colonial state in India, that mostly kept Loreto outside the ambit of the raj, meant that it became possible for experienced Loreto women religious to mediate their own educational freedoms. To this end, much distracting correspondence was deliberately taken up with their male superiors in India, and abroad, arguing for dispensation from Vespers and from participating in feasts for minor European saints. Loreto women justified their requests by arguing that their elevated pastoral responsibilities meant that the order could not regularly gather as one for these observances.[11] Another issue was whether they might be permitted to wear cooler woollen habits in the summer, rather than hot and heavy 'serge' – a matter of physical survival one would think, given the Calcutta climate.[12] Mary Ward's rehabilitation by Rome in 1909 meant that the order in India was able to reaffirm itself as being pontifical, rather than diocesan. This status freed it from the control of the bishops in India – bishops who had previously taken too long to make decisions affecting Loreto and who had restricted the order

from recruiting and sending members to and from other Loreto communities around the world.[13] The new freedom facilitated critical links
with Ballarat in Australia (discussed below) and also the convenient
recruitment of Loreto music teachers from the former French colony
of Mauritius, now a British possession.[14]

Making money

By the early twentieth century, the freedoms that had been cleverly
negotiated by Loreto – both official and unofficial – proved considerable.
These freedoms were consolidated by a skilful strategy of cross-subsidy
funding, presided over by senior Loreto staff, whereby the relatively
high fees paid by middle-class Eurasian girls enrolled in Loreto schools
teaching accomplishments at Darjeeling in the hills, and at the central boarding house in Middleton Row, Calcutta, were used to help
less fortunate girls. Cross-subsidy, and some benefaction from Ireland,
meant that these funds could provide limited revenue streams for day
schools for the very poor, and for genuine Indian orphans in Calcutta
at Loreto's branch schools in the suburbs of Dharamtala, Bow Bazaar
and Sealdah. There was also another boarding school for destitute children at Entally (where Mother Teresa originally worked in the 1940s
as a Loreto sister before starting her own order, the Missionaries of
Charity).[15]

Loreto had another financial advantage: by using many of its educated women religious as teaching staff, it could reduce the amount
it had to pay by way of expensive salaries for European accomplishment teachers. This was a critical advantage over even the competing
St John's Diocesan Girls' High School, administered by the Anglican
order of Clewer sisters in Calcutta. Pay rates for women teachers in
India generally were tightly calibrated and regulated by the state. For
example, in 1917, in the province of Bengal, a woman teacher with a
Bachelor's degree (BA) recruited from Europe (on comparable English
teaching rates) was paid almost twice that of a teacher with a BA gained
in India, while an Indian woman teacher without a university degree
earned only a fraction of that – a wage barely above subsistence level.[16]
The main reason for these stark differentials in remuneration was that
the state used these pay rates to maintain the racial preference that it
had initiated for the education of girls back in 1860. It did so even in
the knowledge that these rates severely restricted the spread of its own
brand of female education. Naturally, this salary calibration also saved
the raj money.

Although even Loreto was required to employ some lay teachers,
by 1917 the Calcutta order also employed thirty-six European Loreto

women religious as teachers. These teachers, who only required living expenses, could deliver instruction of a standard that would satisfy the parent market. Even by 1904, the resultant lower fees of Catholic Eurasian accomplishment schools created enough sectarian crossover (Protestants enrolling in Catholic schools) for the European Code Committee to warn of the total collapse of Protestant college education in northern India.[17] Furthermore, Protestant clergy in India held the state to account for some of this Catholic financial advantage. Protestant clergy were envious of the ability of Catholic brothers and women religious to train their students for the European sporting field in their elite schools. There were also more career opportunities for teachers internal to the Catholic schools, because the European Code Committee still forbade talented Eurasian teachers from holding senior staffing positions in the Martinière schools for Eurasians or in other elite schools, such St Paul's School, Darjeeling.[18] In addition, some women religious came with a 'dowry', paid by parents upon their daughter's entry into the order.

After the First World War, these women religious constituted 46 per cent of Loreto's entire teaching staff, separate from those women religious who provided domestic services. This solid base of cheap-to-employ European teaching women was Loreto's strongest financial advantage, but, more than this, Loreto teaching quality was reinforced by the historicity of Mary Ward's ethic of scholarship and teaching, supported by Christian piety. Along with the discipline of convent community life itself, Loreto teaching quality in India owed just as much to its own professional cloistering as it did to the Western teaching community of women that sparsely populated even the central cities of colonial India.

State anxieties and 'order' mentalities

Another form of Loreto separateness and relative self-sufficiency concerned the raj itself. As a largely self-funding enterprise (receiving only a tenth of the funding given to Protestant girls' schools), Loreto was not usually obliged to formally submit to government inspection, although sometimes it served its interests to do so. For its part, the state's anxiety about Loreto, and other Catholic orders in India, was not so much about the education they offered as about Irish Catholicism itself. Before the 1850s, over one-third of the East India Company army consisted of Irish Catholic soldiers, with many of them only able to speak Irish Gaelic and, therefore, requiring their own Gaelic-speaking Roman Catholic chaplains. By 1880, the figure was still 65 per cent, with most of these soldiers being in the junior ranks.[19] Even those formally educated in Ireland were often bilingual (English and Irish Gaelic), providing a means of communication independent of state surveillance.[20] There were also intellectual crossovers with Ireland proffered by well-situated, non-colonial Indian men. For example, in the 1890s, Swami Vivekananda, Hindu spiritualist and Brahmo Samajist, drew on his interest in Spencer's eugenics to justify his call for his Irish friend, Margaret Noble, to come to India. This was because Noble's Celtic (Irish) blood, according to Vivekananda, best placed her to battle authorities at all levels, as the 'enemy within', on behalf of women on the subcontinent.[21]

In India, the British found it difficult to quantify the functionality of such sectarian undercurrents as any form of coherent threat, particularly during the nineteenth century. However, by 1937, of the over 200 Irish-born women religious who had served at Loreto in India since its inception, only seven of the seventeen who remained were Irish, the rest being Indian-born Europeans or Eurasians. Eight years earlier, in 1929, another three novitiates were reluctantly welcomed from the newly created Yugoslavia, including the later Mother Teresa.[22] It is significant, however, that until 1938 at least, the colonial state still formally forbade a school enrolment comprising of greater than 25 per cent Indian students in central convent schools.[23] And right up until Indian independence in 1947, it continued to formally deny Catholic orders the right to admit Indian women into their respective novitiates, as a means whereby these novitiates might otherwise renew themselves and eventually establish racial assimilation at the centre of their orders.[24] The official ban was circumvented by the Loreto order towards the end of British rule: by 1947, apart from the European sisters, only one woman religious had an Indian name, while thirty-nine others were born in India and carried the name De Costa or De Souza (the name of their baptising priest, and a designation that might still satisfy the state's Eurasian racial test).[25]

Loreto itself contributed to its separateness from both the state and from Roman Catholic patriarchies. Elizabeth Smyth describes the life of a Roman Catholic woman religious, particularly before the Second Vatican Council (1962–5), as being highly regulated:

> by the community's constitutions and customs: how and when she rose and slept, ate and prayed; how she dressed and walked; when and at what she recreated; and all that she did in her congregation and professional life.[26]

In keeping with this practice, the Calcutta-based Loreto order was operational, not as a group of individuals, but as an order controlled internally by its own matriarchy. Strict daily routines of worship reinforced the Christian consciousness of the order; even letters sent home to loved ones were read first by the Mother Superior – unless they were labelled 'conscience letters' (matters raised with a priest in confession). Convent life was probably a significant site in which white women oppressed other white women in colonial India.[27] The inner sanctum of the order also demanded adherence to strict codes of religious observance and Roman Catholic-defined moral behaviour. Even intellect was not a mitigating consideration:

> We are sending S. M. Bernardine Weingartner away as unfit for our Institute. She is highly qualified & very clever, B. A. and B. T., but unfit for community life.[28]

Other argumentative Loreto novitiates, such as M. M. Josepha, were banished to St Catherine's Hospital for the Incurables in Calcutta to follow their vocation as 'seculars' outside the order itself.[29]

Asansol

Race and patriarchy continued to influence the deployment of Loreto's educational resources, particularly when it came to establishing new schools for Eurasians. In the early twentieth century, the Eurasian 'question' still embraced both genders; and where there was a Eurasian boys' school established, so too there must be a sister Eurasian girls' school. This obligation had particular impact on Loreto when the Christian Brothers decided to establish a male Eurasian 'orphanage' in the early 1890s in Asansol, an unattractive and dusty industrial town serving adjacent coal fields 100 kilometres to the west of Calcutta. This came just at the time when the European Code officially hyper-racialised education in favour of Europeans and Eurasians, to the virtual exclusion of Indian girls at state-funded secondary schools in particular.

The Loreto schools at Asansol were justified by the raj in terms of a broader philanthropy. More generally, across the British empire, the race enterprise of empire itself was hardly a matter of contention. For example, in the first decade of the twentieth century, reforming Australian Labour Prime Minister, Andrew Fisher, feared the 'moral damage' that imported Polynesian sugar plantation workers might do in causing the 'deterioration of the white race'. In De Beer's mines at Kimberley, South Africa, 2,000 white supervisors scarcely flinched at the appalling working conditions of their 17,000 African miners.[30] In India, however, the inclination to confidently determine moral matters in terms of racial type also uncovered conflicting patriarchal rationales that sat oddly with Loreto's more focused education agenda for girls.

The Christian Brothers' rationale for setting up its Eurasian boys' school at Asansol, for example, was influenced by its experience in other parts of the empire. The same rationale was contributing to the 'stolen generations' of indigenous children in Australia, whose parents were still living. In India, Christian Brother extraction, until adulthood, of children from the 'low dance of the slums' in Calcutta was really about conversion and Western assimilation. The Christian Brothers later put their rationale for Asansol in the following terms:

> to remove entirely [poor Eurasian girls and boys] from their present sur-
> roundings and never allow them to return until a healthy disgust of their
> previous existence has been fostered, and the habits of clean living and
> thinking have become spontaneous.[31]

The state had a different rationale that led to the same outcome. It saw poor Eurasians in Calcutta in eugenic terms that also justified their removal to Asansol. For the state, their poverty was genetically determined by their slum surroundings 'as an ingrained hereditary habit' likely to lead to social unrest. The poverty was seen as a 'cycle' that rendered poor Eurasians as unemployable for jobs reserved for Europeans and, therefore, without the financial means 'to support them in European habits of life'.[32]

Despite this outside patriarchal policy ambivalence, the move to Asansol in the 1890s obliged Loreto to greatly expand its operations in this city and to establish an expensive new school for girls there as well. By 1892, this Loreto school for local Eurasian girls was almost entirely responsible for the £7,000 debt the order was labouring under: a considerable sum for the time.[33] Furthermore, Loreto's long-standing third Mother Superior, Gonzaga Joynt (b. 1838 – d. 1928), was not inclined to be overly generous in her estimation of the Eurasian phenotype in India. As she saw it, the Eurasian racial 'type' 'seldom produces a strong body or a generous soul'. She held this view even though the fees paid by wealthier Eurasian parents for their daughters' education, in the hills and at the mother convent in Calcutta, kept the whole order operational in Bengal.[34]

Loreto teaching

Loreto's placing in India was therefore complicated and highly depen-dent on often-antagonistic patriarchal and matriarchal governance structures that were mostly internal to the Roman Catholic Church, even on the subcontinent. Despite an outward latency and probable solemnity in the way in which the women in this order connected with forces that restricted their action, internally there were also

Figure 10 Loreto Darjeeling: middle-class schoolgirls taking in the air in the hills. © IBVM (Loreto) Institute and Irish Province Archives (Dublin).

stronger dynamics at work that related to yet another set of influential networks. These networks were principally associated with two key educational areas. The first was Loreto's work in building a curriculum for secondary schooling for more affluent Eurasian girls that was more apposite to their position in India (and not just preparation for the marriage market). The second was Loreto's focus on educating impoverished Indian girls in Calcutta and in their modest outreach stations in and around the city.

In the raj, a strong indicator of how robust any educational institution was in its commitment to the education of females was whether that institution taught girls at secondary level. In most provinces, by 1900, only a handful of government schools offered such schooling and, except for Bengal, and partly due to the influence of Mary Carpenter a generation earlier, there were more teacher training colleges for females (women and girls) than there were well-equipped secondary schools for girls. As for Loreto, its curriculum at secondary level was pitched in direct competition with elite government and Protestant mission institutions in Calcutta and in the hill stations of Darjeeling, Simla and Kurseong, where the traditional accomplishments curriculum was taught.

Accomplishments could only take Loreto so far, however, mostly because of state-based predications. The strong racial bar imposed by the raj on the education of women and girls probably made the accomplishments curriculum more compelling in India than in other parts of the empire. On the subcontinent, the Cambridge middle and upper examinations reinforced the worse features of this curriculum. For instance, the middle-school drawing examination entailed mindless exercises copying flower drawings (European flowers) and other objects of nature, without any scope for creative rendering or interpretation. The didacticism also pointed to a broader academic predication that tended to discourage the work of Froebel and other new movements, which, in India, could otherwise promote the authentic artistic and cultural heritage of a Mughal and Hindu past. Instead, government schooling continued to defend earlier direct artistic replication from Europe. More than this, there was a tendency by the Calcutta government education department, even by 1910, to see the emergence of new Indian art forms in terms of 'degeneracy', using arguments akin to those found in Germany in the 1930s when rejecting its own expressionist art movement: although without the anti-Semitic element.[35] In India, the departmental approach was part of a longstanding Haileybury tradition of identifying Eastern intellectual deficits that then justified stark and misplaced imperial 'remedy'.

However, by the early 1900s there were deeper artistic currents for Loreto to tap into. By this time Schools of Art were emerging in all the main provinces, although most ignored Lockwood Kipling's earlier efforts adjacent to the Lahore 'Wonder House' to faithfully revive India's art heritage, in preference to a Western rendering of it.[36] Some European women teachers helplessly complained that these Schools of Art were located away from the hill stations in the large provincial cities, and were therefore inaccessible to them. In fact, some of these grand-sounding institutions were really industrial schools concerned with woodcarving, weaving and jewellery work.[37] In England, John MacKenzie's work outlines the popular use of motifs and colourings of the Orient in the decorative arts, accompanied by very little cultural and racial relativism.[38] However, at a high artistic level, the work of Abanindranath Tagore (part of the distinguished Tagore family) was already winning recognition in London's artistic circles, with an exhibition at the Tate Art Gallery. Leader of the Bengal school, Tagore sought to modernise and reconfigure Rajput and Mughal artistic styles, and particularly their use of perspective, in order to counter the influence of Western models of art. More significantly, he was the first exponent of *swadeshi* (anti-British, self-sufficiency) values in Indian art. His subtle watercolours were accessible to Loreto students when they visited the Calcutta Museum. There was also the adjacent Government College of Art and Craft, the foyer of which is, to this day, decorated with English Arts and Crafts motifs of the late nineteenth century, part of a creative artistic movement that found its way into Indian artistic circles.[39] It was into this world that Loreto women religious brought their senior students as part of their 'object lessons'; visits that were akin to the purdah schools of India, where Loreto students were conveyed in covered carriages out of hours, away from a prying public.[40]

Loreto's traditional and imported alliance with the Jesuits also offered new pathways of intellectual transmission across the race divides of British India; pathways that were also not coterminous with empire mentalities. In the nineteenth century, Jesuits had connected with Hindus professing *Sadhana-Dharma*: a spiritualism where there is no caste, class, male or female distinction, only measures of fitness and worthiness.[41] Other Jesuits, such as Constans Lievans and John Hoffman at Chotanagpur (240 km west of Calcutta), were to achieve converts in this remote part of India after assisting villagers to challenge raj taxes and land seizures in the law courts. Jesuit *dalit* (untouchable) missions, and the attendant Indian community connections that the Jesuits made with these underprivileged groupings, also worried the British.[42]

Loreto, though not as longstanding in India as their Jesuit brothers, also took its cue from the Jesuit tradition of circumventing the binaries set up by empire to justify Western intellectual and cultural imposition. Crossing the race divide was a key component of Loreto's strategy, as poor Indian girls were taught in its branch schools. So too were Loreto's endeavours to achieve equality in education with men at university level for its most able students. Additionally, Loreto nurtured teacher training for women of the kind that did not just replicate the class-predicated accomplishment curriculum. There were also the scholastic endeavours of Loreto women religious themselves; an example being Sister Maeve Hughes' *Epic Women: East and West*, a work that enmeshed itself in rich Indian epics to make new parallels with ancient Irish literature on women, bypassing England altogether.[43]

High scholarship such as this probably did not make it into the classroom, but sympathetic accounts in the 1920s and 1930s of the Irish Home Rule movement, and leaders such as Eamon de Valera, certainly did.[44] The brothers of many European Loreto women religious were actively fighting against the British in Ireland in the early twentieth century.[45] As Kate O'Malley illustrates, leaders of the rising national movement in India saw events in Ireland as akin to their own struggles for independence from the British.[46] British officials, such as Michael O'Dwyer, Lieutenant Governor of the Punjab, publically identified Indian 'swadeshists' in the Punjab as exporting their ideology back to the Home Rulers in Ireland.[47]

However, despite a sense of a common power struggle in the 1920s at an intellectual level between Irish and Indian nationalists, in fact, from a Roman Catholic point of view, the scene in these two countries was quite different. In Ireland, even in the 1920s, the Roman Catholic Church was not prepared to tolerate critical thinking in its own schools, fearing this would produce individuals likely to question Roman Catholic power over Irish society generally.[48] In India, Roman Catholic power was weaker and there was a different British colonial state to resist. The schooling scene also presented another set of socio-cultural issues, particularly regarding the education of girls.

The anti-English Roman Catholic connections and collaborations in India strengthened the capacity of Loreto to circumvent the most restrictive and unjust aspects of the raj regarding education; and in so doing reinforced the importance of building self-sustaining, *ex officio* communities instead. Additionally, Loreto anti-English feeling could build its credibility among leading liberal national movement leaders. Historically the Jesuits, in particular, had courted state suspicions, even in Europe, with Bismarck expelling them from Germany in 1878 as part of his *Kulturkampf* (culture struggle).[49] From a raj viewpoint, by 1917 Roman Catholic orders were raising official suspicion principally because of their supposed cultural and intellectual infiltrations. The India Office estimated that there were 5,057 'foreign missionaries' in British India by this time.[50]

During the First World War, British Prime Minister Lloyd George uncovered a supposed German plot to infiltrate the British in India from a base in the Andaman Islands off the coast of Eastern India.[51] There was political mileage to be made from this discovery, as it came just after the German sinking of the British passenger liner, the *Lusitania*, in May 1915. As a result, scores of innocent German Jesuits, mostly from south India and from Shillong in Assam, were sent back to England in 1916 to be interned there. Lloyd George favoured doing the same to German women religious, and only German chartable famine relief in India, amounting to £900 in that year, persuaded him to settle, instead, for their confinement to their convents for the duration of the war.[52] Furthermore, the Vatican was advised of the 'propaganda of the German Catholic clergy' in India, and the India Office insisted that the German Jesuits in India be replaced with Italian and Maltese priests.[53]

For Loreto women religious, many of these Jesuits were their confessors, friends and allies in the deep work they were undertaking in local Indian communities. The Mother Superior of Loreto lamented 'even the perfect Apostolic Fr Bulree is to be interned ... nationality their only offence'. These friends were not permitted to return to India even after the war.[54] This confirmed to Loreto an ill-informed, if not cruel, raj that really knew little of the kinship and teaching work Catholic orders had engaged in with local Indian communities

[283]

for at least the prior half century. The brutality of such an intern-
ment process also emphasised the separateness and arbitrariness of
the colonial state.

The Loreto College

More visible institutional links were built across to tertiary education.
Loreto played its part in the initiative of some European and Indian
women to gain access for its students to an academic university education. To this end, Loreto College was one of the first women's colleges
to win access for its senior girls to the Calcutta University exams in
1913, including biology.[55] Loreto women religious strenuously lobbied
for this access so to be able to stake out greater academic distinction
for their bright senior students who were young women, away from
what was on offer from government-run education. These university
exams were academically more demanding than the Cambridge exams,
and they granted access, along with boys of similar age, to the sciences
as well as to Indian languages and intellectualism.

Loreto's strategy to pursue Calcutta University affiliation was probably also initiated because of the dark skin of many of its students who
were classified as Eurasian, a feature that was noticed by department
officials even in the early twentieth century. These girls were less
likely to find good employment among Anglicised communities. As
mentioned in the introduction to this book, the department offered a
contorted explanation for such 'dark skin', going back to the abolition
of slavery in 1833. It is also probable that the Loreto women religious,
themselves, played on the departmental belief to veil their work with
Indian girls, who could now mostly only benefit from their senior-level
education if they were formally classified by the state as Eurasian.[56]

Loreto's Calcutta University affiliation to Intermediate Arts standard in 1913 also included affiliation for a Licentiate in Teaching (LT).
Uniquely, the college was permitted by the inspecting university
professors to combine its Intermediate Arts and its LT college classes; and these latter classes were augmented by the teaching of two
highly qualified secular women from England: Miss Moore and Miss
Connell. Miss Moore and Miss Connell were educated, respectively,
at the Royal University in Ireland and at South Kensington, London.
Both also held Cambridge teaching diplomas, as teachers of method in
science and history, respectively.[57]

The establishment of a teaching college had been at the back
of Loreto Mother Superior, Gonzaga Joynt's mind since the early
1890s. Finding money without the benefit of government grants
was a problem, but the biggest issue at that time for Joynt was the

government's unwillingness to hand over to Roman Catholics, even in part, its preciously conceived teacher training for women, with all the socio-cultural moral implications that the state still saw as accompanying such training.[58]

Loreto was not about transferring feminist mentalities emergent in Europe by this time. Nor was this kind of transferral favoured by a rising India. However, Loreto understood the importance of professional teacher training for its girls, both in terms of finding new professional careers for them and also to stave off any Anglican ascendancy in this kind of academic training for women.[59] In this work, the order was the beneficiary of a close friendship between Gonzaga Joynt and her counterpart in Ballarat, Australia, Mother Gonzaga Barry. Loreto in Ballarat had set up Australia's first teacher training college for women in 1884 (affiliated with Melbourne University in 1906); and, in the twenty-four-year period between 1890 and 1914, Ballarat was responsible for sending seventeen young newly graduated women religious teachers to Calcutta, many of whom went on to enjoy long and successful careers in India.[60] Barry's influence from Ballarat also introduced to India the teaching philosophy of French bishop educator Felix Dupanloup, whose educational philosophy was already influential among Catholic orders in the USA.

> Education is culture and exercise, instruction and order. The teacher cultivates, instructs and labours outwardly but it is essentially necessary that there should be exercise, application, labour within. In education what the teacher does is a trifling matter; what [s]he causes to be done is everything. Whoever does not understand this understands nothing of the work of human education.[61]

Such calls for student-centred learning for Indian women and girls were probably seen as new to India, given the largely false perceptions by most Europeans at the time about the rote learning proclivities of traditional Indian learning in other settings. Although Mother Barry's attached solicitation that her Ballarat trainee teachers be 'good Catholic Teachers ... thoroughly well instructed in our Holy Religion' was hardly a possible aspiration for the sister convent in Calcutta.[62] Nor was the social control of the Catholic Church in India anything like Tom Inglis' characterisation of it in Ireland:

> there was a priest, nun and brother in every corner of society. They presided over schools, hospitals and a wide variety of social welfare institutions ... Like all good authority figures, their supervision and control persisted even in their absence. In the most subtle and yet penetrative forms of power, the supervisory eye of the Church was internalized in the minds and hearts of Irish Catholics.[63]

However, well into the 1930s, and external to Loreto in Calcutta, Loreto superiors in Dublin continued the commodification, in evangelising terms, of a homogenous Loreto product to be spread throughout the world.[64]

Working with the poor

The second distinctive aspect of Loreto's educational labours in India was its work with destitute Indian girls. Central to Loreto's work with the very poor in Calcutta were the unofficial networks of financial subsidy that Loreto in Calcutta set up to channel money from its expensive fee-paying boarding schools in Darjeeling, Simla, Lucknow and Calcutta, to fund Loreto's outreach programmes aimed at imparting basic literacy and numeracy. Building on Hindu ceremonials, poor Calcutta girls were encouraged to visit Loreto House and its branch schools for sweets and a subsistence meal, these being offered in exchange for elementary tutoring and lessons in hygiene. Parents also had to be convinced to allow their daughters to attend school, which involved initiating the parents, many of whom were illiterate, into the structure, process and Western-conceived value of education: something most of them had not experienced before, at least at first hand. The goal was for the parents to allow their daughters to attend school for at least two hours a week, which, with the addition of time spent travelling to and from school, was significant time away from the piecework most girls did as an essential supplement to family income.

All these Loreto strictures and freedoms projected an educational future for girls in India that was different to that offered by government, private-venture or even mission schools. Loreto, and other Catholic orders like it, situated itself in the middle of Indian community life on many interrelated and differentiated levels, emanating out from the central convent compound. These levels included teaching, medical care, encouraging student-outreach programmes inspired by Mary Ward's philosophy, pastoral work and even establishing new commercial industries for Indian women to run.

There were crossovers between these elements that Loreto also mediated. For example, Loreto's outreach programmes were increasingly promoted to government on the basis of providing medical care, an approach already established by the missions to reach broader sections of the Indian female population. This approach was used by Loreto to unofficially increase the enrolment of Indian girls in its poorer schools, and became vital when, even in the late 1930s, the order, like most other European-inspired schooling enterprises for girls, was officially

[286]

restricted to an intake comprising no more than 25 per cent Indian girls, as mentioned earlier in this chapter.[65] To get around the restriction, Loreto conflated medical care with education, justifying the approach in terms of offering Indian girls healthier futures by providing them with the means for at least subsistence livings.[66] The strategy deftly set aside the binary between these two professional turns – nursing and school teaching: a binary that was now solidified in Europe, but not yet confirmed in the Indian communities Loreto served.

Colonial approaches concerning the medical care of Indians, combined with the racial preference of the raj for teaching Eurasian females in its schools and colleges, together helped to define Loreto's countervailing approach in which its Indian girls might now receive both. This approach also reveals a Loreto domain within which obfuscation towards the raj was at its strongest. In a long interview with the author in Dublin, the then eighty-nine-year-old retired Mother Damien insisted upon the significance of Loreto work in this regard at Morapai (a distant mission outpost adjacent to the Ganges river delta). Mother Damien had been the principal of Loreto, Darjeeling in the hills for over twenty years, and had served at the Calcutta convent before that. However, the Morapai outreach, rather than the Loreto central schools, exemplified just how complex, ambitious and *ex officio* Loreto could be, making scrutiny of this outpost an important case study.

Morapai

Reaching the Morapai mission from Calcutta required three hours by slow train and then a canal boat ride through snake and tiger-infested jungle. Morapai itself had long been a Jesuit settlement, and Loreto began by setting up dispensary stations to supply food, medicines and the dressings for wounds, as well as offering outreach visits to treat victims of cholera. Under this cover, a large schoolhouse was built to educate girls, whose manual work paid for most of the entire settlement. The school also embraced, as part of its central business, the education of physically and intellectually disabled Indian children.

Staffing was a serious problem, particularly for outreach posts such as Morapai. There were not enough women religious staff to go around and, given the state's ban on admitting Indian women to the main order, Loreto was forced to work out another strategy. In 1898, the order established an Indian sub-order called the Daughters of St Anne at Ranchi (400 km west of Calcutta) under the jurisdiction of the Belgium Jesuit, Paul Goethals (the first Roman Catholic Archbishop of Calcutta). This strategy was probably inspired by the Daughters of Mary, attached to the Don Bosco schools: a global schooling network

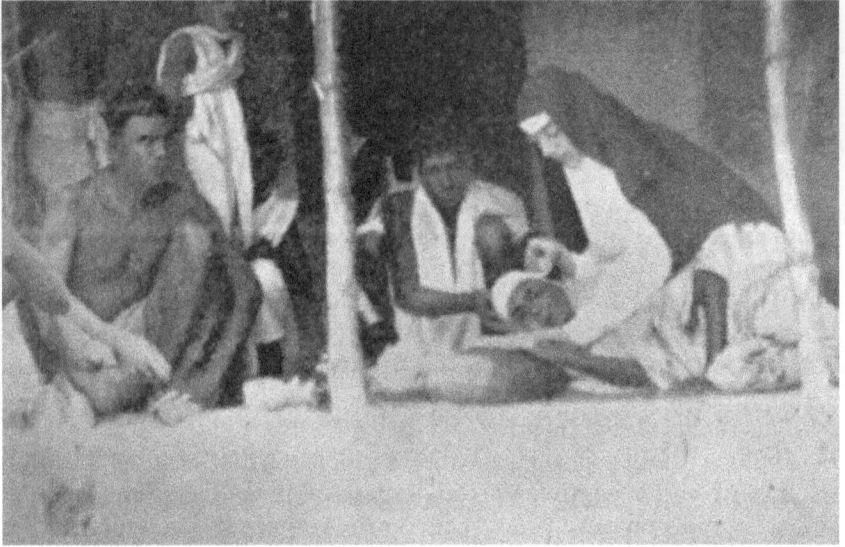

Figure 11 A rare photograph of a Loreto woman religious bandaging the head of a Hindu patient in a village near Morapai. © IBVM (Loreto) Institute and Irish Province Archives (Dublin).

emanating from Italy, which included India in the 1870s. However, the Loreto foundation of the Daughters of St Anne was in breach of government dictums at the time, and only tolerated by the state because of its relatively remote location and likely backlash from Rome if the St Anne sub-order was forcibly disbanded. This questionable legal legitimacy also took the work of the St Anne order underground, to better reach racially excluded Indian women and girls. The St Anne order was originally designed to minister to the 'wild and exotic' females who were Kol tribals of the surrounding Chota Nagpur district, south-west of Calcutta.[67] However, as this order of Indian women religious grew, some of its membership were gradually relocated to other Loreto mission outreach sites, including Morapai.[68]

Even by the turn of the twentieth century, the European Loreto sisters still carried with them Western patronising attitudes towards Indian girls and women, while seeking to promote their education to other Loreto communities abroad. These attitudes also carried through to their views on the Daughters of St Anne. Mother Gonzaga Joynt, writing in 1899 of the teaching of this new Indian Loreto order, observed:

> They are very edifying, pious, docile, laborious & an immense help in teaching and forming our little savages.[69]

[288]

Yet Mother Joynt actively supported the work of the Indian women religious, which transcended anything the state had to offer for teaching destitute Indian girls and she knew that this new order was indispensable if Loreto's outreach was to continue to grow.

The problem remained of how to make the order financially self-supporting. To this end, Morapai established a commercial edge in this part of India manufacturing carpets, pillow lace, machine-woven cloth and hand-knitted fine stockings of superior quality. These goods were competitive in the larger trade with Europe, and not just as charity wares suitable for the local bazaars. Such competitiveness was made possible by research into the newest commercial techniques available at Serampore and Barnagore, in Bengal, whose mastery was presided over by a small community of young widow teachers.[70]

The problematic schooling trade-off for this work was relatively modest: 'taught to read, write, do small sums & trained for domestic duties' was of dubious probity and open to exploitation. Yet the balancing act seems to have worked, with girls enrolled at Morapai not 'trained' for imaginary teaching positions, but at least realistically equipped to earn a modest living in later life by providing goods that had an overseas market (even with Gandhi's later boycotts in favour of 'homespun').[71]

Other complex Loreto outreach communities saw similar expansion and in the twentieth century Loreto managed, in most of its schools, to circumvent the government-imposed limit of 25 per cent Indian schoolgirls. By 1937 in the order's branch schools in Calcutta alone, Loreto, Entally reached 1,000 orphan girls overseen by just twenty women religious. By then, even the poorer Indian schools of Dharamtala, Bow Bazaar and Sealdah (branches of the Calcutta convent) had expanded to about 600 Indian schoolgirls each.[72] Furthermore, the racial 'reach' to Indians was even greater, because Indian girls in all these Loreto communities were expected to share some of their basic literacy and numeracy education in their own communities for one afternoon a week, in accord with Mary Ward's original philosophy.

Christian outreach

By the twentieth century, perhaps because of this rapid community-based expansion, Loreto, like some other Christian missions, was gradually redefining its evangelising agenda. The Christian Brothers and the Jesuits became known for cruel corporal punishment codes that the British had always claimed to be the case in Hindu schools. Yet, for Loreto, the dispersal and scale of the outreach work, in difficult-to-access hot dusty locations, with the immediate need to 'rescue' children, naturally dissipated the possibility for Christian proselytising. Emphasis on humanitarian initiatives, as part of a Christian 'presence', offered better possibilities for the amelioration of the poor, the destitute and girls who were in danger of sexual exploitation. There was also a much more immediate poverty to address, as Mother Gonzaga Joynt told her counterpart, and friend, in Ballarat, Australia:

> Sometimes poor little stray children come to our 'Poor Schools' with a transparent muslin frock and nothing else. To meet such emergencies our sisters keep a supply of undergarments ... Our sisters tell me that often the feeble walk and pallid looks of the children have induced them to enquire as the day advanced if they had breakfast ... answer usually 'no' ... Wonderful how they bear the hunger and faintness so patiently.[73]

Other female education endeavours for Indians, of Western orientation, offered similar outreach programmes away from the classroom but also the chapel. For example, Margaret Hunt, brought up an Anglo-Catholic and a graduate of Bedford College for Women, was stationed at the CMS's Women's Christian College in the 1920s. Hunt confessed 'a kind of weariness for ardent Evangelical piety & any kind of fundamentalism'. Her professional satisfaction, apart from teaching a Western academic English syllabus of Keats, Carlyle and Shelley, came from the College's 'Social Work Friday' where staff and students ventured to neighbouring poor communities, offering gifts and informal education gratis.[74] Furthermore, not all of these broadening endeavours in the later colonial period were necessarily religiously inspired. Margaret Cousins' All India Women's Conference (founded in each major Indian city in the later 1920s), began other multifaceted educational engagement with Indian women through forums such as adult educational centres, milk distribution centres, craft and night schools, crèches and welfare clinics.[75]

Christian orders saw the provenance of their social service agendas as enshrining their European, though not necessarily imperial-inspired, allegiances based on piety. While secular European women's organisations understood their similar social service work more in terms of their role as good citizens in colonial India: their work also unrestricted, as they saw it, from the household constraints of their Indian sisters. However, Loreto's outreach work was still a far cry from the culturally embedded social service narratives of Indians that animated Indian men in particular in the 1910s, even though these same narratives built upon notions of citizenship, which were influenced by such countries as Japan, Australia and the USA.

India-based organisations such as Gopal Gokhale's 'Servants of India', and the welfare strategies of like Indian social service organisations, exerted strong influence in the West, particularly upon student social service in Britain, as well as through the writings and speeches of social progressives such as Beatrice and Sidney Webb and Ramsay MacDonald among others.[76] Other Indian men operated through another set of cultural prisms concerning social service. What might seem as Western ideas of charity and philanthropy were also negotiated by much longer-standing Hindu 'living traditions' such as *sannyas* (developing creativity and alertness) and *brahmacharya* (control of the senses, celibacy) that contributed to Hindu manliness.[77] These philosophies were not based on notions of Indian femininity, and certainly not those from the West. Instead, as Watt argues, north Indian associational life, in particular, mediated social servants by creating separate Indian cross-caste, cross-class and trans-regional solidarities. These solidarities, in turn, gifted to Indian women, as a side benefit, greater access to participate in large-scale relief efforts for the poor, the hungry and the diseased.[78]

Despite scholarship such as that of Maeve Hughes and others after Partition, there is little evidence that Loreto women religious in the 1910s or 1920s were conscious of the cultural Indian way of thinking about social service, although Loreto's rich post-Partition work in Calcutta may have been a different story. At most, the Indian notion of *dāna* (charity) in helping with village uplift, the elderly and others in need, had a superficial commonality with Loreto's own efforts at schooling poor girls for a better Indian life. Furthermore, for Loreto, cross-subsidisation from its wealthier middle-class schools and commercial enterprises to support economic self-sufficiency within its poorer communities was at least a better outcome for Indian girls than the bitterness and poverty that Loreto sisters saw on a daily basis.

Partition

In the late colonial period the raj continued to claim thousands of lower-order girls' schools, even though census data revealed a female literacy rate for Indian girls still stuck at between just 1 and 2 per cent of all school-aged girls.[79] However, the work of Loreto's women religious, and other philanthropic organisations, in imparting even elementary education could lead its students to careers as teachers, nurses, midwives, typists and shopkeepers, albeit on very low pay. This employment could provide a means for these girls to escape the slums and their extortionate landlords; and perhaps even to allow them to enjoy the signifiers of household prosperity, such as brass and copper cooking accoutrements instead of the usual earthenware.

More importantly, these working futures were a kind of vocational middle ground, providing young women with a means of financial support that could be realistically eked out from their surrounding communities. However, the limited social mobility provided by Loreto for underprivileged Indian girls still sat against a backdrop of vast areas of rural poor and city slum dwellers. Underprivileged females, in particular, suffered from overpopulation, the British corrupted markets into which they sold their produce, and these females remained largely untouched by any European education endeavour.

After Indian independence, the new Indian national government rarely granted foreign missionaries residential permits. Yet some religious orders such as Loreto, already firmly anchored within local communities, were able to continue with their work, drawing on Indian women religious to replace their rapidly retiring Irish counterparts. The need for such replenishment by Indians became more acute after Vatican II promoted 'local vocations' for its orders abroad.[80]

Significantly, much of Loreto's counter-positioning in India in relation to the colonial state, whether orchestrated or not, contributed to the order's capacity to navigate Partition when it came in 1947, despite its Christian foundation and European origins. The peculiarity of Loreto's traditional Irish and continental European networks turned out to be a pathway for establishing its anti-imperial bona fides in India. Crippling shortages of women teachers continued, and grinding poverty was visible for all to see, especially among India's oppressed women. As a foil to this oppression, Loreto's credibility as a worthy educational endeavour was actively subscribed to and supported, in particular by Bengal's powerful *bhadralok* (Indian middle-classes). Even by 1919, Michael Sadler's Calcutta University Commission was willing to concede this point, including the Bethune school also in this category, while seeing mission schools as different in this respect, and as catering mostly only for the girls of Christian converts.[81]

Almost a hundred years later, the contemporary education scene in India holds few parallels with the issues that confronted Loreto when dealing with the colonial state. Accomplishments, Eurasian colonial educational hegemonies, and even the feminine identities that forged, in different ways, the teacher and medical care vocations of women in colonial India, would be unrecognisable in modern India. Yet unfulfilled agendas, written by successive Indian governments, World Bank intervention in 1991, and global/NGO imperatives, continue in other ways to measure (mostly defectively) India's emerging 'modernity' using new Western paradigms of literacy and numeracy. The imposition of these paradigms, even when filtered by some socio-cultural sensitivity by state and national Indian governments, has also ruptured much of the connection with this earlier past, even though Loreto had rejected much of the raj, anyway, by the end of the First World War. Paradoxically, the current educational vista in India, many vistas in fact, and Loreto's outreach built around Indian communities still suffering under great poverty, make its networks of action much more local and national but less global compared to the colonial period. Connections between Loreto in India with other Loreto orders around the world are probably less active today than in the colonial period, as Loreto in India works within the realities of educational developments at the national and provincial levels to bring more sustainable futures for the Indian girls it teaches.

Today, Loreto flourishes, with over sixty-seven central schools scattered across north, east and south India, serving mostly Indian girls and with an almost entirely Indian women religious teaching order together with many lay Indian teachers. Loreto's strong social-inclusion programmes are built on connections and networks with surrounding communities. For example, the branch school at Sealdah, Calcutta, referred to earlier in this chapter, today consists of 700 free and 700 fee-paying students. It has five secondary schools attached to it, with 6,260 pupils enrolled, as well as classes with special needs and top-floor rainbow schools teaching basic literacy.[82] The cooperation of the Sealdah Loreto branch with the West Bengal state government involves finding new sites for Loreto outreach schools where micro-credit schemes might subsequently take hold for the future employment of its female graduates. This cooperation has been functional even when past West Bengal governments have been communist in designation. Furthermore, Loreto's Barefoot Training of teachers, in the many informal and outdoor schools throughout Calcutta, has graduated some 7,000 women teachers over the past three decades, many of whom have then turned to teaching in these same schooling communities of girls.[83]

A second Loreto periphery, of much larger scale, lies beyond but is still directly connected to, the Sealdah branch. At this level, Loreto, Sealdah, claims a total outreach of 450,000 women, girls and some boys: mostly underprivileged or destitute and others in abusive domestic child-labour situations. Vocational training – often spurned in India for caste and class reasons – is negotiated as an element of this rescue of Indian girls. Some of these endeavours also involve an ethically difficult interaction with other patriarchies. Most particularly, child slavery exists in *plein-air* brickfields, which are usually located on unwanted land between stagnant water courses and railway lines in parching sun and choking pollution. Here, Loreto women religious, and the secular teachers attached to the order, bargain with the owners

of these brickfields – an uncomfortable de facto recognition of them –
to establish schools after hours for some 1,300 of these children.

Just as stubborn caste, tribal and poverty narratives that particularly isolate women remain in India, so, too, remnants of earlier
periphery-to-periphery European connections and networks are unconsciously embedded in Loreto contemporary work. Pictures of Mary
Ward still hang on the walls of Loreto's precincts; its Roman Catholic
Christian presence still struggles in reconciling the Billings method
of birth control with an overpopulated India; and its women religious
confront sometimes overwhelming imperfections in under-resourced
teaching as measured by Western standards. However, unlike nearly
all schools of the colonial period, Loreto schooling for girls is now
undeniably Indian in its epistemological, pastoral and its pedagogical
configuration.

Notes

1 J. Olson and R. Shadle (eds), *Historical Dictionary of the British Empire* (Westport, CT: Greenwood, 1996), vol. ii, pp. 759–60.
2 Bayly, C. A. *Empire and Information* ..., pp. 365–76.
3 See, for example, A. Amaladas, 'Jesuits and Sanskrit Studies', in T. J. De Sousa and C. J. Borges (eds), *Jesuits in India: In Historical Perspective* (Macau: Xavier Centre of Historical Research, 1992), pp. 214–17.
4 K. Ballhatchet, *Caste, Class and Catholicism in India, 1789–1914* (Richmond, UK: Curzon, 1998), pp. 1–40.
5 M. R. Clark, *Loreto in Australia* (Sydney: University of NSW Press, 2009), pp. 18–22.
6 M. Szpak, 'The life of Mary Ward, her contribution to social and religious education in the seventeenth century and the ministry of education of the Loreto Sisters', 1995. MA thesis, King's College, London.
7 S. Gilley, 'Catholicism, Ireland and the Irish Diaspora' in S. Gilley and B. Stanley, *Cambridge History of Christianity*, vol. 8 (Cambridge: Cambridge University Press, 2006), pp. 250–7;
8 S. Gilley, 'Catholicism, Ireland and the Irish Diaspora' in S. Gilley and B. Stanley, *Cambridge History of Christianity* ..., pp. 250–7; B. Stanley, 'Andrew Walls and the Centre for the Study of Christianity in the Non-Western World' in W. R. Burrows, M. R. Gornik and J. McLean (eds), *Understanding World Christianity: The Vision and Work of Andrew F. Walls* (Orbis Books, 2012); B. Hellinckx, F. Simon and M. Depaepe, 'The Forgotten Contribution of Teaching Sisters: A Historiographical Essay on the Educational Work of Catholic Women Religious in the 19th and 20th Centuries', *Studia Paedagogica*, 44 (Lueven: Lueven University Press, 2009).
9 'Loreto's 125 years', Box H205.3 (LBA).
10 Appended to the letter of Sister Mary, Rajputana Convent, 23/4/1913, Loreto Nuns, 1905–11, 'India', Box 347 (DDA).
11 Mother Mary Bonner to My Lord Archbishop, September 5, 1906, Box 347 (DDA).
12 Mother Mary Bonner to My Lord Archbishop, September 5, 1906, Box 347 (DDA).
13 Account of Mother Damien, former Superior of Loreto, Darjeeling. Interview con-ducted by the author at Loreto Convent, Dublin, October 22, 2009.
14 Gonzaga Joynt to Teresa Bonner, July 10, 1918, Box 18 B16, Loreto Archives, Dublin (LAD).
15 K. Trait 'India- Loreto' Ser. 112 [1], Loreto Archives, Ballarat (LAB).

16 For example, in 1917 in the province of Bengal (of which Calcutta was the capital), a female teacher with a BA recruited from Europe was paid Rs.300 per month (£1 = Rs.15.12), a teacher with a BA gained in India was paid Rs.158 per month and for an Indian woman teacher without a university degree between Rs.15 and Rs.40 a month which was barely above subsistence level. W. W. Hornell, 'Report on Public Instruction in Bengal 1919–20', p. 70 (OIOC) V/24/986.
17 'Committee Upon the Financial Condition of Schools for Europeans in Northern India' (OIOC) V/26/861/1.
18 Rev. C. C. Rodgers, Headmaster of Christ Church Boys' High School, Jubbalpore. Hartog Collection (OIOC) MSS Eur 221/53, f. 83.
19 'Ireland India Missionary Links', India Box 8 (LAD).
20 T. O'Donoghue, *Bilingual Education in Pre-independent Irish-speaking Ireland, 1800–1922* (Ceredigion, Wales: Edwin Mellen Press, 2006), ch. 2 and appendix 1, p. 179.
21 K. Jayawardena, *The White Woman's Other Burden ...*, p. 6.
22 Mary Catherine Joseph, India Box 106 (LAD).
23 'Easter, 1938', Loreto Mission Letter, p. 13, India Box 53 (LAD).
24 Sr Patricia Harris IBVM, 'Celebrating 400 Years of Loreto', September 14, 2009, Bar Convent Conference, York, UK.
25 I am grateful to Sister Cyril Mooney of Loreto, Sealdah, Kolkata for providing me with these statistics.
26 E. Smyth, 'Teaching Sisters, Leading Schools' in E. Smyth (ed.), *Changing Habits: Women's Religious Orders in Canada* (Ottawa: Novalis, 2007), p. 210.
27 Gonzaga Joynt to Gonzaga Barry February 7, 1888, Box 18A/6 (LAD); Mother Mary Teresa Bonner to 'My Lord Bishop', September 5, 1906, Box 347 (DDA); Gonzaga Joynt to Mother Teresa Bonner August 1, 1918, Box 18B/17 (LAD).
28 Gonzaga Joynt to Mother Teresa Bonner, November 15, 1915, Box 18B/12 (LAD).
29 Gonzaga Joynt to Mother Teresa Bonner, July 12, 1915, Box 18B/14 (LAD).
30 D. Day, *Andrew Fisher, Prime Minister of Australia* (Sydney: Harper Collins, 2008), pp. 104–5, 208.
31 A. Mercer, *Fifth Quinquennial Education Report, 1912–17 ...*, p. 131.
32 A. Mercer, *Fifth Quinquennial Education Report, 1912–17...*, p. 131.
33 Gonzaga Joynt to Gonzaga Barry, September 7, 1892, Box 19A/19 (LAD).
34 Gonzaga Joynt to Gonzaga Barry, September 7, 1891, Loreto India Box 18A/18 (LAD).
35 'Quinquennial Report of the Art Section of the India Museum, Calcutta 1912–18' (OIOC) V/24/4477.
36 S. Gujral, *A Brush With Life* (New Delhi: Viking, 1997), pp. 42–44; A. Mercer, *Fifth Quinquennial Education Report, 1912–17 ...*, p. 151.
37 A. Mercer, *Fifth Quinquennial Education Report, 1912–1917 ...*, p. 184.
38 J. M. MacKenzie, *Orientalism: History, Theory and the Arts* (Manchester: Manchester University Press, 1995), pp. 71–2.
39 See also B. M. King, *Silk and Empire* (Manchester: Manchester University Press, 2009), ch. 7.
40 Mother Gonzaga Joynt to 'Archbishop', September 6, 1906, Box 347 (DDA).
41 H. Staffner, 'Jesuit Contribution to Dialogue in India' in T. S. de Sousa and C. J. Borges (eds), *Jesuits in India: In Historical Perspective* (Macau: Xavier Centre of Historical Research, 1992), p. 247.
42 W. Fernades, 'Jesuit Contribution to Social Change in India (16th to 20th Centuries)' in T. S. de Sousa and C. J. Borges (eds), *Jesuits in India: In Historical Perspective.* (Macau: Xavier Centre of Historical Research, 1992), pp. 181–2.
43 Sister M. Hughes, IBVM, *Epic Women: East and West* (Calcutta: The Asiatic Society, 1994).
44 Reminiscence, M. M. Columba Sullivan, Superioress, Buluchistan, 26/6/32 (DDA). I am grateful also to Prof. Jasodhara Bagchi, formerly of Jadavpur University, Calcutta, for confirming this based on her conversations with former Loreto students of this era.
45 Anne Maher, 'Ireland India Missionary Links', India Box 8 (LAD).

46 K. O'Malley, *Ireland, India and Empire: Indo-Irish Radical Connections, 1919–64* (Manchester: Manchester University Press, 2009), pp. 53–89.
47 Speech of Sir M. O'Dywer, April 25, 1917 (OIOC) L/PJ/6/1502, f. 4000.
48 T. O'Donoghue and S. Hartford, 'Contesting the Limond Thesis on British Influence in Irish Education since 1922: A Comparative Perspective', *Comparative Education*, 1:10 (2012), 6.
49 H. Pakula, *An Uncommon Woman: The Empress Frederick* (New York: Simon & Schuster, 1995), pp. 302–6.
50 'Confidential' [1917] (OIOC) L/PJ/6/1467, f. 5170.
51 'Confidential' [1917] (OIOC) L/PJ/6/1467, f. 5170.
52 'Report on German Nuns', December 31, 1919 (OIOC) L/PJ/6/1650 no. 777.
53 'Confidential' [1917] (OIOC) L/PJ/6/1467, f. 5170.
54 Gonzaga Joynt to Teresa Bonner [n.d. 1916], Box 18B1–19 (LAD).
55 Affiliation of Loreto House, Calcutta, to Calcutta University. Education Proceedings (OIOC) P/9193.
56 Hornell, W. W. Bengal Education Proceedings 1915 (OIOC) P/9640.
57 Proceedings Department of Education, March, 1913 (OIOC) P/9193 Appendix A.
58 Gonzaga Joynt to Gonzaga Barry, September 7, 1891, Box 18A/18 (LAD).
59 Gonzaga Joynt to Gonzaga Barry, February 17, 1899, Box H205.3 (LAB).
60 'Australians who went to India' Ser. 112 [8] (LAB).
61 M. M. Hilda Benson in a lecture on Barry's educational philosophy directly using this quotation from Dupanloup's *The Child*. 'Historical Account of the Dawson Street Foundation', Series 33 (LAB).
62 'Gonzaga Barry's Instructions for Running of Training College' (Dawson Street), Series 127, item 2M (LAB).
63 T. Inglis, *Moral Monopoly: The Rise and Fall of the Catholic Church in Modern Ireland*(Dublin: University College Dublin Press, 1998), p. 211.
64 *Loreto Foreign Missions* (Dublin: St Stephen's Green, 1934), pp. 11–15 (LAD).
65 Loreto Mission Letter, 1938, Loreto, India Box 53 (LAD).
66 Mary Catherine Joseph to (?), December 3, 1937, India Box 106 (LAD).
67 Anon, *Loreto's Native Missions in India* ([Calcutta]: Redmond Brothers, 1932).
68 'The Congregation of the Daughters of St Anne', Ser. 112 [2] (LAB).
69 Gonzaga Joynt to Gonzaga Barry, 17/2/1899, Box H205.3 (LAB).
70 'Morapai', January 22, 1936, India Box 113 (LAD).
71 'Loreto Free School and Orphanage, Morapai', India Box 112 (LAD).
72 'Novitiate, Loreto Convent', India Box 106 (LAD).
73 Gonzaga Joynt to Gonzaga Barry, Australia [n.d.] file 18 A/2, Loreto India (LAD).
74 'Papers of Margaret Hunt' (OIOC) MSS Eur F241/2, p. 89.
75 'All India Women's Conference (Calcutta Branch) Annual Report 1953–55' (OIOC) MSS Eur F341/6.
76 G. Brewis, 'Education for service: social service and higher education in India and Britain, 1905–1919' in T. Allender and J. Collins (eds), 'Knowledge Transfer and the History of Education' special issue of the *History of Education Review* 42:2 (2013), 129; N. Owen, *The British Left and India* (Oxford: Oxford University Press, 2007).
77 Watt, C. A., *Serving the Nation* ..., pp. 15–16.
78 Watt, C. A., *Serving the Nation* ..., pp. 6–7.
79 J. A. Richey, Progress of Education in India, 1917–22 (Calcutta: Government Printing, 1923), p. 126 (OIOC) V/24/4423.
80 Anne Maher IBVM, 'Ireland India Missionary Links' [1940–74], India Box 8, p. 14 (LAD).
81 [M. Sadler] *Calcutta University Commission* (Calcutta: Government Printing, 1919), vol. ii, p. 13.
82 [C. Mooney], *Loreto Day School, Sealdah* (New Delhi: Loreto Press, 2009).
83 [C. Mooney], *Loreto Day School, Sealdah* ....

Conclusion

'Learning femininity' in colonial India is one of the simplest and least aggressive phrases that might be used to describe any part of the imperial project. The raj's official rhetorical repertoire intentionally promoted 'female education' as a soft and consistent moral purpose that could only improve the 'condition' of women in India. As this book demonstrates, the reality was very different. The raj deployed a strong race and class agenda, where official gender articulation became a complex but powerful conduit for attempted enculturation from the West. Acknowledgement of this complexity is essential to any successful attempt to make sense of the rich and interesting story of how women educators and learners in India variously came to their classrooms and hospitals during this 112-year period, and of the official mentalities that beckoned them there.

Seeking to understand the vista in these terms requires a longitudinal study, of the kind offered by this book, of the changing interactional features between the state and different female networks. It is apparent that the mentalities of the colonial state concerning women and girls in India changed over time, and were more restrictive, reactive and cognisant than is often supposed. In addition, feminine receptivity, while orchestrated by the colonial state, could also create new learning spaces of female interaction and collaboration that were outside the gender, race and class agendas of empire. In this sense, Western feminine accommodation, and more fragmented Western feminist activism, located *in* India, were not always internal to broader colonial agendas. However, collegial awareness by most of these colonial-aligned women educators was never strong and they were mostly not prescient as to how their daily work might be shaping the colonial domain in India.

These women were powerfully directed by, and themselves directed, various networks that ebbed and flowed during the colonial period. The networks were sometimes strongly coterminous with empire, sometimes controlled by associated agencies (such as the missions) or they could just as easily be engaged by the actions of marginalised groups of women. As this book has shown, these different networks engaged the hopeful CMS missionary teacher of Indian 'orphans' in the 1820s just as much as they did the lonely accomplishment teacher of Eurasians in the 1890s. Some female spheres of action at various colonial peripheries even became new centres of influence in themselves, such as the medical care offered by female missionaries and, late in the nineteenth century, Loreto teaching outreach to Indian women and girls.

State power relations were closely related to the growth and the withering away of these networks concerning Western feminine interaction. Interaction with the limited numbers of women the state sought to direct in India had a strong historicity to it; and the different Western network constellations that had a bearing on this interaction became more overlapping as the colonial period progressed. Furthermore, these overlapping connections responded to Western-identified social and cultural 'deficits' that the colonial state, and other colonial agencies such as the missions, promoted as requiring remedy: deficits which strongly objectified Indian women and their emotional and moral bodies.

The meaning of 'official' and 'the state' also changed over this long time period. These phrases, visible to the British interested in empire, were delineated in the early years of British India by explicit displays of Haileybury bureaucratic procedure and the commercial processes of the East India Company. Later in the nineteenth century, the phrases were articulated as part of the grand imperial project that became known as the British raj. Even the name given to the event that marked a change in the prevailing British belief of what 'the state' meant in colonial India was determined by a Western, morally ascendant view. This event was known as the 'Indian Mutiny' of 1857, rather than the 'Great Revolt', or as it has become termed more recently, 'the first war of Indian Independence'. Beyond this change, however, and before the agonisingly slow moves towards Indian independence that occurred from the 1920s onwards, the colonial state in India needed to project a mythology of immutability to reinforce its message of a stable colonial, and then an imperial, civilising mission. Most of the colonial women referred to in this book saw themselves as acting and reacting within the simplified frame of official self-confidence fed to them through the formal channels of ICS-generated regulations and surveillance. However, for many of these women, their isolation and dispersal brought greater possibilities for spontaneous and creative engagement with Indian females that, in turn, forced the colonial state into new fields of colonial governance and responsibility.

CONCLUSION

As this book has demonstrated, formal placement of the state's female education rhetoric was chiefly through its women teacher and medical carer paradigms. These paradigms also changed over time, being responsive to broader, but changing, colonial network and state power plays that engaged rhetoric about females in India to justify and mask the true nature of colonial rule. Most particularly, during the British colonial interregnum, the raj variously deployed Indian, Eurasian and even European women and girls in artificially constructed Western settings of female professionalism. Here, Western gender codes of femininity and medical care mediated the state's own race and Western class agendas. By the late nineteenth century, when British colonial learning settings aimed to produce a feminine prototype in India, 'Eurasian ladies' were mostly the officially preferred outcome. This educated feminine prototype was to be brown, but not too brown – that is, a mostly Western-oriented Eurasian beneficiary; and a 'lady' not a 'woman' – that is, an accomplished woman of feminine sensibility and bearing, resonant of the English middle-class.

These official narratives, which solidified in the last two decades of the nineteenth century, were far too brittle and constrained ever to be sustained, even within the limited remit of the raj. To Indian intellectuals in the high imperial age, they also rendered fanciful the official claim to be expanding education on the ground to Indian girls. However, such restrictiveness usefully justified the very limited funds the state was actually prepared to spend on female learning on the subcontinent.

The colonial female learning space, as it was formally constructed, also offered little durability. As independence began to look inevitable, middle-class Eurasian women, who had become the chief beneficiaries of Western femininity in the classroom, left India in increasing numbers. A generation later, many other Eurasian women who could not achieve British naturalisation through a European marriage were left to resent the British, as an independent India reduced their status, cut off the possibility of a professional career and 'hounded ... them from post to post' in India.[1] Little evidence remains about how this and earlier generations of Eurasians felt about their predicament, but those accounts that do survive suggest an attitude of serene and bitter disengagement from this group of women, once given preferment by the British but now without possibilities for this preferment.[2] As Elizabeth Buettner illustrates, their disillusionment also had sequel in London, post Indian Independence, which became a place of many meeting points for Indians and Europeans who had once lived in colonial India.[3] Of even greater frailty was the accomplishments canon in India, as was the Western middle-class cultural transfer the state had attempted to impose through this canon a priori in its best funded, racially predicated, girls' schools in the 1880s and 1890s.

The frailty and unsustainability of the colonial 'female education' rubric was partly because state premeditation, without much action concerning Indian women and girls after 1850, infected these professions instead with the raj's broader race and class agendas. Colonial intervention relegated these professions, and a good part of emerging Western feminism, as unworthy to carry forward India's modernity project. The relegation was in addition to, and separate from, the very real cultural barriers Indian nationalism preserved, strengthened and reconfigured for Indian women in the 1920s and early 1930s.

The raj, while keen to tout its female education moral agenda, paradoxically never formally acknowledged the relatively large number of European, Eurasian and Indian women it used to do its bidding. Official raj reportage masked their voice via cynical and impatient ICS officer articulation, which elided any sense of female perception or wisdom. This omission and obfuscation reflected an unequivocally masculine empire, despite the fact that, by 1921 as Geraldine Forbes calculates, there were within the professional classes of women 68,000 medical professionals, another 30,000 employed in educational and scientific fields, and yet others involved in the law and in business.[4] In 1913, those women officially recognised as belonging to the rarefied ranks of the Indian Education Service (IES) amounted to just seventeen – with little increase in their numbers until educational administration was 'decentralised' in 1919.[5] There was also a more troubling female oppression created by a capricious raj and its sometimes abrupt swings in policymaking. Many schoolgirls were placed at risk as a consequence, stranded between two cultures, with a future of destitution before them – a future not helped by the closed colonial classrooms they had once inhabited.

This book recognises different theoretical approaches of past work when considering the dynamic of colonial women, compared to scholarship about their Indian sisters, in the context of rising Indian nationalism. However, although complex, changing state constructions in the colonial sphere about the female learner, teacher and medical carer in colonial India offer some cogency that sustains the theorisation presented here. While the theorisation in this book relates to a putative centre of state direction, and the changing and various networks that drove female interaction relating to this centre, other significant centres of female interaction in colonial India are also identified and examined.

Such cogency identified using the colonial perspective does not belong to the highly charged Indian nationalist side of the story. The cultural and linguistic diversity of India, and its variously multilayered Indian matriarchal and patriarchal arrangements, would firmly resist such an approach, even if there were a stronger evidentiary base with which to work. This side of the political story has produced, instead, a vibrant scholarship of another kind that builds an entirely different picture of Indian women, mostly separate from colonial rule. Using this perspective, Meredith Borthwick contends that non-colonial, Indian writers defined Indian women more in terms of their social role than their behavioural and personality traits.[6] Indian nationalism would give Indian women different roles to those pursued by Indian men when protesting against the British. And, on this theme, Mrinalini Sinha suggests that the Indian female body was a site where nationalist sentiment could find an outlet, while simultaneously excluding women's voices from these very same nationalist debates.[7] Certainly, nationalists aspired to provide an answer to the new social and cultural problems concerning the position of women in modern Indian society, not in terms of their identity, but as a point of difference with perceived forms of cultural modernity in the West.[8]

The ability of the national movement to keep the women's question within the inner domain of national culture, to use Partha Chatterjee's phrase, and away from the arena of the political contest with the colonial state, also owed much to the colonial state itself. 'Female education' had been a critical element in the civilising pretensions of the raj since the 1850s. Yet, for Indian nationalism, as far as it focused on these pretensions at all, the palpable superficiality of the colonial female education message merely signified a vacant ethical and cultural space that could not contest the inner spiritual and domestic domain of the Indian woman; a domain that was projected by the thought of later Indian nationalists.

Away from high politics in the late colonial period, many crossovers concerning the female in India persisted, although as independence approached the interaction began to move well beyond colonial spaces of formal female learning. In the late colonial period, compromises were negotiated concerning hospitality in European households where Europeans and leading Indian nationalists met. By the early 1930s, high-caste Hindus were prepared to eat with Europeans, provided the food was vegetarian; while curry was served at Government House, Lahore when Indians were present as a means of cementing social and political bonds.[9] Of course, there was still the separate world of the British – the 'White man's show' – as Nayantara Pothen illustrates. The Gymkhana Club and other British clubs like it remained places for the 'raj at play' where, before the Second World War, social life was supervised and controlled by European women. These clubs remained bastions of Victorian social values, precedence, strict European protocols and English frippery that extended to the sixteen-button glove.[10] The Western feminine social domain in India was also still robust enough, in these highly exclusionary circles, for women of the 'fishing fleet' to continue to come to India in the hope of landing a husband.[11]

Conversely, other European women, retaining their title of 'Miss', elected to stay in India to teach. Some of these women entered the Indian female civic and social domain, along the lines of Louise Ouwerkerk, Flora Wyld and Leonora G'meiner (who have been discussed in this book), but became female ascetics in their local education situations. Jayawardena illustrates one such early case: that of Margaret Noble in the early twentieth century. Noble, an Irish Protestant, became Nivedita, under the influence of Swami Vivekananda, and began a school for about thirty girls in Calcutta teaching handicrafts, Bengali, English, arithmetic, history and geography, based on the maxim that 'knowledge is supposed to receive a foundation in concrete experience, and all work [should] ... appear to the child in play'.[12] Other examples of European women of this period include the unconventional CMS missionary, Amy Carmichael, in southern India, whose life's work in rescuing *devadasis* (female temple servers) from prostitution involved her choosing to wear Indian clothes and her use of coffee to dye her own skin brown.[13]

In addition, a new genre of Western women's written commentaries on India became popular after the Second World War. For example, Austrian woman Hilda Wernher published the book *My Indian Family* in the USA in 1945, about her daughter's 'mixed marriage' in India to a Bombay Muslim. Wernher's account saw a new kind of inverted cultural negotiation between India and the West, where she supposed her daughter's sanitary customs, her table manners and her social habits might be just as 'amazing and repellent' to her Indian in-laws as widow custom and caste might be to her.[14]

A little earlier, in post First World War colonial India, powerful political imagery was still attached to the female body and her domestic domain, on both sides of the national struggle. This imagery retained much of its earlier potency. General Dyer's massacre of Indians at Jallianwala Bagh, Amritsar on April 13, 1919 was preceded by a serious assault on Miss Marcella Sherwood – a longstanding CMS missionary in the city. The violation of her Western female body, and the reputed refusal of Indian females in an adjacent Indian household to help her after the assault, was a signifier to the British that another 1857-type revolt might be in the offing. This British fear also reprised 'women-in-danger' stories that had diverted polite English society conversations in India for three generations following the Great Revolt.[15] Two days after the Amritsar massacre, Dyer issued his famous 'crawling order', which obliged Indians to crawl on their bellies when travelling down the alley where the Sherwood assault had taken place. As Dyer saw it, this was a means of atonement, appropriating Indian worship rituals.[16]

Nine years later, in 1927, American journalist Catherine Mayo published her exposé *Mother India*. The book objectified Indian women, mostly because Mayo saw their status and 'condition' as reflective of India's broader social ills. The book was to cause an international uproar: so much so, as Sinha argues, that it resulted in a realignment of the correlation between the political and social sphere in colonial India. Two years later, the fierce reaction of Indian writers to Mayo's book saw them blaming the colonial state, instead, for much of the plight of Indian women, and provided the impetus to induce the raj to reluctantly pass the Child Marriage Restraint Act, among other social reform measures, for women and girls.[17]

There were also other tensions created by the nationalist movement in the colonial period that were fought out by Indian women and men about Indian women that went beyond questions of femininity. The conservative quarterly periodical the *Arya Mahila* (Arya Woman), published from 1917 until the 1940s, articulated a revival of eternal *dharma* (an individual's proper conduct), including traditional religious home education for women and girls, without the need for Western education, and a reform of practices that did not otherwise conform to the *śāstras* (ancient rules written in Sanscrit).[18] However, even within this journal, there was no consistent narrative concerning Indian women. In 1923 its editor, Surath Kumari Devi (later Rani of Khairighar, Oudh), was forced accommodate Indian contributions that argued that there was no difference in the 'emotions' and 'the mind' between men and women.[19]

As far as schooling was concerned, some earlier foundations meant that there was never an entirely clear division between colonial and nationalist thought regarding Indian women, even in the very late colonial period. Away from the national political level, the learning domain of Indian females could still convey remnant displays of Western femininity values in the 1930s and 1940s – even when the discussion turned to the sensitivities of preparing traditional Indian brides. Writing with this preparation in mind, Margaret Cousins, as late as 1941, argued:

> Girls themselves are hungry for school and college; their mothers, having been denied education themselves, try to secure it for their girls as a rule in the towns these days; and young men of the middle and upper classes insist on securing educated brides, amongst whose accomplishments should be [Indian and Western] music.[20]

Lady Irwin College (later affiliated to Delhi University), founded a decade earlier under the directorship of Mrs Hannah Sen, offered a one-year certificate course in Home Science in 1932 that was concerned with the running of 'hygienic' households. Eugenic health agendas imported from the West also occupied imperial, nationalist and socialist thinkers and activists at this time.[21]

There was, of course, still important knowledge transfer established in India by the colonial state even after the First World War, including that conveyed by Indian women. Separate from the macro national struggle of the first half of the twentieth century, the idiom and paradigms of knowing were largely Western by this time, although no longer parallel with colonial state power itself. Indian women, in some elite Indian female circles at least, aspired to use this bridge to reach out to a modern national and international world. As D. K. Rukminiamma, one of the first women college graduates in Mysore state, reflected in 1917:

> I have personally come across many high-class orthodox Hindu ladies whose chief regret is that they have had no opportunity to learn English in their younger days and who now evince a very strong desire to remedy this defect. The study of English need not be incompatible along national lines. On the other hand it will promote national interests by facilitating the free exchange of thought not only in India, but also with the world outside, and besides will help our women in their aspirations to take rank along with enlightened women of progressive countries.[22]

While potentially a feminist agenda, it is more significant that a relatively small and separated cohort of Western-educated Indian females now also used their scholarly separateness to partly objectify the Indian 'condition'. As already mentioned in this book, other Indian women, such as those belonging to the Arya Samaj's schools in north India, which were strongly anti-British, also proffered the learning of English as a world language.[23]

By the 1930s a new generation of Indian women educators transcended the barriers of child marriage or widowhood to deliver an education aimed at modernising Indian women along uncompromisingly Indian lines. The Mahakali Pathsala Girls' School in Calcutta successfully taught an academically demanding, orthodox Hindu education, away from the Brahmo Samaj offering, led by the female ascetic Mataji Maharani Tapaswini.[24] In Banaras, Nita Kumar identifies the likes of Sarojini Devi Bhattacharya and Satyavati Devi who, influenced by the thought of Gandhi, sought to teach and set up schools to counter poverty and illiteracy among their Indian sisterhood.[25] These Indian feminists and ascetics were influenced, in turn, by strong but regional

Indian activism of preceding generations. Gail Omvedt identifies the likes of Jyotirao Phule, in the mid-nineteenth century, as an early Indian feminist for his radical thought and work on behalf of Indian women and within the framework of Hindu belief to promote equality between Indian women and Indian men.[26] There was also a lively group of Maharashtrian women, whose Indian feminism was projected by pressing the colonial state to defend them against traditional Indian property rights, to provide protection from abusive husbands, and to help them tackle illiteracy and Indian superstition.[27] In the late colonial period of the 1930s and early 1940s, the activism of Indian females could also extend to that of schoolgirls such as Santi Ghosh and Suniti Chowdhury, who shot dead a district officer in Bengal in December 1931; or to Aruna Asaf Ali and Sucheta Kripalani, who led underground resistance to the British after the entire Congress leadership was jailed in 1942.[28]

The physical colonial heritage concerning females has now mostly disappeared. The red-gravelled and alpine terrain of the hill stations remains, along with some of the elite girls' schools that have a Christian foundation. Some colonial buildings that were once girls' schools still exist in the major cities, usually painted a dusty pink and hidden among bustling local bazaars. These buildings have often been commandeered as government offices or re-badged as elementary language schools. The semiotics of an earlier colonial era regarding female education, in terms of building forms, associated language phrases and even school uniforms, also offers a tempting reference back to a long-past raj when most else is now gone.

After 1947, a new intellectual landscape emerged responsive to an imperfect broader global discourse regarding the oppression of women, as this oppression is understood by feminist thought and gender theorisation. Today, Indian feminist critique is nuanced and often builds outwards from the Indian national domain. It is now both a political and an intellectual pursuit, and the conflation of these two strands has produced an active scholarship about nation-specific issues concerning India. These issues include conceptualising feminist action in terms of 'entitlement' and 'empowerment', if it were to replace the bureaucratic power of Indian males when implementing government policy in culturally complex poor female communities.[29] Some scholars write interrogations concerning gender in India in broader international terms, where 'communities assert their own superiority over the inferiority of others ... [where] nations claim their own purity over the contamination of others ... [and where] the West marks its development over the backwardness of others'.[30] Scholarship in India and about India, from a feminist and a gender perspective, partly concerns how this language is filtered by the Indian state and how strong socio-cultural constituencies at the local level oppress female minorities and exploit their lack of basic human rights. New networks have prized India free from earlier colonial configurations concerning Indian women in ways that are more complete than in the former white dominions of empire. However, many of the relational features of the past that concern the state, Indian and Western patriarchies, caste, global commerce and of course poverty, which continue to contribute to the exploitation of Indian women and girls in India today, remain firmly in place.

Notes

1 Vere Lady Birdwood (OIOC) MSS Eur.T.7.
2 Selections from the edited transcript of Vere Lady Birdwood (October 1973) (OIOC) MSS Eur.T7.
3 E. Buettner, *Empire Families ...*, pp. 239–52.
4 G. Forbes, *Women in Modern India ...*, p. 157. Forbes also sees even these significant numbers as relatively small compared to the numbers of women working in labouring jobs. In 1928, there were 737,000 women domestic workers, with 250,000 women working factories, especially in cotton and jute mills. Another 250,000 women worked in tea gardens and 78,000 in the mines. See also A. R. Caton (ed.), *The Key of Progress* (London: Humphrey Milford, 1930), pp. 155–7 cited in G. Forbes, *Women in Modern India ...*, p. 158.
5 C.Whitehead, *Colonial Educators ...*, p. 58.
6 M. Borthwick, *The Changing Role of Women in Bengal ...*, p. 84.
7 M. Sinha, 'Nations in an Imperial Crucible' in P. Levine, *Gender and Empire* (Oxford: Oxford University Press, 2004), pp. 181–202.
8 P. Chatterjee, *The Nation and its Fragments ...*, p. 117.
9 E. M. Collingham, *Imperial Bodies ...*, pp. 188–9.
10 N. Pothen, *Glittering Decades: New Delhi in Love and War* (New Delhi: Viking, 2012), ch. 2.
11 A. De Courcy, *The Fishing Fleet: Husband-Hunting in the Raj ...*, passim.
12 K. Jayawardena, *The White Woman's Other Burden ...*, pp. 183–8 also citing B. Foxe, *Long Journey Home: A Biography of Margaret Noble (Nivedita)* (London: Ryder & Co., 1975), p. 64.
13 E. F. Kent, *Converting Women: Gender and Protestant Christianity in Colonial South India* (Oxford: Oxford University Press, 2004), esp. ch. 3; E. Elliot, *A Chance to Die: The Life and Legacy of Amy Carmichael* (Old Tappan, NJ: Revell, 1987).
14 H. Wernher, *My Indian Family* (New York: John Day Company, 1945), pp. 221–2.
15 M. Macmillan, *Women of the Raj* (London: Thames & Hudson, 1988), p. 99.
16 P. Bose, *Organising Empire: Individualism, Collect Agency and India* (Durham, NC: Duke University Press, 2003), pp. 37–8.
17 M. Sinha, *Specters of Mother India ...*, pp. 1–22.
18 S. Nijhawan, *Women and Girls in the Hindi Public Sphere ...*, pp. 66–7.
19 S. Nijhawan, *Women and Girls in the Hindi Public Sphere ...*, pp. 69–70.
20 M. E. Cousins, *Indian Womanhood Today* (Allahabad: Law Journal Press, 1941), p. 110.
21 A. K. Sharma, *A History of Educational Institutions in Delhi, 1911–1961* (New Delhi: Sanbun, 2011), pp. 197–201.

22 D. K. Rukminiamma, 'Mysore Economic Conference, 1917' in S. Bhattacharya *et al.*, *Development of Women's Education in India … Documents …*, p. 449.
23 R. Chandra [revised version of] L. Rai, *A History of the Arya Samaj: An Account of its Origins, Doctrines and Activities with a Biographical Sketch of its Founder* (New Delhi: Orient Longmans, 1967).
24 M. Borthwick, *The Changing Role of Women in Bengal …*, p. 100.
25 N. Kumar, *The Politics of Gender, Community and Modernity* (New Delhi: Oxford University Press, 2007), p. 164.
26 G. Omvedt, *Feminism and the Women's Movement of India* (Mumbai: Research Centre for Women's Studies, 1987), pp. 23–4.
27 P. Anagol, 'From the Symbolic to the Open: Women's Resistance in Colonial Maharashtra' in A. Ghosh (ed.), *Behind the Vale: Resistance, Women and the Everyday in Colonial South Asia* (Basingstoke, UK: Palgrave Macmillan, 2008), pp. 36, 37, 42, 43, 44 and 47.
28 S. D. Sharma, *India Marching: Reflections from a Nationalistic Perspective* (Indiana: iUniverse, 2012), p. 133.
29 S. Sharma, *'Neoliberalization' as Betrayal: State, Feminism and a Women's Education Program in India* (New York: Palgrave Macmillan, 2011), ch. 5.
30 R. Ray (ed.), 'Introduction', *Handbook of Gender* (New Delhi: Oxford University Press, 2012), p. 2.

BIBLIOGRAPHY

Primary sources

Archives

Australia

    Baillieu Library, University of Melbourne, Melbourne
    Fisher Library, University of Sydney, Sydney
    Loreto Archives, Loreto Convent, Ballarat
    State Library of Victoria

Canada

    Robarts Library, University of Toronto, Toronto

Great Britain

    Angus Library, Regent's Park College, Oxford
    Bodleian Library, Oxford
    Cambridge University Library, Cambridge
    Main Library Archives, Birmingham University
    Nasser D. Khalili Private Collection, London
    Oriental and India Office Collections, British Library, London
    Rhodes House Library, Oxford
    School of Oriental and African Studies (SOAS) Library, University of London, London

India

    Cambridge Brotherhood Mission Archives, New Delhi
    Jawaharlal Nehru University Main Library, New Delhi
    Loreto Archives, Loreto Convent, Kolkata
    National Archives of India, New Delhi
    Nehru Memorial Museum and Library Archives, New Delhi
    St Stephen's College Library, St Stephen College, New Delhi
    St Xavier's School Library, St Xavier's School, New Delhi
    TATA Institute of Social Sciences Library, Mumbai

Ireland

    Arnold-Forster private family letters, Dublin
    Dublin Diocesan Archives, Dublin
    Dublin Public Library Archives, Dublin
    Loreto Archives, St Stephen's Green, Dublin
    Trinity College Library, Dublin

Pakistan
Punjab Secretariat Library, Anarkali's Tomb Archive, Lahore
Lahore Museum, Lahore

United States of America
Office of the General Assembly, USA Presbyterian Church, 425 Lombard Street, Philadelphia

Contemporary sources

Ackroyd, A., 'The Hindu Mahila Bidyalaya, 1876', a paper read to former pupils and friends in the College for Men and Women, 29, Queen's Square, WC, January 15, 1876 in Tuson, P. (ed.) *The Queen's Daughters: An Anthology of Victorian Feminist Writings on India, 1857–1900* (Reading, UK: Ithaca, 1996)

Adam, W., First Report on Education (1835) in J. A. Richey (ed.), *Selections from the Educational Records* (Calcutta: Government Printing, 1922)

———'Reports on the State of Education in Bengal 1835 and 1838...' reprinted in A. Basu, *Reports on the State of Education in Bengal 1835 and 1838* (Calcutta: Government Printing, 1944)

———'Second Report on Vernacular Education in Bengal (1836)' in S. Bhattacharya, J. Bara *et al.* (eds), *Development of Women's Education in India, a Collection of Documents, 1850–1920* (New Delhi: Kanishka, 2001)

Andrew, E. and Bushnell, K., 'Cantonment Life in India' in P. Tuson (ed.), *The Queen's Daughters* (Reading, UK: Ithaca, 1990)

Anon, *Loreto Foreign Missions* (Dublin: St Stephen's Green, 1934)

Anon, *Loreto's Native Missions in India* ([Calcutta]: Redmond Brothers, 1932)

Bagal, J. C., *Radha Kanta Dev, 1784–1867* (Calcutta, 1957)

Bell, A., *Sketch of a National Institution for Training up the Children of the Poor in Moral and Religious Principles, and in Habits of Useful Industry* (London: J. Murray, 1808)

Beveridge, W. H., *India Called Them* (London: George Allen & Unwin, 1948)

Brander, E., *Kindergarten Teaching in India: Stories, Object Lesson Occupations, Songs and Games* (London: Macmillan & Co., 1899)

British Medical Journal (September 30, 1899)

Bruce, C., *John Lawrence: Saviour of India* (Edinburgh, 1893)

Carpenter, M., *Juvenile Delinquents: Their Condition and Treatment* (London: W. Cash, 1853)

[Carpenter, M.], *Addresses to the Hindoos Delivered in India by Mary Carpenter* (London: Newman & Co., 1867)

Carpenter, M., *Six Months in India* (London: Longmans, 1868)

———*The Last Days in England of the Rajah Rammohan Roy* (Calcutta: The Rammohan Library, 1915)

Caton, A. R. (ed.), *The Key of Progress* (London: Humphrey Milford, 1930)

Chapman, E. F., *Sketches of Some Distinguished Indian Women* (London: Allen & Co., 1891)

Chapman, P., *Hindoo Female Education* (London: R. B. Seeley and W. Burnside, 1839)

———*Hindu In Bengal Female Education* (Surrey: L. and G. Seeley, 1839)

Chatterton, E., *The History of the Church of England in India* (London: SPCK, 1924)

Crane, R. and Johnston, A. (eds.) of the reprint of Steel, F. A and Gardiner, G., *The Complete Indian Housekeeper and Cook* [first published 1888] (Oxford: Oxford University Press, 2010)

Cornelius, J. J., *Rabindranath Tagore: India's Schoolmaster, a Study of Tagore's Experiment in the Indianization of Education in the Light of India's History* (New York: Columbia University, 1928)

Cotton, J. S., *Quinquennial Education Report, 1892–97* (London: HMSO, 1898)

Cousins, M. E., *Indian Womanhood Today* (Allahabad: Law Journal Press, 1941)

———*The Awakening of Asian Womanhood* (Madras: Ganesh & Co., 1922)

Croft, A., *Review of Education in India in 1886* (Calcutta: Government Printing, 1888)

Danvers, F. C., *et al. Memorials of Old Haileybury College* (London: Constable & Co., 1894)

Deed J. (ed.), *Church Work: Mission Life* (London: Wells, Gardner & Darton & Co., 1885)

Dufferin, Countess, *A Record of Three Years' Work of the National Association for Supplying Female Medical Aid to the Women of India, August 1885-August 1888* (Calcutta: Thacker, Spink & Co., 1888)

Dufferin, H. G., 'Preface' in E. F. Chapman (eds), *Sketches of Some Distinguished Indian Women* (London: Allen & Co., 1891)

Edwardes, H. B., *Life of Sir Henry Lawrence* (London: Smith & Elder, 1873)

Francis, F. A., 'Some Municipal Schools in the Punjab' in the *Maria Grey College Magazine* (London: Baines and Scarsbrook, 1891)

Gandhi, M. K., *Basic Education* (Ahmedabad: Navajivan, 1951)

Hamilton-Temple-Blackwood, H. G. [Lady Dufferin], *Our Viceregal Life in India* (London: John Murray, 1889)

Hamilton-Temple-Blackwood, H. G., *The National Association for Supplying Female Medical Aid to the Women of India* (Calcutta: Thacker, Spink & Co., 1886)

Harris, G. F. A., (Inspector General, Civil Hospitals, Bengal), *Triennial Report on the Charitable Dispensaries Under the Government of Bengal for the Years 1908, 1909 and 1910* (Calcutta: Bengal Secretariat Book Department, 1911)

Harvey, R., 'Origin of Leper Work in Nasik' in J. Jackson (ed.), *Lepers: Thirty-One Years' Work Among Them* (London: Simpson & Co. [n.d.])

Howell, A., *Education in British India Prior to 1854 and in 1871* (Calcutta: Government Printing, 1871)

Hunter, W. W., *Report of the Hunter Commission* (Calcutta: Government Printing, 1883)

———'Education Commission Report' Home Department (Education) (Calcutta, 1883) in M. A. Chishti (ed.), *Committees and Commissions in Pre-Independence India, 1836–47* (New Delhi: Mittal, 2001)

Ibbetson, D., *Census of India* (Calcutta: Government Printing, 1883)

Indian Education Policy, 1913 being a resolution issued by the Governor General in Council on the 21st February, 1913 (Calcutta: Government Printing, 1914)

Indian Who's Who of 1937–8 (Bombay: Yeshanand & Co., 1939)

Jex-Blake, S., *Medical Women: A Thesis and its History* (London: Hamilton & Adams, 1886)

——'Medicine as a Profession for Women' in J. Butler (ed.), *Woman's Work and Woman's Culture* (London: Macmillan, 1869)

Karve, D. D., *The New Brahmans: Five Maharashtrian Families* (Berkerley, CA: University of California Press, 1963)

Kelly, S. (ed.), *The Life of Mrs Sherwood* (London: Darton & Co., 1854)

Kipling, R., *Kim* (London: Macmillan & Co., 1901)

Kittredge, G., *A Short History of the Medical Women for India Fund* (Bombay: Education Society's Press, 1889)

Leitner, G., 'History of Indigenous Education in the Punjab Since Annexation and in 1882' in U. Sharma and S. Sharma (eds), *Women's Education in British India* (New Delhi: Commonwealth Publishers, 1995)

Linton, E., 'A Word in Season', *Literary Digest*, October 5, 1895

Long, J. [CMS], *Handbook of the Bengal Missions in Connection with the Church of England* (London: John Shaw, 1848)

Long, J., 'Introduction', *Adam's Reports on Vernacular Education* (Calcutta: Secretariat Press, 1868)

MacKinnon, G., 'Diseases of Women' in W. Byam and R. G. Archibald (eds), *The Practice of Medicine in the Tropics*, vol. 3 (1923) Section xvii, pp. 2471–98

Maria Grey College Magazine (July, 1891) (London: Baines and Scarsbrook, 1891)

Martineau, H., 'Suggestions Towards the Future Government of India, 1858' in P. Tuson (ed), *The Queen's Daughters* (Reading, UK: Ithaca, 2007)

Mill, J., *History of British India*, 3 vols. (London: Baldwin, Cradock & Joy, 1818)

Miss Hamilton's Report, *Lucknow in the Twenty-Third Report of the Indian Female Normal School and Instructional Society* (Birmingham: Josiah Allen, 1875)

Mitra, P. C., *A Biographical Sketch of David Hare* (Calcutta: Basumati Sahitya Mandir, 1877)

Müller, J. C., *Some personal reminiscences of work in the Delhi Medical Mission, 1884–1910* (Buffalo, NY: Richmond Clay, 1910)

Murdoch, J., *Hints on Government Education in India with Special Reference to School Books* (Madras: C. Forster and Co., 1873)

Nathan, R., *Progress of Education in India 1897/98* (Calcutta: Government Printing, 1904)

New York Times, May 3, 1896

Platt, K., *Home and Health in India and the Tropical Colonies* (London: Baillière, Tindal & Cox, 1923)

Robertson, W. N., (Surgeon General, Bengal), *Triennial Report on the Working of Hospitals and Dispensaries under the Government of Bengal for the Years, 1917, 1918 and 1919* (Calcutta: Secretariat Book Dept., 1920)

Rousseau, J., *Émile: or A Treatise on Education* (1762)

Runganadhan, C. S., *History of the City of Madras* (Madras: Varadachary & Co., 1939)

Saha, M., *History of Indian Medicine based on Vedic Literature* (Calcutta: Asiatic Society, 1999)

[Sadler, M.] *Calcutta University Commission* (Calcutta: Government Printing, 1919)

Seal, B., *Comparative Studies in Vaishnavism and Christianity with an Examination of the Mahabharata Legend about Narada's Pilgrimage to Svetadvipa and an Introduction to the Historico-Comparative Method* (Calcutta, 1899)

Sherwood, M., *Stories Explanatory of the Church Catechism* (Baltimore: Protestant Episcopal Female Tract Society of Baltimore, 1823)

Sorabji, C., *India Calling: The Memories of Cornelia Sorabji, India's First Woman Barrister* (London: Nisbet, 1934)

Spencer, A. (ed.), *Memoirs of William Hickey* (London: Hurst & Blackett, 1948)

Steel, F. A. and Gardiner, G., *The Complete Indian Housekeeper and Cook* (Oxford: Oxford University Press, 1902 [reprint] 2010)

Stock, E., *The History of the Church Missionary Society* (London: CMS, 1899)

Stretch, L. M., *The Beauties of History or Pictures of Virtue and Vice Drawn from Real Life* (Paris, 1808)

Surhone, L. M., Tennoe, M. T. and Henssonow, S. F. (eds) [S. V. Pillai], *Prathapa Mudaliar Charithram* [originally published in 1879] (Saarbrücken, Germany: Betascript, 2010)

Swain, C. A., 'Medical Work', *Woman's Foreign Missionary Society of the Methodist Episcopal Church* (Boston, MA: Publications Office, 1906)

Tate, T., *The Philosophy of Education or the Principles and Practice of Teaching* (New York: E. L. Kellogg & Co., 1885) [first edition preface dated 1857]

Taylor, M. A. H., *The Education of Women in India* (St Albans, UK: Bamford, 1910)

The Times, 1859, 1880

Temple, R. C., *Panjab Notes and Queries: A Monthly Periodical* (London: Trubner & Co., n.d.)

Trotter, L. J. *Lord Lawrence: A Sketch of His Public Career* (London: Allen & Co., 1880)

Vaughan, K., *The British Medical Journal*, October 17, 1908

Wace, E. B. and Bourne, F. C., 'Montgomery District, Part A', *Punjab District Gazetteers* (Lahore: Government Printing, 1935 [1933 revised edition])

Weitbrecht, Mrs, *The Women of India and Christian Work in the Zenana* (London: James Nisbet & Co., 1875)

Wernher, H., *My Indian Family* (New York: John Day Company, 1945)

Westcott, Rev. A., *Our Oldest Indian Mission: A Brief History of the Vepery (Madras) Mission* (Madras: Madras Diocesan Committee Publishing, 1897)

[Wilkinson, L.] *A Brief Notice of the Late Mr Lancelot Wilkinson of the Bombay Civil Service with his Opinions on the Education of Natives of India and on the State of Native Society* (Cornhill: Smith, Elder and Co., 1853)

Woman's Herald, 1892

Secondary sources
Articles

Allender, T., 'Anglican Evangelism in North India and the Punjabi Missionary Classroom: the Failure to Educate "the Masses", 1860–77', *History of Education*, 32 (May, 2003)

———'Bad Language in the Raj: The 'Frightful Encumberance' of Gottleib Leitner, 1865–88', *Paedagogica Historica*, 43:3 (2007)

———'Closing Down an Intellectual Interchange: The Gifting of Text to a Colonial India', *Comparativ*, 1 (January, 2012)

———'Learning Abroad: The Colonial Educational Experiment in India, 1813–1919', *Paedagogica Historica*, 45:6 (2009)

———'Robert Montgomery and the Koree Mar (Daughter Slayers): A Punjabi Educational Imperative, 1855–65', *South Asia-Journal of South Asian Studies* (2002)

———'William Arnold and Experimental Education in North India, 1855–59: An Innovative Model of State Schooling', *Historical Studies in Education*, 16:1 (2004)

Arnold, D., 'European Orphans and Vagrants in India in the Nineteenth Century', *Journal of Imperial and Commonwealth History*, 7:2 (1979)

———'White Colonisation and Labour in Nineteenth Century India', *Journal of Imperial and Commonwealth History*, 12:2 (1983)

Atwal, J., 'Foul Unhallow'd Fires: Officiating Sati and the Colonial Hindu Widow in the United Provinces', *Studies in History,* 29:2 (2013)

———'Revisiting Premchand: Shivrani Devi on Companionship, Reformism and Nation', *Economic and Political Weekly*, (May, 2007)

Bear, L. G., 'Miscegenations of Modernity: Constructing European Respectability and Race in the Indian Railway Colony, 1857–1931', *Women's History Review*, 3:4 (1994)

Brewis, G., 'Education for Service: Social Service and Higher Education in India and Britain, 1905–1919' in T. Allender and J. Collins (eds), 'Knowledge Transfer and the History of Education', special issue of the *History of Education Review*, 42:2 (2013)

Burton, A., 'Contesting The Zenana: The Mission To Make "Lady Doctors For India" 1874–85', *Journal Of British Studies*, 35:3 (1996)

Campbell, G., ' The East African Slave Trade, 1861–95: the Southern Complex', *The International Journal of African Historical Studies*, 22:1 (1989)

Caruso, M., 'The Persistence of Educational Semantics: Patterns of Variation in Monitorial Schooling in Columbia (1821–44)', *Paedagogica Historica: International Journal of the History of Education*, 41:6 (2005)

Chambers, J., 'Thomas Tate's Forgotten Philosophy of Education', *Educational Theory*, 13:4 (1964)

Chatterjee, I., 'Monastic Governmentality, Colonial Misogyny, and Post Colonial Amnesia in South Asia', *History of the Present: A Journal of Critical History*, 3:1 (2013)

Chauduri, N. and Stroebel, M., 'Western Women and Imperialism', *Women's Studies International Forum*, 8:4 (1990)

BIBLIOGRAPHY

Coloma, R. C., 'White Gazes, Brown Breasts: Imperial Feminism and Disciplining Desires and Bodies in Colonial Encounters', *Paedagogica Historica*, 48:2 (2012)

Cotè, J., '"The Sins of Their Fathers": Culturally at Risk Children and the Colonial State in Asia', *Paedagogica Historicq* 45:1–2 (2009)

Dyhouse, C., 'Social Darwinism Ideas and the Development of Women's Education', *History of Education*, 5:1 (1976)

Fazli, A. and Kavyani, Y., 'Evaluating the Performance of the Agricultural Bank in Allocating Rural Credits', *International Journal of Academic Research*, 2:6:1 (November, 2010)

Gupta, C., 'Portrayal of Women in Prechand's Stories: A Critique', *Social Scientist*, 19:5–6 (1991)

Hammond, T., "Paidikion": Paiderastic Manuscript', *International Journal of Greek Love* (NY), I, 28:37 (1966)

Hellinckx, B., Simon, F. and Depaepe, M., 'The Forgotten Contribution of Teaching Sisters: A Historiographical Essay on the Educational Work of Catholic Women Religious in the 19th and 20th Centuries', *Studia Paedagogica*, 44 (2009)

Hodges, S., '"Looting" the Lock Hospitals in Madras during the famine years of the 1870s', *Social History of Medicine*, 18:3 (2005)

Jordan, E., 'Making Good Wives and Mothers?', *History of Education Quarterly*, 31:4 (1991)

Kakar, S., 'Leprosy in British India, 1860–1940', *Medical History*, 40 (1996)

Karlekar, M., 'Kadambini and the Bhadralok: Early Debates Over Women's Education in Bengal', *Economic and Political Weekly* 21:17 (April, 1986)

Kishwar, M., 'Arya Samaj and Women's Education: Kanya Mahavidyalaya, Jalandhar', *Economic and Political Weekly*, 21:17 (1986)

Koven, S. and Michel, S., 'Womanly Duties: Maternalist Politics and the Origins of Welfare States in France, Germany, Great Britain, and the United States, 1880–1920', *The American Historical Review*, 95:4 (October, 1990)

Lester, A., 'Imperial Circuits and Networks: Geographies of the British Empire', *History Compass*, 4:1 (2006)

Lutzker, E., 'Edith Pechey-Phipson, M. D.: Untold Story', *Medical History*, 11:1 (January, 1967)

Mashtaq, M. U., 'Public Health in British India: A Brief Account of the History of Medical Services and Disease Prevention in Colonial India', *Indian Journal of Community Medicine*, 34:1 (January, 2009)

Mooney, C., 'Securing a Private Classical Education In and Around Sydney: 1830–1850', *History of Education Review*, 25:1 (1996)

Mund, S., 'Krupabai Sattianadhan: The Portrait of an Indian Lady', *The Ravenshaw Journal of English Studies*, 6:1 (1996)

Nalini, N., 'Gender Dynamics of Missionary Work in India and its Impact on Women's Education: Isabella Thoburn (1840–1901): A Case Study', *Journal of International Women's Studies*, 7:4 (2006)

Nalini, M., 'Pioneer Woman Physician as Medical Missionary to the Women of the Orient, Clara A. Swain, M.D' (1834–1910) in *International Journal of Innovation, Management and Technology*, 1:2 (June, 2010)

O'Donoghue, T. and Hartford, S., 'Contesting the Limond Thesis on British Influence in Irish Education since 1922: A Comparative Perspective', *Comparative Education*, 1:10 (2012)

Phillips, D. and Ochs, K., 'Processes of Policy Borrowing in Education; Some Explanatory and Analytical Devices', *Comparative Education*, 39:4 (November, 2003)

Prakash, G., 'Science "Gone Native" in Colonial India', *Representations*, 40 (1992)

Ramusack, B., 'Cultural Missionaries, Maternal Imperialists, Feminist Allies: British Women Activists in India, 1865–1945', *Women's Studies International Forum*, 8:4 (1990)

Roberts, D. S., ' "Merely Birds of Passage": Lady Hariot Dufferin's travel writings and medical work in India', *Women's History Review*, 15:3 (2006)

Tomaselli, S., 'The Enlightenment Debate on Women', *History Workshop Journal*, 20 (1985)

Tschurenev, J., 'Diffusing Useful Knowledge: the Monitorial System of Education in Madras, London and Bengal, 1789–1840', *Paedagogica Historica*, 44:3 (2008)

Tusan, M. W., 'Writing Stri Dharma: International Feminism, National Politics, and Women's Press Advocacy in Late Colonial India', *Women's History Review*, 12:4 (2003)

Watts, R., Mary Carpenter and India: Enlightened Liberalism or Condescending Imperialism?', *Pedagogica Historica*, Supplementary Series 7 (February, 2001)

Whitehouse, D. and Frith, K., 'Designing Learning Spaces That Work: A Case For The Importance of History', T. Allender (ed.), *'Work! Work! Work!: Work and the History of Education'*, *History of Education Review*, 38:2 (2009)

Books

Allen, C., *Plain Tales From The Raj* (Newton Abbot, UK: Readers Union, 1976)

Allender, T., *Ruling Through Education* (New Delhi: Sterling, 2006)

Amaladas, A., 'Jesuits and Sanskrit Studies' in T. J. De Sousa and C. J. Borges (eds.), *Jesuits in India: In Historical Perspective* (Macau: Xavier Centre of Historical Research, 1992)

Amin, S. and Bhadra, G., 'Ranajit Guha: A Biographical Sketch' in D. Arnold and D. Hardiman (eds), *Subaltern Studies VIII* (Delhi: Oxford University Press, 1994)

Anagol, P., 'From the Symbolic to the Open: Women's Resistance in Colonial Maharashtra' in A. Ghosh (ed.), *Behind the Vale: Resistance, Women and the Everyday in Colonial South Asia* (Basingstoke, UK: Palgrave Macmillan, 2008)

Anagol, P., *The Emergence of Feminism in India, 1850–1920* (Aldershot, UK: Ashgate, 2005)

Andermahr, S., Lovell, T. and Wolkowitz, C., *A Concise Glossary of Feminist Theory* (London, Arnold, 1997)

Arnold, D., *Colonizing the Body: State Medicine and Epidemic Disease in Nineteenth-Century India* (Berkeley, CA: University of California Press, 1993)

Avinashilingam, T. S., *Gandhiji's Experiments in Education* (New Delhi: Government of India, 1969)

Bagchi, A. K., Sinha, D. and Bagchi, B. (eds) *Webs of History: Information, Communication and Technology from Early to Post-Colonial India* (New Delhi: Manohar, 2005)

Bagchi, B., *Pliable Pupils and Sufficient Self-directors: Narratives of Female Education by Five British Women Writers, 1778–1884* (New Delhi: Tulika, 2004)

Bala, P. (ed.), 'Introduction', *Contesting Colonial Authority: Medicine and Indigenous Responses in Nineteenth and Twentieth Century India* (Maryland: Lexington Books, 2012)

Ballantyne, T., *Orientalism and Race: Aryanism in the British Empire.* (Basingstoke, UK: Palgrave, 2002)

Bellenoit, H., *Missionary Education and Empire in Late Colonial India, 1860–1920* (London: Pickering and Chatto, 2007)

Ballhatchet, K., *Caste, Class and Catholicism in India, 1789–1914* (Richmond, UK: Curzon, 1998)

———*Race, Sex, and Class under the Raj: Imperial Attitudes and Policies and their Critics, 1793–1905* (London: Weidenfeld and Nicolson, 1980)

Barrett, T. R., *Calcutta: Strange Memoirs-Foreign Perceptions*(Kolkata: Sankar Mondal, 2004)

Barwick, D. E., *Rebellion at Coranderrk* (Canberra: Aboriginal History Inc., 1998)

Basu, A., 'A Century and a Half's Journey: Women's Education in India, 1850s to 2000' in B. Ray (ed.), *Women of India: Colonial and Post-Colonial Periods* (New Delhi: Bhuvan Chandel, 2005)

———'A Century's Journey, Women's Education in Western India: 1820–1920' in K. Chanana (ed.), *Socialisation of Education and Women* (New Delhi: Sangam, 1988)

Basu, A. and Ray, B., *Women's Struggle. A History of the All India Women's Conference, 1927–2002* (New Delhi: Manohar, 1990)

Bayly, C. A., *Empire and Information: Intelligence Gathering and Social Communication in India, 1780–1870* (Cambridge: Cambridge University Press, 1996)

———*Recovering Liberties: Indian Thought in the Age of Liberalism and Empire* (Cambridge: Cambridge University Press, 2012)

Bell, E. M., *Storming the Citadel: the Rise of the Woman Doctor* (London: Constable, 1953)

Bharathi, K. S., *The Thoughts of Gandhi and Vinoba: A Comparative Study* (New Delhi: Ashok Kumar Mittal, 1995)

Bhargava, M. and Dutta, K., *Women, Education and Politics: the Women's Movement and Delhi's Indraprastha College* (New Delhi: Oxford University Press, 2005)

Bhattacharya, S., Bara, J., Yagati, C. R. and Sankhdher, B. M., (eds.) *The Development of Women's Education in India: A collection of documents 1850–1920* (New Delhi: Kanishka, 2001)

Bordo, S., *Unbearable Weight: Feminism, Western Culture and the Body* (Berkerley, CA: University of California Press, 1993)

Borthwick, M., *Keshub Chunder Sen*(Calcutta: Minerva, 1977)

———*The Changing Role of Women in Bengal, 1849–1905* (Princeton, NJ: Princeton University Press, 1984)

Bose, P., *Organising Empire: Individualism, Collect Agency and India* (Durham, NC: Duke University Press, 2003)

Bourdieu, P., *Language and Symbolic Power* (Cambridge: Polity, 1991)

Brass, P. R., *Language, Religion and Politics in North India* (Lincoln, NE: iUniverse, 2005)

Bold, J. and Hinchcliffe, T., *Discovering London's Buildings* (London: Frances Lincoln, 2009)

Brendon, V., *Children of the Raj* (London: Phoenix, 2006)

Brown, J. M., *Gandhi: Prisoner of Hope* (London: Yale University Press, 1989)

Buettner, E., *Empire Families: Britons and Late Imperial India* (Oxford: Oxford University Press, 2004)

Burbank, J. and Cooper, F., *Empires in World History: Power and the Politics of Difference* (Princeton, NJ: Princeton University Press, 2010)

Burton, A., *At the Heart of Empire: Indians and the Colonial Encounter in late Victorian Britain* (Berkeley, CA: University of California Press, 1998)

———*Burdens of History: British Feminists, Indian Women and Imperial Culture, 1865–1915* (Chapel Hill, NC: University of North Carolina Press, 1994)

Campbell, C., *Race and Empire: Eugenics Thought in Colonial Kenya* (Manchester: Manchester University Press, 2007)

Carton, A., *Mixed-Race and Modernity in Colonial India: Changing Concepts of Hybridity Across Empires* (London: Routledge, 2012)

Chandra, R. [revised version of] L. Rai, *A History of the Arya Samaj: An Account of its Origins, Doctrines and Activities with a Biographical Sketch of its Founder* (New Delhi: Orient Longmans, 1967)

Chatfield, C., *The Americanization of Gandhi: Images of the Mahatma* (New York: Garland, 1976)

Chatterjee, I., *Forgotten Friends: Monks, Marriages, and Memories of Northeast India* (New Delhi, Oxford University Press: 2013)

Chatterjee, P., 'A Brief History of Subaltern Studies' in P. Chatterjee (ed.), *Empire and Nation, Selected Essays* (New York: Columbia University Press, 2010)

———'The Nationalist Resolution of the Women's Question' in K. Sangari and S. Vaid (eds), *Recasting Women: Essays in Indian Colonial History* (New Brunswick, NJ: Rutgers University Press, 1990)

———*The Nation and its Fragments* (Princeton, NJ: Princeton University Press, 1993)

Clark, M. R., *Loreto in Australia* (Sydney: University of NSW Press, 2009)

Cohn, B., *Colonialism and Its Forms of Knowledge* (Delhi: Oxford University Press, 1997)

Collett, S., *Keshub Chunder Sen's English Visits* (London: Sophia Dobson, 1900)

Collingham, E. M., *Imperial Bodies: The Physical Experience of the Raj, c. 1800–1947* (Cambridge: Polity, 2001)

Connell, R., *Gender in World Perspective* (Cambridge: Polity, 2009)

Cooke, G. W., *Unitarianism in America* (Gutenberg: Steiner, Lund and Franks, 2005)

Cox, J., 'Independent English women in Delhi and Lahore, 1860–1947' in R. W. Davis and R. J. Helmstadter (eds), *Religion and Irreligion in Victorian Society: Essays in Honor of R. K. Webb* (New York: Routledge, 1991)

Curthoys, A. and Lake, M., *Connected Worlds: History in Transnational Perspective.* (Canberra: ANU E, 2005)

Darian-Smith, K., Grimshaw, P. and Macintyre, S., *Britishness Abroad: Transnational Movements and Imperial Cultures* (Melbourne: Melbourne University Press, 2007)

Davis, R. W. and Helmstadter, R. J., *Religion and Irreligion in Victorian Society* (London: Routledge, 1991)

Day, D., *Andrew Fisher, Prime Minister of Australia* (Sydney: Harper Collins, 2008)

de Bellaigue, C., *Educating Women: Schooling and Identity in England and France, 1800–67* (Oxford: Oxford University Press, 2007)

De Courcy, A., *The Fishing Fleet: Husband-Hunting in the Raj* (London: Weidenfeld and Nicolson, 2012)

Dewan, D. E., *Education in the Darjeeling Hills: An Historical Survey: 1835–1985* (New Delhi: Indus, 1991)

Dirks, N., *Castes of Mind: Colonialism and the Making of Modern India* (Princeton, NJ: Princeton University Press, 2001)

D'Souza, A., *Anglo-Indian Education: A Study of its Origins and Growth in Bengal up to 1960* (Delhi: Oxford University Press, 1976)

Dutta, K. and Robinson, A., *Rabindranath Tagore: the Myriad-Minded Man* (New York: St Martin's, 1996)

Dyhouse, C., *Students: A Gendered Role* (New York: Routledge, 2006)

Elliot, E., *A Chance to Die: The Life and Legacy of Amy Carmichael* (Old Tappan, NJ: Revell, 1987)

Eraly, A., *The Mughal Throne* (London: Weidenfeld & Nicolson, 2003)

——*The Mughal World* (New Delhi: Penguin, 2007)

Ernst, E., 'Madness and Colonial Spaces: British India, c. 1800–1947' in L. Topp *et al.* (eds), *Madness Architecture and the Built Environment* (London: Routledge, 2007)

Farnie, D. A., *East and west of Suez: the Suez Canal in history, 1854–1956* (Oxford: Clarendon, 1969)

Faye, D., *Jane Austen* (London: British Library, c. 2003)

Fernades, W., 'Jesuit Contribution to Social Change in India (16th to 20th Centuries)' in T. S. de Sousa and C. J. Borges (eds), *Jesuits in India: In Historical Perspective.* (Macau: Xavier Centre of Historical Research, 1992)

Fitzgerald, R., 'From Medicine Chest to Mission Hospitals: The early history of the Delhi Medical Mission for Women and Children' in D. O'Connor (ed.), *Three Centuries of Mission: The United Society for the Propagation of the Gospel* (London: Bloomsbury Publishing, 2000)

——'Rescue and Redemption: The rise of female medical missions in colonial India during the late nineteenth and early twentieth centuries' in A. M. Rafferty *et al.* (eds.), *Nursing History and the Politics of Welfare* (Routledge: London, 1997)

Flemming, L., *Women's Work for Women* (Colorado: Westfield Press, 1989)

Forbes, G., *The New Cambridge History of India: Women in Modern India* (Cambridge, Cambridge University Press, 1996)

——*Women in Colonial India: Essays on Politics, Medicine and Historiography* (Bangalore: Orient, 2005)

——*Women in Modern India* (New York: Cambridge University Press, 2004)

——*Women in Modern India* (The New Cambridge History of India), vol. 4:2 (Cambridge: Cambridge University Press, 1996)

——*Women in Colonial India* (New Delhi: Chronicle Books, 2008)

Foucault, M, 'Two Lectures' in N. Dirks, G. Eley and S. Ortner (eds), *Culture/Power/History: A Reader in Contemporary Social Theory* (Princeton, NJ: Princeton University Press, 1994).

Foxe, B., *Long Journey Home: A Biography of Margaret Noble (Nivedita)* (London: Ryder & Co., 1975)

French, F., *Miss Brown's hospital: the story of the Ludhiana Medical College* (London: Hodder & Stoughton, 1954)

Gandhi, I., *Shreemati Nathibai Damodar Thackersey Women's University* (Bombay: Golden Jubilee, 1966)

George, S., '"Dirty Nurses" and "Men Who Play": Gender and Class in Transnational Migration' in M. Burawoy *et al.*(eds.), *Global Ethnography* (Berkeley, CA: University of California Press, 2000)

Gilley, S., 'Catholicism, Ireland and the Irish Diaspora' in S. Gilley and B. Stanley, *Cambridge History of Christianity* (Cambridge: Cambridge University Press, 2006)

Goodman, J. and Rogers, R., 'Crossing Borders in Girls' Secondary Education' in J. C. Albisetti, J. Goodman and R. Rogers (eds), *Girls' Secondary Education in the Western World* (New York: Palgrave Macmillan, 2010)

Goodman, J. and Martin, J., *Women and Education, 1800–1980* (Basingstoke, UK: Palgrave Macmillan, 2004)

Gorman, D., *Imperial Citizenship: Empire and the question of belonging* (Manchester: Manchester University Press, 2006)

Gottschalk, P., 'Promoting Scientism: Institutions for Gathering and Disseminating Knowledge in British Bihar' in I. Sengupta and D. Ali (eds), *Knowledge Production, Pedagogy and Institutions in Colonial India* (London: Palgrave Macmillan, 2011)

Guha, S., 'Dais to Doctors: The Medicalisation of Childbirth in Colonial India' in L. Lakshmi (ed.), *Understanding Women's Health Issues* (Delhi: Oscar, 1998)

Gujral, S., *A Brush With Life* (New Delhi: Viking, 1997)

Hafkin, N. and Bay, E., *Women in Africa* (Stanford, CA: Stanford University Press, 1976)

Hall, C., *At Home with the Empire* (Cambridge: Cambridge University Press, 2006)

Hartley, C. (ed.), *A Historical Dictionary of British Women* (New York: Routledge, 2003)

Hattersley, R., *The Edwardians* (London: Abacus, 2004)

Hawes, C. J., *Poor Relations: The Making of a Eurasian Community in British India, 1773–1833* (Richmond, UK: Curzon, 1996)

Heimsath, C. H., *Indian Nationalism and Hindu Social Reform* (Princeton, NJ: Princeton University Press, 1964)

Hollis, P., *Women in Public: Documents of the Victorian Women's Movement 1850–1900* (London: George Allen & Unwin, 1979)

Hughes, Sister M. IBVM, *Epic Women: East and West* (Calcutta: The Asiatic Society, 1994)

Humm, M., *The Dictionary of Feminist Theory* (New York: London, 1995)

Hurt, J. S., *Elementary Schooling and the Working Classes* (London: Routledge, 1979)

Huttenback, R. A., *Gandhi in South Africa* (Ithica, NY: Cornell University Press, 1971)

Hyam, R., *Empire and Sexuality* (Manchester: Manchester University Press, 1991)

Inglis, T., *Moral Monopoly: The Rise and Fall of the Catholic Church in Modern Ireland* (Dublin: University College Dublin Press, 1998)

Jayal, N. G., *Indian Diary: Sidney and Beatrice Webb* (Delhi: Oxford University Press, 1987)

Jayawardena, K., *The White Woman's Other Burden: Western Women and South Asia During the British Period* (New York: Routledge, 1995)

Johnston, A., *Missionary Writing and Empire, 1800–1860* (Cambridge: Cambridge University Press, 2003)

Jones, C., *Engendering Whiteness: White Women and Colonialism in Barbadoes and North Carolina, 1627–1865* (Manchester: Manchester University Press, 2007)

Kakar, S., *The Inner World: A Psycho-analytic Study of Childhood and Society in India* (New Delhi: Oxford University Press, 1978)

Kamm, J., *Indicative Past: A Hundred Years of the Girls' Public Day School Trust* (London: George Allen & Unwin, 1971)

Karlekar, M., *Visual Histories: Photography in the Popular Imagination* (New Delhi: Oxford University Press, 2013)

Kent, E. F., *Converting Women: Gender and Protestant Christianity in Colonial South India* (Oxford: Oxford University Press, 2004)

King, B. M., *Silk and Empire* (Manchester: Manchester University Press, 2009)

Knapp, A., *How to Live: A Manual of Hygiene* (New York: Silver: Burdett & Co., 1902)

Kosambi, M., *Pandita Ramabai Through Her Own Words: Selected Works* (New Delhi: Oxford University Press, 2000)

——'The Home as Social Universe' in I. Glushkova and A. Feldhaus (eds), *House and Home in Maharashtra* (Delhi: Oxford University Press, 1998)

Kozlowski, G. C., 'Muslim Women and the Control of Property in North India' in J. Krishnamurty (ed.), *Women in Colonial India* (Delhi: Oxford University Press, 1989)

Kramer, P. A., 'The Darkness that Enters the Home: the Politics of Prostitution during the Philippine-American War' in A. L. Stoler (ed.), *Haunted by Empire: Geographies of Intimacy in North American History* (Durham, NC: Duke University Press, 2006)

Kumar, K., *Poltical Agenda of Education: A Study of Colonialist and Nationalist Ideas* (London: SAGE, 2005)

Kumar, N., *The Politics of Gender, Community and Modernity* (New Delhi: Oxford University Press, 2007)

Lahiri, S., *Indians in Britain: Anglo-Indian Encounters, Race and Identity, 1880–1930* (London: Frank Cass, 2000)

Laidlaw, Z., *Colonial Connections 1815–45: Patronage, the Information Revolution and Colonial Government* (Manchester: Mancherster University Press, 2007)

Lambert-Hurley, S., 'Subtle Subversions and Presumptuous Interventions: Reforming Women's Health in Bhopal State in the Early Twentieth Century' in A. Ghosh, *Behind the Veil: Resistance, Women and the Everyday in Colonial South Asia* (London: Palgrave Macmillan, 2008)

Lambert-Hurley, S. and Sharma, S. (eds), *Atiya's Journeys: A Muslim Woman from Colonial Bombay to Edwardian Britain* (New Delhi: Oxford, 2010)

Lata, M., *Contentious Traditions: the Debate on Sati in Colonial India* (Berkerley, CA: University of California Press, 1998)

Lawrence, D., *Genteel Women: Empire and Domestic Material Culture, 1840-1910* (Manchester: Manchester University Press, 2012)

Levine, P., 'Sexuality, Gender and Empire' in P. Levine (ed.), *Gender and Empire* (Oxford: Oxford University Press, 2004)

Lillard, A. S., *Montessori: The Science Behind the Genius* (New York: Oxford University Press, 2005)

Mann, R. S.,*Culture and the Integration of Indian Tribes* (New Delhi: M. D. Publications, 1993)

Manton, J., *Elizabeth Garrett Anderson* (New York: E. P. Dutton, 1965)

Marland, H., *Health and Girlhood in Britain, 1874–1920* (Basingstoke, UK: Macmillan Palgrave, 2013)

Marshall, N. I., *The Anglo-Indian Absconder Soldier Daddy* (New Delhi: Marshall and Myers, 2011)

Masselos, J., 'The Dis/appearance of Subalterns: A Reading of a Decade of Subaltern Studies' in D. Ludden (ed.), *Reading Subaltern Studies: Critical History, Contested Meaning and the Globalization of South Asia* (London: Anthem, 2002)

McClintock, A., *Imperial Leather: Race, Gender and Sexuality in the Colonial Contest* (New York: Routledge, 1995)

MacKenzie, J. M., *Orientalism: History, theory and the arts* (Manchester: Manchester University Press, 1995)

———*Propaganda and Empire: The Manipulation of British Public Opinion, 1880–1960* (Manchester: Manchester University Press, 1984)

Macmillan, M., *Women of the Raj* (London: Thames & Hudson, 1988)

Marriott, J., *The Other Empire: Metropolis, India and Progress in the Colonial Imagination* (Manchester: Manchester University Press, 2003)

BIBLIOGRAPHY

Mc Dermid, J., *The Schooling for Girls in Britain and Ireland, 1800–1900* (London: Routledge, 2012)

McDonald, L. and Vallée, G. (eds) *Florence Nightingale on Social Change in India* (Ontario: Wilfrid Laurier University Press, 2007)

Midgley, C., 'Anti-slavery and the Roots of "Imperial Feminism"' in C. Midgley (ed.), *Gender and Imperialism* (Manchester: Manchester University Press)

Minault, G., *Gender, Language and Learning: Essays in Indo-Muslim Cultural History* (New Delhi: Permanent Black, 2009)

Minault, G., *Secluded Scholars: Women's Education and Muslim Social Reform in Colonial India* (Oxford: Oxford University Press, 1998)

Mitra, A., *The Financing of Indian Education* (London: Asia, 1967)

Mohanty, C., 'Cartographies of Struggle' in C. Mohanty, A. Russo and L. Torres (eds), *Third World Women and the Politics of Feminism* (Bloomington, IN: Indiana University Press, 1991)

Mohapatra, P. and Mohanty, B., *Elite Women of India* (New Delhi: APH, 2002)

Moi, T., 'Sexual/Textual Politics: Feminist Literary Theory' in C. Belsey and J. Moore (eds), *The Feminist Reader: Essays in Gender and the Politics of Literary Criticism* (London: Macmillan, 1989)

Mommsen, W. J., *The Political and Social Theory of Max Weber* (Cambridge: Polity, 1989)

[Mooney, C.], *Loreto Day School, Sealdah* (New Delhi: Loreto, 2009)

Morgan, A., *J. Ramsay MacDonald* (Manchester: Manchester University Press, 1987)

Morgan, S., *Bombay Anna: The Real Story and Remarkable Adventures of the King and I Governess* (Berkley, CA: University of California Press, 2008)

Mukherji, P., 'Sex and Social Structure' in K. Chanana (ed.), *Socialisation Education and Women: Explorations in Gender Identity* (New Delhi: Sangam, 1988)

Murphy, A. B. and Raftery, D. (eds), *Emily Davies: Collected Letters, 1861–1875* (Virginia: University of Virginia Press, 2004)

Murshid, G., *Reluctant Debutante: Response of Bengali Women to Modernization, 1849–1905* (Rajshahi: Sahitya Samsad, 1983)

Nand, L. C., *Women in the Delhi Sultanate* (Allahabad: Vohra, 1989)

Nijhawan, S., *Women and Girls in the Hindi Public Sphere: Periodical Literature in Colonial North India* (New Delhi: Oxford University Press, 2012)

O'Donoghue, T., *Bilingual Education in Pre-independent Irish-speaking Ireland, 1800–1922* (Ceredigion, Wales: Edwin Mellen, 2006)

O'Hanlon, R., *At the Edges of Empire: Essays in the Social and Intellectual History of India* (Ranikhet: Permanent Black, 2014)

Offer, J., *Herbert Spencer and Social Theory* (New York: Palgrave Macmillan, 2010)

Olson, J. and Shadle, R. (eds), *Historical Dictionary of the British Empire* (Westport, CT: Greenwood, 1996)

O'Malley, K., *Ireland, India and Empire: Indo-Irish Radical Connections, 1919–64* (Manchester: Manchester University Press, 2009)

Omvedt, G., *Feminism and the Women's Movement of India* (Mumbai: SNDT Women's University, 1987)

Owen, N., *The British Left and India* (Oxford: Oxford University Press, 2007)

Pakula, H., *An Uncommon Woman: The Empress Frederick* (New York: Simon & Schuster, 1995)

Phillips, R., *Sex, Politics and Empire* (Manchester, Mnchester University Press, 2006)

Pietsch, T., *Empire of Scholars: Universities, networks and the British academic world, 1850–1939* (Manchester: Manchester University Press, 2013).

Poovey, M., *Making the Social Body: British Cultural Formation, 1830–1864* (Chicago, IL/London: University of Chicago, 1995)

Porter, A., *Religion Versus Empire: British Protestant Missionaries and Overseas Expansion, 1700–1914* (Manchester: Manchester University Press, 2004)

Pothen, N., *Glittering Decades: New Delhi in Love and War* (New Delhi: Viking, 2012)

Prasad, N. V., 'The Litigious Widow: Inheritance Disputes in Colonial North India, 1875–1911' in A. Ghosh (ed.), *Behind the Veil: Resistance, Women and the Everyday in Colonial South Asia* (London: Palgrave Macmillan, 2008)

Pugh, M., *The Pankhursts* (London: Allen Lane, 2001)

Puri, J., *Woman, Body, Desire in Post-colonial India: Narratives of Gender and Sexuality* (London: Routledge, 1999)

Ray, B., *Early Feminists of Colonial India: Sarala Devi Chaudhurani and Rokeya Sakhawat Hossain* (New Delhi: Oxford University Press, 2002)

Ramanna, M., *Western Medicine and Public Health in Colonial Bombay* (Bangalore: Orient Longman, 2002)

Rappaport, H., *Encyclopaedia of Women Social Reformers* (Santa Barbara, CA: ABC, 2001)

Ray, R. (ed.), *Handbook of Gender* (New Delhi: Oxford University Press, 2012)

Robert, D. L., *American Women in Mission: A Social History of Their Thought and Practice*, 4th Edition (Georgia: Mercer University Press: 2005)

Robinson-Dunn, D., *The Harem, Slavery and British Imperial Culture: Anglo-Muslim Relations in the Late Nineteenth Century* (Manchester: Manchester University Press, 2006)

Rowbotham, S., *A New World for Women: Stella Browne, Socialist Feminist* (London: Pluto, 1977)

Roy, A., *Mapping Citizenship in India* (New Delhi: Oxford University Press, 2011)

Rudolph, S. H., Rudolph, L. I. with Mohan Singh Kanota, *Reversing the Gaze: Amar Singh's Diary, a Colonial Subject's Narrative of Imperial India* (New Delhi: Oxford University Press, 2011)

Sangari, K., 'Relating Histories: Definitions of Literacy, Literature, Gender in Early Nineteenth Century Calcutta and England' in S. Joshi (ed.), *Rethinking English: Essays in Literature, Language, History* (New Delhi: Trianka, 1991)

Sargant, N., *Mary Carpenter in India* (Bristol: A. J. Sargant, 1987)

Sarkar, S., *Writing Social History* (Delhi: Oxford University Press, 1997)

BIBLIOGRAPHY

Scharfe, H., *Education in Ancient India* (Boston: Brill, 2002)

Selleck, R. J. W., *James Kay-Shuttleworth: Journey of an Outsider* (London: Woburn, 1994)

Seth, S., *Subject Lessons: The Western Education of Colonial India* (Durham, NC: Duke University Press, 2007)

Seton, R., *Western Daughters in Eastern Lands: British Missionary Women in Asia* (Santa Barbara, CA: Praeger, 2013)

Schriewer, J. and Martinez, C., 'Constructions of Internationality in Education' in G. Steiner-Khamsi (ed.), *The Global Politics of Educational Borrowing and Lending* (New York: Teachers' College Press, 2004)

Shapiro, M., *Childs Garden: The Kindergarten Movement from Froebel to Dewey* (University Park, PA: Penn State University Press, 1983)

Sharma, A. K., *A History of Educational Institutions in Delhi, 1911–1961* (New Delhi: Sanbun, 2011)

Sharma, S., *Famine, Philanthropy and the Colonial State* (New Delhi: Oxford University Press, 2001)

————'Neoliberalization' as Betrayal: State, Feminism and a Women's Education Program in India* (New York: Palgrave Macmillan, 2011)

Sharma, S. D., *India Marching: Reflections from a Nationalistic Perspective* (Indiana Universe, 2012)

Silber, K., *Pestalozzi: The Man and His Work* (London: Routledge and Kegan Paul, 1965)

Simon, B., *The Two Nations and the Educational Structure 1780–1870* (London: Lawrence & Wishart, 1974)

Sinha, M., *Colonial Masculinity; The 'Manly Englishman' and 'The Effeminate Bengali' in the late Nineteenth Century* (Manchester: Manchester University Press, 1995)

————'Nations in an Imperial Crucible' in P. Levine (ed.), *Gender and Empire* (Oxford: Oxford University Press, 2004)

————*Specters of Mother India: The Global Restructuring of an Empire* (Durham, NC: Duke University Press, 2006)

Smyth, E., 'Teaching Sisters, Leading Schools' in E. Smyth (ed.), *Changing Habits: Women's Religious Orders in Canada* (Ottawa: Novalis, 2007)

Spear, P., *The Nabobs: A Study of the Social Life of the English in Eighteenth Century India* (London: Oxford University Press, 1963)

Spivak, G. C., 'Can the Subaltern Speak?' in C. Nelson and L. Grossberg (eds), *Marxism and the Interpretation of Culture* (Chicago: University of Illinois Press, 1988)

Sramek, J., *Gender, Morality and Race in Company India, 1765–1858* (New York: Palgrave Macmillan, 2011)

Srivastava, G., *Women's Higher Education in the Nineteenth Century* (New Delhi: Concept, 2000)

Staffner, H., 'Jesuit Contribution to Dialogue in India' in T. S de Sousa and C. J. Borges (eds), *Jesuits in India: In Historical Perspective* (Macau: Xavier Centre of Historical Research, 1992)

Stanley, B., 'Andrew Walls and the Centre for the Study of Christianity in the Non-Western World' in W. R. Burrows, M. R. Gornik and J. McLean (eds), *Understanding World Christianity: The Vision and Work of Andrew F. Walls* (Orbis Books, 2012)

Stoler, A. L., *Race and the Education of Desire: Foucault's History of Sexuality and the Colonial Order of Things* (Durham, NC: Duke University Press, 1995)

Stokes, E., *The English Utilitarians and India* (Oxford: Clarendon, 1959)

Stopes, M., *Married Love* (London: G. P. Putnam's Sons, 1918)

Streets, H., *Martial Races: The Military, Race and Masculinity in British Imperial Culture, 1857–1914* (Manchester: Manchester University Press, 2004)

Stroebel, M., *European Women and the Second British Empire* (Bloomington: Indiana University Press, 1991)

Sutherland, G., *Elementary Education in the Nineteenth Century* (London: Historical Association, 1971)

Talwar, V. B., 'Feminist Consciousness in Women's Journals in Hindi, 1910–1920' in K. Sangari and S. Vaid, *Recasting Women* (New Jersey: Rutgers University Press, 1990)

Thapar-Björkert, S., *Women in the Indian National Movement* (London: SAGE, 2006)

Theobald, M., *Knowing Women: Origins of Women's Education in Nineteenth-Century Australia* (Cambridge: Cambridge University Press, 1996)

——'"Mere Accomplishments?" Melbourne's Early Ladies Schools Reconsidered' in A. Prentice and M. Theobald (eds), *Women Who Taught* (Toronto: University of Toronto Press, 1991)

Yadav, K. C., *Arya Samaj and the Freedom Movement* (New Delhi: Manohar, 1988)

Ware, V., *Beyond the Pale: White Women, Racism and History* (London: Verso, 1992)

Watt, C. A., 'Philanthropy and Civilizing Missions in India c. 1820–1960: States, NGOs and Development' in C. A. Watt and M. Mann (eds), *Civilizing Missions in Colonial and Postcolonial South Asia* (London: Anthem, 2011)

——*Serving the Nation: Cultures of Service, Association, and Citizenship* (Oxford: Oxford University Press, 2005)

Watts, R., *Gender, Power and the Unitarians in England, 1760–1860* (London: Longman, 1998)

——*Women in Science: A Social and Cultural History* (New York: Routledge, 2007)

Webster, A., *The Debate on the Rise of British Imperialism* (Manchester: Manchester University Press, 2006)

White, A., *The Story of Army Education, 1643–1963* (London: George Harrap, 1963)

Whitehead, C., *Colonial Educators* (London: IB Tauris, 2003)

Williams, S., *Poverty, Gender and Life-Cycle under the English Poor Law, 1760–1834* (Suffolk: Woodbridge, Boydell and Brewer, 2011)

Wilson, A. N., *Victoria: A Life* (London: Atlantic Books, 2014)

Witz, A., '"Colonising Women": Female Medical Practice in Colonial India, 1880–1890' in L. Conrad and A. Hardy (eds), *Women and Modern Medicine* (London: Welcome Trust, 2001)

Zastoupil, L. and Moir, M., *The Great Education Debate* (Richmond, UK: Curzon, 1999)

Zweiniger-Bargielowska, I., *Managing the Body: Beauty, Health and Fitness in Britain, 1880–1939* (Oxford: Oxford University Press, 2010)

Unpublished dissertations and seminar papers

Bubacz, B., 'The female and orphan schools in New South Wales, 1801–1850'. PhD thesis, 2007, University of Sydney

Nelson, A., 'Empire of knowledge: nationalism, internationalism, and the origins of the American University, 1770–1830'. Paper delivered at a Faculty of Education, University of Sydney Colloquium on August 8, 2011

Szpak, M., 'The life of Mary Ward, her contribution to social and religious education in the seventeenth century and the ministry of education of the Loreto Sisters'. MA thesis, 1995, King's College, London

Watts, R., 'Harriet Martineau (1802–77): a liberal Protestant/secular educationalist' a paper delivered on June 26, 2015 at the International Standing Conference for the History of Education (ISCHE 37) Istanbul, Turkey

Wilson, C. A., 'Montessori in India: a study of the application of her method in a developing country'. PhD thesis, 1987, University of Sydney

INDEX

middle-class
Bethune school 243
English/Indian categorisations 72
Eurasians 202–14, 299
European social mobility 92
Indian caste and 241
Loreto cross-subsidisation 275, 291
midwives 164, 182–3, 185, 190–3
missionary medical hegemony 197–8
Missionary Settlement for University
Women 246, 255
missionary status, female medical
professionals 189–90
mission dispensaries 168
mission hospitals 189, 192, 198
missions 129–54
inside the compound 135–9
key female sites 140–6
mission network 131–4
new communities 139–40
outside the compound 146–8
zenanas 148–54
see also CMS; SPG
mission training schools for nurses 198
money, Loreto funding 275–6
monitorial schools/teaching 50, 53, 55,
75, 102, 218
Montague-Chelmsford reforms 254
Montessori 252–4, 262
Montgomery, Lieutenant Governor
Robert 63–4
Morapai 287–9
Morley-Minto reforms 271
motherhood
Carpenter's *Juvenile Delinquents* 98–9
Froebel's kindergarten movement 219
Gandhi's 'better mothers' 233–65
midwives 182–3
racial 147
zenanas 148–54
Mughals 39, 108, 247
Müller, Dr Jenny 184, 193

Nagpur, scandal at 116–23
Naidu, Sarojini 235, 263
Nasik mission school 136–7, 138
National India Association (NIA) 55, 172
nationalism see Indian Nationalism
nationalist spiritual awakening 244–5
native doctors 184–5
native education societies 58, 111

needlework subsidy 147
networks with England, medical
activism 169–74
new demand, medical
professionals 195–7
new feminism 263–5
new knowledge, medical 180–1
new pedagogy
Lawrence asylums 82
Welland school 220–3
new schools, European Code 207–9
Newton, John 47
Nightingale, Florence 172, 186–7
night schools, Bengal 86
normal schools
Carpenter's plan 102–23
Winter's normal school 141–2
Norwood Normal School 83–4
nurses/nursing 190–4, 195–8
see also midwives

orientalism 56–9
orphans 51–2, 66, 218, 275
Eurasian 132, 133, 135, 162
Oudh 60–1, 107
outreach programmes 286, 290
Ouwerkerk, Louise 254, 255, 257, 258

Palamcottah 140–6
Parsis 249–52
Mary Carpenter 100, 105
Montessori school 253–4
Partition 291–4
Patriarchal Roman Catholic
governance 274–5
pay rates 73, 170, 185, 214, 225, 275
Pechey, Edith 170–1
Pestalozzi, Johann 84, 219
physical exercise 162, 255, 262
poor, working with 286–7
'prison schools' 87
private-venture schooling 208–9
professionalism, female medical 178–98
professional learning space 159–74
prostitutes 48, 161–2

Quaker heritage, European women
teachers 239

racial crossover 223–9
'racial motherhood' 96, 147

EU authorised representative for GPSR:
Easy Access System Europe, Mustamäe tee 50,
10621 Tallinn, Estonia
gpsr.requests@easproject.com